INVESTIGATING *your* CaReeR

Teacher's Wraparound Edition

Ann K. Jordan

Career Development Manager
Great Oaks Institute of Technology and Career Development

Lynne T. Whaley

President
Skill Builders

THOMSON

SOUTH-WESTERN

Australia · Canada · Mexico · Singapore · Spain · United Kingdom · United States

THOMSON

SOUTH-WESTERN

Investigating Your Career—Teacher's Wraparound Edition
by Ann K. Jordan and Lynne T. Whaley

Editor-in-Chief
Jack Calhoun

Vice President/Executive Publisher
Dave Shaut

Team Leader
Karen Schmohe

Executive Editor
Eve Lewis

Project Manager
Penny Shank

Production Manager
Patricia Matthews Boies

Production Editor
Colleen A. Farmer

Executive Marketing Manager
Carol Volz

Marketing Manager
Mike Cloran

Marketing Coordinator
Linda Kuper

Consulting Editor
Hyde Park Publishing Services

Manufacturing Coordinator
Kevin L. Kluck

Cover Designer
Lou Ann Thesing

Internal Designer
Tippy McIntosh

Editorial Assistant
Linda Keith

Production Assistant
Nancy Stamper

Compositor
Navta Associates, Inc.

Printer
RR Donnelley, Willard

PHOTO CREDITS
All photos © Getty Images/PhotoDisc, Inc except for the following: pages 8, 189, 240, and 262 © Getty Images/Eye-Wire; page 19 Adrian Arbib/CORBIS, Inc; pages 25 and 198 Getty Images/Digital Vision; pages 40, 85, 89, 137, 143, 153, 236, 247, and 296 © CORBIS; page 82 © Universal Low Vision Aids, Inc. and Magnisight, Inc.

For permission to use material from this text, contact us by

Tel: (800) 730-2214
Fax: (800) 730-2215
Web: www.thomsonrights.com

For more information, contact South-Western, 5191 Natorp Boulevard, Mason, OH, 45040. Or you can visit our Internet site at www.swlearning.com.

TO THE TEACHER

What Makes This Book Different

Investigating Your Career takes a unique approach to career planning that captures the interest of students. The text and supplemental materials engage students by helping them discover who they are and how they can have a satisfying career in the adult world. *Investigating Your Career* taps into students' natural energy, enthusiasm, and desire to do well by asking them to:

- Identify their core passions, talents, and values.
- Investigate career clusters and workplace realities.
- Use practical planning and decision-making tools to develop a personal career plan.
- Practice the job search skills they will need to implement their career plan.

The results are exciting! Students are fascinated to learn more about themselves and are eager to find ways they can have a career that allows them to do the things they like to do.

Investigating Your Career uses a self-discovery process to match a career area to a student and equip each student with the tools needed to develop and implement personal career plans. Students use a variety of approaches in their career exploration, including technology, multimedia, job shadowing, career study tours, and mentors. In addition, the text and supplemental materials help students become more self aware, set goals, manage time, and make informed decisions. Students also learn about work-related issue such as reduction of bias, SCANS competencies, and workplace and workforce expectations. Finally, students learn and practice the job search skills they need to make their career plans a reality.

How This Book Works

Investigating Your Career helps students match their unique characteristics to appropriate careers by involving students in the discovery and decision-making processes. Students who successfully complete this course will be more self-confident about making and taking responsibility for the education and career decisions that affect their life. Using the tools in *Investigating Your Career,* students:

- Identify a career that matches their talents and passions.

- Prepare for that career by creating a practical, personalized career plan.
- Learn skills and acquire tools for success that they can use throughout their lifetime.

The career planning process provides opportunities for students to explore career possibilities, make informed choices, and develop the skills needed for future success.

The proven approach of *Investigating Your Career* benefits the students and teachers like you. Students choose a career based on what *they* want to do. As a result, they develop the ability to make informed decisions about their future, are more excited about learning, and are more motivated to stay in school. Teachers help students make discoveries and learn practical skills that will affect their entire life. As a teacher, you know the satisfaction that comes with making a difference.

ORGANIZATION OF THIS BOOK

The 15 chapters of *Investigating Your Career* are divided into 5 parts, each containing 3 chapters. Every part logically builds on the previous parts, guiding students from the self-discovery process through the successful job interview. Each chapter of *Investigating Your Career* is designed to encourage learning and to place career planning in the context of students' lives.

Part 1: Getting Ready

The first part of *Investigating Your Career* emphasizes the importance of choosing a career that matches students' interests, personality, skills, and values. Students often view work as important for their future but not as something enjoyable or personally fulfilling. *Investigating Your Career* explains that while jobs or careers cannot make a person happy, people can find meaning in their work if they choose work that is meaningful to them. Students learn about themselves—what they enjoy doing and how they are influenced by people in their lives—through assessments and chapter activities. In addition to formal assessments, students explore how informational interviews, job shadowing experiences, career study tours, internships, and service learning projects can help them make informed career decisions.

Part 2: Narrowing the Choices

In Part 2, students begin by exploring general workforce and workplace trends that will influence their future careers.

Investigating Your Career explains how knowledge of current and future career trends involving technology, workforce diversity, and global markets can help students plan their careers. Increasing awareness of the many career possibilities these trends entail encourages students to explore career options they may not have considered.

Most students do not have a single career in mind and are likely weighing several choices for careers. Considering all their options before making a career decision gives students confidence that they are making wise decisions and helps students take charge of their education and career plans.

In the last chapter of Part 2, students use a formal decision-making process and the personalized information they have developed in the first five chapters to choose several careers to explore in a specific career area. Sometimes people worry that students are being forced to make career choices at too early an age. However, students who limit or end their education are making career choices without the benefits of career planning. Career planning gives students a focus for school. Research shows that when students see the connection between schooling and career opportunities, they stay in school longer, work harder, and perform better.

Part 3: Planning

In Part 3, students begin the process of planning their path to achieve career success. Students write the goals they will need to achieve in order to accomplish their education, career, and lifestyle ambitions. Next, students create Action Plans that include strategies for overcoming roadblocks to their success. By learning how to budget their money and manage their time, students develop two practical skills critical to career and life success. Then students analyze, evaluate, and choose among the many career preparation options available to them, basing their choices on the goals they have set. *Investigating Your Career* provides the practical tools students will need to integrate their career goals with their education and training choices.

Part 4: Preparing for the Next Step

Part 4 of *Investigating Your Career* explains the skills and knowledge students will need to be successful in the workplace. Students compare the behaviors employers require and the key skills and competencies the SCANS report identifies as crucial for work success to the skills needed for school success. In the process, students realize that the workplace is not so different from the classroom as they may have thought.

Because most current and future career situations will require employees to work as members of teams, students explore the team concept in depth. In addition, numerous activities throughout the text provide students with practice in applying and developing team skills. Students also learn about different management aspects of the workplace, including how employment laws, types of employment, and employer expectations affect careers.

Part 5: Creating Tools for the Future

The last part of *Investigating Your Career* provides students with the tools and skills they need to continue their career journey outside the classroom as employees or entrepreneurs. Students begin by analyzing how well their job search goals meet or support their career goals. Then students apply proven job search strategies to find appropriate employers. Students prepare for the job application process by developing the practical skills of writing effective resumes and cover letters, selecting references, and completing job application forms. Next, students get ready for the interview process by learning how to research individual employers and how to answer and ask interview questions. Students practice their interviewing skills and plan follow-up strategies that will help them obtain the job they want.

A TYPICAL CHAPTER

Chapters in *Investigating Your Career* have features that benefit both students and teachers because these features promote student learning. The opening page of each chapter, the features interspersed throughout the chapters, and the end-of-chapter activities all make important contributions to students learning how to plan their careers successfully.

Opening Page

The opening page of each chapter lists the chapter objectives. The objectives establish the goals that will motivate the students through the chapter content. The chapter objectives correspond to the main sections of the chapter and to the sections in the summary at the end of the chapter.

The opening page also lists the key terms for the chapter. Each key term is highlighted and defined when it is first used in the chapter. In addition, a glossary on the Career Portfolio and Resource CD includes definitions of all the key terms.

The opening page also frequently includes a quotation related to chapter topics. Class discussions based on these quotations can stimulate interest in the chapter.

An important feature on the opening page is a scenario that is based on the chapter content and is relevant to students' lives. Because these scenarios present familiar real-world situations, students can see at the beginning of each chapter why the topics are important for students' career success. Realistic portrayals of people and situations help students immediately relate to the topic discussed and provide the basis for a class discussion of the chapter content.

Immediately following the scenario, the "What do you think?" feature helps students expand their thinking by asking them to relate the underlying principles of the scenario to their life. The "What do you think?" questions force students to think ahead as well as motivate them to discover the answers and how those answers relate to their situation.

Chapter Features

The following chapter features motivate students in different ways, facilitate learning for different levels of students, and provide a change of pace from reading the chapter.

- *Scenarios*—Scenarios appear throughout the chapters and place concepts in the context of familiar real-world situations. In addition, scenarios often present concepts before the ideas are explained in the text, leading students to an intuitive realization of why and how the concept is important.

- *What do you think?*—These questions appear throughout each chapter and have two primary purposes. One purpose is for the questions to provide a pause for a discussion in which students can think about a specific point before reading further. In this way, the "What do you think?" questions prompt students to discover some of the important points before reading the text. The second purpose of the "What do you think?" questions is to relate points discussed in the text to students' own situation, thereby encouraging them to apply specific concepts to their life.

- *Quotes*—Thought-provoking quotations emphasize the subject matter of the text and help students become aware of the views of notable people concerning careers, work, and success in life.

- *Career Facts*—Factual information related to careers helps expand students' awareness beyond the textbook and brings ideas from the employment world into the classroom. Because they are related to the chapter topics, Career Facts reinforce the concepts described in the text.

- *Career Success Tips*—These bits of advice emphasize how even a small amount of pertinent information can help students be successful in their careers.

- *Real People/Real Careers*—Engaging true stories spotlight interesting careers and career paths and increase students' knowledge of career possibilities and of the different ways people achieve career success. Web sites related to the featured career provide an opportunity for more investigation.

- *In a Nutshell*—A brief summary of the chapter immediately follows the last chapter section. Each summary point corresponds to a chapter objective and reviews the key concepts of a main section of the chapter.

End-of-Chapter Activities

The numerous activities at the end of each chapter apply the concepts discussed in the chapter, help students discover information about themselves, address different learning styles, and customize chapter results to each student. All activities are designed to help students prepare for their future by exploring their career options and developing the skills and qualities needed for career success. The three icons discussed in the following paragraphs identify activities with special purposes.

The **team icon** identifies activities in which students work in teams to complete the activity. Most career situations today and in the future will require employees to have the communication and interpersonal skills necessary to work effectively as members of teams. According to the U.S. Department of Labor, the No. 1 reason people are fired from jobs is for not getting along with coworkers. In addition, growth and advancement opportunities often depend, in part, on an employee's ability to work closely with others. In *Investigating Your Career,* the many team activities closely correlate to the ways in which students will use specialized communication strategies in the workplace. The team process is designed to help all team members learn through every member's participation.

The **portfolio icon** identifies activities that are part of the portfolio-building process. Students should save these activities in their Career Journey Folders. Many of the saved activities are required for subsequent activities in later chapters of the text. In other activities identified with the portfolio icon, students prepare documents and find information they will use throughout their career journeys. For example, students save activities in which they set goals, plan high school classes, develop budgets, write resumes and cover letters, and practice interviewing. All of the activities that students place in their Career Journey Folders help students review the results of their career planning efforts.

The **Internet icon** identifies activities that require students to research topics on the Internet. Students explore a wide range of topics in these activities, such as investigating virtual labs, researching descriptions of possible careers, analyzing possible career preparation options and providers (programs, schools, institutions, individuals, or businesses), and finding the wage or salary ranges for career choices. Students also examine and take several assessments available at Internet sites. The Internet activities allow students to improve their abilities in using this vital resource, to expand their knowledge about career planning topics, and to develop their research skills.

Activities such as the following may be marked with more than one icon:

- When students research wage and salary ranges on the Internet, they place the information they acquire in their Career Journey Folder.
- After students explore SCANS problems and projects on the Internet, they then work in teams to choose and solve a problem or complete a project.
- Once students have practiced interviewing in a team setting, they store the evaluations of their interviewing skills in their Career Journey Folder.

Three types of activities appear in every chapter of *Investigating Your Career.* These activities may or may not also be team, portfolio, or Internet activities.

- ***Coming to Terms:*** Activities that reinforce students' knowledge of some of the terms introduced and defined in the chapter. Rather than having students simply write definitions of the terms, the Coming to Terms activities use various types of applications to reinforce students' understanding of the terms.
- ***Case Challenges:*** Activities that apply chapter concepts to real-world situations similar to students' experiences. Analyzing the short scenarios in the Case Challenges helps students develop problem-solving and critical-thinking skills.
- ***Learning from Others:*** Activities that require students to conduct interviews with people who are already part of the employment world. The interviews provide students with firsthand knowledge about the various requirements for career success and help students develop the interpersonal and communication skills necessary for the job search process.

A few of the activities in *Investigating Your Career* use assessments or self-scoring quizzes designed to encourage student self-discovery. With your direction, students will generally not misunderstand the results of these assessments and self-scoring quizzes. However, if you find any misinterpretation of results, please have students discuss the results with a professionally licensed counselor.

SCANS

The Secretary's Commission on Achieving Necessary Skills (SCANS) Report for America challenged schools, parents, and businesses to help all students develop the basic skills, thinking skills, personal qualities, and workplace competencies employers require. Chapter 10 of *Investigating Your Career* addresses the SCANS skills in the student text to help students define and prepare for the practical skills needed for success in this millennium.

In addition, *Investigating Your Career* provides students with many opportunities to practice and develop the SCANS skills and competencies:

- Students prepare abstracts and summaries of interviews and Internet research and share these reports with the class.
- Students compose cover letters, thank-you letters, and resumes.
- Students apply creative-thinking, decision-making, and problem-solving skills to choose a career and to complete many of the Case Challenges and the activities related to their Career Journey Folders.
- Students take part in many team activities that foster the development of leadership and interpersonal skills and the ability to manage resources effectively.
- Students acquire, evaluate, and interpret information from the Internet and various other resources as they determine and plan the path of their chosen careers.

The entire career investigation process in this book is designed to encourage students' development of the qualities of responsibility, self-esteem, self-management, and integrity and to help students understand and acquire the workplace competencies required for career success.

CAREER JOURNAL

Many students aged 11 to 14 have not yet begun to think seriously about their futures. In fact, this age group is very "now-oriented" and shows the following characteristics:

- Like to be doing activities
- Are preoccupied with identifying their individuality
- Want to figure out how they fit into the world at large
- Like activities that are tailored to their individuality

To help students relate the benefits of career investigation and planning to their "now," *Investigating Your Career* incorporates a pre- and postchapter activity called "Career Journal."

The objective of the two-part journaling activity is to help students relate the chapter content to their personal situation and to begin to take ownership of their career development process. To accomplish this, students are asked to write answers to specific questions at the beginning and end of every chapter. The student journals act as a safe, private reflection tool that helps dreams become real possibilities by showing how they can be attained. The journal captures students' interest by asking them to answer the questions that are so important to them: Who am I? How do I fit into the world?

The first part of the journal activity supports analytical thinking and application focus as well as helps students remember what they already know about the subjects covered in the chapter. The journal questions are designed to increase retention by having students clarify what they would like to know and listing specific questions they hope to answer while studying the chapter. This prereading preparation stimulates students' interest in the chapter content and encourages students to figure out how the chapter content applies to their own life.

The second part of the journal activity continues to support the learning process by acting as a review of the chapter and helping students associate the new material with information they already know. In addition, students are encouraged to use research skills by listing the questions they still have or new questions that have come up about the chapter content and identifying where they can find the answers they need. Finally, students reinforce the "real-world" value of the chapter by writing how they think the chapter content applies to their personal career aspirations.

The pre- and postchapter journal questions appear on the appropriate pages of the *Teacher's Wraparound Edition.* For your convenience, teaching masters are also included on the Instructor's Resource CD.

CAREER PORTFOLIO

Investigating Your Career uses a two-part portfolio-building process. During the first part of the process, each student keeps a Career Journey Folder consisting of (1) all activities marked with the portfolio icon; (2) records of experiences that helped the student make career decisions, such as work samples and assessments; (3) documents related to the student's education and training, such as certificates and letters of recommendation; and (4) personal notes about the student's career journey.

The Career Journey Folder helps students document career goals, education and training plans, and career-related experiences. By looking through the items in their Career Journey Folder, students can see their progress and review why they made their career decisions. In discussing Career Journey Folders with students, you should emphasize that a Career Journey Folder is never finished and will be useful throughout their working life.

During the second part of the portfolio-building process, students use items from their Career Journey Folder to prepare a Career Portfolio for their job search now or in the future. The Career Portfolio is a collection of materials whose purpose is to show students' ability to do a specific job, so the contents of the Career Portfolio change for every job search.

Both the Instructor's Resource CD and the Career Portfolio and Resource CD contain instructions for using the portfolio-building process.

TEAM LEARNING

Working in teams prepares students for the workplace and facilitates peer learning, an effective approach for students with people-oriented learning styles. However, students often have not had enough experience working in teams. Successful teamwork demands not only that teachers be organized, but also that an atmosphere of trust and openness exists in the classroom. As the teacher, you must be willing to give up some control and tolerate some disorder. Prepare students to work together by tightly structuring team activities at first. Some groups may have trouble functioning well enough to complete their tasks, so help them plan for improvement. With enough practice, teamwork will improve, and you will be able to allow groups more freedom.

The team activities in *Investigating Your Career* suggest an appropriate number of team members. Feel free to adjust that number according to the needs of students.

USING ACTIVITIES AND CHAPTER FEATURES

While the activities in *Investigating Your Career* are located at the ends of the chapters, students will benefit most if you assign the activities at the points indicated in the student text. Completing the related activities immediately after students have studied the topics reinforces the material and provides feedback to students. Answers for most of the activities will vary because the goal of the activities is students' self-discovery and development of an individualized career plan. Teaching suggestions are included in the margins of the *Teacher's Wraparound Edition.*

Each of the "What do you think?" features in *Investigating Your Career* appears on a separate teaching master, allowing you to prepare transparencies and use the "What do you think?" questions as focal points for class discussions. The files for the teaching masters are on the Instructor's Resource CD. The filenames refer to the chapter and the order within the chapter. For example, TM02-03 is the third transparency master for Chapter 2.

The margin features in *Investigating Your Career*—the quotes, Career Facts, and Career Success Tips—all provide a change of pace that still reinforces the career planning process. Class discussions of these features will help students relate chapter topics to the real world.

ASSESSING STUDENTS' WORK

Assessment is an integral part of any learning experience. Without some form of assessment, neither you nor students will know if they are learning what they need to know in order to succeed at the next education level or at the workplace. Two assessment approaches work well with *Investigating Your Career*—performance-based assessment and traditional objective assessments.

Performance-Based Assessment

Performance-based assessment is appropriate for many of the activities in *Investigating Your Career* and the *Activities & Projects* book because the primary goals of the text include self-discovery, self-management, and the development of skills in teamwork, communication, and decision making. Achievement of these goals may be easier to assess through teacher observation than through any other form of assessment. Some activities, such as those requiring summaries of interviews, may need to be assessed in terms of evaluating a student's skill in summarizing information and his or her less obvious ability in conducting an interview. Also, although a resume may be graded by how well it meets the criteria of an effective resume, the goal of *Investigating Your Career* is for *all* students to prepare effective resumes. Thus, students should be given the opportunity to edit and rewrite their resumes, using peer review if possible, until they meet the criteria.

Traditional Objective Assessments

Two traditional objective assessments are available as options for use with *Investigating Your Career.* You may wish to purchase one or both of the following products:

- The *Chapter Tests* book includes a two-page test for each chapter. Each test includes true/false and multiple choice questions. The answers to all questions are included in the *Chapter Tests* Teacher's Edition. These tests can easily be used as the primary assessment tool or combined with performance-based assessments to obtain a more complete picture of students' mastery level.

- An **Exam***View*® Electronic Test Bank for *Investigating Your Career* is available from South-Western/Thomson Learning. You may wish to purchase this test-generating software in order to prepare customized assessments. **Exam***View* allows you to print the tests as shown, to print tests that include only some of the questions, or to print tests to which you have added your own questions. **Exam***View* also allows students to take tests over the Internet. Note that to take or publish an Internet test requires Netscape Navigator 4.0 or higher or Internet Explorer 4.0 or higher and an Internet connection. Macintosh users need System 8.6 or higher to access the Internet test-hosting features.

COUNSELORS

The counselor at your school can be a valuable asset for both you and the students in your career planning course. The counselor can support you with class discussions, assist in planning activities, conduct individual student conferences, provide education and career planning information, explain options and help students obtain financial aid, and help in many other ways. Many counselors have professional training in career development.

Counselors who still have primary responsibility for conducting career planning sessions will find *Investigating Your Career* a useful supplement to the regular curriculum. They can use the activities, especially those that involve Internet search and introspection, to help students with their career decision making. The self-administered quizzes and informal assessments provide insight for students to begin group or individual sessions. In addition, the job search material in Part 5 of the text is ideal for preparing students for the pre-admissions process or for future or immediate entry into the job market.

PARENTS AND OTHER FAMILY MEMBERS

Students want information, motivation, and support from their families while making career decisions. Students need the support of parents and family members during the career discovery process because they are the primary influence on students' career decisions. As students move through middle school or junior high school and high school and into postsecondary education and training, parents and family members have a responsibility to help students develop a positive self-image and achieve the goals that will lead to career success.

Each chapter in this *Teacher's Wraparound Edition* includes suggestions for parents and family members. These recommendations will help family members explore many career-related topics with teenagers. An excellent resource for additional information is *Career Coaching Your Kids* by David Montross, Theresa Kane, and Robert Ginn.

You can communicate with the families of all your students by using a monthly or quarterly newsletter, outgoing voicemail messages, or e-mail. You also may wish to publish a collection of students' work and to encourage family members to visit your class. Also, members of students' families may be willing to share their career expertise as guest speakers.

INFORMED INTERNET USAGE

Just because you see something on a computer screen doesn't mean it's true. This point must be emphasized to students and adults alike. The following five criteria will help you and your students evaluate any web site: accuracy, objectivity, timeliness, authority, and coverage. Also keep in mind that technology is not a substitute for teaching; technology is a tool to improve the value of learning.

Teachers should preview all web sites suggested in the text before assigning the Internet activities because:

1. The content of web sites changes often.
2. Without notice and at any time, ownership of web sites may be transferred or sites may be canceled or sold.
3. Schools may have their own specific policies about school-directed Internet use by students.

The publisher and authors are not responsible for changes to web sites or the compliance of suggested web sites with any Internet policies of your school. If your district does not have an acceptable-use policy for technology usage, it is strongly recommended that students and possibly parents or guardians sign one. Students should know that the use of the Internet is a privilege that can be revoked if the policy is not followed.

Because the content of web sites is subject to change without notice, the links listed in the student text or on the Career Portfolio and Resource CD may not have content matching that referenced in the assignment. For problems with broken web links, refer to **www.investigatingyourcareer.com**. In addition, some web sites may require plug-ins for students to view the information. If you or students cannot download the connection, request the technology department at your school to download the necessary information for you.

General Teaching Suggestions

The following teaching suggestions have proven to be successful in the classroom and may be helpful whether you are an experienced or a new teacher. Teaching suggestions for specific chapters appear on the pages of the *Teacher's Wraparound Edition*.

Teaching for Different Learning Abilities

A classroom typically has students with a wide variation in ability, intelligence, and motivation. The first challenge is to identify the special abilities of each student. Learning disabilities can be difficult to detect and classify. Classifying students solely on examination scores and prior classroom performance may be misleading and should be avoided.

The correct assessment of students should be a combined effort of teachers, school counselor and/or special needs staff, parent or guardian, and student. Working together, this team can design an individualized program that will challenge the student and provide adequate opportunity to achieve attainable goals.

Gifted Students

One objective of gifted student programs should be the development of leadership skills. Current literature suggests that four skill areas are involved in the development of effective leadership:

- Cognition—the ability to identify, research, and learn factual knowledge
- Problem solving—the ability to identify problems and develop creative solutions
- Interpersonal communication—the ability to work with other people
- Decision making—the ability to develop and implement realistic goals and evaluate performance of the goals

Most students will enter the classroom with stronger development in some skill areas than others. Thus, for example, a student lacking interpersonal communication skills should undertake projects to develop those skills.

Gifted students may need to move at an accelerated pace. They may not need to work every problem provided. For example, after reviewing a chapter, gifted students may show mastery by answering a few selected questions or completing a complex project.

Limited English Proficiency (LEP) Students

Limited English proficiency (LEP) students are individuals whose native or dominant language is a language other than English. Although these students may be involved in special "English as a Second Language" (ESL) classes, adopting some of the following strategies can significantly improve learning:

- Provide students with translations of key terms before presenting each chapter. Encourage students to use dictionaries.
- Use visual instructional tools, such as posters and bulletin boards, which reinforce concepts in both English and the student's native or dominant language.
- Use simple words in oral presentations and testing materials. Avoid polysyllabic words. Simplify nontechnical vocabulary.
- At early levels, LEP students have limited comprehension of English and can respond with one- or two-word answers. Assess understanding by having students match, choose, move, draw, or point. Students at this level can respond to directions that require them to name, list, categorize, label, or reply with one or two words.
- LEP students require a variety of visual clues to support the lesson and to help them understand abstract ideas. Use

transparencies, textbook illustrations, and software demonstrations to provide these clues.

- Allow for longer pauses when you ask questions. Nonnative speakers need more time to formulate their answers.
- Stress key terms so LEP students learn the language of the workplace.
- Speak directly. Avoid negative constructions and passive verbs.
- Rather than asking students whether they understand what you have said, ask them to restate it in their own words.
- Adjust the length of time allotted to complete assignments and tests.
- Coordinate classroom activities with the school's ESL staff.
- Avoid misinterpreting a nod as understanding. The nod may instead mean that the listener did not understand.
- Be cautious if there are no interruptions or questions. It may mean that very little has been understood.
- In some cultures, "yes" is the response to every question. "Yes" may mean "I heard your question" rather than "I understand."
- In some cultures, giggling or inappropriate laughter may indicate embarrassment at poor comprehension rather than disrespect for the teacher.

Specific Learning Disability (SLD) Students

Adolescence is a period of turmoil and adjustment. What many often view as inappropriate adolescent behavior may, however, be caused by a student's specific learning disability (SLD). The correct assessment of SLD students is difficult because inappropriate adolescent behavior is similar to the typical characteristics of SLD students.

Passive Learners. SLD students avoid making decisions. Instead, they wait for a teacher to provide specific direction.

Poor Self-Concept. Years of failure cause SLD students to have low self-esteem, thus reducing their self-confidence in achieving academic success.

Weak Social Skills. SLD students often have difficulty making and keeping friends.

Attention Deficits. SLD students often lack the ability to concentrate on one topic for an extended period.

Lack of Motivation. Years of failure have conditioned SLD students to doubt their abilities and, therefore, to view their efforts as futile.

Once an SLD student is correctly assessed, the assessment team should work with the student to develop an individualized program with the basic objective of developing functional (life) skills. The student should be counseled to establish challenging yet attainable goals and to provide frequent feedback about his or her achievements. The student's

academic success should be measured on the demonstrated ability to learn as well as the mastery of a body of knowledge. The following general instructional strategies may be effective with SLD students:

- When asking questions in class, ask SLD students questions they are likely to answer successfully until they develop more confidence in your classroom.
- Rotate instructional materials rather than try to complete the entire text. Supplemental instructional materials may include books, business magazines, government publications, and multimedia materials.
- Incorporate current readings from business magazines, newspapers, and the Internet to identify contemporary topics of interest to students.
- Encourage students to maintain a daily log or journal that describes their academic progress. The log may include questions, concerns, and personal impressions about course content and the learning process. Students may share this log, if they desire, with the teacher when updating their individual program.

At-Risk and Reluctant Reader Students

Many factors may negatively impact a student's ability and motivation for academic success. Any student who is a potential dropout may be classified as an at-risk and reluctant reader student. At-risk and reluctant reader students are commonly deficient in mathematics, reading, and language skills. These students provide a unique challenge because teachers have little, if any, power to correct problems in the home environment.

Effective instructional strategies for at-risk and reluctant reader students should be based on the premise that all individuals have a need for achievement and social acceptance. Within the classroom, these needs can be fulfilled by using a curriculum such as this one that provides many opportunities for students to succeed and be recognized for their achievements. Techniques for working with at-risk and reluctant reader students include the following:

- Develop a personal profile of the student. Avoid placing too much significance on past academic performance because past performance may represent a symptom rather than an underlying problem.
- Develop an individualized program with the student that includes both short- and long-term goals. When identifying goals, consider the student's anticipated academic and career goals. Refer to Chapter 7, "Setting Goals," when working with the student to set goals.
- Modify presentation strategies to include more visual displays, and supplement explanations with current, realistic examples.
- Organize field trips and mentor programs to expose students to the workplace environment. See the Learning from

Others activities at the end of every chapter of *Investigating Your Career.*

Visually Impaired Students

Students with mild visual impairments typically take a full program of courses. The nature and degree of students' visual impairments will vary and may include difficulty in reading print, inability to distinguish colors, sensitivity to light, and limited field of vision. Work with each student to adapt appropriate teaching strategies.

There are many sources of alternative teaching materials. Most states have schools for the blind and rehabilitation service agencies that can enlarge the textbook and other printed materials. These organizations also can identify the latest technologies available for helping students.

Work together with the student to develop an individualized program that establishes a time frame for achieving specific learning objectives. The learning objectives should be consistent with the student's anticipated career goals. The time frame should consider the student's impairment and the availability of technical assistance, such as enlarged materials and closed-circuit television.

Hearing-Impaired Students

Hearing impaired refers not only to deaf students but also to those who are hard of hearing. Students who are hard of hearing have a functional sense of hearing and sometimes use a hearing aid. Always face hearing-impaired students when speaking so lip reading is possible. Keep instructions simple and clear. Whenever you can, use printed materials and videos to convey the lesson.

Attention Deficit Disorder (ADD) Students

Students with attention deficit disorder (ADD) are distinguished by critical and persistent difficulties with attention span, impulse control, and occasional hyperactivity. The two types of ADD are attention deficit hyperactivity disorder (ADHD) and undifferentiated ADD. The following are some characteristics that may be displayed by a student with ADHD:

- Fidgets, squirms, seems restless, or has difficulty remaining seated
- Talks excessively, interrupts, intrudes on others, or has difficulty waiting for a turn
- Has difficulty following instructions or sustaining attention
- Is easily distracted and may shift from one uncompleted task to another
- Often loses things necessary for tasks, such as pencils, notebooks, and assignment sheets
- Frequently engages in dangerous actions

Students with undifferentiated ADD primarily exhibit inattentiveness and are not hyperactive. They may have problems with organization and distractibility and may seem quiet or passive.

The following instructional strategies may be helpful with students with ADD:

- Seat students near the teacher's desk, but include them as part of the regular class seating.
- Surround students with good role models. Encourage peer tutoring and cooperative/collaborative learning.
- Avoid distracting stimuli. Try not to place students with ADD near air conditioners, high-traffic areas, doors, windows, or other distractions.
- Maintain eye contact during verbal instruction.
- Make directions clear and concise. Be consistent with daily instructions.
- Repeat instructions in a calm, positive manner, if needed.
- Require a daily assignment notebook in which the student writes down all assignments. The student and parents or guardian should sign the notebook to indicate that assignments have been completed.
- Modify assignments as needed. Consult with special education personnel to determine specific strengths and weaknesses of each student. Develop an individualized education program.
- Make sure to test knowledge and not attention span.
- Keep in mind that children with ADD are easily frustrated. Stress, pressure, and fatigue can break down their self-control and lead to poor behavior.
- Praise immediately any and all good behavior and performance.
- Teach the child to reward himself or herself.
- Encourage positive self-talk.

Students with Dyslexia

There is no widely accepted definition for dyslexia. For most experts, dyslexia exists when normally intelligent children who are exposed to suitable educational opportunities in school and at home experience great difficulty in learning to read and write and in retaining written materials. A visual or auditory problem may cause dyslexia. But not all individuals who have problems with reading have dyslexia. Only a qualified reading professional should make the diagnosis. The following instructional strategies may be helpful with dyslexic students:

- Make shorter reading assignments for a given time period. For example, instead of assigning an entire chapter for one class period, assign the goals, and the scenario at the beginning of the chapter.
- Pair a dyslexic student with a more capable reader who can help emphasize the major points of a reading assignment.

- Emphasize the organization of a chapter before the student begins to read. Point out the relationship between the goals and major headings. A simple diagram or chart of the chapter's organization may help.
- Encourage dyslexic students to create mental pictures of the words. Before assigning reading, use videos, field trips, or photos to provide visual images.
- Have the material read aloud for students with visual dyslexia.
- Model a positive attitude. Self-esteem is critical to a dyslexic student's success.

TEACHING FOR DIFFERENT LEARNING STYLES

Students with different learning styles can use *Investigating Your Career* successfully, in part because of the variety of activities. Teachers can facilitate learning by using a range of approaches when presenting information in the text, including lecture, video, guided discussion, and teamwork. The following paragraphs discuss some of the different learning styles and ways to present the information in *Investigating Your Career* to accommodate these styles.

Print Learners

Print learners prefer to see information in print, preferably printed in words. When learning new concepts, print learners like to read the information and then study an illustration or another visual aid. When you discuss the key terms and concepts in *Investigating Your Career,* refer to the text so print learners can later go back and study the material.

Visual Learners

Visual learners need to "see" the concept and may have difficulty learning when they are asked to read silently. Illustrations and visual aids are especially important to visual learners. By preparing transparencies from the teaching masters and using the transparencies, video, and PowerPoint presentations provided with *Investigating Your Career* in your lectures and class discussions, you will assist students who are visual learners.

Auditory Learners

Auditory learners learn best by hearing and benefit from spoken reinforcement of key ideas. Completing the team activities in *Investigating Your Career* and participating in the class discussions suggested in this *Teacher's Wraparound Edition* aids students who are auditory learners. In addition, you may wish to assign students to list a specified number of important

ideas as they read. After all students have had a chance to complete the reading assignment, call on individuals to read one or two items from their lists. In this way, students who missed key concepts while reading will hear them from their classmates.

Tactile Learners

Tactile learners learn best by touching or handling objects and appreciate activities that use fine motor skills, including writing. Although they may not remember what they saw others do or what they heard, tactile learners remember what they did and how they did it. Many of the activities in *Investigating Your Career* and the *Activities & Projects* book include writing summaries and taking interview notes. Tactile learners also benefit from keying work on the computer. In addition, the teaching suggestions for specific activities include creating artwork or other hands-on projects. Some of the optional activities in the *Teachers' Wraparound Edition* involve learning concepts by playing games.

Kinesthetic Learners

Kinesthetic learners achieve best by taking an active part in instruction. Motion is an important part of kinesthetic learning, including motion that is not specific to the learning process. Simply allowing students to move about the classroom can be particularly helpful to kinesthetic learners. When groups are formed for the many teamwork activities in *Investigating Your Career,* students move to different areas of the classroom. You also may have kinesthetic learners walk to the overhead projector, chart paper, or chalkboard to record information for various class discussions.

Support Materials

Investigating Your Career is supported by a variety of instructional tools that have been carefully designed to assist students' learning and your teaching. Together these materials provide a comprehensive instructional package.

CAREER PORTFOLIO AND RESOURCE CD

The Career Portfolio and Resource CD located in the student text, includes forms and/or worksheets for every end-of-chapter activity. These materials are in individual files with filenames that correspond to the activity number. Students can print the worksheets, or you can print them and provide them as handouts. Some files are in Microsoft Word so students can add their information to the file and save the file on a disk. Students may use some files in future chapters. Students also may prefer to use a computer to update some of their files as they obtain additional information. Some of the files are Portable Document Format (PDF) files, and students will need Adobe Acrobat Reader to view and print these activity forms and worksheets. You can download Adobe Acrobat Reader from the Instructor's Resource CD onto the students' computers, or students can download the software for no charge from the web site **www.adobe.com**.

The Career Portfolio and Resource CD has two PDF files unrelated to the text activities. One file is a glossary of the key terms in the student text. The other file gives students suggestions for using and organizing their Career Journey Folder and provides a form for keeping track of their documents. By making a transparency or providing handouts of TM CJ Folder, you can help students determine categories for organizing their documents.

ACTIVITIES & PROJECTS

The primary student ancillary is the *Activities & Projects* book. Divided into 5 parts and 15 chapters to correlate with the parts and chapters in the student text, this supplement can be used in the classroom, as homework, or as long-term assignments.

Each chapter includes a variety of reinforcement activities, problems, questions, forms, and puzzles to interest and challenge students. An "Imagine" activity that projects students into their own future is among each chapter's activities. The projects that appear at the end of each part provide students with opportunities to work in teams, use a variety of materials, and apply knowledge students have gained from the chapters within that part.

CHAPTER TESTS

The *Chapter Tests* book includes tests for each chapter. Each test includes true/false and multiple choice questions. These tests can easily be used as the primary assessment tool or combined with performance-based assessments.

EXAM*VIEW*®

Exam*View* electronic test bank allows you to create customized tests for all 15 chapters in *Investigating Your Career.* For more information on **Exam***View*, visit the web site **www.examview.com**.

VIDEO

Each chapter in *Investigating Your Career* has a CNN news clip that relates to the chapter content. These clips can be used to initiate discussion at the beginning of each chapter or to stimulate a summary discussion of each chapter. Video discussion guides for each clip are available on the Instructor's Resource CD.

WEB SITE

The web site for *Investigating Your Career,* **www.investigatingyourcareer.com**, provides a variety of interactive career exploration information and search opportunities.

TEACHER'S WRAPAROUND EDITION

This *Teacher's Wraparound Edition* includes a wealth of information to assist you in presenting *Investigating Your Career* to students. The material appears in the side margins and in boxes at the bottom of each core page of every chapter. Teaching suggestions for end-of-chapter activities appear in the margins of the pages.

Side Margins

The following elements appear in the side margins of the *Teacher's Wraparound Edition:*

- *Focus*—This section provides a brief overview of the chapter and prompts you to use the Objectives and Key Terms to help students focus on the content of the chapter. This section also includes a reminder to use the chapter video segment to trigger discussion.

- *Career Journal*—This element appears twice in each chapter and reminds you to have students write Career Journal entries. At the beginning of the chapter, the Career Journal section includes three questions to pique students' interest. Three review questions appear in the Career Journal element at the end of chapter. See page T6 for additional information about the Career Journal.

- *Teach*—Teaching suggestions correlating with the sections of each chapter include tips for presenting the student text material, notes about specific topics, ideas for extending student learning, and additional information to enhance classroom discussion. Some web sites are included in the teaching suggestions; additional links are on the Instructor's Resource CD.

- *What do you think?*—This element is a companion to the "What do you think?" in the *Student Edition* and identifies the appropriate teaching master.
- *Apply*—This element marks an appropriate time to assign one of the activities that appears at the end of the chapter.
- *Enrich*—This element marks an appropriate time to assign one of the activities or projects found in the *Activities & Projects* book.
- *Close*—This element marks an appropriate time to assign chapter wrap-up activities or the wrap-up projects found in the *Activities & Projects* book.
- *In a Nutshell*—This element is a reminder to use the companion element in the *Student Edition* to help students review the chapter objectives.
- *Assess*—This element is a reminder to administer the printed objective tests or a test created with **Exam***View*®.

Bottom Boxes

The following elements appear in the bottom margins of the *Teacher's Wraparound Edition*:

- *Chapter Resources and Materials*—This box on the first page of each chapter lists the ancillary items that are available for the chapter.
- *Online Resources*—This box on the second page of each chapter provides the web address for online resources.
- *Different Learning Abilities*—These boxes appear throughout the chapter and offer teaching suggestions and activities that are appropriate for students with specific learning abilities.
- *Different Learning Styles*—These boxes appear throughout the chapter and offer teaching suggestions and activities that are appropriate for all students and that might be especially helpful for students with specific learning styles.
- *Career Success Tip*—This box is a companion to the Career Success Tip element that appears in the *Student Edition*. The box offers another tip or an activity related to the tip presented on the student page.
- *Career Trend*—This box appears when the student page includes a Career Fact. The element includes information that augments the content of the *Student Edition*.
- *Integrated Academics*—These boxes appear several times in each chapter and offer suggestions for integrating the content of *Investigating Your Career* with other academic areas.
- *Real People/Real Careers*—This element is designed to expand the content and teaching applicability of the Real People—Real Careers feature in the *Student Edition*.
- *Suggestions for Parents and Family Members*—The box on the last page of the chapter includes suggestions for

parents and family members and offers ways families can support teenagers through the aspects of the career planning process relevant to the chapter content

Chapter Activity Pages

The margin copy for the chapter activities section includes an explanation of the purpose of each activity, suggestions for presenting the activity to students, supply lists, and a discussion of the solution and any points pertinent to the activity and student learning.

TEACHER'S EDITION OF ACTIVITIES & PROJECTS

This teacher's resource includes overprinted solutions that will help you direct students in using the *Activities & Projects* book.

TEACHER'S EDITION OF CHAPTER TESTS

Answers to the Chapter Tests book are overprinted in this Teacher's Edition which is available separately.

INSTRUCTOR'S RESOURCE CD

The Instructor's Resource CD, available from South-Western/ Thomson Learning, includes the following materials to help you present the concepts in *Investigating Your Career* and to enhance learning for all students in your class.

- *Teaching Masters.* Every "What do you think?" in the student text is available on a teaching master. The other teaching masters provide information that will add to the text presentation. Either the teaching suggestions for the chapter or specific activities include references to the use of these additional teaching masters. All the teaching masters are PDF files. You can easily review these files using Adobe Acrobat Reader before preparing transparencies or handouts for class discussion. File names for the teaching masters follow a pattern that indicates the chapter number and the order within the chapter. For example, teaching master TM02-03 is the third teaching master for Chapter 2.
- *Internet Links.* These are "hot" links that will connect you directly to the Internet site. The linked sites provide you with information you may find helpful when presenting text material. Please refer to the section "Informed Internet Usage" and review all linked web sites before providing any of the sites to students. For problems with broken web links, refer to **www.investigatingyourcareer.com**.

- **Career Portfolio.** This folder contains instructions, checklists, and tips for using the two-part portfolio building process. Included in the Career Portfolio folder are four explanatory and/or implementation files: (1) CJ Folder, (2) How to Use CJF, (3) Portfolio Building, and (4) Career Portfolio Contents.

- **Career Portfolio and Resource CD.** The Instructor's Resource CD includes all the files on the Career Portfolio and Resource CD, allowing you to print any forms and/or worksheets for student use if students do not have access to a computer.

- **Lesson Plans.** The Lesson Plans on the Instructor's Resource CD are organized by chapter. These help you plan your classes by providing at a glance all the chapter components and program resources available for the chapter.

- **PowerPoint Presentations.** You can use these color slides at the beginning of a chapter to preview the contents of the entire chapter, in appropriate places throughout the chapter, or at the end of the chapter to review the important concepts. In addition, you can print the slides for use as transparencies or print them in the slide/note format for distribution to students for taking notes.

- **Video Discussion Guides.** Video Discussion Guides for each chapter give a synopsis of the video and provide you with questions and activities to assign to students after they view the video.

- **PowerPoint Viewer 97.** This application allows you to access and use the colorful PowerPoint presentations whether or not you have the PowerPoint software program.

- **Adobe Acrobat Reader.** This application allows you to review and print any of the PDF files on the Instructor's Resource CD.

- **Microsoft Word Viewer 97.** This application allows you to view and print Word files if you do not have Microsoft Word software.

- **Suggested Teaching Schedules.** Suggested teaching schedules are provided for traditional class schedules and block schedules. Each schedule provides a sample lesson plan for Chapter 4.

Electronic Media
Limited Warranty

South-Western Educational and Professional Publishing ("South-Western") extends the following warranty to only the original customer:

Warranty Coverage

This warranty covers the media on which the South-Western software/data are recorded. This limited warranty does not extend to the information contained on the media and in the accompanying book materials (the "Software/data"). The media product is warranted against malfunction due to defective materials or construction. This warranty is void if the media product is damaged by accident or unreasonable use, neglect, installation, improper service, or other causes not arising out of defects in material or construction.

Warranty Duration

The media product is warranted for a period of three months from the date of the original purchase by the customer.

Warranty Disclaimers

The following should be read and understood before purchasing and/or using the media:

a.   Any implied warranties that arise out of this sale are limited in duration to the above three-month period. South-Western will not be liable for loss of use of the media or other incidental or consequential costs, expenses, or damages incurred by you, the consumer, or any other user. Furthermore, South-Western will not be liable for any claim of any kind whatsoever by any other party against the user of the Software/data.

b.   South-Western does not warrant that the Software/data and the media will be free from error or will meet the specific requirements of the consumer. You, the consumer, assume complete responsibility for any decisions made or actions taken based on information obtained using the Software/data.

c.   Any statements made concerning the utility of the Software/data are not to be construed as expressed or implied warranties.

d.   SOUTH-WESTERN MAKES NO WARRANTY, EITHER EXPRESSED OR IMPLIED, INCLUDING BUT NOT LIMITED TO ANY IMPLIED WARRANTY OR MERCHANTABILITY AND FITNESS FOR A PARTICULAR PURPOSE, REGARDING THE SOFTWARE/DATA AND MAKES ALL SOFTWARE/ DATA AVAILABLE SOLELY ON AN "AS IS" BASIS.

e.   In no event will South-Western be liable to anyone for special collateral, incidental, or consequential damages in connection with or arising out of the purchase or use of the Software/data. The sole and exclusive liability of South-Western, regardless of the form of action, will not exceed the purchase price of the media.

f.   Some states do not allow the exclusion or limitation of implied warranties or consequential damages, so the above limitations or exclusions may not apply to you in those states.

Further Disclaimers of Warranty

South-Western will extend no warranty where the software is used on a machine other than that designated on the software package.

Media Replacement

Provided that you, the customer, have satisfactorily completed and returned a copy of the License Agreement, South-Western will replace, during the warranty period, any defective media at no charge. At South-Western's option, the defective media must be returned, postage prepaid, along with proof of purchase date.

Please contact South-Western at the address shown below for return instructions before returning any defective media.

South-Western
Media Services
5191 Natorp Boulevard
Mason, OH 45040

Legal Remedies

This warranty gives you specific legal rights, and you may also have other rights that vary from state to state.

Technical Support Hotline

The Technical Support Hotline is available by phone, fax, or e-mail from 8:30 a.m. – 6:00 p.m. EST to help you with any technical problems you may be having with this media product.

Phone: 1-800-423-0563
Fax: 859-647-5045
E-mail: **support@thomsonlearning.com** (24-hour response)

If you identify a problem, please check your hardware to make sure it is working properly. If the hardware is functioning correctly, call the number given. Please have the following information and materials with you when calling the hotline:

- Program or data CD-ROM
- Text

- Instructor's manual
- List of any error messages
- Students' printouts
- Description of the problem
- Computer type and model
- Computer's memory configuration
- Version number of operating system
- Name and version number of commercial software (if applicable)

Please do not permit your students access to the hotline contact information. If you want to order software, call Thomson Learning at (800) 354-9706.

INVESTIGATING *your* CaReeR

Ann K. Jordan

Career Development Manager
Great Oaks Institute of Technology and Career Development

Lynne T. Whaley

President
Skill Builders

THOMSON

SOUTH-WESTERN

Australia · Canada · Mexico · Singapore · Spain · United Kingdom · United States

THOMSON

SOUTH-WESTERN

Investigating Your Career
by Ann K. Jordan and Lynne T. Whaley

Editor-in-Chief
Jack Calhoun

Vice President/Executive Publisher
Dave Shaut

Team Leader
Karen Schmohe

Executive Editor
Eve Lewis

Project Manager
Penny Shank

Production Manager
Patricia Matthews Boies

Production Editor
Colleen A. Farmer

Executive Marketing Manager
Carol Volz

Marketing Manager
Mike Cloran

Marketing Coordinator
Linda Kuper

Consulting Editor
Hyde Park Publishing Services

Manufacturing Coordinator
Kevin L. Kluck

Cover Designer
Lou Ann Thesing

Internal Designer
Tippy McIntosh

Editorial Assistant
Linda Keith

Production Assistant
Nancy Stamper

Compositor
Navta Associates, Inc.

Printer
RR Donnelley, Willard

PHOTO CREDITS
All photos © Getty Images/ PhotoDisc, Inc except for the following: pages 8, 189, 240, and 262 © Getty Images/EyeWire; page 19 Adrian Arbib/CORBIS, Inc; pages 25 and 198 Getty Images/Digital Vision; pages 40, 85, 89, 137, 143, 153, 236, 247, and 296 © CORBIS; page 82 © Universal Low Vision Aids, Inc. and Magnisight, Inc.

For permission to use material from this text, contact us by

Tel: (800) 730-2214
Fax: (800) 730-2215
Web: www.thomsonrights.com

For more information, contact South-Western, 5191 Natorp Boulevard, Mason, OH, 45040. Or you can visit our Internet site at www.swlearning.com.

The Complete Package

The entire **Investigating Your Career** teaching package includes the following:

Text/Career Portfolio and Resource CD (hardcover, 4-color, 320 pages)
Student Activities and Projects Text (softcover, 128 pages)
Chapter Tests, Student Edition (softcover, 32 pages)
ExamView® CD
Video
Chapter Tests, Teacher's Edition
Activities and Projects, Teacher's Edition
Instructor's Resource CD
Teacher's Wrap Edition (hardcover, 4-color, 336 pages)
Teacher's Resource Box
Web site: **www.investigatingyourcareer.com**

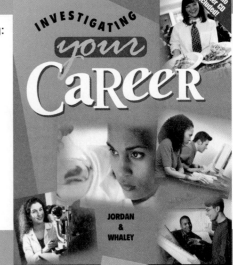

Other Middle School Products Available from South-Western

Integrated Computer Projects
by Momorella and Hohenstein
Integrated Computer Projects is an ideal source of computer literacy projects for students who already have some basic software skills. The text includes non-software-specific basic, intermediate, and advanced projects, as well as a capstone project, covering word processing, spreadsheet, database, presentation, and Internet skills. Students develop critical-thinking and decision-making skills while writing a story, planning a budget, making a presentation, shopping for a computer, solving a mystery, and completing other computer activities.

Text (softbound, 2-color, 168 pages)   0-538-43386-8

Typing Time
by Hoggatt and Shank
Typing Time is a keyboarding software package that teaches students how to type. New-key learning is accompanied by detailed hand animation for correct finger placement. Students are guided through the program and can work at their own pace. A built-in Teacher Utility automatically keeps detailed student records and makes class management a breeze. A text that complements the software is available to reinforce learning.

Windows Site License and User's Guide   0-538-69990-6
Macintosh Site License and User's Guide   0-538-43440-6
Text (softbound, 4-color, 128 pages)   0-538-69992-2
Text (hardbound, 4-color, 128 pages)   0-538-43538-0

Applied Computer Keyboarding
by Hoggatt and Shank
Applied Computer Keyboarding teaches basic keyboarding skills and mastering techniques and then progresses to word processing and business-document formatting. Students learn procedures for business-correct documents needed in every workplace, including MLA-style reports, personal business letters, fliers, and newsletters. *Applied MicroType 3.0* software is available to assist in teaching the alphabetic keyboard and the numeric keypad and holds student interest through games and 3-D models. The software checks selected documents in the text and includes the option to read and hear instructions in Spanish.

Text (hardbound, 4-color, 256 pages)   0-538-43658-1
Applied MicroType 3.0, Windows Site License   0-538-43662-X
Applied MicroType 3.0, Macintosh Site License   0-538-43663-8

THOMSON

SOUTH-WESTERN

Join us on the Internet at www.swlearning.com

Features to Enhance Learning

Chapter objectives set your goals for the chapter. The objectives correspond to both the main chapter sections and the activities.

Each chapter begins with a scenario relevant to your life and to the chapter content. You can see at the beginning of each chapter why the topics are important for your career success.

Key terms are introduced and defined in each chapter. The definitions are also included in a glossary on the Student Resource CD.

What do you think? questions guide you to an informal analysis of how the chapter relates to *your* future. A discussion of these questions will prepare you for success in understanding the chapter topic.

5 Understanding Future Careers

OBJECTIVES

After completing this chapter, you will be able to:

- Examine some characteristics of the Millennial Generation.
- Describe the various types of workforce diversity and their effects on the workplace.
- Identify nontraditional careers for men and women.
- Describe the characteristics of a successful entrepreneur.
- Explain the advantages of global careers.

Key Terms:

- workforce diversity
- prejudice
- discrimination
- culture
- reasonable accommodation
- gender equity
- nontraditional career
- entrepreneur
- market economy
- command economy

Ivan and Reiko met in an e-commerce class at school. They worked on several projects together and found that their personalities and abilities matched very well. Ivan had a way of looking at problems and coming up with various solutions. Reiko brought imagination to their projects with his ability to choose innovative ideas and come up with original marketing ideas. For their final project, they created an award-winning business plan for the state marketing competition. In fact, the plan was so unique that one of the state judges offered them start-up money for their own business. Their only obligation is to continue their education after high school toward associate degrees.

Ivan and Reiko's business plan is to create a wholesale import business that uses their cultural backgrounds. Since Ivan is of Spanish descent and Reiko's family is Japanese, they will import products from Spain and Japan and sell the products to restaurants and specialty food stores that serve or sell Spanish or Japanese food items. Ivan and Reiko plan to take college courses for the knowledge and skills needed to become successful business owners. Ivan wants to take classes primarily in business management, concentrating on accounting, economics and trends, and regulations for their industry. Reiko plans to major in marketing, specializing in advertising and e-commerce to design their computer web site. They will use the site to sell their products and to obtain customer information. Together the young men hope to build a successful food import business slowly, the result of a school project.

What do you think? How might an increase in workers of different races and cultures affect your future career?

Special features

Quotes from authors, leaders, and celebrities add relevance, humor, and motivational thoughts.

Activities are tied to specific sections throughout the chapter, allowing you to test your understanding of key concepts before learning new material. Each main section of a chapter has at least one related activity.

Career Success Tips show how even a small amount of the right information can help you be successful in your career.

Scenarios in each chapter present ideas in familiar real-world situations, allowing you to realize why the topic is important to you.

What do you think? questions throughout each chapter help you think about how a topic relates to *you* and *your* career.

Counselors

Counselors have several responsibilities. One of them is to provide information to guide you as you make decisions for your future. They can suggest courses for you that are based on your activities, talents, grades, and abilities. They can offer selections for researching educational options, such as computer searches. They can set up interviews with employers. In addition, if you choose to use their expertise, they are trained to help you work through the process of career development.

What a counselor does best is help you discover your options. For example, suppose you go to the counselor's office to find out about a career in medicine. Your counselor may ask what particular career you're thinking about—doctor, nurse, dental hygienist, pharmacist, medical transcriptionist. Then the two of you may talk about the courses you should take in high school to prepare for your career. You and your counselor may also talk about other careers in medicine you had not considered—physical therapy, sports medicine, nutrition.

When you have narrowed your career focus and have chosen your education and training pathway, the counselor can help you toward your goal by providing planning checklists, information on courses, suggestions for employment, and tips for taking control of your homework. A counselor is an invaluable resource and has many ways to help you on your *P*A*T*H to Success.*

Use Activity 2-2, "Learning from Others," to find out about the career success of someone you know.

> **66** The future belongs to those who believe in the beauty of their dreams. **99**
> —*Eleanor Roosevelt*

Environmental Influences on Career Decisions

The environment can influence your career decisions in many ways. The following questions are all related to your environment—either your work environment or your social environment. Your **work environment** is made up of the surroundings and conditions of your workplace. Your **social environment** includes the community where you live and work and your lifestyle choices.

- Do you want to stay where you live now? Do you prefer a rural, urban, or suburban setting?
- How important is the outdoors in influencing your choice of career? For example, is mountain biking an important activity for you? Or are you an avid surfer?
- Do you want to have someplace nearby to continue your education?
- Is climate important to you? Do you prefer a change of seasons or a consistent climate?
- Will there be a future for people in your caree... munity where you want to live?
- Do you want to work around people or in isola...

You believe in your business. You are the only one who can make your business successful. Be sure the values and principles that guide your life are the values and principles that guide your business.

Activity 5-7, "Running the Show," is a quiz that allows you to find out if you have an entrepreneurial spirit.

Global Career Opportunities

Businesses today and in the future must consider whether their marketplace includes more than their local area. Companies not only sell products or perform services in other countries but also import materials from companies worldwide. Many businesses believe a global outlook is necessary in order to be competitive and to attract new customers.

CAREER SUCCESS TIP

To help you decide whether you would like working in a foreign country, talk to someone who has worked and lived abroad.

For example, a company in the United States may form a partnership with a company in another country. Both companies profit from such an arrangement because both can reach more customers. Or a company in the United States might reach an agreement with a foreign government to set up an office or a manufacturing plant in the foreign country. The foreign country benefits from increased employment, and the U.S. company benefits from lower manufacturing costs and a larger market for its products or services.

How does this global marketplace affect you? It provides more career options and opportunities. For example, you can consider working for a U.S. company in one of its plants or offices located in a foreign country.

Rema has two major goals in life. She wants to learn to be a good machinist, and she wants to travel all over the world. To become a machinist, she plans to train at the career center during high school. As part of that education, Rema can work at a manufacturing company as a machinist helper while she continues with her classes. Through the company, Rema can reach her second goal. The manufacturing company has branches around the world. She can begin her work in Germany in an international apprentice program. Then she can transfer to another division with the same company in another part of the world. Rema can not only become a good machinist, she can also share her skills worldwide.

What do you think? What are some advantages of being a worker in another country? What are some disadvantages of a global assignment?

Another career option for you to consider is working abroad for a foreign company. For example, employers worldwide need workers with

IN A NUTSHELL

• **I can discuss the characteristics of the Millennial Generation.**

The Millennial Generation, born in 1982 or later, has more freedom in choosing a career than past generations had. In general, the Millennial Generation values family over building a career. As a result, stress levels are lower for this generation. Also, the male and female roles in the workplace are less distinctive for this generation.

• **I can describe the various types of workforce diversity and their effects on the workplace.**

Workforce diversity includes cultural differences, people with disabilities, and gender equity. Having a multicultural workplace enhances both the employees and the relationships with customers. A workplace that is gender equitable provides males and females with equal opportunities. When people with disabilities have appropriate job skills, they can succeed in their careers if given reasonable accommodations. Both employers and employees are expected to respect others' differences and not show prejudice or discrimination. Effective communication unifies a workplace and requires an understanding of workforce diversity.

• **I can i...**

A non...
of 25 j...
traditi...
trade, ...
are oft...
explor...
better ...

• **I can d...**
entrep...

Entrep...
them. ...
organi...
willing...
persist...

• **I can e...**

The gl...
nities. ...
knowle...
I can l...

92

In a Nutshell is a brief summary of the chapter that immediately follows the last chapter section. Each point corresponds to a chapter objective and summarizes the key concepts of a main chapter section.

Employers are becoming more aware of the benefits of hiring workers for nontraditional careers. Employers realize they need to hire the best applicant for a job regardless of the person's gender. A successful nontraditional career depends in part on the employer making the situation comfortable for the employee. For example, businesses that provide sexual harassment training to all employees often have fewer discrimination situations and better cooperation among coworkers.

Use Activity 5-6, "Case Challenges," to investigate stereotypes and equity situations.

Entrepreneurship

Does the thought of owning your own business appeal to you? Have you dreamed of being an **entrepreneur**, a person who creates and manages a business? Starting your own business is a way of combining your passions, skills, and values into a career that *you* control. Being an entrepreneur is not a career choice, but rather a goal for your career plan. It's one of the ways to achieve your *P*A*T*H to Success*.

In his information technology systems classes, Karim learned the skills to install, network, and repair various computer and digital systems. At first, he used his skills at home by networking his family's computers to make a more efficient system. When Karim'...
him to ...
compu...
workin...

Althou...
busines...
both fo...
Then h...
future ...
initial ...
installi...
future ...
for his ...
he grad...
cessful...
employ...

Running a bus...
be prepared t...
seven days a v...
characteristics...
the business b...
of the followi...
to consider sta...

CAREER FACT

By 2010, one out of two Americans will create his or her own career or start his or her own business.

88

When a key term is introduced, it is highlighted and defined.

Career Facts highlight interesting facts, findings, and trends in the world of work.

---

time, he decided to work as an orderly in a rehabilitation center for a year. By working as an orderly, he would get firsthand exposure to careers in physical therapy. Evan thought this experience would allow him to make a firm career decision, one that he would be satisfied with for many years.

Nontraditional careers for men are often in nurturing career fields, such as teaching and caring for the sick. Compared to many traditional careers for men, nurturing careers tend to require less training, have lower pay with fewer benefits, and have fewer opportunities for advancement. Because nurturing careers have typically been undervalued and underpaid, those men who require prestige and a high salary may not be satisfied in these nontraditional careers.

However, the traditional compensation characteristics of a nurturing career are less applicable in the healthcare field due to the high demand for workers. More occupational levels, such as the practitioner level (for example, nurse practitioner) and the assistant level (for example, physician's assistant), have increased career satisfaction factors. Healthcare careers often have higher pay, better benefits, more prestige, and greater advancement opportunities than in the past.

REAL PEOPLE
REAL CAREERS

Internet Radio Station Owner
When did Daniel Anstandig know he wanted to have his own business? At age four, he began selling subscriptions to the family newsletter in his neighborhood. He wrote and sold a neighborhood newspaper in elementary school. He admired his grandfather's work in radio. In fact, Daniel liked the work so much that he built a low-power transformer at age eleven and broadcast a call-in show. At age thirteen, Daniel hung around the college radio station so much that they gave him his own show.
   When he was fifteen, Daniel founded DAER Radio, an Internet radio station. Four years later the station had over 1 million listeners each month. Daniel is the program director. He has attracted nationally syndicated broadcasters, and he writes for one of them. On weekends, he is an IJ (Internet jockey). In addition, Daniel does voice-overs and writes lyrics for advertising. He does all this while balancing his college courses at a major university near Cleveland, Ohio.
   What makes Daniel so successful? He listens to his listeners via live feedback and e-mail. He constantly surveys his audience. "The audience tells us what to play and essentially runs each show," Daniel says. By using his audience as a guide, Daniel Anstandig continues his success.

For more information, investigate:
• Daniel Anstandig at *www.youngbiz.com* in the YoungBiz 100, or use a search engine such as *www.google.com* and the keywords *Daniel Anstandig*.
• becoming an entrepreneur at *www.highschoolstartups.com* or at *www.youngbiz.com*.

Source: "Infotainment Division." *Young Biz. www.youngbiz.com.*

86

PART 2 • • • • • NARROWING THE CHOICES

Real People, Real Careers tell engaging, true stories that spotlight interesting careers and career paths, expanding your knowledge of career possibilities. Web sites provide an opportunity for more exploration.

FEATURES TO ENHANCE LEARNING

Activities

Internet activities allow you to expand your knowledge of topics and to hone your research skills.

ACTIVITY 5-3   Internet Investigation

The Job Access site, *www.jobaccess.org*, works with companies to employ people with disabilities. The site has useful resources and employment information for persons with disabilities and for employers needing employees. Research the Job Access site as listed below.

1. Click on "Job Search" and then on "Job Seeker."
    a. Explore a field of interest or one of the companies listed.
    b. How does the site respect persons with disabilities?

2. Click on "the A.D.A."
    a. Investigate two of the sections. Write a summary of each section.
    b. How would this information benefit individuals with disabilities?

ACTIVITY 5-4   Attitudes

Determine whether the following statements about men and women show a *Traditional Attitude* or a *Nontraditional Attitude*. Why did you choose your answer? Discuss your results with the class.

1. Males have more mathematical ability than females.

2. A male's physical strength allows him to work more efficiently than a female.

3. A woman's first responsibility is to her home.

4. Males and females are equally capable of managing a home.

5. Males are better thinkers than females.

6. If males and females have jobs with the same description, they should get equal pay.

7. Females are more emotional than males.

8. A smart female should downplay her intelligence around males.

9. Females should have the same career options as males.

10. A male's main priority is to provide for his family.

ACTIVITY 5-5   Expectations

Decide whether the following job-relat___
Why did you choose your answer?

1. While researching careers, males a___
gender-appropriate careers.

2. Men and women who have the sam___

94

Your interviews in the Learning from Others activities provide first-hand knowledge about the requirements for career success and help you develop skills for the job search process.

Many activities become part of your Career Journey Folder. You will use these activities to discover your ideal career, to develop your career plan, and to guide you on your career journey.

You complete many activities by working on a team, emphasizing the importance of teamwork in today's workplace and helping you develop team skills.

ACTIVITY 5-1   Learning from Others

You are a member of the Millennial Generation because you were born in 1982 or later. Some of the characteristics of your generation are explained on page 77.

1. Choose someone to interview from one of the generations listed below.
    • Generation X, born 1961–1981
    • Baby Boomers, born 1943–1960
    • Silent Generation, born 1925–1942

2. Interview the person by asking the following questions:
    • What is your generation group?
    • What is (was) your career field? What is (was) your last job title in that field?
    • What were your family's expectations of your personal behavior? Did they expect you to behave better than they did, the same as they did, or worse than they did? Why do you choose that answer?
    • Would you describe your culture as "clean-cut"? Why or why not?
    • Are (were) males and females treated differently in the workplace? Why or why not? If so, how?
    • How do (did) you treat career and family in your life? What are (were) your employer's expectations of your attitude toward your career and family?
    • How much stress do (did) you have in your life? How do you handle too much stress, especially stress on the job?
    • Do you believe you had freedom in choosing your career? Why or why not?

3. Answer the same questions yourself, writing down your responses.

4. Compare your answers with those from the rest of the class.

Rather than having you simply write definitions, the Coming to Terms activities use applications to reinforce understanding of key terms introduced in the chapter.

ACTIVITY 5-2   Coming to Terms

The terms listed below relate to the workplace. For each term, describe a situation where the term applies. The situation may be fact or fiction. Then in small groups, describe a positive ending to the situation.

1. Prejudice

2. Discrimination

3. Workforce diversity

Is starting your own business your dream? Do you have what it takes to eat, sleep, and breathe your business every day of the year? Take this quiz to find out if you have an entrepreneurial spirit.

1. You've never tried racquetball but decide it's time to try your hand at it. In the first five minutes, you miss the ball with every swing and get hit on the back by the ball. What should you do?

   A. Exchange your racquet for in-line skates.

   B. Get out on the court and play again.

2. Are you the one who knows the latest trends, who recommends what your friends should be wearing or reading or listening to or watching?

   A. I have no clue what is in style or what's not—what's hot or what's not.

   B. I seem to be able to predict the latest trends before they become trends. I know what's hot!

3. Have you ever had a hobby? How long did it last?

   A. I've got a closet full of hobbies that I tried for a while.

   B. Of course! People love my latest creations and want to see what I'm currently working on.

4. Those pants you bought yesterday looked great on you in the dressing room in the store. Now you are home, and you find that the color is not flattering at all. What do you do?

   A. Throw them on the floor of your closet and try to forget about the wasted money.

   B. Go back to the store and exchange them for the right color.

5. In the middle of the night, the power goes out—and so does your alarm clock. You wake up late, making you an hour late for work. What do you say to your boss?

   A. Explain why you are late—in minute detail. That explanation makes you even later starting work.

   B. Quickly explain what happened. Work late, making up your time. Then purchase a windup alarm on the way home.

6. Your friend is always late no matter where you are going. When she shows up half an hour late for your dinner together, what do you say when she makes excuses again?

   A. "No problem. Traffic is a problem sometimes."

   B. "If you're late next time, I'm only waiting five minutes."

(See page 98 for a discussion of this qui

---

3. Women cannot be good supervisors because they get too emotional.

4. A man is a better choice to be a sheet metal worker because men are stronger than women.

5. When thinking about possible careers, you should not consider whether a career is only for men or only for women.

6. A woman makes a better nurse than a man does because women are more nurturing than men.

7. Men are better matched for more careers than women.

8. When faced with two candidates—a man and a woman—with similar qualifications, the employer should consider the gender of the job candidate.

9. Employers should consider that women may take time off to have children.

10. Employers should consider that men need to support their families.

In each of the situations below, determine whether the situation shows *Prejudice* or *No Prejudice*. Explain why you chose your answer.

1. On the job bulletin board at the high school is a job opening notice for Powell's Market:

   Girls—Interested in being a grocery cashier? See Mr. Jay at Powell's Market.

2. Brenda loves reading and wants to share her passion with others. She applies to read Books on Tape but is turned down because she is hearing-impaired.

3. Because Natori is of Japanese descent, Ms. Simpson asked him to take information technology courses.

4. After graduating from a community college in computer applications, Donita began creating beautiful brochures and flyers. Because she is an African American, Greater Sycamore Insurance hired her very quickly.

5. Allen is insistent that his wife stay at home and not work until their child enters kindergarten. His reason: "Childcare is women's work."

6. Gary has Down syndrome. Ekkie's Market hired him to bag groceries.

7. In the teacher's lounge, Margaret was overheard discussing her attitude toward the students in her chemistry class. "I like having girls in class better than boys because girls are quieter and more cooperative. With more girls than boys, I can control the class better."

8. "Silvia is from Mexico. We can't hire her for the drive-through after school. She'll just take a siesta, a nap every afternoon."

9. Anita has excellent grades in science and math. Because of her grades and her passion for helping others, her father is glad she is planning a career in medicine.

10. Leatha was born with a clubfoot, which makes her walk with a limp even after many operations. She applied for the physical education teacher position at Clark High but was not asked to interview.

All activities are designed to help you explore your career options, understand the skills and qualities needed for career success, and prepare for your future.

The Case Challenges in each chapter apply chapter concepts to common real-world situations and help you develop your problem-solving skills.

Preface

In a unique approach to career planning, *Investigating Your Career* matches a career area to the student rather than the student to a career area. This approach focuses on each student's needs and guides the student to pursuing a career based on individual talents and passions. *Investigating Your Career* addresses current career trends related to technology, workforce diversity, and global markets; explores investigating careers via job shadowing, service learning, and community mentoring; explains and discusses a variety of career and educational options; and emphasizes self-awareness, goal setting, decision making, reduction of prejudice, SCANS competencies, and economic responsibility. *Investigating Your Career* also promotes future career success by providing students with current and projected career information and by helping them build skills in such vital areas as networking, teamwork, communication, and problem solving.

About the Authors

Ann K. Jordan is the Career Development Manager for the Great Oaks Institute of Technology and Career Development where she oversees career development programs and funds for 114,000 K-12 students, encompassing 36 school districts in southwestern Ohio. Ann is active in the Ohio Career Education Association, serving as Conference committee chair, Board of Trustees member, and currently as President. She was awarded Ohio's Outstanding Career Coordinator Award in 1999. Ann is also active in the Ohio-ACTE organization, working with professional development and the Student Services division. Ann Jordan has also co-authored *Communicating for Success* and *Discovering Your Career* for South-Western, Thomson Learning.

Lynne T. Whaley currently develops and teaches business skills classes for the public and private sector. Since 1999, she has edited or contributed to several career and communication textbooks for South-Western, Thomson Learning. In addition, Lynne has served as Office Occupations instructor and as adjunct faculty at Boise State University. After graduating from the University of Santa Clara, she spent the first 13 years of her career in first-line supervisory, district staff, and large-systems marketing positions at a Fortune 500 telecommunications firm. Lynne has also co-authored *Discovering Your Career* for South-Western.

Acknowledgements

The authors appreciate the contributions, positive recommendations, and constructive criticisms of the following:

Dr. Ernest F. Biller, Coeur d'Alene, ID

Elizabeth Blake, Negaunee, MI

Dr. Mark S. Brown, Columbus, OH

William P. Christos, Cincinnati, OH

Bruce Girouard, Danville, NH

Douglas Haskell, Cincinnati, OH

Mary Jane Hoag, College Station, TX

Belinda McCharen, Midwest City, OK

Mary Lou Millsap, Garland, TX

Sherry Mitchell, Lubbock, TX

B.J. Powell, El Paso, TX

DebAnn Rippy, Kuna, ID

Amy Steketee, New Carlisle, IN

Gemelia Tyler, Hillsboro, OH

Patricia Wetzel, Garland, TX

Table of Contents

Part 5   Creating Tools for the Future

Getting Ready

Chapter 1	**Preparing Your Path to Success**

Your choice of career will affect everything about your adult life—where you live, what your lifestyle is like, and how satisfied you are with your life. By beginning your planning now, you will have a better chance for future success and happiness. Career success starts with your *P*A*T*H to Success*—your passions, attitude, talents, and heart.

Chapter 2	**Influences on Career Choices**

Everything and everyone around you can influence your choice of career. The people you know—your family, teachers, friends, and others—often have the greatest effect on your career decisions. By understanding how influences affect you, you will be able to make the choices that lead to career success.

Chapter 3	**Understanding Yourself**

You are a unique combination of passions, talents, personality, and values. Career assessments can help you discover how your *P*A*T*H to Success* leads to a career plan. Career assessments may involve written answers to questions or informal activities. All assessments help you learn about yourself and what you can achieve.

Part Overview

Part 1: Preparing

Part 1 explains to students why they should begin investigating their careers now rather than waiting until high school or even later. Students need to understand that career success depends on careful and informed preparation. This part introduces students to the *P*A*T*H to Success,* a tool they will use to investigate an ideal career—one that matches their passions, attitude, talents, and heart. Students begin their career journey by learning how people and influences affect their career decisions. Then students continue the self-discovery process through formal and informal career assessment activities.

PART 1

Focus

Investigating Your Career uses a career discovery process. Part 1 provides the background and groundwork for your students' career discovery. Think of your own career discovery process. You may have chosen education because of an influential relative, you may be an educator as a second (or more) career, or you may be a teacher because you were always passionate about helping and improving others. However you chose your career, share the experiences with your students sometime during Part 1.

Chapter 1
Preparing Your Path
to Success

FOCUS

Chapter 1 explains the importance of a satisfying career. By beginning their career planning now, students can set realistic goals and make career choices that will lead to career satisfaction. Following their *P*A*T*H to Success* will help students in the self-discovery process—the start of their career journey.

Use the **Objectives** and **Key Terms** printed in the margin to help students focus on the content of this chapter. Use the **video segment** for Chapter 1 to trigger discussion.

TEACH

Discuss the chapter's opening scenario with students. Point out to students that they must take responsibility for their own education plan, but they don't have to do it alone.

What do you think?

Use **TM01-01**.
Question 1: Students' answers will vary. Make sure students understand that by not planning, they may not have the appropriate skills or education required for the kind of career they want. **Question 2:** Students' answers will vary. Point out that what one person sees as a positive, someone else might see as a negative.

Career Journal

Ask students to spend 10 minutes writing Career Journal entries that answer the following questions:
1. What do you think this chapter will cover?
2. What do you already know about these topics?
3. What three things do you want to learn about these topics?

---

1 Preparing Your Path to Success

OBJECTIVES

After completing this chapter, you will be able to:

• Discuss realistic career expectations.
• Compare the differences in job, occupation, and career.
• Describe the steps in the *P*A*T*H* to Success*.
• Explain why career planning should begin now.
• Describe how career planning supports career success.

❝The purpose of life is a life of purpose.❞
—Robert Byrne, Poet

Key Terms:

• job
• occupation
• career
• career cluster
• transferable skills
• specialized skills

When Adam was in school, he dreamed of earning a living as an artist. Not content to just dream, he decided to investigate how artists make money. He found that artists provide various kinds of artwork for different types of commercial projects. Commercial contracts require that an artist work closely with clients and meet deadlines.

Working with his art teachers, counselor, and family, Adam set goals for his future and developed an education plan. He also chose high school classes that would meet the entrance requirements of art colleges. In his first year of college, Adam realized that he especially liked working with natural materials and that sculpting was his passion. He learned welding not only as an additional way to sculpt, but also as a way to earn money. He started by creating lamps from discarded bus transmissions, working off hours in the college's welding shop. To continue building his skills, Adam transferred to an art college that offered glass blowing, a specialty not taught in many schools.

Today Adam's education and skills support his passion. Adam's creative versatility is valued by employers who use his artwork in architecture, construction, and design. By developing a career plan and making adjustments as he progressed, Adam achieved his dream of earning his living as an artist.

What do you think?
What can happen if you don't plan for your career?
What are the pros and cons of waiting until you're ready—maybe until after college—before planning your career?

2

CHAPTER RESOURCES and MATERIALS

Activities & Projects book
Instructor's Resource CD
• Forms and Worksheets for Chapter Activities 1-1 through 1-6
• Internet Links for Chapter 1
• PowerPoint Presentation for Chapter 1
• Lesson Plans
• Teaching Masters for Chapter 1
• Video Discussion Guide for Chapter 1

Chapter Tests book
ExamView® CD
Video
Web Site

Career Expectations

"What do you want to be when you grow up?" How many times have you heard this or a similar question? Chances are your answer referred to some type of paid or volunteer work because most adults in our society work for a large portion of their lives. Everyone has an idea of what work is and what having a career means.

During her school years, Lucy enjoyed creating pizzas or special cakes for her friends' birthdays. The dinners she prepared for special events were famous. Six months ago Lucy was excited to get a job as an assistant chef at a family-style restaurant. She thought she would be doing work she loved. She did not realize she would be using prepackaged sauces and specific recipes to prepare the side dishes for main entrees. The job is not what Lucy imagined doing when she said she liked to cook, and now she is very unhappy. She keeps working only because she must earn a living.

While attending high school, Rachel was part of the team that wrote and edited the school magazine. She enjoyed researching and organizing information and looked for a job where she could use those skills. Now she is a paralegal in the state prosecutor's office. Rachel cannot wait to get to work each day. She looks forward to investigating the laws, judicial decisions, and legal articles relevant to her cases and to assisting the attorneys during trials. In Rachel's opinion, the days end too quickly.

Why do you think Lucy is unhappy? What are her strengths?

Why is Rachel happy with her work? What are her strengths?

What do you think?

Your Expectations

Even if you do not know what you want to do, you probably have some ideas about what you expect from your career. For example, you may assume you will make a lot of money or travel the world. You may also have general expectations about the type of work you will be doing. Perhaps you think about working in the medical or legal profession. Perhaps you see yourself working in a technical field.

What do you expect from a career?

- Income?
- Reputation or fame?
- Creativity?
- Geographic location?

- Service to others?
- Title and position?
- Balance in your life?
- Use of your strengths?

What do you think?

Point out that career expectations can influence how well people do their jobs and how much satisfaction they derive from their work. Stress that jobs (or even careers) can't make a person happy, but that people can find meaning in their work if they choose work that is meaningful to them.

What do you think?

Use **TM01-02**.
Question 1A: Possible reasons for Lucy's unhappiness include not doing what she enjoys, having expectations that differ from reality, and feeling trapped. **Question 1B:** Lucy's strengths include responsibility and creativity. **Question 2A:** Rachel is doing work she enjoys. **Question 2B:** Rachel's strengths include writing, editing, researching, and organizing.

TEACH

Explain that everyone has career expectations, even if a person has not settled on a specific career. Remind students that it is important to dream big, but that initial career expectations may not be the best fit in the long run.

What do you think?

Use **TM01-03**.
Spend time talking about all eight expectations, and make sure students understand there are no right or wrong answers. What is important to one person is not necessarily important to others.

ONLINE RESOURCES

Check out the web site **www.investigatingyourcareer.com** for teacher resources, student activities, and replacements for broken links for this chapter. To access the teacher resources:

Username: career
Password: investigate

Remind students that it is never too early to start investigating careers. Suggest that they make a point of asking adults about their jobs, occupations, and careers.

What do you think?

Use **TM01-04**.
Students' answers will vary, but their answers should indicate that they realize many teenagers have unrealistic expectations. Wrap up the discussion by pointing out that while the expectations expressed in these statistics are not unrealistic for all teenagers, they are unrealistic for many.

Your Peers' Expectations

A University of Chicago study discovered that teenagers have the following expectations about their futures:

- One in three intends to have a professional career.
- Nearly 10 percent plan to be doctors.
- Few dream about blue collar or service industry jobs.
- Almost all expect to have a high-status job with high pay.
- Many expect to graduate with a bachelor's degree (four or more years of college).
- Many believe a bachelor's degree is a vital tool for success.
- A large majority expect to earn a Ph.D., which requires 8 to 12 years of full-time schooling after high school.

What do you think? How realistic are the expectations expressed in these statistics? Explain your answer.

According to the study, your peers realize that work is important for the future, but they do not necessarily expect to enjoy their work. Many have not yet discovered that the secret to enjoying work is to choose work that uses their strengths. When students know their strengths and learn about career possibilities, they set higher career goals and better understand how to choose a fulfilling career.

For most students, their parents, teachers, and friends—in that order—have the greatest influence on their career decisions. If family members or other adults understand and communicate the rewards of well-chosen work, then students have a clearer understanding of how to choose satisfying careers.

The influence of friends has also proved to be important to students when they choose and prepare for careers. Just as students are more apt to be involved in school activities if their friends are involved in school activities, students tend to be more interested in careers if their friends are interested in careers.

While advice from various sources may be valuable, building a truly successful career will depend on how you use your strengths. Finding out about your strengths is something *you* must learn for yourself.

4

DIFFERENT LEARNING ABILITIES

Attention Deficit Disorder
Divide the class into pairs. If you have ADD students, pair them with a non-ADD student. Have student pairs brainstorm about the dreams they can have for their future careers. Then have student pairs make a list of strengths they have. Have mentor students prompt ADD students to help them discover their strengths. Have student pairs brainstorm about possible careers that might fit their strengths and dreams for their future. Share results as a class.

Based on your own experience, do you agree with the results of the study? Why or why not?

Who or what influences your career decision making? In what way?

 What do you think?

The Reality

According to the College Board, high school students are most likely to select the following careers as their top choices:

1. Marine biologist
2. Physical therapist or sports medicine specialist
3. Doctor
4. Lawyer
5. Teacher

Is it likely that enough jobs in these careers will exist to accommodate all high school students choosing these fields? Why or why not?

What do you think?

In contrast, the Bureau of Labor Statistics (BLS) predicts the following top ten fastest-growing occupations between 1998 and 2008. According to the BLS, these ten occupations will account for nearly 20 percent of the employment growth in these years.

1. Computer engineer
2. Computer support specialist
3. Systems analyst
4. Database administrator
5. Desktop publishing specialist
6. Paralegal and legal assistant
7. Personal care and home health aide
8. Medical assistant
9. Social and human services assistant
10. Physician assistant

In choosing a career, you need to realize that, just as the career demands of ten years ago are not the career demands of today, the career demands of today are not the career demands of the future. Battelle Institute predicts that none of the top ten careers for 2010 currently exist. The *CAM Report* states that when today's kindergartners reach the job market, 90 percent of them will work in careers that do not exist in today's world. Labor trends such as these are important for you to understand as you plan your career. You want to be sure you prepare for a career that will be available when you finish your education or skill training. Chapter 4 will give you more insight into choosing a career that has positive long-term prospects.

Do you have realistic career expectations? Activity 1-1, "Career Planning Quiz," helps check your knowledge about planning for a career.

CAREER FACT

Is your ambition to play a professional sport? Do you know that only 500 of 1,150,000 seniors who played high school baseball signed pro contracts this year? Put your education and training first.

—*adapted from* The Cincinnati Enquirer, *a column by John Erardi*

5

Use **TM01-05**.
Questions 1A & 1B: Students' answers will vary. Make sure students support their answers with reasonable explanations. **Questions 2A & 2B:** Students' answers will vary. Make sure students can explain how the person or thing influences their career choices.

TEACH

Emphasize to students that they must have realistic expectations in order to choose a fulfilling career. Students often focus their attention on careers with high pay and high status while ignoring careers and jobs that are better suited to their abilities and interests.

What do you think?

Use **TM01-06**.
Students' answers will vary. They should realize that there is a limited demand for certain professions.

TEACH

Point out that most of the occupations on the list are service jobs. Students also should realize that the educational requirements for these occupations vary; not all require a four-year college degree.

APPLY

Have students complete **Activity 1-1, "Career Planning Quiz,"** that appears on page 15. Teaching suggestions for this activity appear on page 15, and answers to the quiz appear on page 18. An activity worksheet can be found on the Career Portfolio and Resource CD—**Text Activity 01-1.doc**.

CAREER TREND

Put Education before Sports

Tell students that the high salaries they hear about in baseball go only to a few players at the top. According to information compiled by *Newsweek* in 2002, 63 percent of all the money paid to players goes to the top 20 percent. A star baseball player may earn more than $90,000 per game, while players with fewer than three years of playing in the major leagues may earn as little as $200,000 per year. Minor league players earn even less, most earning less than their peers in other careers.

—*Source:* Newsweek, August 26, 2002, pp. 46–47

Be sure students understand the definitions of job, occupation, and career and how these terms apply to different work situations. Offer students some examples of careers and jobs. Consider using current employment ads to illustrate the difference between a career and a job.

What do you think?

Use **TM01-07**.
Students' answers will vary.

What do you think?

Use **TM01-08**.
To help identify the advantages and disadvantages of frequent job changes, ask students to make a list of reasons why a person might change jobs. Advantages students might identify include better pay, better location, no time to get bored, the chance to meet new people, and the opportunity to learn new skills. Disadvantages students might identify include not able to see long-term projects to completion, not able to demonstrate loyalty, not able to build up a good reputation within an organization, limited opportunities for advancement, and limited opportunities to master skills.

Job, occupation, career—these terms are used constantly. Do they all have the same basic meaning? To make sure there is a common understanding, let's consider the differences.

What do you think?
What do the terms *job, occupation,* and *career* mean to you?
What is your reaction to, that is, your feeling about, each term?

Job

As a student, you may have had at least one job or may have one soon. Your job may be babysitting, delivering newspapers, doing yard work, or assisting in an office. A **job** is a paid position involving a specific place and time and specific tasks set by an employer. A job allows you to save for something, to pay bills, or to put money in your bank account. You choose a job not necessarily because you like what you're doing, but because the immediate benefits meet your needs. Thus, you may choose a job simply because of the money you will earn. On the other hand, you may choose a job because you want to get some experience in a field you are considering for long-term employment.

A job is often temporary. In fact, after the age of 25, a person changes jobs an average of 10 to 15 times throughout a lifetime.

What do you think?
What are some of the advantages and disadvantages of frequent job changes?

Occupation

An **occupation** is a group of related tasks that require special training, education, or experience to learn a specific set of skills. A person with those skills may claim that occupation—whether the person is currently working in a paid job or not. For example, a person trained as an engineer remains an engineer even when not working in a job in that field. People with an occupation often work at several jobs in their field throughout their working life. They may consider their occupation as a job or as a career.

> 66 **Choose a job you love, and you will never work a day in your life.** 99
> —*Confucius,*
> *Chinese Philosopher*

Career

When asked the difference between a job and a career, people often say a career is something for life and a job satisfies a need. A **career** describes a lifetime work history or long-term participation in a particular field of expertise. When choosing a career, many people base their choice on what they like doing and what they want to do the rest of their lives. Instead of considering a career as a way to earn a living, they see a career as an important, positive part of their lives.

DIFFERENT LEARNING STYLES

Kinesthetic Learners
To help kinesthetic learners understand the definitions of job, occupation, and career, divide students into three groups. Have one group make a list of five or six jobs. Have the second group make a list of occupations. Have the third group make a list of careers. Have each group write and perform a skit that demonstrates one of the jobs, occupations, or careers on their list.

All the possible careers in an entire field are called a **career cluster.** For example, nurse assistants, registered nurses, radiology technicians, and doctors all have careers in the health cluster. Regardless of the career cluster, most people begin in an entry-level job. Then they improve their skills and progress to a more complex career. While people do change careers, they do not do so as often as they change jobs. The average adult changes careers between five and eight times.

A Career or a Job?

Many times a person chooses a job based on its location and pay. The person may think, "The job fulfills the needs I have right now. I don't know whether or not I'll like the job, but that's not important in the long run." However, liking a career *is* important in the long run. The career path you choose will affect all aspects of your life—your life outside your work as well as the work you do. Research shows that people who enjoy their careers are more satisfied with their lives. They see a career as an important, positive part of their lives. The closer a career is to your talents and passions, the more fulfilled you will be with your career.

Look at the quotation on the previous page. What do you think Confucius means by the term *job*? What does the quotation mean to you?

What do you think?

REAL PEOPLE

REAL CAREERS

Writer and Producer of Children's Animated CD-ROMs

As a little girl, Theresa Duncan loved toys, games, and storybooks. She thought that storybooks were so imaginative, so full of charm and creativity. "I just never outgrew that . . . imaginative storytelling style," Theresa said as she talked about her passion. That passion inspired her to write her own children's stories on her computer, adding graphics to illustrate them.

Theresa's talent with computers led her to work with a company that produced interactive CD-ROMs. There she learned to animate her stories, making them even more appealing. The skills she learned with the company helped Theresa create an animated children's storybook, *Chop Suey,* which was named CD-ROM of the Year by *Entertainment Weekly.* Since then Theresa has written and produced other interactive adventures for girls in her fairy tale-creating factory. She now has her own company where she writes, develops, and markets CD-ROMs. Theresa's childhood passion for storytelling has stayed with her all her life.

For more information about:
- writing, investigate *www.bls.gov.* Search for "writers and editors."
- graphic design, explore *www.bls.gov.* Search for "graphic designers."

Source: Borst, Terry, and Deborah Todd. "Alt. Screenwriters." September, 1999. *www.wga.org/writtenBy.*

Most young people know they will change jobs throughout their adult lives. They realize they will need to move to companies that place greater value on what they have to offer and that pay them a higher wage. However, students are not aware of the average number of career changes the average person makes during his or her work life. Family members' experiences often influence students' impressions. In rural areas and isolated cities, the average number of career changes is likely to be less than the national average. Explain the meanings of an *average* number of job changes and an *average* person.

What do you think?

Use **TM01-09.**
Question 1A: Students' answers will vary. Students might suggest that in this instance, *job* refers to any kind of work—paid or unpaid. **Question 1B:** Students' answers will vary. Students might focus on the idea that if you enjoy doing something, it will not seem like work.

REAL PEOPLE—REAL CAREERS
Invite Speakers to Class
Have students make a list on the board of careers they are interested in. Vote on the top six. Then arrange the class into six groups. Assign each group one of the careers. Have each group research to find people in their community involved in the career. Suggest that students use the Internet and the local chamber of commerce or other business organizations to help with their research. Have groups invite the people to speak to the class about their careers.

APPLY

Have students complete **Activity 1-2, "Learning from Others,"** on page 15. Teaching suggestions and the solution for this activity appear on page 15. A three-page worksheet for this activity can be found on the Career Portfolio and Resource CD— **Text Activity 01-2.pdf.**

ENRICH

Have students complete **Activity 1-A, "Writing a Thank-You Letter,"** found in the *Investigating Your Career Activities & Projects* book.

In this activity, students write a thank-you letter to the person they interviewed for textbook Activity 1-2. Before mailing, each student's letter should be edited by his or her peers and/or by you.

Each chapter in the student text has a *Learning from Others* activity where students interview someone. Students should thank many of those interviewed with a letter.

Materials: Blank paper or access to word processing software; pens, envelopes, and stamps or access to postage machine

Solution: The solution for this activity appears in the *Teacher's Edition* of *Investigating Your Career Activities & Projects.*

Marcus worked after school in his Uncle Jamul's dry-cleaning business. After sorting dirty clothes, working in the heat of the pressing machines, and watching his uncle labor long hours, Marcus could not understand why his uncle chose to own several dry-cleaning stores. After all, his uncle had a degree in chemistry!

When Marcus asked his uncle to explain, Jamul said that he too had worked for a dry cleaner during his school years. He was fascinated with the chemistry of making clothes bright and clean—the scientific formulas for getting rid of the many kinds of stains and the challenge of cleaning various fabrics. To find out more about chemical interactions, Jamul studied chemistry in high school and college. He has since developed his own cleaning formulas.

Jamul also saw his employer expand from one store to three. Jamul enjoyed figuring out what he would have done if he were the owner. He wanted the challenges of making his own decisions and being involved in all aspects of his own business. To help realize his dream, Jamul took many business classes in college. Now his career includes both of his passions—science and business.

In Activity 1-2, "Learning from Others," you discover how successful people have chosen and planned their careers.

Your *P*A*T*H to Success*

Finding your path to a satisfying career requires careful planning and thoughtful decisions. It is not an easy task, but it is challenging and exciting. You may not realize when you look at career areas that *you* hold the key to discovering your career. That key is self-knowledge. Discovering your career path begins with *you*. You should base your career choice on your passions and your talents.

Your journey to a successful career begins with setting goals. Although your goals may change over time, the things you love to do and the talents you have do not change. By basing your career choice on *you*, your journey will be fulfilling and you will achieve career satisfaction. However, before you can follow your passions and talents to a career, you must know your interests, your values, and your skills. You need to evaluate who you are so you can find out who you can be.

INTEGRATED ACADEMICS
Language Arts

Have students bring a blank notebook to class to use as a career journal. As a class, read the information about *P*A*T*H* on the next page. Provide students class time to write a journal entry about their passions, attitudes, talents, and heart (what they believe is important to their life choices). Tell students what they write is private and they will not be required to share the content of their journals.

Investigating Your Career offers you ways to find the path that will lead to a satisfying career, one that fits your passions and talents. The *P*A*T*H to Success* is one such tool. It will help you begin the self-discovery process.

Passions	Uncovering your passions is the first step on your *P*A*T*H to Success*. *Passion* refers to the strong, positive feelings you experience while enjoying something. Enjoyment is not the same as competence. Being good at something does not necessarily mean you enjoy doing it. Begin to identify your career-related passions by thinking about what makes you happy. What were your favorite play activities as a child? As a teenager, what activities do you choose to do in your spare time?
Attitude	*Attitude* refers to the way you feel. Think about an activity you selected as one of your passions. Are you eager and excited about that activity? Do you excel at it? Enthusiasm, eagerness, and the belief that you can excel make up a positive attitude. A positive attitude helps you believe that you can achieve anything. Choosing a positive attitude is the second step on your *P*A*T*H to Success*.
Talents	*Talents* are natural strengths and abilities. Everyone has talents. The third step of the *P*A*T*H to Success* is to explore new areas until you know your talents. Consider your talents when looking at career areas. By choosing a career compatible with your talents, you can expand your strengths to help your career grow.
Heart	*Heart* refers to what you believe is important to your life choices. The fourth step on your *P*A*T*H to Success*, finding your heart, means answering the questions "What are my values? Who and what are the important influences in my life?" Your answers will help you believe in yourself, choose a lifestyle and career you love, and develop the flexibility and determination you need to reach your goals.

What have past activities, volunteer experiences, or part-time jobs taught you about your abilities, interests, and personality?

What do you think?

How much do you know about your talents and passions? Activity 1-3, "Survey Your Strengths," helps you take the first step to self-discovery.

DIFFERENT LEARNING ABILITIES
Dyslexia
Have students make a list on the board of several careers. Ask students to choose from this list one career they find appealing. Provide students with poster board and several magazines and art supplies. Have students cut pictures from the magazines that represent each letter of their *P*A*T*H to Success*. Then have students use the art supplies to create their *P*A*T*H* visually. Display the projects around the classroom.

TEACH
Emphasize that everyone has a unique *P*A*T*H to Success* and that discovering that *P*A*T*H* is the first step on each student's career journey. Discuss why each part of a person's *P*A*T*H* affects career success and why career satisfaction depends on finding a career that fulfills individual needs rather than on working in a career that fulfills others' expectations.

What do you think?

Use **TM01-10**.
Students' answers will vary. Students who have limited volunteering service and work experience or limited involvement in community activities can base their answers on experiences they have with sports, music lessons, chores, and hobbies.

APPLY
Have students complete **Activity 1-3, "Survey Your Strengths,"** on page 16. Teaching suggestions and the solution for this activity appear on page 16. An activity worksheet can be found on the Career Portfolio and Resource CD—**Text Activity 01-3.doc**.

Why Plan Now?

In the past, career planning was often ignored or put off until a student graduated from high school. At that point, students either accepted the best job they could find—without much regard to whether they found the job interesting—or started college.

In college, career planning was usually as uncommon as it was in high school. If college students were counseled about careers, the emphasis was often on how the students could prepare for available job openings in the labor market. Alternatively, some students may have obtained a degree first and then started thinking about job possibilities. Career research and self-assessments were simply tools students sometimes used to fit themselves into preselected fields with high growth potential.

Until the mid 1980s, people often stayed in one career all their working lives. Any career changes were usually initiated by employers through transfers, promotions, or terminations of employees. On the average, adults changed careers only three times in a lifetime, as opposed to the five to eight times today.

Technological advances and global competition have caused many changes in the workplace. In today's labor market, people need to be independent. Most employers expect employees to plan and implement their own career development. To be successful in this competitive job market, people need to develop two types of skills:

1. **Transferable skills** are similar skills used in various types of careers. For example, transferable skills include the ability to communicate well with others, to identify and solve problems, to set and evaluate goals, to use a computer, to work effectively in a team, and to lead others.
2. **Specialized skills** are skills used in specific occupations. For example, the ability to teach physics and the ability to operate a specific machine are specialized skills.

A broad skill base gives people more career choices and flexibility in their working lives. The flexibility helps people adapt to a changing labor market and avoid becoming burned out in one particular job.

The hot fields in the labor market continue to change rapidly. New technologies, expanding trade, and global economic competition mean greater opportunities and challenges. You can succeed by taking responsibility for your own career and committing to lifelong learning.

CAREER FACT

Old Rule: Become an expert in your career field. That way, your company can't do without you.

New Rule: The more skills you master, the more job and career choices you will have. Your ability to handle varied responsibilities will be invaluable in the long run.

What do you think?

What do you think may happen if you delay planning for your career until you graduate from high school?

Use Activity 1-4, "Coming to Terms," to understand some of the important terms in this chapter more thoroughly.

CAREER TREND
Importance of High School Courses

Create a panel of experts to help with classroom activities and your students. The panel should include two or three business leaders from different-sized businesses, an employment counselor from a placement service, and someone who can represent government employment. Arrange for the committee to visit your class. Divide the class into three groups. Have one group invite the panel members, another group prepare questions for the panel, and the last group introduce the panel members.

Planning for Career Success

Using *Investigating Your Career,* you can DREAM! With a positive attitude that uses your passions, your talents, and your heart, you can use this book to plan for a career. Life is 10 percent what happens to you and 90 percent how you react.

As a big sister, Kathleen liked to play with her younger brothers and sister. She created a family library, planned summer activities, wrote plays, and performed shows to entertain her siblings. In school, Kathleen was in every play, either backstage or onstage, and took part in speech competitions. Her part-time job was working in the local library.

When Kathleen began planning her career, she thought about several choices. She listened to the career ideas of her family, teachers, and friends. Then she thought, "Why do something other people think I should do? Why not do what I love to do?" So Kathleen planned a career as a drama, speech, and English teacher. Her organization and early teaching skills became her working life. What she liked to do, and did well, became her career choice.

CAREER SUCCESS TIP

Use your career plan to guide your selection of classes. Begin preparing for your future now.

What Is a Career Plan?

Your career will be a lifelong journey of self-discovery and accomplishment. A career plan is similar to an itinerary, the proposed outline of a journey. To build your career plan, you will:

- Travel the *P*A*T*H to Success.*
- Research career fields to find career clusters that complement your passions, spark your positive attitude, allow you to exercise your talents, and harmonize with your heart.
- Identify skill requirements in your chosen career clusters.
- Set goals for education, training, and experience.

Finally, you will design your career plan by listing the steps you need to take to reach your goals. As you begin to implement your career plan, you will find you need to be flexible. Life does not always go according to plan. However, if you start planning now, you can use your career plan to help you make decisions that will lead toward the goals you set.

A career plan allows *you* to be in charge. Rather than going through life waiting for a big break—the million-dollar jackpot or the genie in the lamp—you can make your own luck. Why not go through life doing something that gives you satisfaction? Something based on your goals, your talents, and your passions? Something that helps you be happy and productive? Now is the time to design a winning game plan for achieving your dream career.

Have students complete **Activity 1-C, "Community Jobs/Careers,"** found in the *Investigating Your Career Activities & Projects* book.

In this activity, students research a company in the community, identify the different types of jobs the company offers, and classify whether the work is a job or a career.

Students can work individually or in small groups of two or three people. The purpose of the worksheet is to collect brainstorming ideas. To validate or extend this activity, students may research the company's web site to find specific career information.

If students use the Internet, they should use the worksheet to collect their research. To demonstrate how to research a company's career areas, explore **www.thomsoncareers.com**. **Solution:** The solution for this activity appears in the *Teacher's Edition* of *Investigating Your Career Activities & Projects.*

CAREER SUCCESS TIP

How Current Classes Relate to Careers

On the board, make a list of several careers. Ask students to choose one of these careers or to use a career of their choice not listed. Have students write the career at the top of a piece of paper. Then along the left side of the paper, have students make a list of classes they are currently taking. Tell students to leave several lines between each class. To the right of each class, have students jot down ideas about how what they're learning in each class relates to the career.

Career Journey Folder

Explain that the Career Journey Folder is a place for students to store career information during this course and in the future. Have students read "Your Career Journey Folder," which can be found on the Career Portfolio and Resource CD—**CJ Folder.pdf**. Suggest that students print the document and put it in a folder.

What do you think?

Use **TM01-12**.
Ask students to describe several scenarios that might result from such an unplanned trip.

TEACH

Remind students that regardless of how well they plan their careers, they can experience events that force them to take detours from their planned career paths. These detours, however, don't have to take them off track permanently. Along with their career planning, they will prepare for any roadblocks in their path and be able to implement "Plan B."

APPLY

Have students complete **Activity 1-5, "Case Challenges,"** on page 17. Teaching suggestions and the solution for this activity appear on page 17. An activity worksheet can be found on the Career Portfolio and Resource CD—**Text Activity 01-5.doc**.

Throughout this book, you will see the symbol shown in the left margin. This icon suggests that you put a specific document into your Career Journey Folder. Your Career Journey Folder is a place to collect records of experiences that help you make career decisions, such as samples that illustrate your passions and talents, assessments, and much more. You may also add items such as personal notes about your career journey. When you look through the folder, you can review the results of your career planning efforts. Summaries of your personal *P*A*T*H to Success*, results of your career research, and samples of your imagination will all help you in the process of discovering your career.

What do you think? If you lived in California and you wanted to drive to New York to visit friends, what could happen if you left without supplies or a map?

Succeed through Career Planning

Both the planning process and your career plan will give you a head start toward career success. By knowing yourself—your passions, attitude, talents, and heart—you will be able to choose a career.

Finding your career focus helps you concentrate on your education. Setting goals provides a motivation for finishing high school and directing your future education and training. Some students and some parents think career planning should be postponed until after high school or during college. College is not a career plan. The costs of going to college make it an expensive way to experiment with career choices.

Not having a career plan is a direct cause of many students' problems, according to Leon Botstein in *Jefferson's Children*:

- One of five teenagers doesn't complete high school. This means that after 10 to 12 years of school, they will have trouble getting even entry-level work.
- Three out of ten high school graduates finish high school with no plans for further education and training. In reality, they have only begun to develop the skills employers seek and will have a difficult time building a satisfying career.
- Half of the students who go to college never finish. Starting with a career plan could have given them motivation for graduating.
- Without a career plan, college graduates often take positions that are unrelated to their majors, giving up some of the advantages their degrees could have given their careers.

The process of developing a career plan will help you organize and direct your thoughts toward your future in a satisfying career. You will be able to set and achieve goals that allow you to build career success through work *you* have chosen to do.

The case studies in Activity 1-5, "Case Challenges," give you the opportunity to help Sabrina and Julio solve their planning problems and take charge of their futures.

> **"Life is what happens while you're making other plans."**
> —John Lennon, Composer and Musician

DIFFERENT LEARNING STYLES

Kinesthetic Learners

Provide students with art materials, including colored markers and butcher paper, for a class mural. Have students work together to create a mural that illustrates concepts presented in this chapter. Have students use the chapter's key terms and headings for inspiration. Ask a few students to write a song to accompany the artwork and add the lyrics to the mural. Also ask the students to perform their song for the whole class.

Benefits of a Career Plan

At the end of *Investigating Your Career*, you will be able to picture your future because you started planning now. You will have a good idea of where you are going and how to get there. You will be saying yes to the following statements:

✔ School is the place to start the rest of my life. I will take advantage of what my school offers.

✔ Many factors influence my career choice, including my family, my teachers, my counselor, and my friends. I have paid thoughtful attention to those influences in deciding my career area.

✔ I have taken career assessments that helped me identify my passions and talents and some possible career clusters.

✔ I have researched career areas that use my talents and passions. I have investigated the trends for my career in the future. I want to train for a career that will be needed in the future.

✔ I have talked with others in my career area and listened to their advice.

✔ I have investigated the education and skill training needed after high school for my career area.

✔ I am aware of the cost of the education and training for my career area. I know how to look for financial aid opportunities to decrease a financial burden.

✔ I have written down my career plan, including the courses I need now and later in my education. My plan fits my career interests.

✔ Whenever possible, I will work part-time in my career area to gain experience that will help me make my career decision.

✔ I know where to search for jobs and how to go through the job search process.

✔ I have started my Career Journey Folder. The folder includes my career assessment results; my resume; the honors I have received; letters from employers and teachers; samples of my best work; and other items that describe my passions, attitude, talents, and heart. I will update the contents of my Career Journey Folder regularly and continue to use them as guides in making my career decisions.

Activity 1-6, "Internet Application," shows you how to use the Internet as a tool in your journey to discovering your career.

CAREER SUCCESS TIP

Become a strategic thinker about your career. Ask yourself if what you're doing today will become a career skill tomorrow.

A discussion of the checklist on page 13 of the student text will help students see the steps they need to take in order to have a successful and satisfying career. The checklist summarizes the content of the text and is based on students doing the following:
• Gaining the knowledge and skills needed for entry-level employment and for further education and training.
• Developing acceptable work attitudes.
• Tying school experiences into career goals.

APPLY

Have students complete **Activity 1-6, "Internet Application,"** on page 17. Teaching suggestions and the solution for this activity appear on page 17. An activity worksheet can be found on the Career Portfolio and Resource CD—**Text Activity 01-6.doc.**

CLOSE

Invite a high school counselor or successful businessperson to speak to your class about the benefits of investigating career options at an early age.

Have students complete **Activity 1-D, "Guest Speaker Questions,"** found in the *Investigating Your Career Activities & Projects* book.

You may use this generic questionnaire when a speaker is a guest in your class. This form has a dual purpose for students: to take notes on and to provide questions to ask the speaker. For more than one speaker or for a panel of speakers, you may want to give students additional forms.

CAREER SUCCESS TIP

Be a Strategic Thinker

Help students become strategic thinkers about their future careers. Explain that a strategic thinker identifies a goal and plots the steps required to be in the best position to achieve the goal. In their journals, have students make a list of the things they like to do in their spare time. Have students journal about how these current activities might relate to a future career. Also ask students to journal about what activities they want to continue, what activities they want to drop, and what activities they want to add that would be helpful to them in their future career.

IN A NUTSHELL

Remind students about the objectives set forth at the beginning of the chapter, and use this summary to reinforce the concepts presented in this chapter.

Career Journal

Ask students to spend 10 minutes writing Career Journal entries that answer the following questions:
1. How well did what you thought you knew match what the chapter presented?
2. What questions do you now have about the chapter topics, and where do you think you can find the answers to those questions?
3. How will the content of the chapter help you investigate *your* career?

ASSESS

Administer the printed objective test for Chapter 1, available with this package. Test solutions are found in the *Teacher's Edition* of *Investigating Your Career Chapter Tests*. Use the **Exam**View® CD to create your own objective test for this chapter.

IN A NUTSHELL

- **I can identify realistic career expectations.**

  My career will be influenced by how well I learn to understand myself, by the advice and experience of others, by my education and skills training, and by labor market trends.

- **I know the differences in the meanings of the terms *job*, *occupation*, and *career*.**

  Job refers to a paid position involving a specific place and time and specific tasks set by an employer. Occupation describes a group of related tasks that require special skills. Career describes a lifetime work history or long-term participation in a particular field of expertise.

- **I can describe the steps of the *P*A*T*H to Success*.**

  My *P*A*T*H to Success* has four steps: uncovering my career-related passions, choosing a positive attitude, identifying my talents, and finding out what is important to my heart. Following my *P*A*T*H to Success* allows me to choose career fields that are compatible with my talents and passions.

- **I understand why career planning should begin now.**

  Developing a career plan now allows me to direct the focus of my education and skill training in the direction of career fields that suit me. I can choose activities and classes that help me prepare for my future career success.

- **I can describe how career planning supports career success.**

  The career planning process and the career plan I design will give me a head start toward career success. By knowing myself and selecting career fields that require my talents and reflect my passions, I can set goals that will help me finish my education and achieve career success.

Suggestions for Parents and Family Members

Support the Career Investigation Process
Encourage family members to support their children's career investigation. Send a letter to family members with the following suggestions:

1. Talk with your child about his or her career dreams.
2. Spend time together investigating different careers that interest your child.
3. Help your child make a plan of academic study for his or her career choice.
4. Assist your child in developing alternative career plans.

Career Planning Quiz

How much do you know about planning for a career? Decide whether each of the following statements is true or false, and write your answers on a separate sheet of paper.

1. You must work in a career before you can decide whether it's the one for you.

2. Anyone can do any job as long as he or she decides to do it.

3. The average person in the United States spends more time doing work activities than any other type of activity.

4. Most careers in the future will require more than a high school education.

5. The majority of people spend their adult lives in the same career.

6. Just wait—the right job opportunity will come your way.

7. Anyone who plans to work right out of high school needs the same basic academic skills as someone who plans to go to college.

8. If you go to a two-year college, you must transfer later to a four-year college.

9. The best way to get a job is through newspaper want ads.

10. Most high-tech fields, such as digital design, require a bachelor's degree.

11. The No. 1 reason people are fired from jobs is that they don't learn quickly enough.

12. If you have the chance to take additional classes, choose math and science courses.

(See page 18 for a discussion of this quiz.)

Learning from Others

1. Interview one or two people who are successfully employed in a career field that interests you. Some areas to discuss are these:
   - How did you make your career choices?
   - Did you have a career plan? If so, how did you arrive at your plan? If not, why not?
   - How did your values and beliefs influence your career path?
   - What was your education/training path?
   - What were some difficulties you encountered and how did you overcome them?
   - How did the time period during which you were making your career choices affect your career plan?
   - Based on your experience, would you do anything differently? If so, what?

   Summarize your findings for a class discussion or a written report. Tell what you learned from the people you interviewed that will help you in planning your career.

2. Prepare a time line to show the career decisions of one of the people you interviewed.

Activity 1-1: Career Planning Quiz

This activity helps students think about career planning and provides them with a brief introduction to important concepts discussed in this and later chapters. One effective way to use the quiz is as a warm-up activity on the first day of class or when you begin the career section of the course. Have students complete the activity as a type of pretest before they read the chapter. This will help students realize how much they do not know and become more open to learning about careers and career planning. Discuss the quiz with the whole class before students check their answers.

Solution: The answers to the quiz, their supporting facts, and references to later chapters are on page 18 of the student text.

Activity 1-2: Learning from Others

The purpose of Learning from Others activities, which appear in every chapter, is to have students interact with people outside the classroom. In most cases, students will be asked to interview adults already in the career world. In this particular activity, students find out how and when successful people made career decisions.

If the students have similar career interests, they may work in pairs to conduct their interviews. Encourage students to include additional questions about career decisions that interest them. An alternative is to divide the class into small groups and have students share their interview results within the group. If you choose this option, be sure the students are grouped according to similar career clusters. Then each team can report to the entire class. Afterward discuss the similarities and differences of the types of workers in each cluster.

Solution: Answers will vary. Each student should submit one completed questionnaire for each person interviewed, a written summary of what the student discovered about career planning from the interview(s), and a time line for one of the people interviewed.

Activity 1-3: Survey Your Strengths

This activity begins the first stage in the career planning process. Students start to learn about themselves; so instead of trying to match themselves to a career, they will be able to discover a career that matches *them*.

If necessary, explain to students that they should complete the sentences in Question 1 by writing what they liked to play with as children, what they like to do in their free time, and what they think their strengths and passions are.

Emphasize that in Question 2, students should use the suggested questions as the basis for their wishes. The questions give the students focus and help avoid such unrealistic wishes as "I want to be a rock star." Students will use the results of this activity in Chapter 6 when they choose a career cluster.

Solution: Answers will vary according to students' interests. Be sure their wishes are related to careers.

Activity 1-4: Coming to Terms

This activity requires students to question people—not interview them, as in a Learning from Others activity. Then students use their understanding of the definitions of the terms and deductive reasoning to classify the answers. The second part of the activity helps students identify transferable skills they already possess, relate these skills to career possibilities, and work as a member of a team.

For the first part of the activity, allow students to question members of their class and school who have done something to earn money. For the second part of the activity, remind students to choose activities they enjoy doing, they feel pleasure and happiness from doing, and they want to do when they have leisure time. By working in teams, students should be able to identify more skills than would occur to them individually.

This is a good time to begin discussing how school success relates to career success. Include examples of how courses apply to the real world.

Learning about yourself is one of the first steps in discovering your career. The discovery process helps you identify your talents and passions.

1. Complete the following statements on a separate sheet of paper.
   - As a child, I liked . . . .
   - Today I like . . . .
   - My strengths are . . . .
   - Others describe me as . . . .

2. Imagine you find an intriguing bottle on the side of the road. You pick up the bottle and start cleaning off the dirt. And, yes—*Out pops a genie!* You know the drill: The genie must grant you three wishes. The catch (of course there's a catch!) is that this genie is limited to granting career-related wishes only. What is important to you for your future career? Do you have the skills and abilities for that career? What training do you need? What type of lifestyle is best for you? Write the three wishes you would ask the genie to grant.

Job, Occupation, Career

Ask six people, including at least two adults, what they have done to earn money. Based on what each person says, determine whether each considers his or her work a job, an occupation, or a career. Give reasons for your answers.

Transferable Skills

Acquiring many transferable skills increases the number and variety of opportunities available to you. List at least three activities you do, determine what transferable skills you are developing, and name some careers that use those skills.

	Activity	Transferable Skill	Career Area
Examples:	playing computer games	using a computer, problem solving	business owner, any career involving computers
	planning a party	organizing, designing, problem solving	catering, interior design
	serving as an officer in a club	leading, organizing, working with others	business management, politics, business owner, military service

---

As an additional activity, have students analyze their work in school and at jobs. Have students write the transferable skills they are developing in these work situations and describe how these skills relate to various careers. Students should keep work samples that demonstrate their transferable skills in their Career Journal Folders.

Solution: Answers will vary according to students' interests. You may wish to have groups of four or five students discuss their results and then report to the class. After students complete the second part of the activity, tell them to keep their lists for reference as they explore career possibilities.

Case Challenges

 After reading each case study, analyze Sabrina's and Julio's career situations. Do they have career plans? If so, what is wrong with their plans? Then devise a way for Sabrina and Julio to develop effective career plans. Suggest some activities they can do to focus on making clearer career decisions.

1. School doesn't really interest Sabrina. She schedules the classes she needs to graduate on time and takes "fun" classes to fill out the rest of her schedule. All she wants to do is graduate with her friends and start earning money. Sabrina's grades aren't outstanding, but she doesn't plan to continue her education. She just wants to have fun with her friends and pass her classes. She wonders what school has to do with the real world anyway. Working at the fast-food restaurant, Sabrina believes she can cover her expenses on her own. If not, she figures she can use one of the low-rate credit cards and share an apartment with Susie and Petra. Plus, Sabrina has no idea what kind of career she wants.

2. Immediately after high school graduation, Julio plans on going to college for his bachelor's degree. He doesn't know what courses he'll take in college, but he figures he has four years to figure it out. Julio has his college fund, and he thinks his grades are good enough for a scholarship the first year. He knows his parents want him to go to college, so they'll pay his expenses while he makes a decision about his career. He's fairly sure the college advisers tell students what to do, so he wonders why he needs to decide about a college major now.

Internet Application

 Internet web sites provide information about creating a career path. They include stories, career information, and life planning information. Some sites also include assessments you can use to explore your talents, passions, and personality.

1. Investigate at least two areas at each of the following sites. Write down ideas that might be helpful to you in learning about yourself and developing a career plan. If you see any unfamiliar terms, write them down and find their definitions.

   - *www.careerpathsonline.com*
   - *http://motiv8.com*

2. As you investigate each site, look for similarities in ideas and information. Then write statements that describe these common ideas and information.

Activity 1-5: Case Challenges

The purpose of Case Challenges activities, which appear in every chapter, is to have students analyze real-world situations that describe circumstances familiar to students. This particular activity helps students realize the value of early career planning and provides an opportunity for students to improve their teamwork skills.

Divide the class into groups of four or five students. After each group completes its analysis of the case studies, have the group report its results to the class. If your class is small, you can do the activity with the whole class rather than dividing the class into groups.

Solution: Answers will vary. Although students probably will not have the background to make many informed suggestions, they should have some ideas about how to help Sabrina and Julio make clearer career decisions.

Activity 1-6: Internet Application

Internet activities, which appear in every chapter and usually give at least two sites for students to explore, help students develop their research skills and obtain additional information about topics presented in the chapter. The sites in this activity are examples of common career sites. The information in each is similar and adds validity to students' answers to Activities 1-3 and 1-4.

Solution: Answers will vary. Look for definite career planning ideas and concrete terms, such as descriptive adjectives.

Answers for Activity 1-1

You will find more information in *Investigating Your Career* and in the suggested chapters.

1. **False.** Observing people working in careers or interviewing them are two ways to help you decide your career. Chapters 2, 3, and 8 offer more ideas.

2. **False.** How could you possibly have all the specific skills needed for every career? Chapter 3 helps you investigate your talents and passions so you can discover your career.

3. **True.** A career will take up more time in your adult life than relaxation will, so it's important to plan well for your career.

4. **True.** The Department of Labor projects that 85 percent of the careers of the future will require training beyond high school. Only 15 percent of those careers will require a bachelor's degree. Chapter 4 gives more specific information.

5. **False.** The number of times a person will change careers keeps increasing as more and more careers require similar basic skills. Currently, a person changes careers between five and eight times after age 25.

6. **False.** If you wait for a job, you may wait for a long time. Great jobs often come from part-time jobs, referrals from friends, and job changes within the company where you work. Chapter 13 helps you in your job search.

7. **True.** Reading, writing, computing, and listening, as well as critical thinking and problem solving, are the basic skills needed for any career.

8. **False.** Many careers are available with an associate degree. Chapters 8 and 9 assist you in deciding whether to transfer to a four-year college or go to work.

9. **False.** Although the newspaper is useful for researching the job market, most jobs come from referrals. This topic is discussed in Chapter 13.

10. **False.** High-tech fields generally require training beyond high school but often don't require a bachelor's degree. Chapters 8 and 9 give you more information.

11. **False.** The No. 1 reason people are fired from jobs is that they cannot get along with their coworkers. The second reason is that they have an attendance problem.

12. **True.** The fastest-growing occupations between 1998 and 2008, as identified by the BLS, all involve math and/or science skills.

Influences on Career Choices

Doug's passion was discussing politics. Whether he was talking about a presidential election or about the political correctness of a school mascot—he thrived on the conversation. So when writing about his passions in his Career Journey Folder, Doug knew he needed to mention his love for politics. However, Doug didn't think he wanted to run for political office in the future. How would he be able to satisfy his overwhelming passion for politics without becoming a politician?

Then Doug talked to Mrs. Garden, his journalism adviser. She pointed out that in the writing he did for the school paper, Doug investigated problems, interviewed people, and wrote his opinions. Wasn't he essentially discussing politics? She also reminded Doug of his excellent grades in his English and government classes, which gave him a solid foundation for a career as a political reporter or columnist.

Mrs. Garden suggested that Doug work during the summer at a weekly newspaper to find out if a career in journalism fit his passion for politics. Doug followed her suggestion. At the *Forestville Reporter*, he is now stimulating political discussion for a wide audience while reporting on local politics.

When you think about your future career, whose opinions are important to you—parents or other relatives? teachers? peers? employer? counselor?

What do you think?

OBJECTIVES

After completing this chapter, you will be able to:
- Describe how influences can affect career decisions.
- Analyze how people influence you and your decisions.
- Determine your preferences for a work environment.
- Identify the values that influence you.

66 **A closed mind is a good thing to lose.** 99

—*Anonymous*

Key Terms:
- influence
- work environment
- social environment
- values
- motivation
- intrinsic
- extrinsic

Chapter Overview

Chapter 2 Influences on Career Choices

FOCUS

Chapter 2 discusses the many factors that influence students' career decision making. People—especially family members, teachers, friends, counselors, and employers—have the greatest influence on career choices. Students' values and their work- and social-environment preferences also influence their career decisions.

Use the **Objectives** and **Key Terms** printed in the margin to help students focus on the content of this chapter. Use the **video segment** for Chapter 2 to trigger discussion.

TEACH

A class discussion can help students begin to see the many influences on career choices. Start the discussion by having students recall their earliest career ambition. Ask them to identify the important people in their lives who encouraged (or discouraged) them toward that career. Then ask students how their early career ambitions were affected by the people they identified.

What do you think?

Use **TM02-01**.
Students' answers will vary.

Career Journal

Ask students to spend 10 minutes writing Career Journal entries that answer the following questions:
1. What do you think this chapter will cover?
2. What do you already know about these topics?
3. What three things do you want to learn about these topics?

CHAPTER RESOURCES and MATERIALS

Activities & Projects book
Instructor's Resource CD
- Forms and Worksheets for Chapter Activities 2-1 through 2-6
- Internet Links for Chapter 2
- PowerPoint Presentation for Chapter 2
- Lesson Plans
- Teaching Masters for Chapter 2
- Video Discussion Guide for Chapter 2

Chapter Tests book
Exam*View*® CD
Video
Web Site

20

Influence

> **We shape clay into a pot, but it is the emptiness inside that holds whatever we want.**
>
> —*Tao Te Ching, Wisdom of Ancient China*

The word **influence** means the power of people or things to cause an effect on others indirectly. Everything and everyone around you influences you every day. You may not consciously think about how the person, place, idea, experience, or thing influences you. However, your life and the choices you make will be affected.

Influences may be positive or negative. For example, if you are allergic to cats and work as a veterinary technician in a small animal clinic, then your surroundings have a negative influence on you.

Also, some influences are stronger than others and have a greater effect on your behavior and decisions. For example, if you respect and admire someone or believe a person is knowledgeable, then the advice and opinions of that person are likely to have a strong impact on you.

Although influence is not manipulation or direct persuasion, influence still affects you and your decisions. In this chapter, you will determine what has some bearing on your career decisions—in other words, who or what influences you. Then as you travel along your career path, you can decide what advice or experiences you will allow to influence your career decisions.

Activity 2-1, "Things You Love to Do," will help you begin to see what may influence your career decisions.

People Who Influence Career Decisions

Information about work comes from many sources. Of all these sources of information, the people you know will have the greatest influence on your career decision making. Family members, teachers, peers, community members, and many others give advice, provide part-time jobs, and share experiences. In addition, listening to others talk about their work influences your perception of work and various careers.

Observing and investigating how work affects people both positively and negatively can give you much information. Sometimes in talking with people about their careers and where they work, you can tell just by their tone of voice that they are happy with their careers. You can tell they enjoy waking up each morning and heading off to work.

Learning why people work, finding out what makes them happy or unhappy with their careers, listening to them talk about their workday, and watching their interactions on the job are some of the ways you can research careers. Your observations can provide information that ultimately may help you make decisions about your own career.

Parents and Other Family Members

What do you think?

Do your parents or other family members look forward to going to work most of the time, or do they reluctantly get ready each day?

How do they generally act and talk about their jobs or careers?

According to the Ohio Career Development Services, the greatest influence on your career decision making is your family. Your parents and other family members provide the basis for your initial ideas and beliefs about work. In particular, the way they react to their work situations can influence your perception of work and various careers.

Constanza loves her career as a cosmetologist. She is delighted by how people's faces light up with pleasure after she has completed her transformations with scissors and chemicals. She has a knack for bringing out the beauty in her customers, flattering their appearances with her skill. Her knowledge of color and her skill at creating new shades of nail polish, hair color, and makeup make her one of the most sought-after cosmetologists in her part of town.

Though working with people and beauty is her passion, Constanza never reveals her love of her career at home. In fact, Constanza comes home from work every day complaining—about her customers, her aching feet, and the shop owner. However, she also spends several hours of her free time each week researching new products, volunteers monthly at the local cosmetology school, and gives an annual presentation about her profession for Career Day at the area high school.

Constanza's daughter, Donna, hears her mother's grumbling every day, but also sees her dedication to her profession. Because of her mother's behavior, Donna has mixed feelings about a cosmetology career. She wonders how she can get a clear understanding of the profession.

Even though you may get conflicting messages about a particular career from the behavior of your parents or other family members, you should not ignore their advice when you create your career plan. Family members know you well and can help you make sound career decisions.

What do you think?

Use **TM02-02**.
Questions 1 & 2: Students' answers will vary. Encourage students to identify conversations and actions that support their ideas.

ENRICH

Have students complete **Activity 2-B, "Visit Your Hobbies,"** found in the *Investigating Your Career Activities & Projects* book.

In this activity, students use the list of hobbies from Activity 2-A. Then they make a list of places they could visit to learn more about their hobbies and related careers.

Collecting the list of places to visit will help you in planning field trips and speakers and creating a list of web sites. Publishing the list of web sites for parents and family members will connect home with the students.
Solution: The solution for this activity appears in the *Teacher's Edition* of *Investigating Your Career Activities & Projects*.

DIFFERENT LEARNING ABILITIES

Auditory Learners

Have students use a tape recorder to interview three different people about their careers. Students should ask what the person likes and dislikes about his or her chosen career. As students listen to their taped interviews, have them make note of the mixed messages they may be getting about their own future careers. Hold a class discussion about the mixed messages society gives to young people about careers. Help students sort out the messages that may be helpful to them.

What do you think?

Use **TM02-03**.
Questions 1A & 1B: Students' answers will vary. Encourage students to talk about all kinds of interests. **Questions 2A & 2B:** Students' answers will vary.

TEACH

Discuss how parents and family members may have a negative influence on students' beliefs about work. In a study by the Families and Work Institute, when children were asked what they wished they could change about their family's work life, a common response was, "I wish my family would be less stressed about work." Only 41 percent of children thought their parents enjoyed their work. However, an average of 65 percent of family members actually did enjoy their work. Help students understand that family members may be letting off steam, and not accurately conveying the way they really feel about their work.

TEACH

Use the Listening Tips shown on **TM02-04** as a transparency or handout in a class discussion of family expectations. Encourage students to use these tips when interacting with family members or other adults.

Expectations

What do you think?

Do you share a common interest with a family member? What is it?

Would you pursue that interest as a career? Why or why not?

Your family has expectations for you, hopes and dreams for your future. These expectations influence your personality, passions, interests, talents—and your choice of careers. You may find you are expected to fulfill career dreams based on someone else's talents and passions. You may be expected to follow in the footsteps of family members or to join them in their business or profession. Or you may be cautioned against pursuing the careers practiced by members of your family.

Michael's dad, Lou, has a small successful dental practice. Lou has always dreamed of working with his son Michael and eventually turning the business over to him. Michael has helped his dad in the office since he was twelve. He helped sterilize instruments, cleaned equipment, and ran errands. While he worked with his father, Michael closely observed the work of a dentist. In high school, Michael worked in a dental lab, making dentures and crowns. Michael's experience helped him decide that he doesn't want to become a dentist. He likes working with people, but he's more interested in a career in advertising.

Lou had a difficult time accepting his son's decision. He wondered whether all his hard work to build a dental practice was for nothing. Michael talked to his father about his decision. Michael explained how he wanted to follow his father's example to build a career from the ground up—how he wanted to work in advertising and eventually start his own agency. Lou listened carefully. He saw more clearly how he and Michael were alike in their passion for their work but different in their interests.

If you think your family expects you to follow a career path that doesn't really fit you, take the initiative to show them the success you have had in your courses, extracurricular activities, and part-time jobs—anything related to a possible alternative career. By doing this, you set the stage for your family to listen to and support your dreams.

CAREER SUCCESS TIP

Welcome helpful criticism. You may be able to identify things about yourself that you want to change. Accept and learn from criticism that seems to make sense to you.

Encouragement

By supporting and guiding you, the members of your family can help you develop and pursue your career focus. Your family can support your search for possible careers that will allow you to use your unique talents and passions. Encouraging you to take challenging courses so you can explore your career interests is one of the most important ways your family can help you create plans and goals for the future. Your family's encouragement to expand your talents and passions can help you find your *P*A*T*H to Success.*

22

PART 1 • • • • • • GETTING READY

CAREER SUCCESS TIP

Welcome Helpful Criticism

Tell students that helpful criticism will help them do better at their work. Unhelpful criticism will not. To help students understand the difference, explain that helpful criticism lets them improve their work while unhelpful criticism is just complaining for no helpful reason. If a supervisor offers friendly and helpful suggestions, students should listen and pay attention without getting defensive. They will want to try to incorporate the suggested changes into their work.

You should discuss your talents and passions with your parents and other family members. Talk about what you like and how you want to find out more about possible career opportunities. If you really like to do something and you do it very well, that passion—if you pursue it—is often the foundation for a happy and successful career. The encouragement of your family can give you confidence in the direction you choose for the rest of your education and training.

Teachers

What have been your favorite courses in school?

What do you think?

What are some possible careers related to those courses?

Teachers influence your career decisions almost as much as your family does. For example, recall this chapter's opening scenario in which Doug's career decision was influenced by his journalism adviser. Students are in contact with classroom teachers every day during the school year and are often comfortable discussing their futures with approachable teachers or advisers. This is especially true if the student is interested in a career involving a teacher's subject matter. For example, suppose you are taking Spanish and believe you have a talent for foreign languages. In this situation, your Spanish teacher is a natural resource about career opportunities for Spanish majors.

Your English teacher can have a major influence on your career no matter what your interests are. You may think English classes relate only to a few occupations, such as writing books, journalism, or editing. However, every career requires workers to have effective communication skills, skills that are developed in English classes. Effective communication skills include having the ability to give and follow instructions accurately, to persuade people to a particular point of view, and to write in an organized style with correct spelling and grammar. Workers in every career must read material related to job skills, and every employee needs to explain problems to supervisors and other workers. For example, in addition to writing diagnostic summaries and repair recommendations, an auto technician may skim an average of 150 pages of manuals a day!

Your math teacher will also have an influence on your career success. Some careers use math directly every day, such as engineers, accountants, and respiratory therapists. However, do you realize that mathematics plays an important part in the careers of funeral directors, electricians, broadcast technicians, and glass blowers? Yes, even glass blowers must know math and science. Each type of glass needs a specific temperature to make it malleable, and each style of shaping and blowing requires precise temperature adjustments.

CAREER FACT

Eighty-seven percent of employers surveyed by *The Chronicle of Higher Education* think communications skills are critical for their employees. Fifty percent think computer skills are as important as communications skills.

What do you think?

Use **TM02-05**.
Question 1: Students' answers will vary. **Question 2:** Students' answers will vary. Make sure students can explain the connection between the courses and the possible careers.

TEACH

All teachers have a strong influence on students' career choices. Subject-matter teachers may think their courses are separate from career planning and they have nothing to do with students' career decisions. However, these teachers influence students' interest in their courses and in careers related to the subject. In fact, only family members have a greater influence on students' career choices. In hands-on learning classes, teachers have an even stronger influence. By working with staff members, you may be able to find ways (such as in-service sessions or printed or e-mail updates) to help teachers realize the strength of their influence.

CAREER TREND
Fastest-Growing Occupations
According to the America's Career InfoNet, many of the fastest-growing occupations are technology/computer-related careers. The careers include computer software engineers, computer support specialists, computer software/system engineers, network/computer systems administrators, and network/systems data communications analysts. Discuss with students that they will need knowledge of technology for careers that will be in demand.
—*Source: www.acinet.org*

Ask students how extracurricular activities and the advisers and coaches of those activities might influence their career decision making. Help students identify ways activities can develop skills related to careers. Students who feel challenged and engaged at school are more likely to perceive how activities relate to their career goals.

TEACH

Students may have other strong influences not covered in this chapter. For example, students may want to choose a career because they perceive it as appealing or glamorous. Careers portrayed on popular television shows, in current events, and in hit movies often are considered by students to be their first choices. Following a career path for this reason can lead to dissatisfaction if students' perceptions of the careers do not coincide with their talents or with the real world.

Teachers are excellent resources for learning about your skills and behaviors. Many activities and courses in school require the same behaviors used in the workforce. Teachers know whether you are flexible and can adapt to change. Observing you in action shows them whether you can work cooperatively in a team; have leadership skills; and are organized, punctual, and dependable. Teachers can be impartial and truthful with you when discussing your work qualities. Some of your behaviors may need to change for you to succeed in a career field, so the comments teachers make can help you improve.

Which teachers are the most helpful? The ones who know you well and who have been pleased with your work are the obvious choices. They are the ones you should approach first for career advice. Begin by talking to them about what you have enjoyed in their classes. Ask for suggestions about how the skills learned in their classes can help you develop your career focus. Teachers enjoy talking with students after class about their subjects and have much insight and experience to offer. These discussions not only help give you confidence to take charge of your future but also provide you with a wealth of information.

REAL PEOPLE
REAL CAREERS

Space Scientists

Steve Chien became fascinated with artificial intelligence while he was still in high school. He thought the opponents in computer games were not challenging and so devised ways to make them more challenging. Now he is part of a team that works on projects at NASA's Jet Propulsion Laboratory. These projects will allow a spacecraft to go places where it has never been before. His work with rovers and self-directed spacecraft intrigues him now as much as tinkering with computer games did in the past.

Ken Nealson always cared more about his science classes than he did about any other subjects. Now he is following his passion for science in a career at NASA. In his work, Ken studies how life arises and thrives in some of earth's extreme environments, such as Antarctica. The results of his studies will help those who explore other planets. Ken is also working on a project that is searching for life in outer space. Just the prospect of extraterrestrial life thrills him. Ken hopes to develop new methods of detecting life. (NASA cares as much about life detection as it does about space missions.) Who says life has to be like it is on earth?

For more information about:
- NASA careers, investigate *www.nasa.gov*. Explore *Navigating NASA's Strategic Enterprises,* and then look at some of the topics that follow.
- engineering careers, explore the National Society of Professional Engineers site at *www.nspe.org*.

Sources: "Official Bio—Steve Chien." *NASA. http: www.nasa.gov*
"Kenneth H. Nealson." *NASA. http:www.nasa.gov*

REAL PEOPLE—REAL CAREERS
NASA Careers
Have students work in small groups to investigate careers with NASA. Suggest that students use the Internet site listed in the text on this page for their research. Students may also contact NASA directly for information. After each group has chosen a career to work with, have student groups prepare an oral presentation about the career. Presentations are to include visual aids. Each member of the group is to be responsible for a part of the presentation. Display the visual aids around the room.

Peers

You influence your friends—and they influence you—every day in many ways. That influence may include what clothes to wear, where to eat after the football game, what classes to take, and what music CDs to buy. But how much influence should your friends have on your future life and your career? You may want to continue hanging out with your friends after you finish school, but do you want to build *your* future around your friends' lives?

Many of Kita's classmates admired her creative way of dressing. She used the most unlikely combination of accessories in her outfits and received many compliments for her style and flair. Her talents included a unique eye for color and design. She also liked creating displays and posters. With these qualities, Kita seemed destined for a career in fashion design or interior decorating.

Shauna, Kita's best friend, wanted to move to Chicago and work as a receptionist after graduation. Since Chicago was known for its famous designers and decorators, Shauna asked Kita to go with her. Shauna's plan was intriguing to Kita, but it would mean postponing her plans for fashion design school. Still, Kita was excited about moving to Chicago and sharing an apartment with Shauna.

Excitedly Kita called her close friend Linda and told her about her plans for Chicago. Linda asked Kita if fashion design was still her career goal. Kita quickly said yes. Then Linda suggested that Kita think about sharing an apartment with Shauna during the summer but starting school in the fall. Linda told Kita that if she let Shauna influence her, she would be putting her education and career plans on hold.

After talking with Linda, Kita wasn't sure what to do. Living in Chicago with Shauna sounded so exciting! Kita finally decided that delaying her career dream was not what she wanted to do. Fashion design was her passion, and she was eager to begin her education. She hoped Shauna would understand and agree to share an apartment in Chicago for the summer.

Discuss the influence of peers. Students often pursue the same activities and interests their friends pursue. Thus, if a student's friends enjoy learning and are involved in school activities, the student is likely to be involved in school activities and often is interested in postsecondary education. Similarly, if a student's friends are interested in the world of work, the student also is interested in the world of work.

DIFFERENT LEARNING STYLES

Kinesthetic Learners

Have kinesthetic learners work as a team to write several scenarios that demonstrate peer influence. Have these students act out their scenarios for the whole class. Encourage students to make their scenarios entertaining. Give them different prompts and types of influences if they need help. Allow students to use music, props, and costumes for their scenarios. After the scenarios are completed, have the students lead a class discussion on the influence of peer pressure and different ways to cope with it.

> **"You are in charge of your own attitude—whatever others do or circumstances you face. The only person you can control is yourself."**
>
> —Marian Wright Edelman, Author and Children's Activist

Often talking to your friends allows you to consider other people's viewpoints. Their advice may help you consider other possibilities when making your decisions. But never forget your goals and your passion. Keep in mind that your friends' influences can be either positive or negative. Use your judgment to decide whether to take your friends' advice when you make your career decisions. Your friends may have good intentions, but they may not truly understand what is best for you in the long run. While your friends' opinions are important to you, analyze their advice in terms of *your* interests.

Employers

Parents, other family members, teachers, and peers are not the only people who can influence your career choice. Your employer at a part-time or summer job may also influence your decisions about a career.

Joining the Explorers was a wise choice for Manuel. He was interested in firefighting and was eager to make a decision about whether to pursue it as a career. One of the Explorer groups linked Manuel with the Anderson Fire Department, where he now works and can see firsthand the daily labors of a firefighter. During school breaks, Manuel has a paying job with the fire department, cleaning the station. Though he isn't able to go out on fire calls, he does participate in Explorer fire training. During his interview for the job, Manuel spoke with Ms. Farrell, the supervisor of the fire department. He wanted her to know that he considered the part-time job to be a testing ground for his career focus.

To help Manuel with his career decision, Ms. Farrell gave him scheduling duties and other routine work. His Explorer training offers different aspects of a career in firefighting. Manuel likes working with the equipment and teaching fire safety. He finds the work in firefighting challenging, though he isn't sure he is ready to face the dangers and hazards of the career.

Ms. Farrell is helping Manuel with his career because helping him can also help the fire department. She hopes Manuel is a good employee who will work each summer and holiday break while in school. Hopefully, Manuel can work for the Anderson Fire Department full-time after he receives his training and certification.

There are several ways in which an employer can influence your career choice and help you make career decisions. You don't have to have something as formal as a part-time job to benefit from an employer. You can observe an employee at his or her workplace or interview someone who works in a career field that interests you. Even working as a volunteer can help you understand the skills necessary for a successful career. Chapter 3 discusses these research options in depth.

INTEGRATED ACADEMICS
Computer Sciences

Arrange students into groups of four or five to create a spreadsheet on careers. Have each group list the types of people who may influence their career decisions. The students may include additional categories to those indicated in the textbook. Have each group print out its spreadsheet and then report to the class. Reports may include students' impressions on each category of people who may influence their career decisions. Post the spreadsheets around the classroom.

Counselors

Counselors have several responsibilities. One of them is to provide information to guide you as you make decisions for your future. They can suggest courses for you that are based on your activities, talents, grades, and abilities. They can offer selections for researching educational options, such as computer searches. They can set up interviews with employers. In addition, if you choose to use their expertise, they are trained to help you work through the process of career development.

What a counselor does best is help you discover your options. For example, suppose you go to the counselor's office to find out about a career in medicine. Your counselor may ask what particular career you're thinking about—doctor, nurse, dental hygienist, pharmacist, medical transcriptionist. Then the two of you may talk about the courses you should take in high school to prepare for your career. You and your counselor may also talk about other careers in medicine you had not considered—physical therapy, sports medicine, nutrition.

When you have narrowed your career focus and have chosen your education and training pathway, the counselor can help you toward your goal by providing planning checklists, information on courses, suggestions for employment, and tips for taking control of your homework. A counselor is an invaluable resource and has many ways to help you on your *P*A*T*H to Success*.

Use Activity 2-2, "Learning from Others," to find out about the career success of someone you know.

> **66** The future belongs to those who believe in the beauty of their dreams. **99**
> —*Eleanor Roosevelt*

Environmental Influences on Career Decisions

The environment can influence your career decisions in many ways. The following questions are all related to your environment—either your work environment or your social environment. Your **work environment** is made up of the surroundings and conditions of your workplace. Your **social environment** includes the community where you live and work and your lifestyle choices.

- Do you want to stay where you live now? Do you prefer a rural, urban, or suburban setting?
- How important is the outdoors in influencing your choice of career? For example, is mountain biking an important activity for you? Or are you an avid surfer?
- Do you want to have someplace nearby to continue your education?
- Is climate important to you? Do you prefer a change of seasons or a consistent climate?
- Will there be a future for people in your career field in the community where you want to live?
- Do you want to work around people or in isolation?

TEACH

TEACH

Students may not consider lifestyle preferences or social environment when they make career decisions. Point out that just as a career affects a person's satisfaction with life, a person's life outside of work can affect his or her satisfaction with a career. In addition, career satisfaction includes more than just liking the type of work. For example, even if a person enjoys all the tasks associated with a career, the career will not be satisfying if the person prefers to interact with others but the career requires working alone. As you discuss the questions on page 27 of the student text, encourage students to think of additional ways their work and social environments can influence their career success.

APPLY

Have students complete **Activity 2-2, "Learning from Others,"** on page 33. Teaching suggestions and the solution for this activity appear on page 33. A two-page worksheet for this activity can be found on the Career Portfolio and Resource CD—**Text Activity 02-2.doc**.

DIFFERENT LEARNING ABILITIES
Limited English Proficiency Students
Pair students who have limited English proficiency with a native English-speaking student. Ask students with limited English proficiency to outline the chapter in their native language. Outlines are to include headings, key words with definitions, and a short summary of the information under each heading. Have English-speaking students write questions about the chapter to ask the limited English proficiency students. Then have students discuss any questions that are answered incorrectly to assure understanding of the material.

Some of these questions may seem strange to you. For example, why would a climate change, such as having snow, influence a career path? However, climate is sometimes a factor in making a career choice. For some people, the changing seasons are important to their mental health. They seem to be able to focus on work better when they have changing weather. Others are the opposite and want consistency in temperature.

CAREER SUCCESS TIP

You will need effective interpersonal skills to achieve career success. Those skills include teamwork, self-confidence, dedication, and understanding others.

By identifying the environments in which you want to work and live, you will be better able to narrow your career focus. Some careers must be near certain natural resources. For example, marine life is normally studied in a coastal community or in a zoo or an aquarium. Other careers, such as convention event planner or computer network troubleshooter, require frequent travel. For those careers, you could probably live wherever you want, although you may not be home much of the time.

Your work environment involves much more than the climate and the geographic area in which you live. The atmosphere of your workplace and your interactions with others are important factors in your work environment. Your career success will depend partly on knowing the type of workplace you prefer.

Use Activity 2-3, "Environment Preferences," to determine some important environmental influences on your career choice.

Influence of Values on Career Decisions

What do you think?

What makes people successful in a career?

What does success mean to you?

What will make you feel successful in a career? earning a large income? having an important title and position? being famous? having the respect of others? being independent? being able to develop innovative products? providing service to others? Your answer is influenced by your values. Your **values** are the things that are important to you. Your values are also the **motivation** behind your goals and decisions—the reasons why you set specific goals and make certain decisions.

Your perception of success depends on your personal values, the values of your family and culture, and your economic values. If your career is based on your values, you will be happy with your life and career and you will consider yourself successful. Because you are the only one who knows your values, only you can define what success means to you and only you can determine what motivates you to achieve success.

☞ CAREER SUCCESS TIP

Effective Interpersonal Skills

Explain to students that most employers agree that effective interpersonal skills play an important role in career advancement. Have students work in four small groups. Have each group discuss how they are learning teamwork, self-confidence, dedication, and understanding of others on a daily basis. Ask students to discuss how these interpersonal skills help their lives and how lack of these skills hinder their lives. Have each group give an oral report on its discussion. Ask students to keep a journal for a week on how they use these skills in their own lives.

Personal and Family Values

Your family began instilling its values in you when you were born. These values are the standards that your family members emphasize. While each family has its own set of values, the way individual family members interpret those values might vary.

Elizabeth's family believes in serving others. Ever since she was a little child, her parents have included her in church activities that benefit their community. In addition, Elizabeth's mother has always worked in the local polling place on election day. One of Elizabeth's earliest memories is of passing out the "I Voted Today" pins. Throughout her school years, Elizabeth has worked in a soup kitchen for the homeless and asked her teachers to save hotel soaps and shampoos for the women's shelter. Naturally, her family's influence has resulted in Elizabeth believing that helping others should be part of her life, including her career. She is exploring careers in teaching, social services, and healthcare.

The guidance provided by your family's values can be comforting. You know what to expect until you determine your own unique values. As you develop your own set of values, you may take part of your family's values and add new values that are especially important to you. You may begin with your father's streak of independence and your mother's trust in people, add your grandmother's thriftiness and your cousin's love for justice, and finish off with your own belief in community service—all to form your own personal value system.

Elaine believes in her work. She is honest, though she prides herself on being the one who is usually different. That creativity results in her web site designs being award winners. Her use of stimulating colors and graphics makes the sites eye-catching. Elaine will not give up her standards of what is right and true. She knows she has her family to thank for her values. Elaine's family taught her honesty, so her designs do not attempt to deceive those who view them. Her mother's artistic sense is part of Elaine's character, and her father's precision guides her in studying computer language. In her work, Elaine retains the values of her upbringing.

Activity 2-4, "Values That Motivate You," helps you pinpoint those values that motivate you to do your best.

What do you think?

Use **TM02-07**.
Students' answers will vary. Make sure students realize that understanding and accepting cultural diversity in the workplace is important to career success.

TEACH

In a class discussion, encourage students to talk about the expectations and values of their cultures. Although Chapter 5 discusses in depth the societal expectations related to male/female careers, you may wish to have students explore ways their cultures view some careers as appropriate for men and some as appropriate for women.

APPLY

Have students complete **Activity 2-5, "Case Challenges,"** on page 35. Teaching suggestions and the solution for this activity appear on page 35. An activity worksheet can be found on the Career Portfolio and Resource CD—**Text Activity 02-5.doc**.

Cultural Expectations and Values

What do you think?
Does your cultural heritage impose expectations that influence your decisions?

You may have certain beliefs and behaviors because of your culture—your social, ethnic, or religious background or perhaps even the community where you live. The expectations and values of your culture may influence your work values. Your answers to the following questions will help you begin to identify your cultural values and expectations and their effect on your work values.

- Is helping others important in your culture?
- Should work permit you to make beautiful things and to add beauty to the world, as many Asian cultures advocate?
- Is caring for the environment something that is important to you and your culture?
- Should the world outside your community be avoided, as the Amish culture believes?
- Will the groups that your culture does business with affect your choice of careers?

> The Navajo tribe has expectations for Shasheem and the other members of her tribe. Her Native American upbringing has helped form her values through its expectations. Whether she continues to live on the reservation or leaves to work in the state capital, Shasheem will have the core values her family and her tribe instilled in her, such as respect for her elders. She knows that working in front of a television or still camera is frowned upon in her culture, so Shasheem will avoid careers that involve film and photographs of her. Her heritage is important to Shasheem, so the small modifications she must make are minor choices for her. She will always respect the Navajo customs and will never abandon her beliefs.

You may be unaware of many of the cultural expectations that can influence your career decisions. Their influence is often very subtle. By analyzing the things that are important in your culture, you can identify ways your culture influences your decisions.

The case studies in Activity 2-5, "Case Challenges," give you the opportunity to analyze some of the influences on career decisions.

Economic Values

What kind of lifestyle do you want in the future? Do you want to acquire the latest electronic gadgets, a luxury car, and designer label clothes? Or do you want to buy a home, marry, and raise a family? No matter how you answer, all types of lifestyles involve money—and having money usually means earning an income.

> *" Success seems to be connected with action. Successful people keep moving. They make mistakes, but they don't quit. "*
>
> —*Conrad Hilton, Founder of Hilton Hotels*

INTEGRATED ACADEMICS
Visual Arts
Remind students that values are the things that are important to them and that their values are the motivation behind their goals and decisions. Have students keep a list of several decisions they make during the next week. Then have students create a chart. Across the top of the chart include the following categories: personal and family values, cultural expectations and values, and economic values. Have students list their decisions under one of the categories.

How important is money in your life right now?

If you had to choose *either* a career in which you were unhappy but made a great deal of money *or* a career in which you were happy but made very little money, which would you choose?

What do you think?

Your economic goals are related to your values. In making career decisions, you often need to determine how important money is to you. Which of the following is most important to you?

- A career that fulfills your passions and talents
- A career that allows you to pay the bills and have some money for extras and savings
- A career that provides you with a large income
- A career that provides you with prestige and status

Some careers have **intrinsic**, or internal, rewards. In these careers, the feelings that the career provides you are more important than the money you receive. Other careers offer **extrinsic**, or external, rewards. In these careers, the monetary rewards and benefits are of more significance to you than the work you perform.

You may choose to work at a nursing home for the extrinsic rewards you receive. With the paycheck you receive, you can buy concert tickets, CDs, clothes, books—whatever items you choose to spend your money on. On the other hand, you may choose to volunteer at a nursing home for the intrinsic rewards, receiving no pay for your efforts. You enjoy helping elderly people and making their lives a little less lonely.

Another factor influencing income levels is education. The Bureau of Labor Statistics (BLS) reports that the more you learn, the more you earn—and the less likely you are to be unemployed. This fact does not mean you need to have a bachelor's degree or higher to earn a high wage, but it does mean you must continue to improve your education over your lifetime to earn a high wage. In truth, education often pays simply because employers believe educated workers learn tasks more easily and are better organized—which may or may not be true. The biggest reason for variety in income is the difference in occupations people enter as a result of their education level. For example, anyone with a college degree may enter a career that requires less education if he or she meets the other job requirements.

The amount of your income is only one factor in determining whether your career is satisfying. Although everyone needs money, very few people choose a career based solely on income. Other factors include the nature of the work, the potential career advancement, and the working conditions. One of the most important factors is for your career to be based on your values. Only you can determine which factors will have the most influence on your career choices.

CAREER FACT

Income has an effect on people's health. Studies have shown that the more money people make, the healthier they are.

What do you think?

Use **TM02-08**.
Question 1: Students' answers will vary. Help students to see how money influences their lives even though they are not yet financially independent. **Question 2:** Students' answers will vary.

TEACH

Monetary rewards generally are important to preteens and teenagers. Ask students what they think the purpose of a job is. Then ask what they think the purpose of a career is. If they answer "to make money" in both instances, explain why they likely will have little career satisfaction. Point out that career satisfaction requires doing work you enjoy; working every day at a job you hate, regardless of the amount of money you earn, will not make you happy.

CLOSE

Have students write the objectives from the beginning of the chapter on a piece of paper. Then have students write a paragraph or two about how each objective was met and how each objective applies to their lives. Have students work with a classmate to discuss each objective and their learning. Ask for several volunteer pairs to recap their discussion for the whole class. Be sure to have different student pairs speak to the different objectives.

CAREER TREND

Peace Corps

Many young people are more interested in adventurous careers and providing service to the world than they are in earning a large salary. These young people might consider the Peace Corps. As of April 1, 2002, there were 6,046 Peace Corps volunteers working in 72 countries. Sixty-one percent of the volunteers are female, and 92 percent of the volunteers are single. Although education beyond high school is not a requirement, most Peace Corp volunteers have a college degree (85 percent), and some (13 percent) have graduate degrees.

—*Source: www.peacecorps.gov/about/facts.cfm*

Have students complete **Activity 2-6, "Coming to Terms,"** on page 36. Teaching suggestions and the solution for this activity appear on page 36. An activity worksheet can be found on the Career Portfolio and Resource CD—**Text Activity 02-6.doc**.

IN A NUTSHELL

Remind students about the objectives set forth at the beginning of the chapter, and use this summary to reinforce the concepts presented in this chapter.

Career Journal

Ask students to spend 10 minutes writing Career Journal entries that answer the following questions:
1. How well did what you thought you knew match what the chapter presented?
2. What questions do you now have about the chapter topics, and where do you think you can find the answers to those questions?
3. How will the content of the chapter help you investigate *your* career?

ASSESS

Administer the printed objective test for Chapter 2, available with this package. Test solutions are found in the *Teacher's Edition* of *Investigating Your Career Chapter Tests*. Use the **Exam*View*®** CD to create your own objective test for this chapter.

Use Activity 2-6, "Coming to Terms," to understand some of the important terms in this chapter more thoroughly.

IN A NUTSHELL

- **I can describe how influences affect my career decisions.**

  Everything and everyone around me influences me and my decisions. Influences may be positive or negative. Some influences are stronger than others, and these strong influences are likely to have an impact on my career decisions. By determining who and what influences me, I can find out what advice and experiences affect my career decisions.

- **I have analyzed how people influence me and my decisions.**

  My family is the basis for my initial ideas and beliefs about work. Teachers may also have a strong influence on my career decisions. My peers' opinions are important to me, but I must analyze their advice in terms of my interests and passions. An employer can help me make career decisions by providing me with experience in a field that interests me or by allowing me to observe an employee. My counselor can provide information and options that help me make my career decisions.

- **I have determined my work and social environment preferences.**

  My work environment is made up of the surroundings and conditions of my workplace. It includes the atmosphere of my workplace and my interactions with others as well as the geographic area and climate where I work. My social environment includes the community where I live and work and my lifestyle choices.

- **I have identified the values that influence me.**

  My values are the things that are important to me. They are the motivation behind my goals and decisions. The values instilled in me by my family will influence my choice of career and will affect my personal value system. My cultural heritage may also impose expectations and values that can influence my work values and career choices. My economic values will determine the balance of intrinsic and extrinsic rewards I choose for my career.

Suggestions for Parents and Family Members

Supporting Career Choices

Help parents support their children's career choices by providing them with the following suggestions in a send-home letter:

1. Emphasize positive behaviors in your home by respecting teens' career choices and supporting their interests. Communicate openly and avoid controlling behaviors such as making decisions for teens.
2. Allow teens to choose their own career rather than forcing them to fulfill your expectations.

Things You Love to Do

Analyzing the things you like to do will help you begin to understand some things that influence your career decisions.

1. On a separate sheet of paper, list 20 things in life you really love to do.

2. Code your responses using the following. (You may use more than one symbol.)

   • Place a **$** before any item that costs *money* to do.
   • Put an **R** in front of any item that involves some *risk*. The risk might be physical, intellectual, or emotional.
   • Record an **F** before the items you think a *family member* would have had on a list if he or she had been asked to make a list at your age.
   • Place a **P** before items you prefer doing with *people* and an A before items you prefer doing alone.
   • Place a **5** by the items you probably would not list in *five* years.

3. Which of the categories in Question 2 influences you most? Why?

Learning from Others

How much do you know about the careers of people who influence your career decisions? Interview one of your parents or a relative about his or her current career. Use the questions below as interview guidelines.

1. Where do you work now?
2. How long have you been with your current employer?
3. What is your specific job title? What is your job description?
4. What products or services does your employer provide? Who are the customers?
5. What qualifications are needed for this career? (Include the specific training or education needed.)
6. What communication skills are needed for this career? What math skills are needed? What technology skills are needed?
7. How has this career changed over the years? How has technology affected it?
8. What is the best thing about this career? Why?
9. What is the worst thing about this career? Why?
10. What was the first paying job you had? How did it help with your current career?
11. Why did you choose your current career?
12. What is your advice for preparing for career success?

After completing the interview, answer the following question: How did the results of the interview influence your thinking about career choices?

Activity 2-1: Things You Love to Do

This activity leads students to an appreciation of how the influences covered in this chapter affect them. The informal assessment pinpoints the influence—economic values ($), risk (R), family (F), work environment (People or Alone), and students' current situation (5)—on some of students' favorite activities.

Students may find the results of this activity helpful in correlating assessment results later in this chapter and in Chapter 3. Chapter 6 uses results from many of the assessments to help students discover their ideal career area.

Solution: Answers will vary. The last category may include extracurricular activities, organizations with mostly teen members, risk-taking activities, and high school courses. Be sure students realize which categories influence them most and why.

Activity 2-2: Learning from Others

According to many studies, parents and family members are the primary influences on a student's career decision-making process. This activity often reveals how much influence a parent or family member has on a student's career decisions and whether the influence is positive or negative.

If you have not provided students with a handout of **TM02-04**, you may wish to use it to introduce the activity. The Listening Tips are beneficial for both students and family members. You can use **TM02-04** as a transparency or a handout.

Solution: Answers will vary. The summarizing answer to the concluding question is almost as important as the interview because it helps determine the family's work ethic and whether the family influence is positive or negative for the student. Note that a family influence may be negative due to outside influence, such as a student's peers, or teenage rebellion. Some teenagers automatically choose the opposite of what a parent or family member suggests.

A general discussion of the interview results is important to the whole class. Try to help students understand why and how their families influence them. Many students and parents believe they know each other well, and the interview results may surprise both of them. Keep personal details confidential when discussing the interviews to avoid talk among your students about their peers.

Activity 2-3: Environment Preferences

In this activity, students identify their community and climate preferences and their ideal lifestyle—all environmental factors that influence career decisions. The sooner students write down their dreams, the better. Students can always modify their dreams, but capturing their dreams' essence is important in this early stage of the career journey.

Tell students to imagine both a weekday and a weekend day. Suggest that they consider who else might be living with them, the weather, their lifestyle, their coworkers, their leisure activities, and their responsibilities. Don't suggest that they consider their family; let them think of that possibility for themselves. Also suggest that students list regions of the country rather than naming specific places.

Suggest that, if possible, students print their answers and results from the web site *Ideal Life Style Inventory* to use in later chapters when making a career choice, designing a budget, and choosing a place to live. You may want to extend the number of years for both sections of the activity to age 30, 40, or even older.

Solution: Answers will vary. Make sure students use concrete adjectives and descriptive phrases to describe their community and climate preferences. In addition to the items listed on page 34 for their ideal lifestyle, encourage students to include other items, such as specific types of recreation, arts and culture, and types of transportation.

Activity 2-4: Values That Motivate You

This activity shows students how their personal values might affect their performance at school. The activity also relates their work in school to their work on a job, reminding students that school motivations and performance will carry over to work motivations and performance. As emphasized in Chapter 1, students need to realize that school is their primary job right now. However, they also need to know that success in school is directly related to success in a career.

Solution: Answers will vary. Some students may be surprised by their results because they are unaware of how their values influence their motivations.

Community and Climate Preferences

Included in the environmental factors that create career satisfaction are the climate, location, and type of community in which you live and work. On a separate sheet of paper, describe your preferred community, including its environmental factors. Then list the benefits of the community you prefer.

- Examples of climate: humid or dry, changing or consistent
- Examples of location: small town or big city, rural or suburban area, nearby lake or ocean, hills or mountains or flat land
- Examples of benefits: close to mass transit, family-oriented, healthcare availability, cost of living, education availability, neighborhood safety

Ideal Lifestyle

Go to *www.bgsu.edu/offices/sa/career/process/exercise.html* and take the *Ideal Life Style Inventory*. As described at the end of the inventory, use your *very important* choices to allow yourself to dream about what your life will be like when you are in your early 20's. Use as much detail as possible, including such things as your coworkers, leisure activities, responsibilities, family, and so on.

From the following list, select six items that motivate you to do your best work in school. Write them on a separate sheet of paper. Remember, school is your current job—grades and knowledge are your pay, classmates are your coworkers, and so on.

1. Good pay
2. Career advancement
3. Respect of others
4. Being the top performer
5. A nice work space
6. Freedom to do projects my own way
7. Rewards or bonuses
8. Job security
9. Ability to do a good job
10. Approval of the boss
11. Nice coworkers
12. More money
13. The chance to plan what I do
14. Feelings of importance
15. Nice working conditions
16. Giving support to others
17. Recognition from others
18. Opportunity to do new things
19. The chance to talk to other people
20. Being interested in what I am doing

If you selected items:	Then you may be motivated by:
1, 2, 7, 8, 12	security
5, 11, 15, 16, 19	working with other people in nice surroundings
3, 4, 10, 14, 17	prestige and achievement
6, 9, 13, 18, 20	independence and personal satisfaction

Do you see a pattern? Which of your values influence your motivations?

After reading each case study below, discuss the case with a small group of your fellow students. Use the following questions to get your group started. After you have analyzed each case using these questions, decide what advice, if any, your group would give to the person involved.

- What is the *motivation* of the person in the case?
- What personal *values* might have motivated a particular career choice?
- What is the work *environment* choice?
- What other influences might have played a role in the case?

1. Charles teaches high school economics and enjoys working with students. Stephanie, his wife, is a certified public accountant (CPA) with a large company. She works an average of 60 hours a week, including many Saturdays. Their first baby is due in two months. Both Stephanie and Charles believe one parent should stay home with the new baby while the other parent works. But who should stay home and who should work? Both Charles and Stephanie can take three months off from their jobs when the baby is born. However, Charles has made business contacts in the community through his work and has been offered a position as a bank officer. This new job will pay more than his present job. Should Charles take the banking job, or should he leave his teaching job to stay at home until their child enters school? Should Stephanie return to her well-paying job as a CPA?

2. Alana likes her job as a carpenter. She works for a company that produces Broadway shows in major U.S. cities. She is in charge of the team that investigates the tour theaters and works with the set designer to customize the shows' sets. Alana travels to each city and stays with her team until the problems are solved. Looking to the future, Alana is thinking about starting her own company in New York City. She has a lot to consider. Should she begin taking college courses in business management? Should she retrain for another position? Should she look for a way to cut back on her travel now?

3. Bobek is fascinated with running a kitchen in a restaurant. He is the pastry chef at Ginseng, a trendy vegetarian restaurant in Atlanta. However, he is not entirely happy because he hasn't been promoted to head chef, the person who makes the decisions in the kitchen. One of Bobek's customers has offered him the opportunity to be the head chef of a family restaurant in a town on the coast of Washington state. Bobek now has a problem. Should he leave the bustling atmosphere of his hometown, Atlanta, to become the head chef of a family restaurant in a small town thousands of miles away? Or should he wait until he finds a head chef position in Atlanta? He knows he can be successful as a head chef. He's just not sure what to do.

4. Marguerite received her associate degree as a registered nurse (RN) from the local community college. Because she is a single parent, she prefers working as a nurse for patients in their homes, which provides her with flexible hours. Though she enjoys nursing, the hours for home-based nursing care aren't always steady. Sometimes the pay doesn't cover her family's expenses. When Marguerite's friend told her about job openings at the post office, Marguerite took the test and became a letter carrier. She now works regular hours. However, she wonders if she made the right decision. She misses medicine and her contact with patients. Should Marguerite go back to school to become a surgical nurse, a skilled position with regular hours? Or should she continue her job as a letter carrier?

Activity 2-5: Case Challenges

In this activity, students analyze real-world situations involving work environment choices, personal and work values, and lifestyle choices. Also, students are introduced to situations emphasizing the difficulties of balancing work, family, and children—situations where no one decision is clearly better than another, and each choice is based on different criteria and has different consequences. These real-world situations involve dilemmas that many students will face in the next 10 years. The cases will help students develop both critical-thinking and team skills.

Divide the class into groups of four or five students to analyze the cases. Then have each group report its results to the class.

Solution: Answers will vary. Students need to realize that there is no one right decision and that the values and motivation of the people involved determine the best decision in each case. Be sure students include answers to the bulleted questions for each case.

Activity 2-6: Coming to Terms

This activity explores the influences of personal values, cultural expectations, and economic values and helps students clarify their understanding of these influences. The results of the personal values part of the activity provide validity for Activities 2-3 and 2-4 and will help students narrow their career choices in Chapter 6. By writing down their values and cultural expectations, students will have a better understanding of their actions.

You may need to provide additional explanation about the meanings of *intrinsic* and *extrinsic*. An *intrinsic* motivation comes from *inside* a person. An *extrinsic* motivation comes from *outside* a person. Some motivations may be both intrinsic and extrinsic. Guide students through the start of this part of the activity. Students also may benefit from working in pairs or small groups for this part of the activity.

Solution: Answers will vary.

Every aspect of a career is subject to many influences. The influences mentioned in this chapter are:

- People—including parents or other family members, teachers, peers, employers, and counselors.
- Environment.
- Values—personal and family values, cultural expectations and values, and economic values.

Personal Values

Take the values assessment at **_www.adm.uwaterloo.ca/infocecs_** by clicking on "Students," then on "Career Services," and finally on "Self-assessment" and "Values."

1. After taking the assessment, write down any other values that are important to you.
2. On a separate sheet of paper, list the five values that are most important to you. Choose your five values from those values you rated **1** on the assessment and from the others you listed. Give reasons for your choices.

Cultural Expectations

Your culture is your social, ethnic, or religious background or the community where you live. Your culture may expect you to behave or believe in specific ways and can influence your decisions. Answer the following questions on a separate piece of paper. (If you don't think you are influenced by your culture, answer the questions based on the expectations of a close friend's culture.)

1. What is your cultural heritage?
2. How do the expectations of your culture influence your life?
3. How might the expectations of your culture influence your career decision?
4. How can you make your own career decision and still respect your culture?

Economic Values

Your motivation for working is often related to the type of reward you receive. On a separate sheet of paper, list at least six types of work you do and the reward that motivates you. Determine whether your motivation is *intrinsic* or *extrinsic*. You do not necessarily have to be given money for the work.

	Type of Work	Motivation	Intrinsic or Extrinsic
Examples:	completing an assignment	learning more	intrinsic
		getting better grades	intrinsic and extrinsic
	mowing yard	money	extrinsic
		family's respect	intrinsic
		pride in good-looking yard	intrinsic

Understanding Yourself

3

OBJECTIVES

After completing this chapter, you will be able to:

- Recognize how assessments can help focus your career journey.
- Identify types of formal assessments.
- Explain how to use formal assessment results.
- Describe types of informal assessments.

Key Terms:

- *Internal Career Design*
- self-assessments
- formal assessments
- interest inventories
- ability assessments
- personality assessments
- work values
- informal assessment experiences
- career fair
- informational interview
- job shadowing
- internship
- service learning

Martene is confused. She is ready to schedule her high school classes, but she's overwhelmed. Her mother keeps asking what she wants to do after high school graduation. Her counselor has reminded her twice that it is time she develop a career focus and plan. In addition, she must complete her schedule for all four years of high school! Martene has no idea what career to pursue. There are so many choices. She could just scream.

How is she supposed to make these decisions, she wonders. Her Aunt Cario is a nurse. Martene thinks she might like nursing, although she really doesn't like to be around sick people. She loves to argue, so maybe she should be a lawyer. She also likes speaking and politics, but the courses her Uncle Rob had to take to become a lawyer don't sound too interesting to her. All Martene knows is that she wants to work with people.

Martene's English teacher, Mr. Yates, saw her struggle with her questions. He took her aside and asked about her interests, her extracurricular activities, and her favorite classes. Then he suggested she talk to her counselor about taking some assessments that would help her identify her personality traits, abilities, and interests. He told her the assessment results might point her toward career areas unique to her. He said she could use that information (plus her activities, favorite classes, and hobbies) to help choose her classes. She could create her career plan and start on her *P*A*T*H to Success*.

What can happen if you don't have a *P*A*T*H to Success*?

What do you think?

Chapter Overview

Chapter 3 Understanding Yourself

FOCUS

In Chapter 3, students use career assessments to help them discover how their *P*A*T*H to Success* leads to a career plan. Formal assessments help students relate their passions, talents, personality, and values to a career area. Informal assessment experiences provide firsthand knowledge about careers to assist students in their career decision making.

Use the **Objectives** and **Key Terms** printed in the margin to help students focus on the content of this chapter. Use the **video segment** for Chapter 3 to trigger discussion.

TEACH

Discuss the chapter's opening scenario with students. Emphasize that when people know themselves, they can choose and prepare for a career that will be satisfying for many years. They can discover a career that matches their passions, personality, and values and uses their talents.

What do you think?

Use **TM03-01**.
Students' answers will vary.

Career Journal

Ask students to spend 10 minutes writing Career Journal entries that answer the following questions:
1. What do you think this chapter will cover?
2. What do you already know about these topics?
3. What three things do you want to learn about these topics?

CHAPTER RESOURCES and MATERIALS

Activities & Projects book
Instructor's Resource CD
- Forms and Worksheets for Chapter Activities 3-1 through 3-6
- Internet Links for Chapter 3
- PowerPoint Presentation for Chapter 3
- Lesson Plans
- Teaching Masters for Chapter 3
- Video Discussion Guide for Chapter 3

Chapter Tests book
ExamView® CD
Video
Web Site

37

TEACH

Ask students how many of them know someone who just "happened" into a career. Some people graduate from an education or training program and *then* think about looking for a job and starting a career. They have not planned what they want to do for much of the remainder of their lives. They have not really considered whether the career that has found them is the career best suited to their talents and interests. When people don't have a strong passion for a career and don't use their talents, they may drift from job to job and eventually become stuck in a job with no future.

What do you think?

Use **TM03-02**.

Students' answers will vary. Encourage students to think about all kinds of positive characteristics. Ask students to think about all aspects of their lives.

> **❝ I was brought up to believe that how I saw myself was more important than how others saw me. ❞**
>
> —*Anwar Sadat, Egyptian President*

When have you really thought about who you are? You may have often compared yourself to others—your parents, family members, peers, or celebrities. However, what do you really know about yourself?

No one else in the world has your combination of talents and passions. You are unique. The passions, attitude, talents, and heart of your *P*A*T*H to Success* combine into making you the person you are. In addition, the things you like to do, the ways you are talented, and your personality help define your *Internal Career Design*. Your unique *Internal Career Design* matches your interests, abilities, personality, and values to an ideal career for you.

Your skills, interests, beliefs, and values—plus your likes and dislikes—are very important in helping you understand and appreciate who you are. When you know these things about yourself, you will be able to discover your *Internal Career Design* and begin to choose your career path. Learning about yourself may take some time. You are a complex person. Be patient and think about all your complexities as you learn more about yourself.

What do you think?

What are some of your positive characteristics that make you unique—different from your friends and relatives—such as writing songs, telling stories, solving mysteries?

Assessments

One way to learn about yourself is through assessments. You may be thinking, "Assessments. Aren't those types of tests? Why take a test to find out what kind of person I am? Isn't that what *thinking* is supposed to do? I can just think about what type of person I am and then write it down. That's my assessment, right?"

However, if *thinking* alone could assess who you are and identify your career path, then wouldn't everyone have a satisfying career? Finding a career path requires more than just thinking. Assessments provide information that will help you choose a career based on your talents and passions. By using all your unique qualities to guide you on your *P*A*T*H to Success*, you can find a satisfying career. Then in the future, you won't look back, as many people do, and dream about what you could have done and the life you could have had.

Magazines, web sites, and information in counselors' offices are full of assessments. You can take an assessment to find out if you are color blind. You can do brainteasers to assess your problem-solving skills. You can even take a test to find out how well you sleep at night. These are all informal assessments and are based on what you think. Formal assessments are based on the research of others.

PART 1 · · · · · · GETTING READY

ONLINE RESOURCES

Check out the web site **www.investigatingyourcareer.com** for teacher resources, student activities, and replacements for broken links for this chapter. To access the teacher resources:

Username: career
Password: investigate

Career assessments focus on the activities you like, your natural talents and abilities, and the characteristics of your personality. They focus on what makes you unique. You can match the results of these assessments with your experiences and use the career clusters to discover your *Internal Career Design*.

Career assessments assist you in investigating, identifying, and recognizing those interests, personality traits, abilities, values, attitudes, and individual preferences that will help you succeed. Analyzing assessment results can help you decide what you want from your career and how you want your life to unfold. Thus, career assessments also help you set your career goals and your life goals. Once you have set goals, you can identify the steps needed to take action. Postponing these decisions will only delay your *P*A*T*H to Success*.

With so many instruments available, careful selection of career assessment tools is necessary so you will have an accurate basis for making decisions and planning your career. Self-assessments, combined with formal assessments and informal assessment activities, can give you a wide view of the options and the career areas that complement your natural talents and abilities.

> Have you ever taken an assessment—at school, at work, or from a magazine?
>
> What did the results tell you?
>
> **What do you think?**

You want your career to be a part of you. You want your career to allow you to follow your passions. The challenge is how to realize more about yourself and how to use the information you acquire. Learning about yourself by taking assessments is one of the first steps toward helping you find your ideal career. All the pieces of your *Internal Career Design* will eventually fall into place, and you will understand why your career journey makes sense for you.

Self-Assessments

The questions you answer in a self-assessment can begin to help you learn more about yourself. **Self-assessments** are based on what you think. You generally take them in unstructured settings with no time limits. A self-assessment may be a list of questions or a checklist. Although a self-assessment may not include an explanation of the results, the knowledge you gain is a good foundation for your career plan.

Activity 3-1, "Inventorying Interests and Abilities," is a self-assessment that can help you determine your interests and abilities.

Have students complete **Activity 3-A, "Looking at Personal Experiences,"** found in the *Investigating Your Career Activities & Projects* book.

This activity helps students identify their interests and abilities as they list classes and projects they have enjoyed. Although the activity serves the same purpose as Activity 3-1, the different approach may be helpful for some students.

After students complete the brainstorming and categorizing, organize the class into small groups to complete the second page. Students can use their results in Chapter 6.
Solution: The solution for this activity appears in the *Teacher's Edition* of *Investigating Your Career Activities & Projects.*

Have students complete **Activity 3-B, "Evaluate Your Skills"** found in the *Investigating Your Career Activities & Projects* book.

In this activity, students evaluate their skills/abilities using a specific list. This activity serves the same purpose as the abilities portion of Activity 3-1, but it uses a different approach. The second page of the activity is optional.
Solution: The solution for this activity appears in the *Teacher's Edition* of *Investigating Your Career Activities & Projects.*

Formal assessments are based on the research of others and are created by publishing companies that specialize in assessments. Often you will take a formal assessment in a group setting, using either a computer or paper and pencil. The publishing company may charge a fee for the assessment and/or the scoring. Formal assessment results are usually more extensive than those from self-assessments.

Formal assessments are used in several situations. You may take them to help you with career planning decisions. Employers may use them to help with hiring decisions. Colleges and universities may use them for admissions. Four categories of formal assessments can be used to help you match your interests, talents, personality, and values to a career—to discover your *Internal Career Design.*

Interest Inventories

What do you like to do? Given several choices of activities, which would you pick? **Interest inventories** are designed to help you relate your interests to occupational areas.

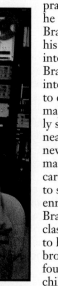

Brandon was consumed with sports, especially baseball. When he could, he was either playing in a game at a nearby field or practicing with a team. In the winter, he would pore over sports magazines. Brandon's interest inventory revealed his love for sports and also showed an interest in public speaking. However, Brandon didn't know how to tie those interests to a career. So when he went to college, he chose an education major even though he was never really satisfied with his choice. Then a nearby state university established a new masters program in sports information. Brandon realized that a career in this area would enable him to satisfy both of his interests, and he enrolled in the first class. Today Brandon is finishing broadcasting classes at a community college to add to his expertise and is starting to broadcast college sports. He has found a career that continues his childhood love of sports and allows him to follow his life's passion.

The format of interest inventories varies. Sometimes you must choose between only two activities, and sometimes you have several choices.

DIFFERENT LEARNING ABILITIES
Hearing Impaired
Have students with impaired hearing sit near the front of the classroom. As often as possible, face them when you speak. When other students ask a question or give an answer, repeat the question or answer to make sure hearing-impaired students can hear the question or answer. When other students are giving a report, ask them to face the hearing-impaired students. When lecturing, check with the students several times to make sure they are able to hear you.

In any case, you are selecting what you like to do. After you take an interest inventory, the publisher of the assessment often provides some occupational areas or choices that tend to match your interests. In Chapter 6, you will use interest inventory information in discovering your *Internal Career Design*.

> **What do you think?**
>
> What are some of the interests you have developed? What are some careers that would allow you to use these interests?

Ability Assessments

If you are interested in something, the next question is "Do you have the ability to do it?" **Ability assessments** measure how well you perform specific tasks and whether you can master certain skills. Usually, publishing companies design the assessments and score them for a fee.

Azad decided to take an ability assessment to learn about himself. He had been thinking about a career as an architect, but his test results showed that his math ability wasn't high enough. Azad learned some other interesting things. He learned that his art and verbal skills were high. So he decided to investigate careers in web site and graphic design. These careers would use his creative skills and not depend so much on math ability.

In Activity 3-2, "Coat of Arms—Interests and Abilities," you will begin to discover your *Internal Career Design* by recording the results of the self-assessment in Activity 3-1.

Personality Assessments

Do you like to plan ahead and find the solutions to potential problems before you encounter them? Or would you rather plunge right into a task, working to solve the problems as you discover them? Do you like to work with people? Or would you rather work on your own, meeting with other people only when you report results? Do you like to make decisions alone after weighing the facts? Or would you rather work with others to reach a decision as a group? All of these choices are part of your personality. A **personality assessment** reveals the traits that make up your personality.

The results of a personality assessment can tell you your behavior style, that is, the temperament that best describes you. Also, the results often suggest how you may perform in various social and personal settings. In addition, you find out the type of work environment that fits your personality traits. Knowing your traits can help you decide on a specific career within a career cluster. For example, if you want to work in a medical field, you can become a nurse practitioner, where you interact with many people, or a medical technician, where you work alone in a laboratory setting much of the time.

> ❝ Knowing your purpose, personality, and passion enable you to realize the course you are starting. Then succeed as you move forward. ❞
>
> —*Lou Stoops,*
> *Positively Speaking*

Use **TM03-06**.
Question 1A: Students' answers will vary. Possible answers include building things, dancing, participating in sports, playing games, solving puzzles, and talking. **Question 1B:** Students' answers will vary. Make sure students draw a logical connection between the activities and the careers.

APPLY

Have students complete **Activity 3-3, "Coat of Arms—Personality and Work Values,"** on page 51. Teaching suggestions and the solution for this activity appear on page 51.

ENRICH

Have students complete **Activity 3-C, "Your Personality,"** found in the *Investigating Your Career Activities & Projects* book.

This activity serves the same purpose as Part 1 of Activity 3-3 in the textbook. It is a simpler assessment than the Keirsey Temperament Sorter in Activity 3-3. You may have students include their results of this activity with the results of Activity 3-3, or the results of Activity 3-C may replace the *Personality Test* results for the activity.

Solution: The solution for this activity appears in the *Teacher's Edition* of *Investigating Your Career Activities & Projects*.

Personality assessments were originally used only to discover problems. Now these assessments help match a person's personality traits to those of top performers in certain career areas. In fact, employers may use the results to assess the behaviors of potential employees and to determine how teams of employees will interact.

A personality assessment can help you determine whether you will be successful in a particular job. One test helps you measure six important values. The results give you some idea about how you will approach a job. The values measured are how practical you are, how much you like to achieve, how much variety you like, how decisive you are, how orderly you are, and how goal oriented you are.

What do you think? What are some activities that you enjoy because they fit your personality? How could these personality traits help you in a career?

Work Value Assessments

Why does someone choose a certain career? What are the reasons a person wants to work? Is it to earn an income, to acquire status, to earn respect from others, to gain independence, to provide service to others, or some other reason? The reasons a person works depend on the individual and make up a person's work values. **Work values** are the things about an occupation that are important to you. An assessment of work values helps you discover your reasons for wanting to work and also helps you find characteristics of occupations that appeal to you.

CAREER SUCCESS TIP

There are people who were born to do the job you can't stand. Let them! Saying no to a job you hate and yes to a life's work that feeds your true soul demands courage, patience, and optimism.

Joaquim loved books. Ever since he started to read, he was hooked. He knew he wanted to have a career that involved books. When Joaquim took interest assessments, the results supported his love for books. Joaquim spent even more time with books when he began his part-time job in the local library. But how should books be a part of his career? Should he get a degree in library science? To help him find his career path, he took an assessment to reveal his work values. The assessment showed that a position in a library would not be a good fit for Joaquim. He needed independence in a career. He also needed financial security.

Joaquim knew that because of his need for independence and his love of books, he wanted to own a bookstore some day. He decided to work for a bookstore chain after school to gain experience and explore the retail book business. Through Joaquim's work at the bookstore, he found he would need business management courses, especially in small business ownership, accounting, and marketing. With these courses in mind, Joaquim developed his career plan. He set goals to get the education and financial backing for his independent bookstore. Joaquim may open a bookstore in town or launch a bookstore online. Whatever Joaquim chooses, he is in charge of his career and is looking forward to being surrounded by the books he loves.

CAREER SUCCESS TIP

Follow Your Bliss

Tell students that Joseph Campbell, an internationally recognized authority on world mythologies, offers the advice to people to follow their own bliss. By this, he means that in his study of cultures worldwide, he found the most successful people were those who were fulfilled by their work. To help your students follow their own bliss, have them describe what they believe is their ideal career if they could do anything they wanted. Encourage them to use their imaginations with this exercise.

Why do you enjoy your favorite activities? What are the things about the activities that are important to you?

In Activity 3-3, "Coat of Arms—Personality and Work Values," you will use the Internet to continue to discover your *Internal Career Design*.

Formal Assessment Results

Formal assessments are useful because they measure skills and interests and give you insight into yourself. However, formal assessments are only the beginning of your search for the career for *you*. It is what you *do* with the results of the assessments that is important.

Keep the following ideas in mind when analyzing your formal assessment results:

Different assessments appeal to different people. Assessments ask questions in different ways and request different types of answers. One assessment may ask you to choose between two answers, neither of which is appealing to you, such as choosing between drafting and accounting. You may have no interest in either drawing or math. Another assessment may ask you to indicate how you would react in a particular situation. You may find that you like one type of assessment more than another.

No one assessment is completely accurate. Assessments reflect your responses. Your answers may change from day to day according to how you feel. The assessment results may also change over time as you add to your experiences. You are better off using the results of assessments as suggestions for new ideas. Don't think of the results as the absolute truth.

Different assessments give different results. Some people may like a certain skill assessment. Just because an assessment is right for your best friend doesn't mean it's the best one for you. If you don't like an assessment, try another one. Also keep in mind that you can get some strange results whether you like or dislike a certain assessment.

Keep in mind that you are unique. Because assessments tend to categorize people into types, you may believe you are not exceptional, but one of a group of people. Though others may have similar traits, you are unique in your combination of talents and passions.

Taking more than one assessment will give you a better picture of yourself. Personality, interest, ability, and work value assessments are all different. Taking all types of formal assessments, plus experiencing informal assessments, will help you move more clearly toward discovering your *Internal Career Design*.

CAREER FACT

To hire an engineer, Thomas Edison would give each candidate a light bulb and ask, "How much water will it hold?" One way to measure used gauges and took up to 20 minutes. The second way was to fill the bulb with water and then measure the water, which took only 1 minute. Edison hired anyone who used the second, more creative way.

Use **TM03-07**.
Question 1A: Students' answers will vary. **Question 1B:** Students' answers will vary.

TEACH

A class discussion based on the points found on pages 43 and 44 of the text will help students understand how to interpret their formal assessment results. They need to realize that assessments are only tools they can use to learn more about themselves. Assessments cannot identify students' ideal careers and cannot make career decisions for them.

CAREER TREND
Interests and Success

A current trend is for people to look for careers that suit their personalities. Stanford University Press, in collaboration with CPP, Inc., creators of *Strong Interest Inventory®*, an interest assessment for adults, offers a free report that compares the reader's interests with interests of successful people in different careers. Have students obtain the report at **http://discovery.skillsone.com**. They can use the report to see how their interests fit with those of successful people in different careers.

—*Source: http://discovery.skillsone.com*

APPLY

Have students complete **Activity 3-4, "Learning from Others,"** on page 51. Teaching suggestions and the solution for this activity appear on page 51. An activity worksheet can be found on the Career Portfolio and Resource CD—**Text Activity 03-4.doc.**

ENRICH

Have students complete **Activity 3-D, "Imagine . . . ,"** found in the *Investigating Your Career Activities & Projects* book.

In this activity, students complete a diagram that depicts their present abilities and their future needs—what they need to be able to do and what skills they must learn. Consider diagramming a sample using one of the scenarios on page 41 or 42 in the student text.

Solution: The solution for this activity appears in the *Teacher's Edition* of *Investigating Your Career Activities & Projects.*

TEACH

Informal assessment experiences will reinforce the career decision-making process. Also, students may need to participate in an internship or a service learning project in order to fulfill a class or graduation requirement. All of the following need to be part of every informal assessment experience: relevance to students' courses, necessary workplace skills, teamwork, community partnership, connection between learning and earning, and introduction to a career.

You know more about yourself than any assessment can tell you. If assessment results point you toward being a landscape architect but you are allergic to grasses and leaf mold, then steer clear of that career path. If your love of solving complex problems leads you to the career area of mechanical engineering but you would much rather work outdoors, then consider another type of engineering. For example, civil engineering would regularly take you away from an office.

The assessment does not tell you everything. Assessment results give you a lot to think about, but they do not determine your career path by themselves. You should use the results along with other activities to help you discover your *Internal Career Design.*

Remember that assessments cannot make your decisions for you. Assessments are only tools that will help you identify your talents and interests. They can confirm your belief in your strengths. They can reassure you that the career plan you have started on is the right track. The information from the assessments is one of the resources for your *P*A*T*H to Success* and should be included in your Career Journey Folder for you to use to discover your *Internal Career Design.*

Activity 3-4, "Learning from Others," will help you analyze how a successful person has used his or her interests, abilities, and skills in choosing a career.

Informal Assessment Experiences

In the assessments described so far, you answer questions using paper and pencil or a computer. However, another type of assessment can be very valuable. **Informal assessment experiences** are activities in which you work in a specific career or observe someone working in a career.

> Lu had always wanted to become a veterinarian. She loved puppies and kittens and had enjoyed training her intelligent dog, Pooka. When Lu had the opportunity to spend a day observing her vet, Dr. Zapata, she naturally jumped at the chance to see a veterinarian in action. However, after seeing surgeries, broken bones, skin rashes, blood tests, and euthanasia procedures performed on both small and large animals, Lu changed her mind about her career choice. She decided she would explore the world of animal training rather than work with sick animals.

Informal assessment activities give you insight into specific career areas and offer many advantages. Informal assessments such as career fairs, informational inerviews, job shadowing, internships, and service learning can help you:

• Acquire firsthand knowledge about types of jobs in a career field and their requirements.
• Understand the world of work and its positive and negative aspects.
• Discover your *Internal Career Design.*

INTEGRATED ACADEMICS
Communication
Have students work with a partner to create an informal assessment practice. Ask students to read the information on page 44 through the top of page 48. Next, have students create a scenario where one person is working in the career and the other person is interviewing, job shadowing, or interning. Have students work through their scenario for about five minutes and then switch roles. Finally, have students work with a different partner and repeat the process.

Career Fairs

Career investigations take many forms. Research in the library and Internet searches are certainly useful. So is a career fair. At a **career fair**, you can find job leads and learn about different companies. You can talk with many employers in just one day.

Informational Interviews

An informational interview will give you additional insight. An **informational interview** is a discussion with someone who works in the career area you are considering. Sometimes an informational interview is your only option for obtaining firsthand knowledge about a career.

- Bella is under the age of 18 and cannot ride with a deputy in a squad car to find out about her county's law enforcement. So she sets up an informational interview with Deputy Mooney to obtain answers to her questions.
- Jim cannot enter the research and development lab to observe a chemist. The company restricts access to prevent disclosure of trade secrets. So he arranges an informational interview by telephone with the lab's head chemist.

In an informational interview, you are in charge and you direct the questions. However, it is often beneficial to send some of your questions to the person you are interviewing before the interview appointment. The information will help him or her prepare answers for questions that may be unfamiliar or require research.

> What are some of the career areas or businesses you would like to investigate?

CAREER SUCCESS TIP

Build a network of people who know your character and qualifications, such as people you can talk to in informational interviews. Stay in touch with as many people as possible.

What do you think?

Job Shadowing

Sometimes an informational interview isn't enough. You may need to see someone actually working at the career. **Job shadowing** is an informal assessment activity in which you spend several hours following a worker at the job location. By simply observing the worker and asking questions, you will learn a tremendous amount about a career area through job shadowing or a career study tour.

> When Tomàs was three years old, he found a screwdriver on the kitchen table and started experimenting with it, copying what he had seen his father do. Tomàs's love of taking things apart grew into a love of electricity. He began rewiring appliances and lamps for his family and neighbors and recently started a part-time job putting together stereo systems for the local appliance store. After developing a strong interest in his math and physics classes, Tomàs knew that being an electrician was the career for him.

CAREER SUCCESS TIP

Building a Network

Help each student create a network notebook that organizes the network of people who know the student's character and qualifications. Suggest students use 4" by 6" index cards or an address book. Ask that students leave space between each entry for notes. Each entry should include the person's name, address, phone number, e-mail address, and relationship to the student and any comments the student wishes to make. Have students begin building their network with family members and friends and then add coworkers and acquaintances. More in-depth information about networking is found in Chapter 13.

You may wish to invite a guest speaker who can describe the internship program at a local company and answer students' questions about interning. Another possible speaker is the person in your school who coordinates your school's relationship with the business community and who can discuss the career areas in which internships are available and how students are selected for participation.

" You have talents. You have a lot of what it takes. Your strong points can open doors. Know what your strengths are; now build on them. "

—*CollegeView Career Center*

The best route to becoming an electrician was to take apprenticeship career/technical courses at the career center and then continue the apprenticeship with the local electrician's union. With all that training ahead of him, Tomàs realized he must be positive his career choice was the right one.

Tomàs talked about his situation with his counselor and his math teacher. He took their advice and made appointments to job shadow both a residential electrician and a commercial electrician, each for one day. The job shadowing experiences will help Tomàs make his career decision.

How can you find people to job shadow in the specific career areas that interest you? You should first consider your relatives and family friends because it is probably easiest to arrange to job shadow one of them. If they do not work in careers you wish to pursue, talk to the teacher of your favorite class, the teacher of your career course, the career development coordinator, or your counselor. Any of these people should be able to give you the names of companies you can contact to arrange a site to shadow. They may even be able to coordinate a shadowing site for you. In fact, job shadowing may be part of your class curriculum or may be arranged as part of a special event, such as "Take Your Child to Work Day" on the fourth Thursday in April or "Groundhog Shadowing Day" on February 2.

Learning business etiquette and knowing some of the details of the workplace surroundings ahead of time will enrich your job shadowing. Some experiences may require additional preparation. For example, job shadowing in a hospital may require completing an orientation on patient confidentiality and working around disease-causing germs. Be prepared for the shadowing experience to take from two to six hours.

Sharing the results of your job shadowing day with your class will give all of you insight into many career areas and into the working world. For example, several types of workplaces may offer similar career opportunities. Advertising agencies, manufacturing companies, and hospitals all need accountants, desktop publishers, and writers. However, the job shadowing experiences for each type of business will be very different.

DIFFERENT LEARNING ABILITIES
At-Risk and Reluctant-Reader Students
Many at-risk and reluctant-reader students may be unable to understand the correlation between their personal interests and a future career. They have not learned how they can use their talents to help them in the job market. To encourage these students, have them work with a peer mentor. Have mentors help the at-risk and reluctant-reader students write an assessment of their talents, strengths, and interests. Have the pair brainstorm possible occupations that fit these talents, strengths, and interests.

What are some businesses or people you could job shadow to help you discover your *Internal Career Design?*

What do you think?

The case studies in Activity 3-5, "Case Challenges," will help you identify and analyze the benefits of various assessments.

Internships

An **internship** provides practical experience working in a specific career. Internships essentially offer a way to "test-drive" a career before committing to it. An internship is a better way to confirm your career path than job shadowing is because you have a longer time to experience a career. Some interns may be paid; others volunteer. An internship provides experience that may lead to a job or even to entry into a career.

> During the Webster School's job shadowing day, Renata worked in the city clerk's office. She was fascinated by the workings of the office and the details of the citizens' lives. As a result of her questions and interest in the work, Renata was offered a nonpaying internship to explore careers in civil service. The experience proved very useful. Renata now has a strong interest in government. That interest has resulted in her choosing to study city government and planning. "You should experience the work for yourself. If you don't, you won't know whether you'll like it," Renata told her class.

REAL PEOPLE
REAL CAREERS

Animal Keeper

Ayéssa Rourke respects and loves nature and wildlife, works well in a team, and is physically strong. Her career as an animal keeper at the Los Angeles Zoo makes use of her talents and passions. Ayéssa improves the quality of life for captive animals, helps educate the public, and contributes to the preservation of the environment.

In her daily job, Ayéssa cleans and maintains exhibits of animals and other displays; observes animal behavior, noting any unusual behaviors that may require medical care; and administers and assists in veterinary procedures. In other words, she works mostly with healthy animals, but at times, she will take care of sick ones. Ayéssa also keeps records and charts, gives talks and demonstrations, and answers questions from the public. Her job duties use her math, science, English, and public speaking skills.

Ayéssa's advice for someone who is considering a career in animal keeping is to volunteer at a veterinary clinic, humane society, zoo, or wildlife preserve. Ayéssa actually spent more time volunteering than she spent in class studying for her associate degree in animal management/zookeeping technology.

For more information about animal keeping:
- explore the American Association of Zoo Keepers site at *www.aazk.org*.
- explore The American Zoo and Aquarium Association at *www.aza.org*.

Source: Pouncey, Margaret. "Talk to the Animals." *My Generation*, Jan. 2001, 28.

CHAPTER 3 · · · · · UNDERSTANDING YOURSELF

47

What do you think?

Use **TM03-11.**
Students' answers will vary. Offer suggestions of local businesses that will allow students to shadow employees.

APPLY

Have students complete **Activity 3-5, "Case Challenges,"** on page 52. Teaching suggestions and the solution for this activity appear on page 52. An activity worksheet can be found on the Career Portfolio and Resource CD—**Text Activity 03-5.doc.**

ENRICH

After reading Chapter 3, have students complete **Activity 3-E, "Self-Awareness Puzzle,"** found in the *Investigating Your Career Activities & Projects* book.

This activity uses most of the Key Terms in a word search double puzzle.

Solution: The solution for this activity appears in the *Teacher's Edition* of *Investigating Your Career Activities & Projects.*

REAL PEOPLE—REAL CAREERS
Working with Animals

Obtain written permission from students' parents for an off-campus visit to your local humane society, zoo, animal park, or other animal-related organization. Contact the organization to ask for a tour and lecture to be given to your students about the organization and what it is like to work with animals. If volunteer opportunities are available, give extra credit to students who volunteer. Check with the organization to see how student volunteers are doing.

What do you think?

Use **TM03-12**.
Students' answers will vary.

──── TEACH ────

After students have completed service learning experiences, ask them briefly to describe their experience to the class. In particular, ask whether the project was a true reciprocal arrangement—the student learning from those he or she served.

What do you think?

Use **TM03-13**.
Students' answers will vary. Students should understand that service learning benefits both parties.

──── APPLY ────

Have students complete **Activity 3-6, "Coming to Terms,"** on page 52. Teaching suggestions and the solution for this activity appear on page 52. An activity worksheet can be found on the Career Portfolio and Resource CD—**Text Activity 03-6.doc**.

──── CLOSE ────

Have students complete **Project 1, "Career Collage,"** found in the *Investigating Your Career Activities & Projects* book.

In this activity, students use their career-related wishes from Activity 1-3 to create a collage. Students may work in pairs; however, each student should create a personal collage. Display the collages around the classroom.

Solution: The solution for this activity appears in the *Teacher's Edition* of *Investigating Your Career Activities & Projects*.

After an internship, you may decide not to pursue the career you experienced—and not choosing a career area is as important as having an internship support your career path. Your career decisions will affect all aspects of your future life. Thus, you will benefit from learning early in life whether a specific career is right for you.

What do you think? What factors would influence your decision to take a longer informal assessment experience, such as an internship?

Service Learning

In a **service learning** program, you volunteer your time to help the community so you can meet a course or graduation requirement. In choosing your service learning project, you focus your volunteering experience to build skills for the workplace and to help determine the focus of your career path.

CAREER ★ SUCCESS TIP

A great way to experience various types of volunteering is to make a day of it. Your community often has days designated for projects, such as cleaning the riverbank, parks, or schools or tutoring. Look for the opportunities.

Jamal became involved in Habitat for Humanity, an organization that helps low-income families build their own homes. His church group began its construction project on weekends. Jamal then learned his work with Habitat provided service learning hours required by his school. Jamal worked on a team with Habitat. As a result, he learned to communicate more directly with different types of people. Through his volunteer work, Jamal experienced the rewards of working for others. What he learned about himself and others was also important in understanding himself.

Karen's service learning project involved working with residents at the Bartlett Nursing Home. By taking oral histories of the residents, Karen learned a lot about the history of the city of Bartlett. More importantly, she learned about the residents' rich experiences. She had always known writing would be part of her career. Now she knew she wanted to work with senior citizens in her future.

Service learning involves mutual give-and-take. While you give of your time and talents, you learn from the people you serve. A service learning project can easily become part of your Career Journey Folder and can help you discover your *Internal Career Design*. Service learning can also serve as a type of internship by focusing on a specific career area.

What do you think? What are some of the rewards you can gain from a service learning experience?

Use Activity 3-6, "Coming to Terms," to understand some of the important terms in this chapter more thoroughly.

✊ CAREER SUCCESS TIP

Service Learning Opportunities

Have students work in groups of four to brainstorm about volunteer opportunities in your community. Make a list on the board, and vote on the top three. Appoint three committees and assign each to investigate and report on one of the selected opportunities. The reports should say how volunteers get involved, what they can expect, and what is expected of them. Vote on the three opportunities, choosing one. Set an extra-credit volunteer day when members of the class can volunteer together. Make transportation arrangements so all students have the opportunity to volunteer. Students should submit a written or an oral report on their experience.

- **I can recognize how assessments help focus my career journey.**

Career assessments help me learn about myself by identifying my interests, personality traits, abilities, and values. Analyzing the results of the assessments can help me decide what I want from a career and how I want my life to unfold. Assessments will help me set the goals that will start me on my *P*A*T*H to Success*.

- **I can describe different types of formal assessments.**

Formal assessments are based on the research of others. Interest inventories can help me relate my interests to occupational areas. Ability assessments measure how well I perform specific tasks and whether I can master certain skills. Personality assessments reveal the traits that make up my personality. Assessments of work values help me identify the things about an occupation that are important to me. Formal assessments can help me match my interests, talents, personality, and values to a career—to help me discover my *Internal Career Design*.

- **I can explain how to use formal assessment results.**

Although formal assessments are useful because they help me determine my skills and interests and give me insight into myself, they cannot make my career decisions for me. The results should be included in my Career Journey Folder so I can use them to discover my *Internal Career Design*.

- **I can describe types of informal assessment experiences.**

Informal assessment experiences are activities in which I can observe or participate in a specific career. At a career fair, I can find job leads and learn about different companies. In an informational interview, I interview someone who works in the career area I am considering. In job shadowing, I spend several hours observing a worker at the job location. In an internship, I get experience working in a specific career. In a service learning program, I volunteer my time to help the community so I can meet a course or graduation requirement. Informal assessment experiences can help me acquire firsthand knowledge about a career, understand the world of work, and discover my *Internal Career Design*.

> **" Happy are those whose purpose has found them. "**
> —*Anonymous*

Remind students about the objectives set forth at the beginning of the chapter, and use this summary to reinforce the concepts presented in this chapter.

Career Journal

Ask students to spend 10 minutes writing Career Journal entries that answer the following questions:
1. How well did what you thought you knew match what the chapter presented?
2. What questions do you now have about the chapter topics, and where do you think you can find the answers to those questions?
3. How will the content of the chapter help you investigate *your* career?

ASSESS

Administer the printed objective test for Chapter 3, available with this package. Test solutions are found in the *Teacher's Edition* of *Investigating Your Career Chapter Tests*. Use the **Exam**View® CD to create your own objective test for this chapter.

Suggestions for Parents and Family Members

Assisting with Assessment
Parents and family members can assist students in assessing their talents and interests for future careers. Following are a few suggestions to offer parents:

1. Talk with your children about their interests to help them clarify their natural abilities.
2. If your children are interested in your work, let them shadow you or take a career study tour.
3. Introduce your children to organizations that provide insights into their fields of interests.

Activity 3-1: Inventorying Interests and Abilities

This activity helps students identify the type of interests important to them and the kinds of abilities in which they are skilled. Though the results are not normed, the activity gives students an idea of what they enjoy doing and what they do well.

To help students identify and classify their interests and abilities, you can suggest that students think about their participation in various activities. Examples include family or school projects, hobbies, jobs, and volunteer and extracurricular activities. You may also wish to use TM03-04 as a transparency or a handout to help students think of situations in which they used various skills or explored interests.

The Instructor's Resource CD includes additional web sites for interest and ability assessments. One of the sites, **www.onetcenter.org**, is sponsored by the Department of Labor.

Solution: Answers will vary. Students will use their results in Activity 3-2 and in Chapters 6 and 13.

Activity 3-2: Coat of Arms— Interests and Abilities

This activity summarizes students' results from Activity 3-1 and provides students with a visual representation of their most important interests and of the abilities in which they have the most skill.

Students should write their passions—interests that are most important to them—in the bottom left-hand portion of the Coat of Arms. In the bottom right-hand portion, students should write their talents—abilities they believe they do well. These two portions form the base of each student's Coat of Arms.

If students prefer, they can draw symbols or cut pictures from magazines to represent their interests and abilities. Encourage students to use colors.

Solution: Answers will vary. Students will complete their Coat of Arms in Activity 3-3.

Print the graphs for this activity from your CD, or use the handout from your teacher if a computer is not available. Put dots in the appropriate places in the graphs. Then connect the dots for each graph. A portion of the Interests Graph is shown below as an example.

Interests

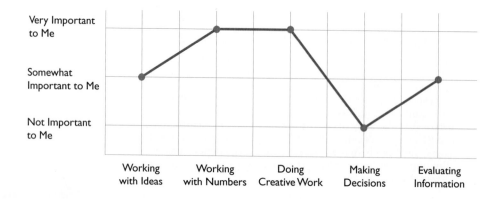

Evaluating yourself helps you realize who you are now. Print the **Coat of Arms** from your CD, or use the handout from your teacher if a computer is not available. In this activity, you will fill in the interests and abilities that create the unique you. You will also use the same Coat of Arms in Activity 3-3.

1. Find the items you marked "Very Important to Me" on the Interests Graph in Activity 3-1. Write the words or draw symbols for them in the space marked "Interests" on the Coat of Arms.

2. Find the items you marked "Very Good at This" on the Abilities Graph in Activity 3-1. Write the words or draw symbols for them in the "Abilities" section on the Coat of Arms.

ACTIVITY 3-3 Coat of Arms—Personality and Work Values

Evaluating yourself helps you realize who you are now. Use the same **Coat of Arms** that you used in Activity 3-2. In this activity, you will fill in the personality traits and work values that create the unique you.

1. Take the *Personality Test* at <u>www.myfuture.com</u>. Click on "Work Interest Quiz." Click on "Personality Test" and take the test. Print the results. Write the major temperament types or draw symbols for them in "Personality Traits" on the Coat of Arms.

2. Take the *Work Interest Quiz* at <u>www.myfuture.com</u>. Print the results. Write the top two work types or draw symbols for them in "Work Values" on the Coat of Arms.

ACTIVITY 3-4 Learning from Others

Interview an adult about his or her career journey in choosing a career. You may choose the same person you interviewed in Activity 1-2, someone in a career that fascinates you, or someone you admire. You may choose to job shadow the person, observing for at least two hours at his or her workplace. Below are suggested questions to use during the interview.

1. What were your favorite courses in school?

2. What extracurricular activities did you enjoy most?

3. What did you like to do with your family and friends?

4. What did you like to do with your free time?

5. What were your favorite hobbies and interests?

6. Which of your special skills are most valuable to you? Why?

7. What achievements make you most proud?

8. Why did you select your career?

9. What did your parents do? How did this affect your career decision making?

10. As a child, what did you want to be when you grew up?

Activity 3-3: Coat of Arms—Personality and Work Values

This activity helps students identify their personality traits and work values. The activity provides students with a visual representation of their personality traits and most important work values.

The personality traits on the web site given in the student text are divided into four categories that are broken down into four parts per category, or 16 possible personalities. The quiz page has links to the definitions of each type. Emphasize to students that no single personality type is better than another.

The Instructor's Resource CD has additional web sites for personality and work value assessments, plus web sites for other types of assessments.

After taking the assessments on the web site and printing the results, students should write their top two work values in the top left-hand portion of the Coat of Arms and write their personality traits in the top right-hand portion.

Encourage students to use colors for a more visual representation. You may want to display the completed Coats of Arms in the classroom, but be sure students eventually place their Coats of Arms in their Career Journey Folders.

Solution: Answers will vary. Each student's Coat of Arms will represent his or her individual *P*A*T*H to Success*. You may wish to invite your school's counselor to the class at this time to discuss assessment results in general. Then students can meet individually with the counselor.

Activity 3-4: Learning from Others

This activity helps students understand that there is no one "right" way to choose a career. Class discussion should reveal that some career choices are made early in life and some careers are still evolving.

Some students may choose to interview the same person they interviewed in Activity 1-2. If they interview the same person, they should refer to the time line they created in Activity 1-2 and then ask the additional questions listed in the text. You may also want them to update the time line they created in Activity 1-2 so it includes the results of this activity.

A discussion of the interview results is important to the class. The shared experiences should increase students' understanding of the different ways people choose a career and the different paths to career success. Students may want to save their results in their Career Journey Folders.

Solution: Answers will vary.

Activity 3-5:
Case Challenges

This activity helps students develop their analytical and team skills and checks their understanding of the circumstances in which different types of assessments are helpful.

You may wish to have a class discussion in which each pair of students shares its decisions.

Solution: Answers will vary. Students may choose more than one assessment for each case. Suggested answers are as follows:

1. Informational interviews, a career study tour, and job shadowing will allow Todd to see that academic courses, especially in math and science, are an integral part of welding careers.

2. Work value and personality assessments will give Stella the information she needs. Also, an ability assessment will confirm whether she is capable of doing the job.

3. Yao has the required interest, but he needs personality and work value assessments to see if he is suited to the pace of emergency room work. Also, taking an ability assessment will help Yao find out whether he has the necessary skills for the job.

Activity 3-6:
Coming to Terms

This activity reinforces students' understanding of informal assessment experiences and helps them develop their team skills. By requiring a situation description, the activity thoroughly checks students' knowledge.

Have students work with partners, or divide the class into groups of three or four students. Make sure students can define each term before describing or creating their situations.

Solution: Students' situations will vary.

After reading each case study, discuss the case with a partner. Which type of assessment would help the person in each case? Why? (You may have more than one answer.) Give examples.

1. Todd is a bright student who has definite goals in life. However, he questions why he should do classroom work that he thinks has nothing to do with his future goals. His father and uncle are welders, and he really likes helping them. He wants to learn welding. However, Todd's counselor and teachers are encouraging him to take academic courses that would prepare him for a bachelor's degree.

2. Stella especially enjoys working with people. She job shadowed both a marketing director and a teller at Streamwood Savings and Loan. She found the experience exciting, and she enjoyed interacting with customers. Streamwood Savings and Loan has offered her an after-school job. However, Stella is not sure she has the qualifications to work in the banking industry, and she wonders whether she would like this type of career.

3. After an informational interview with the emergency room manager at Midtown Hospital, Yao was offered a day of job shadowing there. He was thrilled! He was able to observe not only how the team members interacted with the patients, but also how they worked with optimum speed and efficiency. In the late morning, when only a few patients were admitted, Yao learned several computer operations used to check the maintenance of some of the equipment. The computer training was interrupted when a patient with a smashed finger needed to be escorted to radiology. At the end of the day, Yao had mixed emotions. He had found the work exciting, but was also worried. Did he have what was needed to work in the emergency room every day? How could he tell?

Informal assessment experiences include situations in which you participate in an activity and then analyze the results to help you discover your *Internal Career Design*. On a separate sheet of paper, describe a situation in which you have used or could use each of the following informal assessment experiences. You may want to use some of your answers from the "What do you think?" activities. Be as detailed as possible.

1. Informational interview

2. Job shadowing/Career study tour

3. Internship

4. Service learning

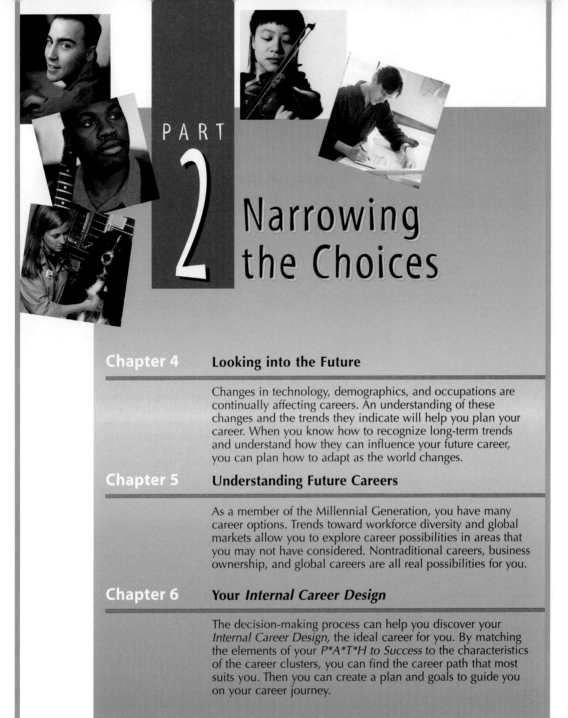

Part 2: Narrowing the Choices

Part 2 explores various aspects of careers, beginning with an investigation of career trends and how they can affect students' future careers. By recognizing long-term career trends and understanding their influence, students can plan how to adapt as the world changes. Trends toward workforce diversity and global markets will require students to adapt to a changing workplace but also will allow students to pursue nontraditional careers, business ownership, and global careers. After students are aware of all their career options, they use the decision-making process to narrow their career focus. By matching their *P*A*T*H to Success* to the characteristics of the career clusters, students discover their *Internal Career Design* and begin to plan their career journey.

PART 2 Narrowing the Choices

Chapter 4 — **Looking into the Future**

Changes in technology, demographics, and occupations are continually affecting careers. An understanding of these changes and the trends they indicate will help you plan your career. When you know how to recognize long-term trends and understand how they can influence your future career, you can plan how to adapt as the world changes.

Chapter 5 — **Understanding Future Careers**

As a member of the Millennial Generation, you have many career options. Trends toward workforce diversity and global markets allow you to explore career possibilities in areas that you may not have considered. Nontraditional careers, business ownership, and global careers are all real possibilities for you.

Chapter 6 — **Your *Internal Career Design***

The decision-making process can help you discover your *Internal Career Design,* the ideal career for you. By matching the elements of your *P*A*T*H to Success* to the characteristics of the career clusters, you can find the career path that most suits you. Then you can create a plan and goals to guide you on your career journey.

PART 2
Focus

The term *trends* is important to Part 2. Use the following activity to confirm students' knowledge.

Create a list of things that influence students' lives. These influences could be inventions, services, material goods, and systems, all with a direct impact on their lives. Then discuss what careers are involved with these influences. What type of education/training do these careers need? What subject areas are needed to prepare for these careers? Then list the commonalities of the discussion. The commonalities are trends.

Chapter Overview

Chapter 4
Looking into the Future

Chapter 4 explains how past and current trends can affect students' future careers. Students learn how to use information about past and ongoing changes in career fields to make predictions about future career areas. By researching current career trends and analyzing workplace and workforce trends, students can futurecast so they can make informed career decisions.

Use the **Objectives** and **Key Terms** printed in the margin to help students focus on the content of this chapter. Use the **video segment** for Chapter 4 to introduce the chapter.

TEACH

Discuss the chapter's opening scenario with students. Point out that Oscar's decision is based on his research.

What do you think?

Use **TM04-01**.
Question 1: Answers should focus on the idea that careers of today might not be the careers of tomorrow.
Question 2: Students should understand that there are a variety of careers within an occupation.

Career Journal

Ask students to spend 10 minutes writing Career Journal entries that answer the following questions:
1. What do you think this chapter will cover?
2. What do you already know about these topics?
3. What three things do you want to learn about these topics?

---

4 Looking into the Future

OBJECTIVES

After completing this chapter, you will be able to:

- Describe how trends can affect future careers.
- Explain how past and present changes in career fields can affect future careers.
- Examine how workplace and workforce trends are changing the way people work.
- Research sources in order to futurecast—make predictions based on trends.

Key Terms:

- trend
- futurecasting
- demographics
- labor force
- service occupations
- e-commerce
- cross training
- lifelong learning
- telecommuting
- job sharing

According to his mother, listening is Oscar's gift. People talk to Oscar about almost anything because he listens and is interested. Oscar wants to learn about human behavior and how people interact with each other, so he plans to take as many courses in social sciences and literature as possible. Through his school's service learning program, Oscar is able to work with people in different communities and cultures in his area. He likes working with senior citizens the most. After talking with his guidance counselor, Oscar investigated various career fields. His research always pointed him to a career in gerontology, the study of aging in older people.

Oscar wants to decide what to do with a career in gerontology. Should he research senior citizens to study the process of aging? Should he study about planning and providing services to older people? Working with others to help older people find solutions for their problems is something Oscar does in his volunteer work. He sees that his volunteering makes a difference. With a degree in gerontology, he can help people live longer—regardless of the specific career he chooses. Though Oscar doesn't need to decide his exact career interest now, he does know through his research that the field of gerontology is growing because people are living longer. His career will be in demand. His research verifies that fact.

What do you think?

Why do you need to predict the future for your career field? Isn't a doctor always a doctor and a carpenter always a carpenter?

CHAPTER RESOURCES and MATERIALS

Activities & Projects book
Instructor's Resource CD
- Forms and Worksheets for Chapter Activities 4-1 through 4-5
- Internet Links for Chapter 4
- PowerPoint Presentation for Chapter 4
- Lesson Plans
- Teaching Masters for Chapter 4
- Video Discussion Guide for Chapter 4

Chapter Tests book
ExamView® CD
Video
Web Site

Futurecasting

You are bombarded daily with information—from the Internet, television, radio, newspapers, and people you know. How do you know what information is important for you and your future? One way is to analyze the information to look for trends that indicate how your world may be changing. A **trend** is a general movement in a recognizable direction over the course of time.

> What are some trends that affect your everyday life—for example, what you wear, what music you listen to, and what movies you see? **What do you think?**

This chapter introduces some trends that serve as a starting point for making predictions of how the world might change. In *Investigating Your Career*, making predictions based on trends is called **futurecasting.** The key to successful futurecasting is identifying those trends that may be important to your career. An effective way to identify trends is by making insightful analyses based on the information you receive daily.

Recognizing trends may help you make predictions about your career in the following areas:

- Whether your career will be there when you begin working
- Whether there will be a need for your career throughout your employment future
- How your career might change in the next couple of decades

Keep in mind that predictions based on trends can be wrong because no one can foresee the future with perfect accuracy. Unusual twists in national or global politics, unanticipated economic changes, world health catastrophes, and extreme or unexpected weather conditions can all affect current predictions.

Activity 4-1, "Trends Quiz," helps check your knowledge about current and past trends that can affect your career field.

Changes in Career Fields

Trend watching is vital to futurecasting because the employment outlook is changing rapidly. In addition, change is not isolated to the United States, but is occurring all over the world. Some trends may affect your life in the near future; others may not have an effect for 10 or 20 years. By recognizing long-term trends and thinking about how they may influence your future career, you can plan how to adapt as times change.

Some of the changes that are occurring now or that have occurred in the past indicate trends that can strongly affect your future. In particular, changes in technology, demographics, and occupations will continue to influence career fields.

Discuss the following statement with students: Perhaps the only thing that can be said with certainty about work today and in the future is that there are fewer age limits and no consistent, predictable working life. Encourage students to identify some specific career trends in the statement and how the trends they identify might affect them. For example, fewer age limits identify a trend toward older people in the workforce. Students' communication skills and career choices might be affected because they would be expected to work effectively with people of many different ages. Then ask students what types of trends might help them make predictions about the career areas in the bulleted list on page 55 of the text.

> **What do you think?**

Use **TM04-02**.
Students' answers will vary. Encourage students to think about their daily activities to explain the influence of trends.

APPLY

Have students complete **Activity 4-1, "Trends Quiz,"** that appears on page 71. Teaching suggestions for this activity appear on page 71, and answers to the quiz appear on page 75. An activity worksheet can be found on the Career Portfolio and Resource CD—**Text Activity 04-1.doc.**

ONLINE RESOURCES

Check out the web site **www.investigatingyourcareer.com** for teacher resources, student activities, and replacements for broken links for this chapter. To access the teacher resources:

Username: career
Password: investigate

TEACH

Students need to realize why computer and web skills are vital to many careers. Point out that many companies use the Web for much of their research and for almost all information distribution within the organization. The Internet makes work more efficient by providing faster, better, and cheaper access to information.

Technological Changes

During the past three decades, the employment world has been evolving from the Industrial Age to the Digital Age. The Digital Age is based on the technological changes that began with the computer and that now affect everyone's life and nearly all careers.

CAREER SUCCESS TIP

Learning does not stop after you are out of school. It is a lifelong process. In order to succeed, you need to adapt to future changes by acquiring new skills.

In the 1960s, David received his bachelor's degree in agricultural and mechanical engineering. He began his career designing and revamping farm machinery parts for a major company. To create his designs, David used a drawing board and pencil and did his calculations with a slide rule. After David completed his drawings, a drafter redrew them on specialized paper. The paper was put through a blueprint machine where it underwent a chemical transformation. The paper became a permanent blueprint, or copy, of the drawing.

Today David is astounded at the transformation of mechanical engineering. Now he does the majority of his drawings on a desktop computer and performs the necessary calculations on a graphic calculator. A drafter may assist him, but David prefers using the computer to make his revisions and final drawings himself. The computer stores his drawings and produces any required number of immaculate copies, not blueprints. In addition, David is able to e-mail his drawings to customers for approval and use them in videoconference presentations.

The technological changes David experienced during the last 30 to 40 years are phenomenal, but not unusual. Although no one predicted the technological revolution, everyone has experienced it. The trend toward increased use of digital technology is expected to continue as technological breakthroughs occur at an incredible rate.

Since IBM first introduced its desktop personal computer (PC) to the public in 1981, PCs have become smaller and more powerful. Laptops are replacing some PCs, and handheld personal digital assistants (PDAs) are increasing in popularity. Cellular phones, introduced to the public in 1983, now are in nearly every household—and pocket or purse. Don Norman, former chief technology officer of both Apple Computer and Hewlett Packard, predicts that by 2020, 100 percent of the United States population will have absorbed digital technology into their lives. In an extremely short span of time, digital technology has reshaped the way society works, communicates, and even thinks.

What's behind the technological revolution? A strong economy is one of the main forces behind the technological changes. A strong economy provides businesses with funds to experiment with and to develop new products, which increases competition among companies. Strong economic growth also provides more income for people to purchase new technological devices.

CAREER SUCCESS TIP

Lifelong Learning

Invite one or two guest speakers to speak to your class. One speaker could be someone from a local college or university who works with nontraditional, or older, students. The other speaker could be a nontraditional student who is currently taking college classes. Have students prepare questions about the changes in enrollment and courses the university has made in the last few years. Ask the adult student to explain why he or she started or returned to college and how doing so affected his or her career.

How will technological changes affect you and your career? In the last ten years, employers have struggled to keep up with the constant need to fill an increasing number of new high-tech positions. Many of these positions did not exist even five years ago. Also, according to Jim Treacy, chief operating officer of TMP Worldwide Inc., information technology and other computer areas haven't reached a peak yet. Companies will continue to compete for their share of the market and for their share of workers who have the appropriate skills. Thus, if you have the appropriate skills, you will have a better chance of career success.

Demographic Changes

Demographics are information about a population, such as employment numbers, ethnic background, age, education, and so on. When making your career decision, you need to consider the demographics of the United States in general and the labor force in particular. Changes that are occurring in both populations will affect the careers of the future. The **labor force**, defined by the U.S. Department of Labor, consists of all persons age 16 and older who are working or who are actively seeking employment. Among the demographic changes that may affect your career are an older labor force, more two-career families, and the increasing ethnic diversity of the U.S. population and the labor force.

Age-Related Changes

How might the age of the labor force influence your career choice?

What do you think?

A change in the U.S. population that has already had an effect on employment is the increase in life expectancy. As the number of older people in the population increases, any career field that provides services to senior citizens has more employment opportunities. Some of these careers are in established industries, such as travel planning, elder care, and home healthcare. Others are in new areas, such as the development and staffing of wellness centers. In addition, more health-related career areas will open as healthcare technology increases.

The aging of the baby-boomer section of the population is another age-related change that has affected careers. Baby boomers form the largest population group in the United States, and workers over age 45 are the largest workforce group now and for at least the next ten years. As a whole, baby boomers are prosperous. Their prosperity has created career opportunities in areas that provide goods and services to them. For example, auto manufacturers have produced cars designed to appeal to them. Because the baby boomers are getting older, new career areas are opening. For example, new careers in medical research are appearing as pharmaceutical companies create drugs to treat the effects of aging and cosmetic firms develop antiaging creams and new sunblock lotions.

CAREER TREND

Career Trend Predictions

According to the U.S. Department of Labor's *Occupational Outlook Handbook*, by 2010, the civilian labor force is projected to increase by 17 million people. By 2010, 158,000 million people will be part of this workforce. The youth labor force (ages 16–24) is expected to grow more rapidly than it has in the past 25 years. The Asian and Hispanic ethnic groups are projected to grow more rapidly than African Americans or other ethnic groups. Men will enter the labor force at a greater rate than women.

—*Source: **www.bls.gov***

Changes in Families

Two demographic changes that have affected the labor force are the decrease in single-wage-earning families and the increase in single-parent households. The Bureau of Labor Statistics (BLS) reports that in 51 percent of couples with children, both parents have careers. Fifty-nine percent of women who have infants are in the workforce. How can these changes affect your career?

Masaki, a physical therapist at a rehabilitation hospital, has a hectic schedule that often forces him to work overtime. His wife, Annu, owns a specialty clothing store at the local mall.

As in many retail businesses, Annu's store has a high employee turnover rate. To make sure her business is running smoothly and efficiently, Annu must often work long hours at the store. With their careers filling so much of their time, Masaki and Annu have little time for the daily chores at home. What little free time they have, they want to spend with their children. Both Annu and Masaki believe that guiding and interacting with their children is more important than cooking or cleaning or cutting the grass. However, both also realize that daily chores must be done.

Masaki and Annu decide that the only solution to their dilemma is to pay others to do some of their routine chores. First, Masaki and Annu hire a cleaning service. Now Lorie cleans their house once a week. Freed from weekly cleaning, the family has more time for leisure activities on weekends. Next, Masaki and Annu set up a contract with a landscape maintenance company. Now Jon Paul and his crew trim the grass every Monday and take care of yearly maintenance chores. The fee that Annu and Masaki pay for this service saves them many hours that are better spent with their family. Finally, Annu and Masaki order takeout food or pick up prepared dinners at the grocery during the week. They do their gourmet cooking and baking on weekends when everyone in the family can enjoy participating.

Because of demographic changes involving the structure and goals of families, the labor force has changed. Many workers are buying outside services, such as yard maintenance and cleaning services. Thus, if you can provide a service that allows people more leisure time, you increase your chance of a successful career. Also, because of increases in both two-career families and single-parent households, many

DIFFERENT LEARNING ABILITIES

Visually Impaired

Some students with visual impairment may benefit from an audio recording of printed material. Make arrangements for volunteers to record reading assignments—from the textbook and other appropriate sources.

women join or return to the workforce before their children begin school. Thus, the childcare industry is growing, and there will be a need for any career related to childcare services.

Ethnic Diversity

A change occurring in both the U.S. population and the labor force is the increase in minorities. How does this diversity in ethnic background affect you and your career? In many professions, knowing a second language can lead to career success. Many large companies have customers and offices around the world, so learning the customs of other cultures will help you communicate effectively. In addition, the ability to build successful relationships with coworkers of diverse backgrounds will increase your career success.

Occupation Changes

Changes in occupations have occurred in the past and continue to occur. The reason is due, in part, to changes in demographics and technology. The industrial revolution, which was the result of technological changes, caused workers to move from the farm to the factory. After World War II, companies that manufactured goods further reduced the workforce of the farming industry, which used to be the largest employer in the United States. Farming occupations continue to decrease.

Today manufacturers are no longer the largest employers. In fact, manufacturing occupations are declining. Since 1970, **service occupations**, jobs in industries that provide services rather than goods, have outnumbered manufacturing occupations.

A change in demographics—more people living longer—has caused service occupations to increase in the healthcare field. In addition, new healthcare jobs are being created to provide more services in less expensive ways. For example, nurse practitioners, who receive more training than registered nurses but less training than doctors, can provide basic medical care at a lower cost.

Many manufacturing jobs have changed because of technological advances. For example, think about how technology has changed the machine tool industry. In the past, machine operators set machines manually and then physically operated the lathes and drills. Today operators simply insert a computer disk to run the machines. In this case, while workers still produce the same product, the skills needed for the job have changed a great deal.

Changes in occupations will affect many careers—including yours. Now and in the future, workers in nearly all occupations must be computer literate and be able to adapt to new and increasingly complex computer applications. New technology means an increased need

> 66 **I'm fascinated by people and their capacity to innovate. You know there is no end in sight.** 99
>
> —*Abraham Peled, CEO/NDS Group*

TEACH

Discuss how the demand for goods and services affects labor market trends. Explain that demand is the quantities of a good or service consumers are (1) willing to buy and (2) able to buy at (3) various prices during (4) a given time period. All four elements must be present for demand to exist. When demand for a specific good or service increases, more workers are needed to produce the good or service and more jobs are available in that career field. When demand for a specific good or service decreases, fewer workers are needed to produce the good or service and fewer jobs are available in that career field. Providing examples may help students understand that their career success depends in part on the demand for the good or service that their career field (company) supplies.

DIFFERENT LEARNING STYLES
Visual Learners

Provide visual learners with colored markers and several sheets of paper. Ask them to draw symbols or some representation that helps them comprehend and retain the information in the textbook. Encourage visual learners to keep a notebook of their drawings to help them prepare for the end-of-chapter test and end-of-year tests. Periodically post some of the drawings in the classroom to give other students ideas of how to arrange their visual notebooks of the text material. Print and tactile learners also may benefit from this process.

for employees who have technological knowledge and higher reading, communication, and math skills. These skills play an important role in getting a job and in developing a career.

Activity 4-2, "Learning from Others," will help you discover how a career area has changed over the years.

Trends in Career Fields

The key to futurecasting is identifying trends. Two types of trends important for your career are workplace trends and workforce trends. Workplace trends are changes employers are making in order to be more efficient or competitive. Workforce trends are changes employees are making to allow them to meet their personal and professional goals and responsibilities. Identifying these two types of trends can help you predict future changes in career fields.

Workplace Trends

In today's workplace, *competence*, not educational background, often defines an employee's value. With a need to fill positions, especially those that did not exist five years ago, companies are more willing to hire employees who have unconventional training. For example, someone without a degree but with specialized job skills may beat out a college graduate for a job. According to the BLS, 10 of the largest 13 industry employers rank specialized training ahead of a college degree when they are searching for people to fill highly technical positions.

CAREER FACT

Individuals in Generation X and the Digital or Millennial Generation (people born after 1960) are technologically oriented, culturally diverse, and more globally aware than the generations before them.

As an example, the BLS predicts that three fast-growing careers in the next ten years will be air traffic controllers, elevator installers and repairers, and dental hygienists. None of these careers requires a bachelor's degree. Why air traffic controllers? The increase of airline travel and the increase in retirement travelers mean more flights. Why elevator workers? Use of mass transit is increasing due to overcrowded highways and the high cost of fuel. Mass transit uses elevators and escalators to move people to and from trains and to and from gates and terminals within an airport. So constant upkeep is necessary. Why dental hygienists? Dental hygienists already perform some of the work for dentists, such as cleaning people's teeth. Because of the shortage of dentists, hygienists are expected to do even more of the work. Also, the number of dental cavities has increased 100 percent in the past few years. The American Dental Association expects that cavities will continue to increase as people consume more soft drinks and bottled water, which contains no fluoride.

Another workplace trend is contracting work. Work previously done by a business's employees is now contracted out, or sent out, to other businesses that specialize in particular skills. A business can save money hiring specialized workers for a project. Examples of work that is commonly contracted are security services; grounds maintenance; payroll services; advertising services; and computer services, networking, and repair.

The growth of e-commerce is also an emerging workplace trend. **E-commerce**, or electronic commerce, is the buying and selling of goods and services via the Internet. E-commerce is changing the way people shop. So companies must change the way they do business. Firms may need to branch out by offering both web-based retailing and regular buying and selling. In addition, when people shop less often at retail stores, the demand for package delivery services, such as FedEx and UPS, increases.

REAL PEOPLE
REAL CAREERS

Contract Worker—Computer Support Specialist

Lana McKinney, an information technology contractor, often feels like a substitute teacher or a mercenary—she goes to where she is needed. She might install a network for one firm, then rush off to devise a wireless system for another. Lana works for a new company every few months, learning new skills and meeting new people at every location.

After she graduated from high school, Lana earned her bachelor's degree in business and computer education and became a teacher. When her school district began to install technology, including working with servers and networks, Lana became interested and took courses in hands-on informational technology at the community college.

Information technology is a career field that is constantly changing as new technology is invented. Information technology workers must continually update their knowledge—or their skills will fall behind those of others in their field. The basis of a high school information technology curriculum includes business courses that offer experience with computers, computer classes, the problem-solving aspects of math classes, and the discovery elements of science courses.

Lana McKinney began her contracting career two years ago and enjoys being able to work in many different areas of information technology. She wouldn't have as much variety in projects if she worked in only one company. Now after each project is complete, Lana is off to new and different experiences at the next company.

For more information about:
• computer support specialists, the second fastest-growing occupation for the next decade, search *www.itaa.org*.
• experience in contract work, search *www.cehandbook.com*.

Source: Harrison, Crayton. "Techno-advisers Enjoy Flexibility." *The Cincinnati Enquirer*, 16 April 2001.

ENRICH

Have students complete **Activity 4-A, "Futurecasting Interview,"** found in the *Investigating Your Career Activities & Projects* book.
Solution: The solution for this activity appears in the *Teacher's Edition* of *Investigating Your Career Activities & Projects*.

In this activity, students interview people who have 15–20 years in their current career. The questions in this activity forecast the career area.

You can assign this activity as a new interview activity or as additional questions for students to use when interviewing the first two categories of people in Activity 4-2 of the textbook—those who have less than 5 years in a career or those who worked for 15–20 years in their career.

REAL PEOPLE—REAL CAREERS
Computer Support Specialists

Arrange students into two groups. Assign each group one of the web sites listed in the textbook. Have one group research computer support specialists. Ask students to look for information about what computer support specialists do and what training is needed, as well as other important information. Have the other group learn about contract work. Ask students to find information about how contract workers get jobs and who pays them, as well as other information. Ask both groups to report on their findings to the other half of the class.

Two other important trends in the workplace that will continue to affect your career are the increase in world trade and the emphasis on teamwork in the workplace. Employment in the Digital Age will require different skills and attitudes from those needed in the past.

The Global Marketplace

What do you think? What influence do other countries have on you now? How might the growing global marketplace influence your future?

In the past, most businesses in the United States competed with other businesses within the United States. In the Digital Age, U.S. businesses have fierce competition from countries all over the world and the U.S. economy is linked to economic and political changes in nations around the world. Indeed, what happens in South Korea or France can affect the state of Missouri or even the entire United States.

> ❝There are not two worlds—education and work. There is one world . . . life.❞
>
> —Willard Wirtz, former U.S. Secretary of Labor

Halia has two loves—science and travel. Her career goal is to be a chemist for the Haskell Corporation. After talking to her uncle, who works for Haskell, Halia knows the first thing she must do is finish college, getting her degree in chemistry. Then after being hired by Haskell, she can be placed wherever the company needs her. She can end up anywhere in the world. The chance to work outside the United States at one of the Haskell plants is the reason Halia wants to work for the company. Halia's interest assessment shows her to be creative and flexible—essential skills for a successful career with a global company.

If Halia is placed at a plant in another country, she knows she will have to adapt quickly to the customs, language, and different ways of doing business to survive day-to-day living. As an Arab-American U.S. citizen, Halia already has experience learning how to be flexible by attending U.S. schools. Although Halia's skills as a chemist will be valuable, her ability to adapt quickly and successfully to different work situations is just as important to the Haskell Corporation. Haskell's managers realize that their employees around the world are their ambassadors and are critical to the success of the company. What an exciting career Halia has ahead of her!

International trade has expanded the world's marketplace. Modern communications technology, such as the Internet, has made today's workplace a national—and often global—one. The global marketplace has caused several changes that affect employment in the United States. To expand their markets, many U.S. companies have formed partnerships with companies in other countries, increasing their need for employees. Other U.S. companies have moved their manufacturing plants to countries that pay lower wages than those in the United States, decreasing their need for American workers. Finally, by having a larger market in which to sell their products, many U.S. industries

INTEGRATED ACADEMICS
Music

Arrange students into four or five small groups. Assign each group a foreign country. (Choose countries where information about their music is readily available.) Have students research the music of that country and the types of jobs that surround the country's music industry. Suggest that students use the Internet for research and/or contact their country's embassy. Hold a celebration of music in the classroom where students play the music of their researched country.

(such as the industrial machinery, electronics, and transportation industries) have seen significant job growth.

How might this trend toward a global marketplace affect you and your career? The American workplace has seen increased cultural diversity in both the customers and employees of U.S. employers. Knowing how to interact with workers from different cultures, knowing how to speak different languages, and discovering different ways of solving problems are increasingly important skills for employees of today and tomorrow.

Teams

| What are the advantages and disadvantages of working on a team? | What do you think? |

Many workers today are learning different ways to work. Instead of being closely supervised, they are expected to identify and solve work-related problems, manage their own work schedules, and work together with coworkers and customers. According to Alan November, Educational Technology Planner, this trend "is not just limited to well-educated white collar workers." For example, a John Deere welder in Illinois now uses computer and telecommunication networks to communicate with a welder in Germany. Through their communication systems, they manage a network of robot welders and work together to do their work more efficiently.

Companies must respond quickly to changes in technology, customer demands, and global competition. As a result, management techniques have changed. The emphasis now is on teams. Teams are usually made up of workers who are brought together to complete a specific task. Each team member may be skilled in one area, such as technology or finance. Teams also have more control over their work than workers had in the past. However, team members are often evaluated on the success or failure of the team, rather than on individual performance.

When a project is finished, team members may move on to new teams and new projects. So team members need skills that can be used in more than one situation. The idea of teams supports cross training. In **cross training**, employees prepare for several workplace roles, rather than just one job. Cross training is a major trend of today's workplace.

Why is the trend toward teams important for you? Although employers want to know what specialized skills you have, they also want you to be skilled in many other areas, especially in communicating and cooperating as a member of a team. As you discover your *Internal Career Design*, keep in mind that various skills are important to career success in the Digital Age.

CAREER SUCCESS TIP

Participation in cross-training programs is a good strategy for enhancing career success. Cross training on the job is becoming common as a way to deal with staffing changes.

In the Digital Age, the trend is toward workers creating their own careers rather than applying for exact job descriptions. Ask students what this trend will mean for the workforce. In your discussion, emphasize how career customization will require creativity and problem-solving skills. Mention that employers may value transferable skills more highly than specialized skills for some types of jobs.

APPLY

Have students complete **Activity 4-3, "Case Challenges,"** on pages 72–73. Teaching suggestions and the solution for this activity appear on pages 72–73. An activity worksheet can be found on the Career Portfolio and Resource CD—**Text Activity 04-3.doc**.

> "Everyone has to learn to think differently, bigger, to open up to possibilities."
>
> —*Oprah Winfrey, television host, producer, actor*

Digital-Age Employment

The traditional workplace has certainly changed. Today employers want workers who have a wide range of skills and who can contribute to many areas of a business. Employers in the Digital Age also value employees who can make effective day-to-day decisions and communicate those decisions to customers. The success of a company often depends on its relationships with customers and the community.

Adaptability and change are key ingredients in today's businesses and for today's workers. Change means more than adjusting job titles and classifications. Companies and their workforces need to be self-directed and self-motivated. Businesses need to adapt their products and services to meet changing markets. They must be able to access information and work with people all over the world.

What should you do to make yourself more adaptable in the Digital Age? Employers are interested in what you can do. Demonstrating your skills and having the certifications to prove your ability are important. Attitude is also key. Being positive about yourself, being passionate about what you do, and having confidence in your ability can help you advance in your career. In addition, because change is occurring rapidly in the Digital Age, you need to be innovative and willing to learn new products and procedures.

Activity 4-3, "Case Challenges," provides you with an opportunity to apply workplace trends to real-life situations.

Workforce Trends

Workforce trends include international competition, the team concept, and other workplace changes in the Digital Age. These changes have led employers to demand workers who are well educated and highly skilled. However, workplace trends aren't the only thing you need to consider as you make career decisions. Trends are also taking place in the workforce.

Some workforce trends are taking place because workers are reacting to workplace changes. Others are based on employees looking for ways to improve their working conditions, to meet their responsibilities outside of work, or to improve their lifestyles. Important workforce trends involve transferable skills, lifelong learning, and work scheduling.

Transferable Skills

In response to workplace changes, workers have become adept at switching gears quickly to pursue new opportunities. To do this, they have developed their transferable skills. Transferable skills are portable and allow you to move from one career to another, from one work site to another. For example, if you know how to run complicated computer applications and complex machinery, you can easily transfer from one career area to another.

DIFFERENT LEARNING ABILITIES

Attention Deficit Disorder

When asking questions during class, refer students to the paragraph from which you are taking the question. Make questions open-ended so students can easily find the answers. Avoid questions that can be answered *yes* or *no* because it is too easy for students to be wrong, thereby increasing the frustration level of ADD students. Prompt students if needed. Always praise students for providing the correct answers.

Maddie was always inside a computer—adding a sound card, rewiring a system, or networking her friends' computers together. When she wasn't working with computers, she was interacting with people. Maddie decided that nursing would be a good career field for her because she would be able to work with people and computers. In addition, her research showed that nurses were always in demand.

After she finished nursing school, Maddie had several employment options. She chose to begin her career in the cardiac intensive care unit at the Ohio Clinic. She liked the fact she would be in contact with people and complex machinery on a daily basis. She also thought she would like the work schedule because the 37-hour/three-day workweek would give her four days off to work on computers.

However, after 18 months in the cardiac unit, Maddie realized nursing was not for her. She dreaded the work schedule and was more excited by her days off than she was by her days at work. Her work in the cardiac unit simply didn't allow her enough opportunity to satisfy her passion for working with computers and networks. So Maddie quit her job at the Ohio Clinic and moved back to her hometown.

Maddie applied for work at the local cable company, which was looking for someone to install cable modems and networks for high-speed Internet access in small businesses and private homes. The recommendations from people for whom Maddie had done work in her off-hours persuaded the cable company to hire her. Interacting with people and working with computers gave Maddie the satisfaction she needed—and the experience to become a contract employee for a computer-consulting firm two years later.

Transferable skills are valuable resources that can provide you with options when changes occur in the workplace. Improving your transferable skills is one way you can adapt to future trends in career fields. In addition to computer-related skills, effective communication and math skills are transferable skills that will be in high demand in the future.

TEACH

Emphasize that knowledge of math, science, and technology is essential to future career success. Students should try to take more courses in these areas than the minimum required. Whether students will directly use math, science, or technology in their careers is irrelevant; the industry they work in will use these courses. Therefore, all employees need to have a working knowledge of them.

DIFFERENT LEARNING STYLES

Kinesthetic Learners

Arrange students into groups of four to six. Provide poster board for student groups. Ask groups to create an advertising poster that promotes lifelong learning. To help develop their posters, students may contact colleges and universities with programs for nontraditional students to ask for advertising brochures. Display all posters in the classroom.

Use **TM04-06**.
Students' answers will vary. Students should recognize the need for learning new skills to keep up with changes in technology.

What do you think?

Use **TM04-07**.
Students' answers will vary.

ENRICH

Have students complete **Activity 4-D, "Flexible Scheduling,"** found in the *Investigating Your Career Activities & Projects* book.

In this activity, students investigate flexible scheduling as a workforce trend. In addition, the collecting, organizing, and analyzing of data help students understand scientific sampling and surveying.

Students can interview one or two people in pairs or individually. If some students have trouble with transportation, they can interview people with flexible part-time schedules in school, such as cafeteria workers or bus drivers.

Use the second sheet to compare class results unless time is an issue. After the interviews are completed, ask students what they've discovered about the need to be flexible in a retail career. Then extend the discussion to similar flexible work schedules in other career areas.
Solution: The solution for this activity appears in the *Teacher's Edition* of *Investigating Your Career Activities & Projects*.

Lifelong Learning

What do you think? Why isn't the education you receive before you start your career enough?

Education is not as structured as it once was. Learning the basic skills of reading, computing, writing, and listening is no longer sufficient. Today, because of changes in technology and the workplace, emphasis is placed on helping you prepare for career success. For example, the relationships between skills and real problems common in the working world are explored in many classes.

For you to be successful in the changing workplace, your education cannot stop with high school or college or beginning on-the-job training. Your education must continue throughout your working life. **Lifelong learning**—the constant improving of your education—is necessary for nearly all occupations. In fact, 85 percent of jobs will require further education. Those that do not are primarily service industry jobs, such as restaurant servers and cashiers, where employees start at low pay and have little opportunity for growth in wages or position.

Lifelong learning does not necessarily mean going back to a traditional school. One option for continuing your education is e-learning—using educational materials and courses available on the Internet. E-learning sites offer valuable tools, such as curriculum modules, troubleshooting exercises, certification courses, job previewing, and online simulations. These courses and other activities, which can be accessed at home or on the job, provide education solutions for people whose schedules do not permit going to a university or another facility. Through learning environments that simulate the workplace, e-learning also offers "just-in-time instruction" when employees need specialized preparation.

CAREER FACT

For the first time in history, most children are more comfortable with and knowledgeable about an innovation central to society than their parents are. That innovation? The Internet.

Work Scheduling

What do you think? How important is it to you to be able to manage your own schedule?

Flexible work schedules are fast becoming the norm, not the exception. Many employees no longer work five 8-hour days each week. Instead, many work four 10-hour days or work fewer than 40 hours a week. Nor do many employees go into an office every day. **Telecommuting,** working at home while linked by technology to one or more company offices, has become increasingly common. Telecommuting was originally designed as a way for companies to cut costs and, at the same time, help working parents balance work and family life. Many telecommuters prefer this way of working even though they may average well over 50 hours a week at home and spend additional time at a conventional office.

CAREER TREND
Online Job Searches

As the emphasis on lifelong learning increases, colleges and universities have recognized the need to offer online courses. Have students work in small groups. Assign one group local colleges and universities, assign another group out-of-state institutions, assign another group foreign institutions, assign yet another group virtual institutions, and so on. Have student groups go online to investigate an institution in their category. Students are to find what courses are offered and how the courses are administered and graded. Have groups give oral reports of their findings.

When Paul's second child was born, he asked his company if he could telecommute. He needed more flexibility in his work schedule so he could take care of the children. On a typical morning, Paul serves his children breakfast. At the same time,

he may be on his cell phone sharing a budget revision with his manager. Paul makes sure the bus picks up his son for school. Then he is likely faxing revisions through his computer and e-mailing reports.

Paul works four days a week in his office at home, driving into the company office on Thursdays. There he shares space with four other employees who have work schedules similar to his. The nontraditional work arrangement allows Paul to be part of his children's lives. The flexible work schedule also eliminates childcare problems. In exchange, Paul's company has fewer offices to equip and maintain—and has a happy, hard-working employee who is valued by his employer.

Other types of flexible, nontraditional work arrangements include independent or on-call contract workers, part-time workers, temporary employees, and job sharing. In **job sharing**, two employees split a full-time position. They split duties, vacation days, and so on, and each receives half the pay and benefits.

Nontraditional work arrangements offer benefits and drawbacks. The flexibility of the positions allows workers to reach a better balance between their careers and personal lives and to gain new experiences in various types of careers and businesses. However, some employers only reluctantly agree to unconventional work arrangements because they are not really convinced the business will benefit. These employers may give the impression that nontraditional workers are less dedicated and less loyal. Although employers may benefit from lower costs and higher productivity, their nontraditional employees may not receive worker benefits and may risk unplanned unemployment. In any case, trends indicate that the traditional roles of employer and employee are being redefined.

Use Activity 4-4, "Technology Trends—Virtual Labs," to explore some e-learning options of virtual laboratories.

APPLY

Have students complete **Activity 4-4, "Technology Trends—Virtual Labs,"** on pages 73–74. Teaching suggestions and the solution for this activity appear on page 73. An activity worksheet can be found on the Career Portfolio and Resource CD— **Text Activity 04-4.doc**.

INTEGRATED ACADEMICS
Visual Arts

Ask students to imagine they are working in their career choice. They have made arrangements to work from a home office. Brainstorm with students what their perfect office space would look like. Remind them it should fit their individual likes and the type of job they will be doing. Provide students with poster board, magazines, and art supplies. Students may also use computer graphics. Have students design their perfect office space. Display the pictures of offices in the classroom.

What do you think?

Use **TM04-08**.
Students' answers will vary.

━━ TEACH ━━

Emphasize that the Bureau of Labor Statistics is a valuable resource for the career decision-making process. The BLS web site, **www.bls.gov**, has many charts and statistics related to the workforce and the workplace. The site has information about six of every seven jobs, identifying what people in the occupation do, where they work, their working conditions, the training required, the job outlook, and the median weekly pay. In addition, the BLS site provides the *Occupational Outlook Handbook* online and updates it every three months. The *Handbook* presents industry trends, the employment outlook, tips for job seekers, and detailed descriptions of a wide variety of occupations.

What do you think?

Use **TM04-09**.
Students' answers will vary.

What do you think? To futurecast, you need to forecast one or two decades ahead. How might your career change throughout your life?

Jobs in technology are the future. The microprocessor is in many devices, making society more computerized. The BLS, which is the major U.S. agency that provides future employment outlooks, predicts that 65 to 70 percent of tomorrow's workers will need one to three years of technical training beyond high school. In addition, according to the BLS, the Internet is the most important factor in the top ten fastest-growing jobs. One out of every 12 positions in information technology is not filled. That means workers will be needed in ever-increasing numbers. In the next decade, more than half of all U.S. employees will work for companies where information technology is a vital part of the business.

For the next decade, the BLS makes the following predictions:

- The U.S. economy will remain healthy with moderate growth and strong foreign trade.
- Workers over age 45 will account for a larger share of the labor force, and employers will continue to employ more women.
- The workforce will be more racially diverse as minority groups grow faster than the Caucasian population.
- Service and retail occupations will have the most job openings.
- The two fastest-growing industries will be computerized data processing and home healthcare.
- Careers requiring higher levels of education will grow faster. However, most careers will not require a bachelor's degree.

What is the best way to prepare for tomorrow's careers? Education is the answer and lifelong learning is the key. Education does not necessarily mean obtaining a bachelor's degree. Education can take place on the job, in an Internet course, and in various types of classrooms and facilities. Technology and the workplace are continually changing, and the greatest danger to career success is to become out of date. The modern world is undergoing a leap in creativity and productivity, and the workplace of the future needs a flexible, educated workforce. You can be part of that workforce.

What do you think? How can you make sure your passions, interests, and talents lead you to a career that will *have* a future?

Remember the first question in Activity 4-1? How many inventions did you and your classmates write down? These are just the inventions that have been created since you were born! Change is occurring at an ever-faster rate every day.

DIFFERENT LEARNING ABILITIES

Gifted Students
Provide gifted students a chance to use their imaginations by writing, casting, and filming a video. Have students brainstorm about what their lives will be like 20 years from now. Give them the following questions for their futurecasting: What will their lives be like? What types of careers will many of them be in? Will more education be needed? How will lifelong learning affect their lives? How will technology have changed? How will society have changed?

You need to plan for a career in a business or an industry that will grow. So how can you be knowledgeable about ongoing and future trends? How can you investigate what the trends may mean for your career? Try some of the following suggestions:

- Put business news on your reading list. Follow the trends by skimming weekly news and business magazines. If you have access to the Internet, cost is not a factor because you can read these publications online.

Business Week	*www.businessweek.com*
Time	*www.time.com/time*
Newsweek	*www.msnbc.com/news/NW-front_Front.asp*
USA Today	*www.usatoday.com*

- Stay current with financial news at:

Nightly Business Report	*www.nightlybusiness.org*

- For keeping up to date with employment trends, check these web sites:

The BLS offers employment projections through news releases, data, and publications such as the *Occupational Outlook Handbook* and the *Occupational Outlook Quarterly*. *www.bls.gov*

America's Career InfoNet provides both occupational and economic information. *www.acinet.org/acinet*

The U.S. Census Bureau site includes tools such as maps, employment statistics, and data and trends in many areas, including population, education, and immigration. *www.census.gov*

The Wall Street Journal's
College pages *http://collegejournal.com*
Career pages *http://careerjournal.com*

This chapter offers a broad perspective of workplace and workforce trends. Reading and watching the sites and news sources mentioned above, plus investigating other resources, will help you identify employment trends and make predictions. You will be able to plan a career for the future—a career that is dynamic and responsive to change in the years ahead.

66 The size of your world is determined by how much you explore. 99
—*Anonymous*

ENRICH

Have students complete **Activity 4-E, "Imagine . . . .,"** found in the *Investigating Your Career Activities & Projects* book.

This activity gives students practice in identifying trends and in predicting changes that might occur in the future because of trends they identify. Students can explore one site or more if time permits. They should justify their conclusions not only with hypotheses, but also with data from the site(s). Students may work individually or with a partner. **Solution:** The solution for this activity appears in the *Teacher's Edition* of *Investigating Your Career Activities & Projects.*

CLOSE

Have students work in two teams. Assign Team 1 the first half of the chapter and Team 2 the second half. Have each team write 20 questions about this chapter. Teams who write the questions must also know the answers. Have teams line up opposite each other. Have Team 1 ask the first question. If Team 2 answers it correctly, it gets a point. If not, it loses a point. Next, Team 2 asks Team 1 a question and the process continues.

DIFFERENT LEARNING STYLES

Auditory Learners

To help auditory learners understand and assimilate the textbook material, call on different students to read sections of the chapter. After a student has read a few paragraphs, ask another student to paraphrase the material. Next, have a second student read a few paragraphs; then ask a series of questions about that section. Have a third student read another section. Ask three students each to write a question from this section, and then have other students answer these questions.

APPLY

Have students complete **Activity 4-5, "Coming to Terms,"** on page 74. Teaching suggestions and the solution for this activity appear on page 74. An activity worksheet can be found on the Career Portfolio and Resource CD—**Text Activity 04-5.doc**.

IN A NUTSHELL

Remind students about the objectives set forth at the beginning of the chapter, and use this summary to reinforce the concepts presented in this chapter.

Career Journal

Ask students to spend 10 minutes writing Career Journal entries that answer the following questions:
1. How well did what you thought you knew match what the chapter presented?
2. What questions do you now have about the chapter topics, and where do you think you can find the answers to those questions?
3. How will the content of the chapter help you investigate *your* career?

ASSESS

Administer the printed objective test for Chapter 4, available with this package. Test solutions are found in the *Teacher's Edition* of *Investigating Your Career Chapter Tests*. Use the **Exam**View® CD to create your own objective test for this chapter.

 Use Activity 4-5, "Coming to Terms," to check your understanding of some of the Digital Age terminology in this chapter.

IN A NUTSHELL

- **I can describe how trends may affect my career.**

  Trends indicate how my world may be changing. I need to identify trends that will affect employment and occupations so I can predict whether my career will exist when I begin working, whether my career will be needed throughout my employment years, and how my career might change in the next 10 or 20 years.

- **I can explain the past and present changes in career fields that may affect my career.**

  In the last 30 years, the employment world has evolved from the Industrial Age to the Digital Age. Changes in technology, demographics, and occupations will continue to influence my career. In particular, I need technological knowledge and reading, communication, and math skills for career success.

- **I have studied how workplace and workforce trends are changing how people work.**

  Workplace trends are changes employers are making in order to be more efficient or competitive. Workplace trends include an emphasis on technological skills, a move toward contracting employment, the growth of e-commerce, the increase in global trade, and an emphasis on teamwork. Workforce trends are changes employees are making to allow them to meet both their personal and professional goals and responsibilities. Workforce trends involve transferable skills, lifelong learning, and work schedule flexibility.

- **I have researched sources so I can futurecast.**

  By using various sources to observe long-term trends, I can make predictions about future workplace and workforce changes. I can structure my education and career plans to make sure I have the skills and flexibility I need to be successful. Futurecasting helps me choose a career that will be there for me when I'm ready.

Suggestions for Parents and Family Members

Helping Students Identify and Analyze Trends

Following are suggestions to give to parents and family members so they can better help their children identify and analyze career trends:
1. Encourage your child to take a variety of courses, including courses in math, science, and technology. He or she may want to take extra courses in the summer.
2. Continue your own lifelong learning, especially in math, science, and technology.
3. Keep an open mind about your own abilities to learn new information.

How much do you really know about the future? Will you be good at futurecasting? Let's see how much knowledge you have about changes and trends in career fields. Answer the following questions on a separate sheet of paper. Note: The term *careers in the future* means careers in the next ten years.

1. What year were you born? What are at least three inventions that have been created for public use since you were born?

2. What is the average number of jobs a person has in his or her lifetime after the age of 25?

3. What is the average number of careers a person has in his or her lifetime after the age of 25?

4. In the next ten years, what career area will have the most job openings?

5. In the next ten years, what will be the fastest-growing career cluster?

6. How many of the top ten careers of the future exist today?

7. What type of elective courses should you take in high school to prepare for careers in the future?

8. What percentage of careers in the future will require a bachelor's degree?

9. What percentage of careers in the future will generally need little or no training or education?

10. Which of the following age groups includes the largest number of people?

   • The Digital or Millennial Generation, born in 1982 or later
   • Generation X, born 1961–1981
   • Baby boomers, born 1943–1960
   • Silent Generation, born 1925–1942

11. In the next ten years, which racial group will be the largest percentage of the labor force?

12. In what year was the cellular phone introduced to the public?

13. In what year was the Internet available to the general public?

14. Who makes more computers, IBM or General Motors?

15. What invention has made the most impact on your generation?

(See page 75 for a discussion of this quiz.)

Activity 4-1: Trends Quiz

This activity provides an overview of important current and future career trends and helps students realize the value of futurecasting.

You may wish to have students complete the activity as a type of pretest before they read the chapter. Often when students realize how much they do not know, they are more open to learning how to future-cast. Discuss the quiz with the whole class before students check their answers.

Solution: The answers to the quiz and their supporting facts are on page 75 of the student text. Note that some of the information in the quiz is found in Chapter 5.

Activity 4-2: Learning from Others

Through the interviews in this activity, students learn how to identify trends by analyzing how a career area in which they are interested has changed.

If you have time constraints, ask groups of three students who have similar career interests to work together. Each group member interviews one person, and then group members pool results to create the time line. Activity 1-2 provides a sample of a time line. As an alternative to a time line, students could create a table to show career changes visually.

Solution: Answers will vary. In a class discussion, point out the changes within each career area included in the interviews. Then compare the various career areas to help students identify the similarities and differences. Discuss how the similarities may indicate general trends applicable to many careers and how the differences may indicate trends in only a specific area.

Activity 4-3: Case Challenges

This activity increases students' awareness of the different directions a career based on a particular field of interest can take. By using the questions related to each case to analyze the possible career paths of another person, students learn how to make informed decisions about their own careers.

Divide the class into groups of four or five students. Each group analyzes the case studies and reports its results to the class. If your class is small, you can do the activity with the whole class.

Solution: Answers will vary. Students need to realize that no one decision is the only correct one. They should explore all possibilities and back up their answers with information from the chapter. Students should include the following points in their answers:

Case 1: As a hands-on artist, Eric might not earn enough money to live on. As a commercial artist, Eric would probably have to use a computer, which he does not like. However, Eric likes commercial art, and he could work for a variety of companies. Eric could compromise by combining both

72

In order to see how careers have changed over the years, interview three people who are in a career field that appeals to you. You may choose a career field based on your assessment results in Chapter 3. With your subject's permission, you may want to tape record your interview. The following questions can help you get started. Share the results of your interviews with your class.

1. Interview the following three people:
   - A person who has worked in the career less than 5 years
   - A person who has worked in the career for 15–20 years
   - A person who has retired from the career or from a related field

   Possible interview questions:
   - What made you decide on _____ as a career?
   - What was your education and training path?
   - What are the benefits of your career?
   - What are the challenges of your career?
   - How has your career changed since you've been part of it (for example, technology, paperwork requirements, customer expectations, and customer service)?
   - Have you changed jobs in this career area? If so, why?
   - Have you changed careers within this career field? If so, why? If not, why not?
   - What are some positive things that have occurred in your career because of changes in technology or society?
   - What are some negative things that have occurred in your career because of changes in technology or society?

2. Use the results of your interviews to prepare a time line covering the last ten years that shows the change in the career field you selected.

After reading the following case studies, meet in small groups to determine a possible career direction for the person in each case. (Your group may have more than one answer.) The discussion should include answers to the questions following each scenario. Futurecast using the information in this chapter.

1. Eric knows he wants to be part of the art world; however, he doesn't want to be a "starving artist." He likes commercial art—creating art that sells products or services. As a commercial artist, Eric would do work for one or more companies or for an advertising agency. Eric's dilemma is that he is unsure which direction to take for his career. He really wants to be a hands-on artist using his pencils and brushes, but computers are used in many companies.

   a. What are the positives and negatives of his choices?

   b. Is there a compromise? What is it?

   c. What might the future hold for a commercial artist?

types of art as a commercial artist. Eric should be prepared for the increased use of technology and decreased use of hands-on techniques in commercial art. Also, some form of commercial art will likely continue to be needed for companies in every field.

Case 2: Being a traditional lawyer might frustrate Flavia, who enjoys working with technology more than working with people. Flavia could consider a law career involving Internet use or intellectual property to combine technology skills with

interest in law. However, her skills in technology might make her more suited to developing software for law firms. Because she enjoys reading about the history and background of law cases, Flavia should also consider a career as a researcher for a law firm. A firm that specializes in technology-related cases would allow her to pursue both her passions.

Case 3: Edwina can specialize by working with educational tours or tours to certain parts of the world. Another travel-related career would be

2. Although she's taking business technology courses through her career center, Flavia knows she may eventually want to pursue a career as a lawyer. Right now she is a paralegal for a large law firm. The firm appreciates Flavia's attention to detail and her creative use of computer applications. In fact, she has designed several new spreadsheet solutions for logging cases. Flavia also enjoys researching the law, especially on the Internet. She spends many of her off-hours reading about the history and background of law cases.

   a. Consider the following directions Flavia might choose to complete her education:
      • A traditional lawyer (If so, which specialty?)
      • A law practice technologist who develops software for law firms
      • Another career related to law
   b. What are the positives and negatives of each choice?
   c. What might the future hold for each choice?

3. Edwina's passion is travel. She dreams of seeing the world by combining travel with her career. During the summer after her sophomore year in high school, Edwina interned with a local travel agency that planned and guided tours. Because of her age, she could not go on tours outside the country. However, she was able to accompany her employer on several trips to resorts. The internship convinced Edwina that her career plan is on the right path. While interning, Edwina discovered one drawback of working as a tour guide for a travel agency. Tour guides do not make much money; travel is the major benefit of the occupation. In addition, many people who planned tours through travel agencies in the past now use the Internet to research and book trips. However, there are alternative careers that involve travel. For example, a meeting planner organizes conferences at various locations and an adventure travel planner organizes and guides adventure experiences.

   a. What are some other career fields related to travel that Edwina hasn't considered?
   b. What are the positives and negatives of each career choice?
   c. What might the future hold for each career choice?
   d. If, in the future, Edwina decides to stay in one location and raise a family, will she be able to continue in her career? Explain your answer.

ACTIVITY 4-4   **Technology Trends— Virtual Labs**

 Learning and teaching have changed during the past few years, especially due to increased technological changes. Virtual learning is now possible in many areas and enhances courses, training, and laboratory work. In addition, virtual learning stretches the laboratory beyond the classroom and extends workplace training.

The following sites are some of the virtual labs you can visit. Many of the sites are interactive and cover a variety of subjects. These self-paced sites demonstrate learning by doing, not just learning by viewing. They often offer real-world solutions to real-life simulations.

1. Investigate at least one or two categories in two sites. If a site is animated, you may have to download one or more plug-ins on your browser. See your teacher if a plug-in is not on your network.

online researcher and guide. As Edwina has discovered, tour guides who work with individual customers do not earn much money. However, tour guides who have corporate accounts earn more money and still have travel as a benefit. Use of travel agents may decline because of commission cuts from the airlines and the ease of making travel plans on the Internet, but overall travel is likely to increase because of retiring baby boomers. By specializing in tours that appeal to this segment of the population, Edwina could earn a good salary and be able to travel. Internet travel research is another career alternative. However, Edwina would not be able to indulge her passion for travel.

Activity 4-4: Technology Trends— Virtual Labs

Exploring virtual learning sites helps students understand a trend in education that will affect them regardless of the career they decide to pursue.

Discuss the implications for teachers of the trend toward virtual learning to help students see how technology can affect future careers. Point out that in virtual learning, teachers interact with students on an individual or a small-group basis rather than in a large-group setting. Teachers also must be information managers in the virtual-learning setting.

Students can investigate additional virtual-learning sites by doing an Internet search using the key phrase *virtual learning*. Note that you must preload the plug-ins necessary to experience virtual sites if your technology program does not allow students to download them.

Solution: Answers will vary. A class discussion of students' opinions of this form of education may be worthwhile.

Activity 4-5: Coming to Terms

This activity checks students' understanding of some workforce and workplace trends that will affect their future careers.

Have students work in small groups of four or five students or with a partner. You may want to discuss students' descriptions in class.

Solution: The descriptions of career situations will vary.

---

2. Write down answers to the following questions for each of the two sites you investigate.

a. What are the benefits of the site's technology? How is the site virtual? (A virtual site provides a simulated environment in which the participant experiences the environment through sights and sounds. In addition, the participant's actions partially determine what happens in the environment.)

b. What are the positive aspects of the site?

c. What are some drawbacks to using this site?

d. How practical is this site versus a real-life laboratory or simulation?

e. How can this site give a person a technological head start on his or her career?

Sites to investigate:

- *www.biointeractive.org* This site is run by the Howard Hughes Medical Institute and includes many types of virtual laboratories, animations, virtual exhibits in a museum setting, and interactive activities.
- *www.itg.lbl.gov/vfrog* Dissect a digitized frog virtually as part of the Lawrence Berkeley National Laboratory's "Whole Frog" project. You can also build a virtual frog.
- *http://vcourseware5.calstatela.edu/GeoLabs* Geology Labs Online has such labs as the Virtual Earthquake and Virtual River-Flooding.
- *http://set.lanl.gov/sports/main.htm* The Physics of Sports site helps students learn about math, science, social studies, and other courses through many types of sports.
- *www.mislab.com* This site offers training for both business and education and provides hands-on training for computer support and networking certification courses. This site is a typical for-profit e-learning site.

ACTIVITY 4-5   **Coming to Terms**

The terms listed below are related to workforce and workplace trends. For each term, describe a career situation in which the term would apply. Choose a specific career field for your description. Choose the field based on your assessment results in Chapter 3, or choose a field that interests you. Be as detailed as possible.

1. Lifelong learning

2. Service occupations

3. Cross training

4. Telecommuting

5. Job sharing

1. **The answers for this question will vary.** Compare your answers with those of your classmates.

2. **10–15 jobs.** The average person changes places of employment often in his or her lifetime, using the transferable skills needed to adapt to different work sites.

3. **5–8 careers.** Lifelong learning is important as people change careers more frequently in their lifetimes. Again, having transferable skills that cross over into different career areas is important.

4. **Retail service occupations.** The key term here is *job openings* because retail occupations have high turnover rates. This classification, which includes retail salespeople, cashiers, and restaurant servers, is 15 percent of the labor force. To be hired for a retail occupation, a person often needs little or no education and training.

5. **Computers/technology or health.** One out of every five of the fastest-growing careers will be computer-related. The four fastest-growing occupations for the next ten years are projected to be computer engineers, computer support specialists, computer systems analysts, and database administrators. These occupations are expected to increase by 108 percent, 102 percent, 94 percent, and 77 percent, respectively. Many of the other fastest-growing occupations are projected to be in healthcare.

6. **None.** A tricky question—and answer. The projected top ten careers for the next 10–25 years include some careers that are in the formative stages and that may ultimately exist in an entirely different form. Some of these careers are artificial intelligence technicians, bionic medical technicians, cryonics technicians, and automotive fuel-cell battery technicians.

7. **Math, science, and technology.** As you can see from the answers to Questions 5 and 6 above, the top careers for the future and the fastest-growing careers all involve math, science, and/or technology.

8. **15 percent.** Only 15 percent of careers will *require* a bachelor's degree, but 85 percent will require training and/or education beyond high school. Almost all careers will require lifelong learning.

9. **15 percent.** Most of these jobs will be in the retail service occupations. See Question 4.

10. **Baby boomers.** The baby-boomer group is beginning to retire, so the workforce needs replacements for them. Also, this group is interested in purchasing technology and in staying young and healthy as long as possible. Any careers connected with the interests of this group, such as the healthcare industry, will grow.

11. **No one racial group will dominate.** Minorities will grow faster than the Caucasian population.

12. **1983.** Cellular phones have become a part of nearly every family's life in an extremely short time.

13. **1988.** Personal use of the Internet didn't really take off until the early 1990s. The majority of society will use the Internet and digital technology by 2005, and 100 percent will adopt them by 2020.

14. **General Motors.** General Motors does not make laptops or personal computers, but it does make computerized programmable memory systems for vehicles. These systems automatically control a vehicle's mechanical systems.

15. **The Internet.** Most people in your generation are more comfortable with and knowledgeable about the Internet than most adults are.

Chapter Overview

Chapter 5 Understanding Future Careers

FOCUS

As members of the Millennial Generation, students must consider several important issues before they choose their future careers. Because of the increase in workforce diversity, Millennials need to know about expectations in a diverse workplace, communication with different cultures, people with disabilities, and gender equity. For Millennials, choosing careers also involves examining nontraditional career opportunities, having global awareness, and considering entrepreneurship.

Use the **Objectives** and **Key Terms** printed in the margin to help students focus on the content of this chapter. Use the **video segment** for Chapter 5 to introduce the chapter.

TEACH

Discuss the chapter's opening scenario with students. Ask students if they have ever thought of owning their own business.

What do you think?

Use **TM05-01**.
Students' answers will vary.

Career Journal

Ask students to spend 10 minutes writing Career Journal entries that answer the following questions:
1. What do you think this chapter will cover?
2. What do you already know about these topics?
3. What three things do you want to learn about these topics?

---

5 Understanding Future Careers

OBJECTIVES

After completing this chapter, you will be able to:

- Examine some characteristics of the Millennial Generation.
- Describe the various types of workforce diversity and their effects on the workplace.
- Identify nontraditional careers for men and women.
- Describe the characteristics of a successful entrepreneur.
- Explain the advantages of global careers.

Key Terms:

- workforce diversity
- prejudice
- discrimination
- culture
- reasonable accommodation
- gender equity
- nontraditional career
- entrepreneur
- market economy
- command economy

Ivan and Reiko met in an e-commerce class at school. They worked on several projects together and found that their personalities and abilities matched very well. Ivan had a way of looking at problems and coming up with various solutions. Reiko brought imagination to their projects with his ability to choose innovative ideas and come up with original marketing ideas. For their final project, they created an award-winning business plan for the state marketing competition. In fact, the plan was so unique that one of the state judges offered them start-up money for their own business. Their only obligation is to continue their education after high school toward associate degrees.

Ivan and Reiko's business plan is to create a wholesale import business that uses their cultural backgrounds. Since Ivan is of Spanish descent and Reiko's family is Japanese, they will import products from Spain and Japan and sell the products to restaurants and specialty food stores that serve or sell Spanish or Japanese food items. Ivan and Reiko plan to take college courses for the knowledge and skills needed to become successful business owners. Ivan wants to take classes primarily in business management, concentrating on accounting, economics and trends, and regulations for their industry. Reiko plans to major in marketing, specializing in advertising and e-commerce to design their computer web site. They will use the site to sell their products and to obtain customer information. Together the young men hope to build a successful food import business slowly, the result of a school project.

What do you think?
How might an increase in workers of different races and cultures affect your future career?

CHAPTER RESOURCES and MATERIALS

Activities & Projects book
Instructor's Resource CD
- Forms and Worksheets for Chapter Activities 5-1 through 5-8
- Internet Links for Chapter 5
- PowerPoint Presentation for Chapter 5
- Lesson Plans
- Teaching Masters for Chapter 5
- Video Discussion Guide for Chapter 5

Chapter Tests book
Exam*View*® CD
Video
Web Site

Millennials

Millennials, or the Digital Generation, is the name given to the people born in 1982 and later. You are a Millennial. You have a level of freedom in choosing your career that past generations did not have.

> Pedro was born a few years after IBM introduced its personal computer to the general public. Good timing, because without computers, Pedro might not have discovered his passion. As soon as he had access to a computer, Pedro knew he had found his future career. In fact, Pedro decided that working on a computer was more enjoyable than eating or sleeping. Pedro's abilities went far beyond the computer classes at his middle school. He created web sites for his friends' amusement and dreamed of combining creativity on the computer with owning his own business.
>
> With the aid of his counselor and his family, Pedro enrolled in web design and networking courses at a nearby career/technical high school. The school accepted him because of his excellent grades in English, math, and technology classes. After his high school training, Pedro can take industry-specific network certification tests, which will add the industry expertise he needs for the workplace. If he gets high grades in his technical courses, Pedro will also acquire credits toward an associate degree at the local community college. Pedro plans to work part-time in his field during high school and be well on his way to having his own web design business.

The book, *Millennials Rising*, by Neil Howe and William Strauss reveals some interesting discoveries about your generation, discoveries learned from surveys of students and teachers:

- Your family expects you to have better personal behavior than their families expected of them. In other words, your family wants you to behave better than they did at your age.
- Your culture is more clean-cut than any group since the 1930s.
- You celebrate being one of two distinct genders, but expect gender differences not to affect employment opportunities.
- Female Millennials are the pacesetters who set the standards for their peers.
- As workers, you will demand that employers adjust to your need to build careers and families at the same time.
- You will insist on having less stress in your life than your family had.

As a Millennial, you will be affected by trends occurring in the workforce and the workplace. Trends toward workforce diversity and global markets will expand your employment options and allow you to explore career possibilities in areas that you may not have considered.

Use Activity 5-1, "Learning from Others," to compare some characteristics of your generation with those of another generation.

> 66 Work has become a part of who we are, not just what we do. 99
>
> —*John Izzo and Pam Withers, Values Shift*

ONLINE RESOURCES

Check out the web site **www.investigatingyourcareer.com** for teacher resources, student activities, and replacements for broken links for this chapter. To access the teacher resources:

Username: career
Password: investigate

TEACH

Emphasize that by law, employers cannot discriminate in hiring on the basis of race, national origin, religion, gender, disability, or pregnancy. Discuss how and why employers should overcome their prejudices and achieve the goal of nondiscrimination. Ask students what types of policies companies can set and how employers can foster nondiscriminatory actions by their employees. In your discussion, include how the actions of managers or supervisors influence the behavior of the workers they manage or supervise. Ask students how they think they might be influenced by the actions of their supervisors.

The American population has changed in the last decade and now includes more people of diverse races and cultures. This change has carried over to the workplace, creating a new workforce. **Workforce diversity** means the workplace includes a variety of workers with different backgrounds, viewpoints, experiences, and ideas. In essence, the face of the workforce is changing to include more women, more ethnic minorities, more immigrants, and more people with disabilities.

Effects of Workforce Diversity

Workforce diversity brings new ways of thinking about careers. Instead of picturing a certain career being performed by a person of a particular race and sex, a variety of images may come to mind. These changes in the workforce require changes in how workers and employers are expected to behave and changes in how workers communicate.

Expectations in a Diverse Workplace

As a member of the future workforce, you will be expected to respect others' differences and not show prejudice or discrimination. **Prejudice** means to prejudge, usually unfavorably, or to classify a whole class of people as though everyone who falls into the category behaves, thinks, and feels the same way. **Discrimination** occurs when people act on their prejudices. In a diverse workplace, you are free to pursue a career based on your passion instead of your race, gender, or culture.

Many students take cooking classes because they enjoy blending different flavors and ingredients together. However, when

Ju Mengtou began culinary training after high school, he told his instructors he wanted to be an artistic chef—one who excelled in the look as well as the taste of food. When Mengtou was ready for work experience, the school's placement representative did not consider his ethnic background and assigned him to places without any particular Asian influence.

Currently, Ju Mengtou is a garde manger chef and is responsible for preparing cold foods in a professional kitchen. A garde manger chef has to be a combination of painter, architect, and chef because the attractive visual display of cold food is as important as its taste.

DIFFERENT LEARNING ABILITIES
Attention Deficit Disorder
Help ADD students write down all the headings in the chapter. Point out that students also should include any headings for features. Have students look at each heading before they read the material and predict what they will learn. Have students describe to you or to the class any prior knowledge they have about the topic. If there is time, have ADD students read the material aloud. After reading, have them describe what they just read.

Employers are also expected to avoid discrimination. The Equal Employment Opportunity Commission (EEOC) enforces legislation that ensures equity in the workplace. Equity includes equal pay and freedom from employment discrimination on the basis of race/color, national origin, religion, gender, disability, or pregnancy. For that reason, the EEOC has developed guidelines to prohibit discrimination on the basis of "physical, cultural, or linguistic characteristics of a national group or discrimination due to manner of speaking or accent."

The workplace should be a welcoming place that fosters respect and celebrates the uniqueness of all who work there. Employers who believe in the benefits of a diverse workforce realize that it promotes creativity and helps them understand their customers. From their employees, employers can learn how to develop products and services for their increasingly diverse customer base.

Communication in a Diverse Workplace

Approaches to spoken, written, and nonverbal communication vary among people with different backgrounds and viewpoints. Your communication style consists of three components: *how* you say or write something, *when* you say or write it, and *why* you say or write it. Miscommunication generally results because one individual's style of communication differs from another person's. At some point in your career, you will work with a coworker whose communication style differs from yours. Communicating effectively with all your coworkers and supervisors is a necessity no matter what career field you enter.

> What are some situations in which miscommunication has affected you?

What do you think?

The following guidelines can help you communicate effectively with other workers:

- Take time to learn about other communication styles. The time will benefit you and your workplace.
- Make an extra effort to communicate effectively. Concentrate on creating clear, concrete, accurate, courteous, and complete messages.
- Remember that different communication styles may be used among people of different age groups, economic classes, education levels, work experiences, and personalities.
- Analyze what might be causing misunderstanding. Be aware of your assumptions and the expectations of your audience.
- Use language that promotes trust and agreement in what you say or write, including e-mails. Avoid jokes, words, or expressions that may reflect prejudice, such as those based on ethnicity, race, gender, disability, or age.
- Above all, respect differences. Don't judge people because of the way they speak, act, or dress.

> " There is no future in any job. The future lies in the person who holds the job."
>
> —*W. G. Crane,* English Designer

What do you think?

Use **TM05-02**.
Students' answers will vary.

TEACH

In your discussion of communication, ask students to describe workplace situations where being able to speak a second language is advantageous. Also ask what accommodations students think should be made for employees who do not speak the primary workplace language. Explain why English has become the language of business worldwide.

To help students understand miscommunication, offer examples from your own experiences or from the media. Ask students for their experiences with miscommunication.

ENRICH

Have students complete **Activity 5-A, "Career Opinions,"** found in the *Investigating Your Career Activities & Projects* book.

This activity increases students' awareness of their stereotypes about careers. They write a career that comes to mind for each word in a list of adjectives.

Discuss the oversimplification of opinions, attitudes, and judgments expressed by students and often by the business world. The discussion is more important than the answers to the activity.

Solution: The solution for this activity appears in the *Teacher's Edition* of *Investigating Your Career Activities & Projects.*

CHAPTER 5 • • • • • UNDERSTANDING FUTURE CAREERS   **79**

DIFFERENT LEARNING STYLES

Visual Learners

Have students choose a favorite television show that depicts different characters trying to communicate with one another. The communication may take place in the workplace or within the characters' families. Have students observe spoken and nonspoken communication among the characters. Hold a discussion about students' observations. Then have students draw a cartoon that depicts how the characters interacted with one another. Cartoons may include dialogue. Display the cartoons around the room.

APPLY

Have students complete **Activity 5-2, "Coming to Terms,"** that appears on page 93. Teaching suggestions and the solution for this activity appear on page 93. An activity worksheet can be found on the Career Portfolio and Resource CD—**Text Activity 05-2.doc**.

TEACH

You may wish to discuss some aspects of religious choice in the workplace using the following questions: When should an employer restrict religious dress? Should employees be able to decide when they work *after* they've been hired? Should religious beliefs have reasonable accommodation? Should employees be able to interfere with coworkers' religious beliefs?

Discuss the Career Success Tip using as examples the various cultures reflected in the student body.

What do you think?

Use **TM05-03**.
Students' answers will vary.

Good communication can unify a workplace, but lack of communication can divide coworkers. The challenge for today's employer is ensuring that workforce diversity is a source of strength rather than tension. Promoting understanding in a diverse workplace is an important employer goal. However, employers are not solely responsible for achieving this goal. You and all other employees share in the responsibility.

Activity 5-2, "Coming to Terms," helps you understand some of the key terms related to workforce diversity.

Cultural Differences in the Workplace

One of the results of workforce diversity is that the workplace now includes a wide variety of cultures. **Culture** is a set of learned attitudes, behaviors, and traditions that make up a way of life. You share the culture of your workplace with all your coworkers; however, your personal culture may be different from theirs.

The winter holiday season is always a hectic time of year at the radio station. Customers need special advertising written, disc jockeys put in longer hours with more personal appearances, and vendors send more packages. All this activity makes Sherm's job harder because he is responsible for delivering copies, supplies, packages—everything that needs to go from one place to another at the station. What makes the holiday season even more difficult for Sherm is that he must work during special times important to his religion, especially Sunday evenings, Christmas Eve, and Christmas Day. However, the radio station never closes, and his boss has indicated that he needs Sherm to work at least three hours each day.

After overhearing Sherm discussing his dilemma with a coworker, Ben looked at his work schedule. Because Ben was a copy assistant in the advertising department, he wasn't scheduled to work past noon on Christmas Eve, and he never worked the Christmas holiday or Sundays. Yet working at those times didn't bother Ben because he was Jewish. Ben talked to Sherm and offered to work during Sherm's special holiday times. In exchange, Sherm offered to work if Ben was scheduled on Jewish holidays or on Saturdays when he had religious services.

CAREER SUCCESS TIP

Improve your interpersonal skills by becoming more culturally aware. Read books on other cultures, take cultural awareness classes, and keep an open mind.

What do you think? Think about times when you met people of different cultures at school, work, or community events. When has a difference in culture been an advantage for you? When has it been a disadvantage?

Your culture connects you to others of the same background; however, your culture can also separate you from those who do not share it. Does this mean you should hide your culture to avoid problems in your workplace? No. Use your cultural differences to help your coworkers, your workplace, and your customers. For example, if you

CAREER SUCCESS TIP

Become Culturally Aware

To help students become more culturally aware, hold a Celebrating Cultures Day. Arrange students into groups of three or four. Assign each group a culture. Have groups research their cultures, including the food, music, types of jobs that relate specifically to that culture, and the working conditions in those jobs. Have each group give an oral presentation about the types of jobs and working conditions. As part of their presentations, have student groups play the culture's music and bring a food of that culture for classmates to taste.

speak a second language, offer to serve as an interpreter or translator for customers who share that language. Explaining some of your culture's traditions, sharing food customs, and teaching basic words and key phrases to coworkers often improves the workplace atmosphere. You may become more comfortable talking about your culture when you have more exposure to other cultures.

Persons with Disabilities

Persons with disabilities are part of today's workplace. Rather than isolating people with disabilities from other workers or developing separate businesses for them, companies are now hiring more individuals with disabilities as part of the mainstream workplace. As more people with disabilities succeed in their careers because of equal employment opportunities, both business and society will benefit.

> How does an employer benefit from hiring a person with a disability? **What do you think?**

In your school, you may be familiar with the effects of the Individuals with Disabilities Education Act (IDEA). This act ensures that all children with disabilities have access to "a free appropriate public education which emphasizes special education and the related services designed to meet their unique needs." The Americans with Disabilities Act (ADA) provides the same assurances to the workplace that IDEA provides to education.

Erica feels as though she was always meant to be an employee of Children's Hospital. She works as a data processor, a placement made through her career/technical school's business program. Despite the fact she is legally blind, Erica has not experienced any discrimination by her coworkers or other members of the hospital staff. Occasionally she visits some of the patients, and they are very accepting of her blindness. When Erica started her job, the hospital made some accommodations for her disability, including a magnifier for her computer monitor, a large-print calendar, and a talking desk clock. Those accommodations allow Erica to perform her job as well as any sighted person.

The ADA provides protections for a qualified individual with a disability. A qualified individual is someone who has a disability as defined by the ADA. Under the ADA, a person has a disability if he or she has a physical or mental impairment that substantially limits a major life activity, such as hearing, seeing, speaking, thinking, walking, breathing, or performing manual tasks. A qualified individual also must have the skills to perform the desired job.

Most importantly, qualified people have a right to request a reasonable accommodation during the hiring process or on the job. A **reasonable accommodation** is a change or an adjustment to a job or the work environment from the way things usually are done. An

CAREER FACT

U.S. census data shows that minority-owned businesses are growing at nearly four times the rate of all U.S. firms.

TEACH

You may wish to invite a person with a disability or an advocate of persons with disabilities to speak to the class about the problems someone with a disability can encounter in the workplace and about how a disabled person's coworkers can contribute to the person's career success.

What do you think?

Use **TM05-04**.
Students' answers will vary.

ENRICH

Have students complete **Activity 5-B, "Learning about Requirements,"** found in the *Investigating Your Career Activities & Projects* book.

This activity increases students' awareness of the physical requirements for careers and how persons with disabilities can use this type of knowledge to make career decisions. Students also rate themselves to see if they meet the physical requirements of the career.

Students may research more than one career. Emphasize that some careers have physical limitations for many people, not just for persons with disabilities. For example, a commercial pilot must have nearly perfect eyesight. Compare class results if time permits.
Solution: The solution for this activity appears in the *Teacher's Edition* of *Investigating Your Career Activities & Projects*.

CAREER TREND

Growth of Minority-Owned Businesses

According to the U.S. Commerce Department's Census Bureau, minority-owned businesses grew from 2.1 million firms to about 2.8 million firms between 1992 and 1997. While most U.S. firms grow at a rate of about 7 percent, minority firms grew at a rate of 30 percent. Hispanics firms make up the largest number of minority-owned businesses in the United States. Asian and Pacific Islander minority-owned firms have the largest share of business revenues. For more information on minority businesses, have students check the U.S. Census web site at **www.census.gov**.

The Newly Designed MagniSight Explorer easier to read, write a become independent at home, school, wor

accommodation, such as Erica's computer monitor magnifier, allows people with disabilities to perform job functions and enjoy equal access to places available to other individuals in the workplace. If you think you might need an accommodation during the application process or while on the job, you can request a reasonable accommodation at any time before or after you start working.

The ADA also protects individuals with disabilities from harassment because of their disability. A remark about a person with a disability, such as "Let me work on Saturday—he has enough trouble getting his regular work done," is a harassing statement. Also making offhand remarks about a disability, even a temporary condition such as a pregnancy, is considered harassing behavior.

 Use Activity 5-3, "Internet Investigation," to explore resources for individuals with disabilities.

Gender Equity in the Workplace

For hundreds of years, men and women have been treated differently and have had unequal opportunities in the workplace, in education, and in everyday life. Fortunately, changes in society and modern technology have moved the workplace toward more **gender equity**—equal opportunity regardless of gender. The EEOC regulates some of the legislation that ensures gender equity, including equal pay for men and women who perform equal work and freedom from discrimination in all aspects of employment.

What do you think? How has gender equity affected your life at school or at work?

Beginning thousands of years ago, the roles played by men and women were based on division of labor. Men were the providers. They hunted and gathered food, collected wood to make the fires, and protected others from harm. Women were the nurturers. They prepared the food and cared for the children and others in the community who were weak. Because of these traditional roles, women have typically chosen nurturing careers, careers that would allow them to stay at home and raise their families. The careers women chose also tended to be similar to the typical nurturing roles they had in the home—nursing was caring for the sick, teaching was educating the children, and secretarial work was assisting the male bosses.

82

PART 2 • • • • • NARROWING THE CHOICES

INTEGRATED ACADEMICS
Language Arts
Ask students to interview two adult women who are part of the workforce. The women should be different ages and have different work experience. One woman should be young with only a few years' experience. The other woman should have many years' experience. Have students ask these women how they experience gender equality in the workplace. Are they treated differently than men? If so, how? Hold a class discussion on students' findings.

Edith was not of the Millennial Generation; she was born much earlier. In fact, Edith grew up at a time when women had certain careers and men had certain careers. Her mother was a teacher, a common career for women, and Edith followed in her mother's footsteps. As a preteen, Edith was involved in church activities, helping to teach Sunday school and working with children during the summer. The time she spent with children resulted in babysitting jobs during junior high and high school. Edith's interest in children led her to major in early childhood education with an internship in the university's preschool. After graduation, Edith continued with her love of teaching children, eventually creating a much-needed preschool at her church. Edith was well matched to her career. However, if she had been a Millennial, her options would have been much greater.

Gender equity means working toward breaking down barriers that have traditionally maintained a segregated workforce. For example, employers increasingly define childcare and work and family balance as *family* issues, not *women's* issues. Only a few years ago society expected women to work for pay while they were single and to leave the labor force after marrying and having children. As men become more involved in parenting, they are more vocal about having flexibility in their work roles so they have time for their responsibilities as parents. Responsibilities toward children and aging parents increasingly affect both female and male employees.

Use Activity 5-4, "Attitudes," to analyze peoples' attitudes concerning the roles of men and women.

> **"The real danger is in not encouraging one half of the world's minds and potential. Which half—the male half or the female half?"**
>
> —*Susan McLester,* Technology & Learning

APPLY

Have students complete **Activity 5-4, "Attitudes,"** on page 94. Teaching suggestions and the solution for this activity appear on page 94. An activity worksheet can be found on the Career Portfolio and Resource CD—**Text Activity 05-4.doc**.

TEACH

Some students will need a more in-depth discussion of the traditional, versus nontraditional, workforce.

Some male students may believe that increased employment of women in nontraditional careers leads to discrimination against men. Reassure them that this has not been the case in the years of the EEOC regulations.

In the reading and discussing of nontraditional careers, do not overemphasize traditional male and traditional female careers. That discussion could lead to more stereotyping and students disregarding a career because it has been labeled nontraditional. This possibility is especially important to consider when teaching middle school students.

Nontraditional Employment

If you are a male and are asked "Would you consider being a secretary or a kindergarten teacher or a dental hygienist?" what would you answer? If you are a female and are asked "Would you consider becoming a mechanic or an air traffic controller or a firefighter?" what would you answer?

Many male and female students have not been exposed to careers that do not fit the traditional work models for men and women. Those careers are referred to as nontraditional careers. In a **nontraditional career**, one gender consists of 25 percent or less of the workers in the particular occupation. Workforce diversity has promoted an interest by both men and women in pursuing nontraditional careers.

What are the bonuses of working in a nontraditional career? What are the challenges?   **What do you think?**

What do you think?

Use **TM05-06**.
Students' answers will vary.

DIFFERENT LEARNING ABILITIES
Gifted Students
Nontraditional employment offers challenges that gifted students, and others, may find exciting. Have students choose three nontraditional careers; the careers should vary in the type of education and training needed. Working in small groups or pairs, have students list the positive and negative aspects of the three nontraditional careers chosen. Discuss the results as a class.

Nontraditional Careers for Women

Women are becoming more interested in mechanical and technical nontraditional careers. This increased interest is partly due to the shortage of technical workers, especially in auto repair, manufacturing, and computer-aided design. Some women are also breaking new ground by selecting a nontraditional career. They are choosing careers in which they may be the only woman working with an all-male crew.

In high school, Rhonda did whatever her friends did. So when her friends took business office courses, Rhonda took them too. After graduating from high school, Rhonda got a position as a clerk in a firm that promised excellent raises and good advancement. However, after nearly two years on the job, Rhonda saw that her future at the company would be behind a desk. Rhonda also realized she needed a change of scenery in her job; she could not keep working in the same place at the same desk day after day. She decided to explore becoming a pipefitter.

Rhonda became an apprentice pipefitter and trained to set up, install, and maintain piping systems, including those used for heating, cooling, and sprinkling. Rhonda climbed scaffolding, worked outside before walls were raised on new buildings, and helped renovate heating systems. Many jobs lasted only a few weeks in one location—just what Rhonda wanted. She had variety and independence; plus the pay was outstanding. Pipefitters are skilled union workers, and even when Rhonda was training, she earned more money hourly than she had behind a desk. The major drawback to Rhonda's new career was that she was a woman. She was the first woman many pipefitters had worked with, and she had to prove herself by working harder and better than many of her male counterparts. The effort was worth it. Rhonda completed her apprenticeship successfully and became one of the most sought-after pipefitters in the area.

Nontraditional careers for women often pay higher wages than traditional careers do. According to the U.S. Department of Labor, women entering nontraditional careers earn 20 to 30 percent more than women in traditional female careers. Although only 2 percent of women in the workforce are presently in skilled trade and technical occupations, women like Eleanor Baum are helping to promote nontraditional careers for women.

Eleanor chose a nontraditional career as an engineer, and although she enjoyed the work, her acceptance as a female engineer was not always smooth. When Eleanor started her first engineering job and talked to her male coworkers, her supervisor accused her of flirting. Eleanor eventually changed management's view of female engineers to one of equality. Today Eleanor is a role model for female engineers. As the dean of engineering at Cooper Union in New York City, Eleanor Baum has made engineering a popular career option for

CAREER FACT

Successful women have several factors in common: a supportive parent, a belief that they can make a difference, and participation in sports or organized clubs.

—from *See Jane Run,* by Sylvia Rimm

CAREER TREND

Growth in Number of Women in the Workplace

According to the U.S. Department of Labor, 63 million women work in the United States. They are 46 percent of the total civilian labor force in the United States. By 2008, it is estimated that women will make up 48 percent of the labor force. For more information, have students access the following web site: **http://eserver.org/feminism/facts-on-working-women.txt**.

—*Source: www.dol.gov/wb/wb_pubs/hotjobs02.htm*

women. Through her encouragement, the number of female engineering students has grown to 38 percent.

Nontraditional careers for women often offer higher salaries, desirable benefits, and better advancement opportunities—all important for providing career satisfaction. However, nontraditional careers often require additional training that can range from a short period of time to the longer education time needed to receive a professional degree.

Nontraditional Careers for Men

The Bureau of Labor Statistics (BLS) customarily applies the term *nontraditional careers* to women because of the discrimination and inequity of pay common in traditional women's careers. However, men are also entering nontraditional careers, particularly in the healthcare field. Healthcare careers (such as physical therapist assistants, registered nurses, and surgical technicians) are considered nontraditional careers for men. These careers are needed right now and will continue to be in demand in the future.

Rather than taking the advice of his parents and counselor to plan his career in high school, Evan graduated from high school without any career focus. Evan simply didn't know what direction to take. He believed he should take his time until he was sure about what he wanted to do for the rest of his life. He didn't want to plan and study for a career and then realize he had made the wrong choice. Evan also assumed that after he went to college for two or three years, he would know what career he wanted to pursue and would then decide on his major. However, after two years in college, Evan couldn't declare his major because he still did not have a concrete career goal.

Evan's thoughts kept returning to a career that fascinated him because of his friend John. That career was physical therapy—working with people who had been injured and needed rehabilitation, such as John, who had been injured in a car accident. In talking with his college adviser, Evan found out that labor projections predicted a high demand for males in physical therapy careers for the next decade. However, Evan was cautious. Instead of plunging ahead and taking additional college courses at this

Ask students' opinions about why males take more math and science courses than females do. Explain that the common denominator in the disparity between men's wages and women's wages is the amount and kind of math and science courses taken. The current trend is for females, beginning in middle school, to take fewer advanced courses and have less success in those courses. Ask your students for suggestions on ways to encourage females to take more math and science courses in school.

ENRICH

Have students complete **Activity 5-C, "Personality Traits,"** found in the *Investigating Your Career Activities & Projects* book.

This activity provides another way for students to discover their attitudes by having them label adjectives that describe personality traits as *female, male,* or *both*.

Some students may see the list of words as primarily male or female; others may see most words as having both male and female connotations. Class discussion should focus on *why* the students made their choices.

Solution: The solution for this activity appears in the *Teacher's Edition* of *Investigating Your Career Activities & Projects.*

DIFFERENT LEARNING STYLES

Visual Learners

Have students create a visual album of nontraditional careers. Students may use photographs, magazine cutouts, drawings, computer-generated graphics and designs, and other art materials. Encourage students to be creative with this project. Have students share their albums in small groups.

Have students complete **Activity 5-D, "Imagine . . . ,"** found in the *Investigating Your Career Activities & Projects* book.

In this activity, students generate a list of all the aspects of home, family, and work life that would be affected if, by the year 2020, total equality of employment opportunities existed. Then students are asked to recognize ways they could eliminate bias and stereotyping.

Students can work with a partner or individually. Have them share their results with the class. Also discuss what students can do to reach the goal of total equity (Question 4). **Solution:** The solution for this activity appears in the *Teacher's Edition* of *Investigating Your Career Activities & Projects.*

TEACH

You may need to have further class discussion of nurturing careers versus other types of careers.

time, he decided to work as an orderly in a rehabilitation center for a year. By working as an orderly, he would get firsthand exposure to careers in physical therapy. Evan thought this experience would allow him to make a firm career decision, one that he would be satisfied with for many years.

Nontraditional careers for men are often in nurturing career fields, such as teaching and caring for the sick. Compared to many traditional careers for men, nurturing careers tend to require less training, have lower pay with fewer benefits, and have fewer opportunities for advancement. Because nurturing careers have typically been undervalued and underpaid, those men who require prestige and a high salary may not be satisfied in these nontraditional careers.

However, the traditional compensation characteristics of a nurturing career are less applicable in the healthcare field due to the high demand for workers. More occupational levels, such as the practitioner level (for example, nurse practitioner) and the assistant level (for example, physician's assistant), have increased career satisfaction factors. Healthcare careers often have higher pay, better benefits, more prestige, and greater advancement opportunities than in the past.

REAL PEOPLE
REAL CAREERS

Internet Radio Station Owner

When did Daniel Anstandig know he wanted to have his own business? At age four, he began selling subscriptions to the family newsletter in his neighborhood. He wrote and sold a neighborhood newspaper in elementary school. He admired his grandfather's work in radio. In fact, Daniel liked the work so much that he built a low-power transformer at age eleven and broadcast a call-in show. At age thirteen, Daniel hung around the college radio station so much that they gave him his own show.

When he was fifteen, Daniel founded DAER Radio, an Internet radio station. Four years later the station had over 1 million listeners each month. Daniel is the program director. He has attracted nationally syndicated broadcasters, and he writes for one of them. On weekends, he is an IJ (Internet jockey). In addition, Daniel does voice-overs and writes lyrics for advertising. He does all this while balancing his college courses at a major university near Cleveland, Ohio.

What makes Daniel so successful? He listens to his listeners via live feedback and e-mail. He constantly surveys his audience. "The audience tells us what to play and essentially runs each show," Daniel says. By using his audience as a guide, Daniel Anstandig continues his success.

For more information, investigate:
- Daniel Anstandig at *www.youngbiz.com* in the YoungBiz 100, or use a search engine such as *www.google.com* and the keywords *Daniel Anstandig.*
- becoming an entrepreneur at *www.highschoolstartups.com* or at *www.youngbiz.com.*

Source: "Infotainment Division." *Young Biz. www.youngbiz.com.*

REAL PEOPLE—REAL CAREERS
Young Entrepreneurs

Have students access the site **www.highschoolstartups.com** to learn about the experiences of young entrepreneurs. In small groups, have students brainstorm possible small businesses that they could start while still in school. Encourage students to be imaginative. Instruct each group to write a brief description and prepare a two-minute oral presentation about the business. Have a representative of each group present the group's business idea to the class.

Use Activity 5-5, "Expectations," to examine some job-related gender expectations.

Expanding Your Career Options

Gender equity is about creating opportunities and changing stereotypes. Don't ignore a career opportunity just because you think the career is for someone of the opposite sex. By considering both traditional and nontraditional careers, you will have a better chance to find your P*A*T*H to Success. The following examples of nontraditional careers may help you think about expanding your options:

Women
- Attorney
- Electrician
- Dentist
- Forester
- Funeral director
- Airline pilot
- Architect

Men
- Childcare worker
- Speech therapist
- Home health aide
- Cosmetologist
- Librarian
- Elementary school teacher
- Receptionist

What nontraditional careers appeal to you? **What do you think?**

Don't be discouraged from entering a nontraditional career because of the myths below. The fact that follows each myth gives a more accurate view.

- *Women aren't strong enough physically for many nontraditional careers.* The Occupational Safety and Health Administration (OSHA) has guidelines on lifting and other tasks that take into consideration the male and female bodies. Besides, many women do physical work in traditional female careers such as nursing. Many nontraditional careers for women do not require physical strength.
- *Nontraditional careers cause isolation from others of the same sex.* As employers hire more women and men for nontraditional careers, this problem will disappear. Also, even traditional careers can cause isolation.
- *Nontraditional careers take jobs away from others.* Every person is entitled to work. Employers hire the person with the best skills and training qualifications.
- *Women don't have the math or technical skills to work in a skilled trade.* In general, female students do not take enough math courses. That trend is changing as schools encourage more females to take math and technical courses. Women are just as capable as men in learning and applying math, science, and technology skills.
- *Men don't have the nurturing ability to care for children.* Many men show nurturing ability in caring for children. The numbers of men teaching elementary school is increasing, and many men are single parents. In addition, not all women necessarily have nurturing abilities. Each individual has unique characteristics.

Have students complete **Activity 5-5, "Expectations,"** on pages 94–95. Teaching suggestions and the solution for this activity appear on page 94. An activity worksheet can be found on the Career Portfolio and Resource CD—**Text Activity 05-5.doc**.

TEACH

Have students share their perceptions of the stereotypical myths listed on page 87 of the text. Ask them why they think these myths exist and what can be done to correct mistaken beliefs.

What do you think?

Use **TM05-07**.
Students' answers will vary.

ENRICH

Have students complete **Activity 5-E, "Early Expectations,"** found in the *Investigating Your Career Activities & Projects* book.

This activity helps students realize that career choices may change from nontraditional to traditional or vice versa as students get older. Students should interview two people if at all possible. Determine the grade level of the younger students according to the availability of lower grade levels in your school. Encourage students to compare their career choices with those of the younger students.
Solution: The solution for this activity appears in the *Teacher's Edition* of *Investigating Your Career Activities & Projects*.

INTEGRATED ACADEMICS
Visual Arts
Have students locate and collect magazine pictures to create a visual representation of nontraditional jobs for men and women. Refer students to the list on page 87 of the text to help them begin. Provide students with butcher paper to create a wall mural. Several days before beginning the project, have students collect magazines and bring them to class. For extra credit, have students create a time line that shows the progression of women entering nontraditional fields of employment.

Have students complete **Activity 5-6, "Case Challenges,"** on page 95. Teaching suggestions and the solution for this activity appear on page 95. An activity worksheet can be found on the Career Portfolio and Resource CD—**Text Activity 05-6.doc**.

TEACH

Discuss with students the six qualities of successful entrepreneurs found on text pages 89 and 90. The introduction to the six qualities is found at the bottom of page 88. Be sure students understand the reasons these qualities are necessary for success. Also have students brainstorm situations where owning a business can be both a positive and a negative experience. Emphasize that students who are seriously considering starting their own business need to obtain a great deal more information than can be included in this text.

Employers are becoming more aware of the benefits of hiring workers for nontraditional careers. Employers realize they need to hire the best applicant for a job regardless of the person's gender. A successful nontraditional career depends in part on the employer making the situation comfortable for the employee. For example, businesses that provide sexual harassment training to all employees often have fewer discrimination situations and better cooperation among coworkers.

Use Activity 5-6, "Case Challenges," to investigate stereotypes and equity situations.

Entrepreneurship

Does the thought of owning your own business appeal to you? Have you dreamed of being an **entrepreneur**, a person who creates and manages a business? Starting your own business is a way of combining your passions, skills, and values into a career that *you* control. Being an entrepreneur is not a career choice, but rather a goal for your career plan. It's one of the ways to achieve your *P*A*T*H to Success*.

CAREER FACT

By 2010, one out of two Americans will create his or her own career or start his or her own business.

In his information technology systems classes, Karim learned the skills to install, network, and repair various computer and digital systems. At first, he used his skills at home by networking his family's computers to make a more efficient system. When Karim's aunt found out about his technology skills, she hired him to expand the memory and do some internal changes to her computer. Soon Karim had so many technology jobs that he was working several evenings a week and most weekends.

Although he was still in high school, Karim wanted to start a business based on his computer jobs. He wrote down his goals, both for the next few months and for the next several years. Then he created a business plan that included both initial and future expenses and income. Karim realized he would have some initial expenses, such as buying equipment and tools and installing a voicemail system for his business, in addition to future expenses. Though school and work sometimes competed for his time, Karim persisted and kept the business going. When he graduated from high school two years later, Karim had a successful, established business. He was even able to hire an employee so he could take classes toward his associate degree.

Running a business involves more than having a great idea. You must be prepared to eat, sleep, and breathe your business 24 hours a day, seven days a week. Successful entrepreneurs share many common characteristics. These characteristics are needed not only for starting the business but also for keeping the business going. If you have most of the following qualities of a successful entrepreneur, you may want to consider starting your own business.

CAREER TREND

Healthcare for the Self-Employed

A study by the National Association for the Self-Employed (NASE) states, "More than two-thirds of micro-business owners say they are unable to afford health insurance for themselves or their employees." According to NASE, seven in ten small businesses do not provide healthcare coverage for their employees. There are 24.5 million Americans families in which the head of the house is self-employed or works for a small company. Students may wish to consider health benefits in making career decisions.

You can set goals and create the steps to achieve them. Starting your own business requires planning. Your plan should list what you need to start the business, including the education required to manage all aspects of the business from start-up to balancing the books. For the business to succeed, you also must have a plan for the immediate future as well as for five or ten years from now. Visualize how your business will fit into the economy. In addition to defining your goals, your plan will help you set limits, such as not expanding too fast or not hiring employees before you need them.

You are willing to ask for advice. Other small business owners and local business groups are great sources of advice for entrepreneurs. An entrepreneur cannot be afraid to ask for help when needed. Businesses often fail because owners believe they can find the solutions for problems by themselves. They end up asking for help too late—when the business is beyond help.

You have good organizational skills. Organization means planning, but it also means keeping all aspects of the business under control. You must be able to set priorities and stick to them. Paperwork must be kept under control and completed on time. Details are an important part of a business. Organization also includes time management. As a business owner, you will often need to work long hours. Managing your time and setting priorities will help your business be successful.

You see problems as challenges and are willing to develop alternative solutions. Creativity and enthusiasm fuel a business. An entrepreneur sees an unfulfilled need, creates a solution, and starts a business. Creativity and hard work keep the business going. Entrepreneurs face the challenge of finding the right solutions to problems. They must often make personal sacrifices to keep the business successful.

You are enthusiastic and persistent—and optimistic. Starting your own business takes courage and enthusiasm. Your passion drives your initial enthusiasm to start your business and to manage your career. Continuing with the business and making it successful, despite many ups and downs, takes persistence. You can't give up easily, or your business will flounder. You also need to be optimistic, to look at the positive side of events and not be discouraged. You will need energy and enthusiasm to remain optimistic.

Have students complete **Activity 5-F, "How to Become a Millionaire,"** found in the *Investigating Your Career Activities & Projects* book.

This activity tests students' knowledge of facts about millionaires. The results show students they are unlikely to achieve wealth without self-discipline, including planning and making sound choices. Wise choices lead to becoming an entrepreneur, a more likely millionaire.

Solution: The solution for this activity appears in the *Teacher's Edition* of *Investigating Your Career Activities & Projects.*

DIFFERENT LEARNING ABILITIES
Dyslexia
Have students with dyslexia copy the headings from the textbook. After they read the material, have students ask or write questions about what they just read. Then under each heading, have students create a diagram or word picture that helps them better understand and remember the material. Encourage students to be creative with their visual images of the material. Have students share their visual representations to give other students ideas.

APPLY

Have students complete **Activity 5-7, "Running the Show,"** on page 96. Teaching suggestions and the solution for this activity appear on page 96 and answers to the quiz appear on page 98. An activity worksheet can be found on the Career Portfolio and Resource CD—**Text Activity 05-7.doc**.

TEACH

Students can learn a great deal about other cultures by studying the business customs of foreign countries. Because of the increase in workforce diversity, this knowledge will be helpful for all students, not just those considering global careers. Having students research customs on the Internet and inviting businesspeople of other cultures to speak to the class will increase students' awareness.

What do you think?

Use **TM05-08**.
Students' answers will vary. Remind students that what one person sees as an advantage might be seen as a disadvantage by someone else.

You believe in your business. You are the only one who can make your business successful. Be sure the values and principles that guide your life are the values and principles that guide your business.

Activity 5-7, "Running the Show," is a quiz that allows you to find out if you have an entrepreneurial spirit.

Global Career Opportunities

Businesses today and in the future must consider whether their marketplace includes more than their local area. Companies not only sell products or perform services in other countries but also import materials from companies worldwide. Many businesses believe a global outlook is necessary in order to be competitive and to attract new customers.

CAREER SUCCESS TIP

To help you decide whether you would like working in a foreign country, talk to someone who has worked and lived abroad.

For example, a company in the United States may form a partnership with a company in another country. Both companies profit from such an arrangement because both can reach more customers. Or a company in the United States might reach an agreement with a foreign government to set up an office or a manufacturing plant in the foreign country. The foreign country benefits from increased employment, and the U.S. company benefits from lower manufacturing costs and a larger market for its products or services.

How does this global marketplace affect you? It provides more career options and opportunities. For example, you can consider working for a U.S. company in one of its plants or offices located in a foreign country.

Rema has two major goals in life. She wants to learn to be a good machinist, and she wants to travel all over the world. To become a machinist, she plans to train at the career center during high school. As part of that education, Rema can work at a manufacturing company as a machinist helper while she continues with her classes. Through the company, Rema can reach her second goal. The manufacturing company has branches around the world. She can begin her work in Germany in an international apprentice program. Then she can transfer to another division with the same company in another part of the world. Rema can not only become a good machinist, she can also share her skills worldwide.

What do you think?
What are some advantages of being a worker in another country? What are some disadvantages of a global assignment?

Another career option for you to consider is working abroad for a foreign company. For example, employers worldwide need workers with

---

CAREER SUCCESS TIP

Working Abroad
Have students look at different web sites to learn more about working in foreign countries. The names and addresses of some appropriate sites appear below.

Alliances Abroad: **www.alliancesabroad.com**
LEAPNow: **www.leapnow.com**
BUNAC: **www.bunac.com**

i-to-i: **www.i-to-i.com**
EscapeArtist.com: **www.escapeartist.com**
GoAbroad.com: **www.goabroad.com**

information technology skills. New information technology occupations are created every day. Employers have trouble filling at least 1 out of 12 jobs in the field. Many foreign companies are employing high-tech workers from other countries to fill the positions. As a temporary worker, you can often obtain a visa to work in another country because of the lack of skilled workers in these nonagricultural specialty occupations.

If you work in another country, you may be starting a career as well as entering a new culture, perhaps with a different language. Even if you work for a U.S. company, you will need to adjust to living in another culture, perhaps one with different attitudes, values, and behaviors. People base their on-the-job and social behaviors on the unique viewpoint of their culture. To be successful in a job in a foreign country, you will need to adapt your behavior to that of the culture where you work and live.

Working in another country is an excellent way to learn about and understand another culture. You can expand your knowledge, both in the working world and in your personal life. Seeing other cultures and learning other languages offer interesting and challenging opportunities and responsibilities. Working abroad may also have some disadvantages, such as adjusting to a new culture and being separated from familiar surroundings and friends and family. However, if you learn some of the disadvantages in advance, you will have a more accurate picture of working abroad and can increase your chances of success.

For example, U.S. workers have a great deal of independence because the United States has a **market economy**, sometimes referred to as free enterprise. In a market economy, individuals and businesses are free to make their own decisions as they buy and sell in the marketplace. Businesses are generally privately owned and are free to operate for profit in a competitive system. The government does not interfere in business, except to pass and enforce regulations to protect the public interest and keep the U.S. economy in balance. Other countries around the world have a command economy. In a **command economy**, the government owns, manages, and regulates the production and distribution of goods and services. Although you are a U.S. citizen, when you work in a country with a command economy, you must conform to the country's economic employment system.

With the current world population consisting of 57 percent Asians, 21 percent Europeans, 8 percent Africans, 7 percent North Americans, and 7 percent South Americans, much of the world exists outside of the United States. Why not expand your career options and explore this outside world?

Activity 5-8, "Global Employment Opportunities," will give you insight into employment opportunities in different types of economic systems.

CAREER FACT

Americans who come back to the United States after working abroad are often amazed by the emphasis that U.S. workers put on time. According to *World Traveler,* work is given top priority in the United States, with family and friends second. In the rest of the world, the priorities are often reversed.

TEACH

You may wish to discuss the Career Fact on page 91 of the student text. Ask students for their ideas about why workers in most of the rest of the world have different priorities concerning work, family, and friends than U.S. workers do.

APPLY

Have students complete **Activity 5-8, "Global Employment Opportunities,"** on page 97. Teaching suggestions and solutions for this activity appear on page 97. An activity worksheet can be found on the Career Portfolio and Resource CD—**Text Activity 05-8.pdf.**

ENRICH

Have students complete **Activity 5-G, "Global Awareness,"** found in the *Investigating Your Career Activities & Projects* book.

In this activity, students use their interviewing skills to learn how a retail store in their community does business globally. Students may conduct interviews in pairs or individually. If transportation is a problem for interviewing, invite a guest speaker from a local retail store. Another alternative for finding the answers to the questions is to have students investigate a web site of a company whose products they use. Encourage students to share their results in class.
Solution: The solution for this activity appears in the *Teacher's Edition* of *Investigating Your Career Activities & Projects.*

CAREER TREND
Working Overseas
Students may wish to investigate work in a foreign country. Finding jobs in another country presents a challenge. Finding overseas jobs begins with a good resume that includes work experience and education. A good way to start is to search for overseas jobs at JobsAbroad.com (**www.jobsabroad.com**). This site provides information on different types of jobs in a variety of countries. Warn students to investigate carefully and to protect their personal security when using the Internet. Not all sites are legitimate.

Invite a human resources person from a local company to speak to your class about the importance of gender equality in the workplace. Have students make a list of companies in your area. Write these names on the board, and then vote on the company from which the class wants to invite the speaker. Have students make a list of questions they want to ask. Make sure the class writes a thank-you note to the speaker.

IN A NUTSHELL

Remind students about the objectives set forth at the beginning of the chapter, and use this summary to reinforce the concepts presented in this chapter.

Career Journal

Ask students to spend 10 minutes writing Career Journal entries that answer the following questions:
1. How well did what you thought you knew match what the chapter presented?
2. What questions do you now have about the chapter topics, and where do you think you can find the answers to those questions?
3. How will the content of the chapter help you investigate *your* career?

ASSESS

Administer the printed objective test for Chapter 5, available with this package. Test solutions are found in the *Teacher's Edition* of *Investigating Your Career Chapter Tests*. Use the **Exam***View*® CD to create your own objective test for this chapter.

IN A NUTSHELL

- **I can discuss the characteristics of the Millennial Generation.**

  The Millennial Generation, born in 1982 or later, has more freedom in choosing a career than past generations had. In general, the Millennial Generation values family over building a career. As a result, stress levels are lower for this generation. Also, the male and female roles in the workplace are less distinctive for this generation.

- **I can describe the various types of workforce diversity and their effects on the workplace.**

  Workforce diversity includes cultural differences, people with disabilities, and gender equity. Having a multicultural workplace enhances both the employees and the relationships with customers. A workplace that is gender equitable provides males and females with equal opportunities. When people with disabilities have appropriate job skills, they can succeed in their careers if given reasonable accommodations. Both employers and employees are expected to respect others' differences and not show prejudice or discrimination. Effective communication unifies a workplace and requires an understanding of workforce diversity.

- **I can identify nontraditional careers for men and women.**

  A nontraditional career is one in which one gender consists of 25 percent or less of the workers in the occupation. Nontraditional careers for women include mechanical, skilled trade, and technical careers. Nontraditional careers for men are often in healthcare and other nurturing fields. I should explore both traditional and nontraditional careers to have a better chance at finding my *P*A*T*H to Success*.

- **I can describe the characteristics of a successful entrepreneur.**

  Entrepreneurs can set goals and create the steps to achieve them. They are willing to ask for advice. They have good organizational skills. They see problems as challenges and are willing to develop alternative solutions. They are enthusiastic, persistent, and optimistic. They believe in their businesses.

- **I can explain the advantages of global careers.**

  The global marketplace provides career options and opportunities. By working in a foreign country, I can expand my knowledge, both in the working world and in my personal life. I can learn about other cultures and learn new languages.

Suggestions for Parents and Family Members

Supporting the Career Discovery Process
Parents and family members can support their child's career discovery process:

1. Discuss changes in how employees are perceived in today's workplace as compared to when you began working.
2. Be an unprejudiced role model in speaking about persons with disabilities, people from other cultures, and different genders.
3. Encourage your child to consider careers based on his or her interests rather than on stereotypes.

Learning from Others

You are a member of the Millennial Generation because you were born in 1982 or later. Some of the characteristics of your generation are explained on page 77.

1. Choose someone to interview from one of the generations listed below.

   • Generation X, born 1961–1981
   • Baby Boomers, born 1943–1960
   • Silent Generation, born 1925–1942

2. Interview the person by asking the following questions:

   • What is your generation group?
   • What is (was) your career field? What is (was) your last job title in that field?
   • What were your family's expectations of your personal behavior? Did they expect you to behave better than they did, the same as they did, or worse than they did? Why do you choose that answer?
   • Would you describe your culture as "clean-cut"? Why or why not?
   • Are (were) males and females treated differently in the workplace? Why or why not? If so, how?
   • How do (did) you treat career and family in your life? What are (were) your employer's expectations of your attitude toward your career and family?
   • How much stress do (did) you have in your life? How do you handle too much stress, especially stress on the job?
   • Do you believe you had freedom in choosing your career? Why or why not?

3. Answer the same questions yourself, writing down your responses.

4. Compare your answers with those from the rest of the class.

Coming to Terms

The terms listed below relate to the workplace. For each term, describe a situation where the term applies. The situation may be fact or fiction. Then in small groups, describe a positive ending to the situation.

1. Prejudice

2. Discrimination

3. Workforce diversity

CHAPTER 5 • • • • • UNDERSTANDING FUTURE CAREERS

93

Activity 5-1: Learning from Others

This activity helps students realize how other generations' attitudes toward workforce diversity, work, and family are different from students' attitudes.

After the interviews are completed, you may wish to divide the class into groups of three to six students. Each group should include students who interviewed people from each of the other generations. Students should compare the attitudes of other generations with the attitudes of their generation. Then have the groups report their results to the class.

Solution: Answers will vary. Discuss the similarities and differences between the students' generation and the various generations of the people students interviewed.

Activity 5-2: Coming to Terms

In this activity, students clarify their understanding of terms related to workforce diversity by describing a situation in which the term applies.

Before students begin the activity, explain that they should not just use the term in a situation. The situation should show the definition of the term. Encourage students to describe an actual situation, if possible. If the situation is negative, have students write a solution to make the situation positive. Divide students into groups of four or five students to complete the activity.

Solution: Answers will vary. Have groups describe some of their situations to the class. Then as a class, brainstorm additional solutions to negative situations to help students see beyond their prejudices.

Activity 5-3: Internet Investigation

Investigation of a web site designed to help disabled people find employment should help students improve their understanding of people with disabilities.

The web site, which is an excellent resource for both employers and employees, contains information for people with disabilities, including rights and employment opportunities. Tell students to explore a site before answering the questions and creating their summaries. Explain that an *abstract* is a summary of the main points, usually written as a list. A *summary* generally is written in paragraph form.
Solution: Answers will vary but should be specific and concrete.

Activity 5-4: Attitudes

This activity helps students discover whether their viewpoints on gender equity are traditional or nontraditional.
Solution: Statements 4, 6, and 9 show a nontraditional attitude; the others show a traditional attitude. Discussion should focus on the reasons why students and other people have traditional or nontraditional attitudes.

Activity 5-5: Expectations

In this activity, students extend their investigation of their attitudes regarding gender equity to career-related areas, helping them discover whether they are considering all their career options.
Solution: Statements 2 and 5 show *gender equity*. Encourage discussion to allow students to express their opinions. Although students may easily identify the statements as inequitable or equitable, they may agree with inequitable statements or disagree with equitable statements. Class discussion should emphasize the reasons the statements are equitable or inequitable. Be sure to point out the EEOC guidelines where applicable.

The Job Access site, **www.jobaccess.org**, works with companies to employ people with disabilities. The site has useful resources and employment information for persons with disabilities and for employers needing employees. Research the Job Access site as listed below.

1. Click on "Job Search" and then on "Job Seeker."
   a. Explore a field of interest or one of the companies listed.
   b. How does the site respect persons with disabilities?

2. Click on "the A.D.A."
   a. Investigate two of the sections. Write a summary of each section.
   b. How would this information benefit individuals with disabilities?

Determine whether the following statements about men and women show a *Traditional Attitude* or a *Nontraditional Attitude*. Why did you choose your answer? Discuss your results with the class.

1. Males have more mathematical ability than females.

2. A male's physical strength allows him to work more efficiently than a female.

3. A woman's first responsibility is to her home.

4. Males and females are equally capable of managing a home.

5. Males are better thinkers than females.

6. If males and females have jobs with the same description, they should get equal pay.

7. Females are more emotional than males.

8. A smart female should downplay her intelligence around males.

9. Females should have the same career options as males.

10. A male's main priority is to provide for his family.

Decide whether the following job-related statements show *Gender Equity* or *Gender Inequity*. Why did you choose your answer?

1. While researching careers, males and females should gather information only on gender-appropriate careers.

2. Men and women who have the same specialized skills can do the same job.

3. Women cannot be good supervisors because they get too emotional.

4. A man is a better choice to be a sheet metal worker because men are stronger than women.

5. When thinking about possible careers, you should not consider whether a career is only for men or only for women.

6. A woman makes a better nurse than a man does because women are more nurturing than men.

7. Men are better matched for more careers than women.

8. When faced with two candidates—a man and a woman—with similar qualifications, the employer should consider the gender of the job candidate.

9. Employers should consider that women may take time off to have children.

10. Employers should consider that men need to support their families.

ACTIVITY 5-6   **Case Challenges**

In each of the situations below, determine whether the situation shows *Prejudice* or *No Prejudice*. Explain why you chose your answer.

1. On the job bulletin board at the high school is a job opening notice for Powell's Market:

   Girls—Interested in being a grocery cashier? See Mr. Jay at Powell's Market.

2. Brenda loves reading and wants to share her passion with others. She applies to read Books on Tape but is turned down because she is hearing-impaired.

3. Because Natori is of Japanese descent, Ms. Simpson asked him to take information technology courses.

4. After graduating from a community college in computer applications, Donita began creating beautiful brochures and flyers. Because she is an African American, Greater Sycamore Insurance hired her very quickly.

5. Allen is insistent that his wife stay at home and not work until their child enters kindergarten. His reason: "Childcare is women's work."

6. Gary has Down syndrome. Ekkie's Market hired him to bag groceries.

7. In the teacher's lounge, Margaret was overheard discussing her attitude toward the students in her chemistry class. "I like having girls in class better than boys because girls are quieter and more cooperative. With more girls than boys, I can control the class better."

8. "Silvia is from Mexico. We can't hire her for the drive-through after school. She'll just take a siesta, a nap every afternoon."

9. Anita has excellent grades in science and math. Because of her grades and her passion for helping others, her father is glad she is planning a career in medicine.

10. Leatha was born with a clubfoot, which makes her walk with a limp even after many operations. She applied for the physical education teacher position at Clark High but was not asked to interview.

This activity checks students' understanding of when a situation or statement shows prejudice.

You may choose to divide the class into groups of four or five students or to analyze the cases as a class activity. Make sure students understand the definition of *prejudice* before they start the activity.

Solution: Cases 6 and 9 show *no prejudice*. In a class discussion, emphasize why the statements are prejudicial or not prejudicial by applying the EEOC, ADA, and equity information from the text.

Activity 5-7: Running the Show

This activity helps students determine whether they are suited for a career as an entrepreneur.

Rather than using a list of characteristics, this lighthearted quiz describes situations in which students' reactions determine their suitability as entrepreneurs. Class discussion should focus on the answers to the quiz and why the answers reveal who would make a good entrepreneur. Also have students list the characteristics of an entrepreneur they identified from the quiz.

Solution: The answers to the quiz and support information are found on page 98 of the student text.

Is starting your own business your dream? Do you have what it takes to eat, sleep, and breathe your business every day of the year? Take this quiz to find out if you have an entrepreneurial spirit.

1. You've never tried racquetball but decide it's time to try your hand at it. In the first five minutes, you miss the ball with every swing and get hit on the back by the ball. What should you do?

   A. Exchange your racquet for in-line skates.

   B. Get out on the court and play again.

2. Are you the one who knows the latest trends, who recommends what your friends should be wearing or reading or listening to or watching?

   A. I have no clue what is in style or what's not—what's hot or what's not.

   B. I seem to be able to predict the latest trends before they become trends. I know what's hot!

3. Have you ever had a hobby? How long did it last?

   A. I've got a closet full of hobbies that I tried for a while.

   B. Of course! People love my latest creations and want to see what I'm currently working on.

4. Those pants you bought yesterday looked great on you in the dressing room in the store. Now you are home, and you find that the color is not flattering at all. What do you do?

   A. Throw them on the floor of your closet and try to forget about the wasted money.

   B. Go back to the store and exchange them for the right color.

5. In the middle of the night, the power goes out—and so does your alarm clock. You wake up late, making you an hour late for work. What do you say to your boss?

   A. Explain why you are late—in minute detail. That explanation makes you even later starting work.

   B. Quickly explain what happened. Work late, making up your time. Then purchase a windup alarm on the way home.

6. Your friend is always late no matter where you are going. When she shows up half an hour late for your dinner together, what do you say when she makes excuses again?

   A. "No problem. Traffic is a problem sometimes."

   B. "If you're late next time, I'm only waiting five minutes."

(See page 98 for a discussion of this quiz.)

| ACTIVITY 5-8 | **Global Employment Opportunities** |

A Venn diagram is a visual way of comparing two different ideas. Print the Venn diagram from your CD, or use the handout from your teacher if a computer is not available. You will use the Venn diagram to compare and contrast the employment opportunities of the market economy in the United States and an economic system in the international job market, particularly a command economy. (See page 91 for more explanation of these types of economic systems.) You will write the unique, or different, characteristics in either the left or right sections and the common, or similar, characteristics within the overlapping section.

Refer to characteristics of each type of economic system listed below.

1. In the overlapping part of the circles, write the characteristics that are similar in both systems. What characteristics do the market economic system and the command economic system have in common?

2. In the parts of the circles that do not overlap, write the characteristics that make each system different. How are the market economic system and the command economic system different?

The overlapping part shows what is similar about the two economic systems. The other parts outside the overlapping part show what is not similar about the two systems.

Features of Market Economy

Jobs created by entrepreneurs
Demand for labor comes from the demand for consumer goods and services
Incomes based on achievement, education, and skills
Wide variety of occupations and skills
Equal employment opportunity under the law
Market changes determine wages and salaries
Demand for training and technical skills
Promotion based on merit and performance
Individual rewards to motivate employees
Government protection of worker health and safety
Combined private and government-sponsored retirement systems

Features of Command Economy

Production decisions made by planners
Demand for labor determined by the central plan
Incomes based on more equal distribution of wealth
Wide variety of occupations and skills
Equal opportunity under the law
Jobs created to provide employment for all
Wages established by the planning system
Demand for training and technical skills
Group rewards to reach output goals
Government protection of worker health and safety
Government-sponsored retirement system

CHAPTER 5 • • • • • UNDERSTANDING FUTURE CAREERS

97

Activity 5-8: Global Employment Opportunities

This activity helps students understand how workers are affected by the economic system of the country in which they work. Using a Venn diagram to compare the market economy in the United States and the command economy of other countries shows students the value of a visual display for detailed data. Depending on the level of students, you may have them do this activity as a class or in small groups. Discuss all terms with students before beginning the activity. Give examples as needed.

Before students begin the activity, discuss the importance of the world market for careers of the future. Point out that almost every business buys or sells its products or services globally. In addition, some students will choose to work directly with or in countries other than the United States.

Solution: The characteristics common to both economic systems are (1) wide variety of occupations and skills, (2) demand for training and technical skills, (3) government protection of worker health and safety, and (4) government-sponsored retirement system. Students should show these characteristics in the intersecting portion of the circles. The remaining characteristics should be included in the appropriate portions of the circles that do not intersect. Note that students need to separate the retirement system characteristic of a market economy into two parts, including government-sponsored retirement system as a common characteristic and private retirement systems as a characteristic of only a market economy.

1. The correct answer is **B.** Every entrepreneur is defeated occasionally (maybe even again and again) but keeps trying.

2. The correct answer is **B.** Yes! Entrepreneurs need to know the latest trends. If you aren't up on the latest trends, your new business will have a very dusty inventory in the back room.

3. The correct answer is **B.** Your business takes passion and commitment. Just because running a business has boring parts doesn't mean you should abandon it. You must stick to it through the excitement and the hard work.

4. The correct answer is **B.** Every entrepreneur must be able to accept problems and find solutions—without wasting resources, such as money. If you ignore a problem, you don't move forward, and an entrepreneur must continuously move forward.

5. The correct answer is **B.** You must be able to adjust to any situation as an entrepreneur. You can't let little things stop you—or waste your time.

6. The correct answer is **B.** When it comes to business, time is money. You must be polite and assertive. You won't succeed in business if you allow customers or employees to mistreat you this way.

You have what it takes to be a successful entrepreneur if you have more **B** answers than **A** answers in this quiz. If you have four or more **B** answers, you have an entrepreneurial spirit. Good luck!

Your *Internal Career Design*

6

Matthew Nadro's ideal career would be based on music. His passions are playing the bass guitar and composing music. But he knows that in the near future, he is unlikely to be able to support himself by his music alone. Matthew wants to find a career he will enjoy, perhaps one that uses his writing ability and allows him some free time to work on his music. Matthew knows he needs to make a career decision now so he can confirm the rest of his school schedule. He must also plan for additional education and training after graduation. He just doesn't know how to make a career decision. Matthew decides to talk to his counselor, Ms. Beckner, to see if she can help.

When Matthew and his counselor discuss his career options, Ms. Beckner shows him a step-by-step decision-making process. The process can help him find a career path that will allow him to use his creativity and writing ability and to follow his passion for music. Then she gives Matthew an ability assessment. The results indicate that Matthew would likely excel in sales or advertising. A sales career offers flexible hours that would allow Matthew to pursue his music. However, after job shadowing a salesperson, Matthew realizes he does not have the outgoing personality needed for sales.

Matthew plans to investigate advertising careers and further develop his writing skills. He also decides to continue working with Ms. Beckner to find an ideal career based on his passion for music.

How will you discover a career that is based on your passions? **What do you think?**

99

OBJECTIVES

After completing this chapter, you will be able to:
- Describe the decision-making process.
- Explain why you need to make a career decision now.
- Identify the benefits of making a good career decision.
- Examine possible career decisions.
- Choose your *Internal Career Design*.
- Create a plan to carry out your career decision.
- Monitor the success of your career decision.

Key Terms:
- self-understanding
- career maturity
- career satisfaction

Chapter Overview

Chapter 6
Your *Internal Career Design*

FOCUS

In Chapter 6, students use the decision-making process to help them discover their most suitable career path. In this pivotal chapter of *Investigating Your Career*, students match the elements of their *P*A*T*H to Success* to the characteristics of career clusters to discover their *Internal Career Design*. Then they begin to create a plan to implement their career decision and monitor its success.

Use the **Objectives** and **Key Terms** printed in the margin to help students focus on the content of this chapter. Use the **video segment** for Chapter 6 to introduce the chapter.

TEACH

Have students reread the opening scenario and identify the decision-making steps Matthew has taken so far in deciding on his career path. In subsequent sections of this chapter, students will learn more about Matthew and his decision-making process.

What do you think?

Use **TM06-01**.
Students' answers will vary. Answers should focus on the need to identify passions.

Career Journal

Ask students to spend 10 minutes writing Career Journal entries that answer the following questions:
1. What do you think this chapter will cover?
2. What do you already know about these topics?
3. What three things do you want to learn about these topics?

CHAPTER RESOURCES and MATERIALS

Activities & Projects book
Instructor's Resource CD
- Forms and Worksheets for Chapter Activities 6-1 through 6-8
- Internet Links for Chapter 6
- PowerPoint Presentation for Chapter 6
- Lesson Plans
- Teaching Masters for Chapter 6
- Video Discussion Guide for Chapter 6

Chapter Tests book
Exam*View*® CD
Video
Web Site

99

What do you think?

TEACH

Explain that in the first five chapters of the text, students have read information and completed activities in order to understand themselves and their *P*A*T*H to Success,* to learn about influences and trends that affect their career decisions, and to broaden their awareness of their career options. Now students will use what they have learned to make their career decision.

APPLY

Have students complete **Activity 6-1, "Decision-Making Process,"** that appears on page 116. Teaching suggestions and the solution for this activity appear on page 116. An activity worksheet can be found on the Career Portfolio and Resource CD—**Text Activity 06-1.doc.**

ENRICH

Have students complete **Activity 6-A, "Decision-Making Defense,"** found in the *Investigating Your Career Activities & Projects* book.

In this activity, students use the decision-making process presented on page 100 to solve the dilemmas for each case.

Solution: The solution for this activity appears in the *Teacher's Edition* of *Investigating Your Career Activities & Projects.*

What do you think?

What important decisions have you made in your life? What steps did you use to make those decisions?

You can't choose a career by throwing a dart at a list. You need an organized, logical method to make an informed career decision. The following decision-making process can help you discover your *Internal Career Design,* the ideal career for you. This chapter explains how to use the process to make your career decision.

1. **Understand that you must make a decision.** Choosing a career now will allow you to direct the focus of your education and skill training. You can select activities and classes that will help you prepare for your future career success. Your decision will give you a head start in preparing for the five to eight careers you will likely have over your lifetime.

2. **Identify the benefits of making a good decision.** By following your *P*A*T*H to Success,* you can choose a career that is based on your passions, attitude, talents, and heart. A career choice based on your *P*A*T*H,* your ideal lifestyle, and your climate and community preferences is likely to provide you with satisfaction in both your work life and your personal life.

3. **Consider all possible decisions.** Look at each career cluster. The clusters show the possible careers in a field. By looking carefully at the passions, attitude, talents, and heart associated with each cluster, you can select the cluster that matches your *P*A*T*H.* Answer questions such as these: Am I passionate about the career? Can I succeed in the courses needed for the careers listed in the cluster? What are the positives and negatives of the cluster?

4. **Make a decision.** Select the career cluster that best matches your *P*A*T*H to Success.* Then identify one or two careers within the cluster that are closest to your passions, attitude, talents, and heart and that match your lifestyle preferences. Although you will change and evolve, your passions and talents—and your *Internal Career Design*—are unlikely to change.

5. **Create a plan to carry out your decision.** Your plan will outline your goals and the steps necessary to achieve your goals. Your plan will help keep you on track by making sure that each step takes you closer to your career goal.

6. **Monitor the success of your decision.** Check your plan and your progress periodically to make sure you are on track. If you need to make any changes in your decision or in the steps necessary to carry out your decision, you can modify your plan before you go too far in the wrong direction.

In Activity 6-1, "Decision-Making Process," you will check your understanding of the logical steps for making a decision.

> 66 When I was growing up, I always wanted to be somebody. Now I wish I had been more specific. 99
>
> —*Lily Tomlin, Entertainer*

ONLINE RESOURCES

Check out the web site **www.investigatingyourcareer.com** for teacher resources, student activities, and replacements for broken links for this chapter. To access the teacher resources:

Username: career
Password: investigate

Understand You Need to Decide Now

In previous chapters, you thought about influences on your career choice, explored many types of assessments, considered workplace and workforce trends, and looked at how workforce diversity has expanded your career options. By now you realize that career planning is more than simply thinking about the question "What do I want to do when I grow up?" You realize that career planning involves more than taking an interest inventory or a personality assessment. You realize that your life can take many different directions and that you can choose many different career paths.

Through your classes and activities, you are mastering transferable skills that give you the flexibility to pursue various careers. Now you can also begin developing the specialized skills necessary for a specific career. The time is right for you to choose your career and decide the direction your career will take.

"How can I choose my career now?" Clarissa wonders. "I have so many options, I have so many interests, and I feel strongly about so many things." Clarissa faces choosing between two of her passions. If she chooses to follow her passion for cooking, she needs to take more math and chemistry classes. But if she decides to follow her passion for art, she needs to take visual art courses, such as computer graphics and photography. Each course of study has different requirements. Clarissa needs to make her decision before the end of her sophomore year. If she doesn't, she probably will have to take extra courses after high school. Clarissa wants to choose a career path now.

The secret to choosing a satisfying career is to base your choice on your talents, your passions, and your personal goals. Then achieve your chosen career by developing and following a plan. Planning allows *you* to be in charge. Rather than going through life waiting for the right career to find you, plan the career that will give you satisfaction. The time is right for deciding your career direction and designing your plan.

Use Activity 6-2, "Nine Boxes of Life," to review the important aspects of your life.

TEACH

This first step in the decision-making process reinforces the premise in Chapter 1 that students need to begin their career journey now. Emphasize that before students make education or training plans and before students graduate from high school, they must investigate career options. Although students can change their career direction, they need to investigate career choices now so they make practical plans for their future.

Review the subject transferable skills, which was presented in Chapter 1, with your students. Like Clarissa, they may have skills that will give them a choice of several of their passions/career areas.

APPLY

Have students complete **Activity 6-2, "Nine Boxes of Life,"** on page 116. Teaching suggestions and the solution for this activity appear on page 116. An activity worksheet can be found on the Career Portfolio and Resource CD—**Text Activity 06-2.pdf**.

DIFFERENT LEARNING ABILITIES

Gifted

Have students interview three adults and ask the following questions: How old were you when you decided on your career? How did knowing your career at that point in your life help or hinder you in your career? Tell students to write down each person's responses during the interview. During class, have students meet in a group to tally the responses and list the results on the board. Hold a class discussion on the results and what they show.

People who love their careers do work that matches their passions and talents, their interests and strengths. A well-chosen career gives people a sense of accomplishment. People who enjoy their careers live more satisfied lives overall. These people see a career not only as a way to earn money but also as an important, positive part of their lives.

If your career is based on your *P*A*T*H to Success*, you will benefit by having a satisfying and fulfilling career. Each of the following elements of the *P*A*T*H to Success* is important to discovering your ideal career.

CAREER SUCCESS TIP

The career path you choose will affect all aspects of your life—your life outside your work as well as the work you do. So be sure your career is based on something you love to do.

- **Passion** is what fascinates you, what you especially enjoy doing, what jump-starts your imagination. Your passion is what made you happy as a child and what you love to do now. You never object to spending your spare time on your passion.
- **Attitude** is an emotion, such as the positive way you feel when you think about an activity you enjoy. A positive attitude will make you feel as though you can accomplish anything.
- **Talents** are those abilities that enable you to do something well. The satisfaction of working in a career field that matches your talents will encourage you to develop your capabilities, advance your career, and explore new challenges.
- **Heart** refers to what you think and feel is important about a career. If you follow your heart and work hard, you're bound to go farther in a career. Being happy and fulfilled is more encouraging than working every day in a career that is not a good fit for you.

Charting your *P*A*T*H to Success* will help you discover your *Internal Career Design*. Your passions, attitude, talents, and heart will guide you as you begin your journey toward your career.

The uncertainty about his career decision is beginning to make Matthew Nadro feel discouraged. So many of his friends have already determined a career direction. After talking to his counselor again, Matthew realizes he will be better able to focus on choosing a career path if he links his career choice to his *P*A*T*H to Success*. Then his courses in school will have a new significance because they will relate to his career direction. He believes his future will be clearer when he makes a career decision.

To help make a decision, Matthew charts his *P*A*T*H to Success*, as shown in Illustration 6-1. He includes his passions, attitude, talents, and heart. He also lists his ideal lifestyle and climate and community preferences because he knows these elements also contribute to a satisfying life. After he completes his chart, Matthew realizes he is already feeling better. He knows he is on his way to finding a career that will support him and allow him to enjoy his passions.

Illustration 6-1   Matthew Nadro's chart

Passions (Interests)	Doing creative work Composing and playing music Writing Reading
Attitude (Personality)	Artistic Sensory Precise
Talents (Skills/Strengths)	Verbal communication Ability to compose music Writing ability Ability to play music
Heart (Values)	Likes to work alone Is reflective and reserved Considers family important
Ideal Lifestyle and Climate and Community Preferences	Prefers solitary workplace Must live in or have mountains nearby Prefers suburban or even more isolated location

Use Activity 6-3, "Charting the Course," to list your *P*A*T*H to Success* results from earlier chapters.

Consider All Possible Decisions

How do you choose a career? Should you take the advice of other people? Sometimes listening to others may confuse you. Some people may tell you the economy is uncertain so you should be cautious. Others will tell you to take risks. Some people may advise you to go to college. Others may recommend finding a job as soon as possible after high school. Confusion only adds to the dilemma. This time of your life is supposed to be exciting because you have so many options. But sometimes having so many options is the problem.

So how *do* you choose a career? Begin by exploring many career possibilities before you make a commitment. Then match what you know about yourself through assessments and other activities to the options. Consider everything. You might be surprised by how well you match some career areas you hadn't even considered.

APPLY

Have students complete **Activity 6-3, "Charting the Course,"** on page 116. Teaching suggestions and the solution for this activity appear on page 116. An activity worksheet can be found on the Career Portfolio and Resource CD—**Text Activity 06-3.pdf**.

DIFFERENT LEARNING STYLES
Kinesthetic Learners
Using the chart on this page as a model, have students make up one 3" by 5" note card for each category, putting the categories (Passions, Attitude, and so on) on the left side of the card. Ask students to begin walking around the room while carrying their cards. While the students are walking, play several CDs representing different types of music. Tell students to stop whenever they have a thought that describes them and to write it on one of their cards. Take about 15 to 20 minutes to do this exercise.

To help students understand the benefits of making a good career decision, you may want to use the following activity: Have students take off their shoes and put them on the wrong feet. Then have them walk around the room. Ask them how they feel. Make two lists on the board or on chart paper of adjectives that describe (1) how shoes feel when they fit and (2) how shoes feel when they don't fit. Then make the transition from shoes that don't fit to a career that doesn't fit. Ask students for adjectives that describe a career that fits and for adjectives that describe a career that doesn't fit, recording their responses in two more lists. Finally, discuss the similarities in the shoe lists and the career lists.

Basis for Your Decision

Before you can make an informed career decision, you need to know yourself. You must accept all your qualities—positive and negative—before you truly understand yourself. You want to base your career decision on you—on your passions, talents, and values.

Self-Understanding

To recognize your talents or skills, you need to achieve **self-understanding**, a clear insight or knowledge about yourself. In other words, you need to understand yourself. Achieving self-understanding is not easy. Often you have more knowledge about a friend or family member than you do about yourself.

Ana is Julia's younger sister. People compare her with Julia in a lot of ways. Julia plays the piano beautifully, and so does Ana. Julia does well in school, as does Ana. Julia likes to help people, so Ana tries to do the same. When Julia became active in her church youth group, Ana became involved too.

When asked to describe herself, Ana often points out Julia's positive talents, instead of her own. When asked about her own talents, Ana is at a loss for words. She believes she knows more about her sister than she does about herself. Yet Ana's outstanding qualities are unmistakable to others. She is quite capable and adaptable. She can find her way wherever she goes. When her family moved from Ohio to Denver, she made new friends and found a part-time job within a week. Ana is positive about any situation. Her optimistic attitude is encouraging to those around her. However, before Ana can make an appropriate career decision, she must come to realize her own talents.

You cannot select the right career if you do not know yourself. Achieving self-understanding sounds easy. After all, who spends more time with you than you do? However, true self-understanding means more than identifying your positive and negative traits. True self-understanding means working to build on your strengths and improve your weaknesses. Strengths and weaknesses are part of you, and you need to know both to have insight into the best career area for you.

INTEGRATED ACADEMICS
Mathematics
Show students several different types of graphic organizers. Then have students use the organizer on page 103 as a model to create a graphic organizer that shows their own passions, attitude, talents, heart, and ideal lifestyle as well as climate and community preferences. Call on volunteers to share some of their answers. Write these on the board under the categories. Add categories, such as male and female responses. Tally all the responses. Discuss the similarities and differences in the responses.

Assessment Results

You have considered many factors that influence your career decision. You have also used formal assessments to survey your interests, personality, strengths, and values. The advice you receive and the results of assessments are guides that help you discover the career area that suits you. Because you change as your experiences change, you can gain additional insights and explore various career options through informal assessments such as informational interviews, job shadowing activities, internships, and service learning projects.

When you believe you have a good understanding of your passions, attitude, talents, and heart, you can match your formal assessment results and your exploration experiences to career cluster descriptions. You can find out what career cluster and what careers best match your *P*A*T*H to Success*. After you choose a career cluster, additional informal assessment experiences will help you be sure that the cluster and careers you have chosen are appropriate for you. Everything you learn about yourself through assessment activities and exploration experiences is involved in discovering your *Internal Career Design*. Your ideal career depends on all the things that make you unique.

Career Clusters

A career cluster is an entire group of careers in one broad area. Under the umbrella of each career cluster are many different types of careers. For example, the Arts and Communication cluster includes web designers, graphic artists, television producers, sculptors, architects, entertainers, and broadcasters. Although these careers seem very different at first glance, they have several common interest and skill requirements. Also, many of the people whose careers are in the same cluster share certain personality traits.

Now that you have begun to discover your *Internal Career Design*, you need to analyze the career clusters to find the career path that most suits you. Illustration 6-2 on pages 106 and 107 describes the characteristics of the six career clusters and lists some of the career areas in each cluster. As you examine each cluster, look first for your passions. Your passions will lead you along the path to your ideal career. Then think about your talents, personality, and values.

Consider each career cluster carefully. Before accepting or rejecting a cluster, review all of its characteristics and think about how they compare to yours. Also look at *all* of the clusters before you choose—you may find your best match is in an area you do not expect.

In Activity 6-4, "Case Challenges," you will have an opportunity to match career clusters to people described in case studies.

CAREER FACT

An accounting professor saw one of his students, Carolyn Davidson, working more on graphic designs than accounting. He asked Carolyn to create a logo for his new shoe company. The "swoosh" she designed made Nike famous and Carolyn $35 richer.

TEACH

The term *career pathway* is used in some areas instead of the term *career cluster*. Career pathways/career clusters are great ways for students to begin their career selection process without making their decision too narrow. Some high schools are designed on an academic or career pathway system in which students take courses only in their cluster.

APPLY

Have students complete **Activity 6-4, "Case Challenges,"** on page 117. Teaching suggestions and the solution for this activity appear on page 117. An activity worksheet can be found on the Career Portfolio and Resource CD—**Text Activity 06-4.doc**.

CAREER TREND
Work World Projections

Hold a class discussion about what students imagine the work world will be like 10, 20, 50, and 100 years into the future. Have students project what the trends of the future will be. For example, will robots and robotic equipment replace people for manufacturing and service jobs? If so, how will this affect students hoping to work in manufacturing? Explain to students that by projecting future trends, they can choose careers that have a strong future.

Examine the six career clusters with students. Encourage them to expand their thinking and not immediately accept or reject any clusters. You may wish to have students explore why people who have the characteristics of a cluster find satisfaction working in some of the career areas listed. Ask students if they think a person is likely to have *all* the characteristics of a cluster. Be sure students understand the meanings of the characteristics of the career clusters and are thoroughly familiar with all six clusters before they choose a cluster in the next section.

Illustration 6-2 Career Clusters

Arts and Communication	Business and Management	Environment and Agriculture
Passions • Performing or writing • Being creative and original • Using imagination • Using music, art, drama, or writing • Sharing information and ideas	**Passions** • Creating order • Working with words • Knowing the proper procedures and standards • Valuing consistency	**Passions** • Planning and organizing • Working with hands or using technology • Working outdoors and/or with animals • Analyzing problems
Attitude • Self-motivated • Sensitive • Persistent • Creative and enjoys being different	**Attitude** • Organized • Honest, dependable, and responsible • Detail-oriented • Works well with others	**Attitude** • Analytical • Curious • High energy • Common sense
Talents • Innovative style • Mechanical ability • Art, music, drama, or writing ability • Gift for recognizing details in surroundings, including colors and shapes	**Talents** • High energy level • Mechanical ability • Good with words • Thinking skills • Organizing and leading ability	**Talents** • Understanding of living systems • Problem-solving ability • Math and science ability • Ability to classify and to devise strategies
Heart • Likes to create original ideas or objects • Likes to make beautiful things • Likes to work alone • Needs variety in activities	**Heart** • Likes working closely with other people • Likes a pleasant work environment • Likes coordinating events • Needs job security	**Heart** • Likes to work independently • Likes to learn how systems work • Likes to work alone • Likes challenge of solving problems
Career Areas to Consider • Commercial art • Advertising • Fine art • Journalism or writing • Printing • Editing • Floral arranging • Architecture	**Career Areas to Consider** • Accounting • Marketing • Sales • Public relations • Business management • Information processing • Paralegal • Business owner	**Career Areas to Consider** • Ecology • Agricultural engineering • Naturalist • Park ranger • Veterinary medicine • Marine biology • Landscaping • Agricultural sales

DIFFERENT LEARNING ABILITIES
Dyslexia
Arrange students into four groups: Arts and Communication, Business and Management, Environment and Agriculture, and video crew. Have each group write a song that explains the Passions, Attitude, Talents, Heart, and Careers to Consider. Next, have student groups perform their songs for the whole class. Have the video crew tape each group performing its song. Use the videos as part of the chapter review.

Illustration 6-2 Career Clusters (continued)

Health Services	Human Resources/Services	Technology, Science, and Engineering
Passions • Working with people • Using math, science, and/or technology • Researching and investigating • Fascination with details	**Passions** • Interacting with others • Leading or facilitating • Working with people • Fascination with human nature	**Passions** • Building and repairing things • Working with tools • Working with hands • Driving or working on trucks, cars, or equipment
Attitude • Caring • Sensitive • Good stress management • Investigative	**Attitude** • Caring about other people's feelings • Outgoing • Dependable • Respected by others	**Attitude** • Quiet • Curious • Individualistic • Practical, common sense
Talents • Excellent memory • Ability to adapt to all kinds of people • Ability in math, science, and/or technology • Attention to detail	**Talents** • Ability to work with all types of people • Planning and organizing ability • Good verbal skills • Problem-solving ability	**Talents** • Communication skills • Math, science, and technology ability • Analytical and problem-solving ability • Mechanical ability
Heart • Likes to care for sick or disabled people • Likes detailed projects • Likes solving problems • Values wellness activities	**Heart** • Likes to help people • Likes to work closely with others, including coworkers • Wants to understand others' situations • Wants to make things better for others	**Heart** • Likes to work alone • Takes pride in accomplishments • Likes to investigate the "why" of things • Needs job security
Career Areas to Consider • Athletic training • Biomedical research • Dental hygiene • Nursing • Paramedic • Pharmacist assistant • Mortician • Psychology	**Career Areas to Consider** • Social work • Lawyer or paralegal • Childcare • Cosmetology • Firefighting • Teaching • Human resources • Psychology	**Career Areas to Consider** • Construction • Computer technician • Drafting • Manufacturing • Truck driving • Auto mechanics • Mechanical engineering • Electrician

TEACH

Emphasize to students that careers exist in each cluster for people with various education and training levels. Also point out that careers can span more than one cluster because people often have passions and talents that do not exactly match the characteristics of one cluster. However, one cluster will usually be a better match than the other cluster, as in the scenario on page 110, and is referred to as the primary career cluster. Ask students for examples of careers other than teaching that may span two clusters.

DIFFERENT LEARNING STYLES
Print Learners
Have students write a short story about an imaginary character who lives 20 years in the future and is living the perfect lifestyle while working at the perfect job. Tell students to be specific in the descriptions of their characters' lives. Ask for volunteers to read their stories to the class. After reading several stories, hold a class discussion on what students think their lives will be like in the future.

107

Have students reread Matthew's scenarios on pages 99, 102, and 108. Then discuss the specific ways his *P*A*T*H to Success* fits the Arts and Communication career cluster. In Activity 6-5, students complete checklists similar to Illustration 6-3 for all six career clusters.

Make a Decision

After you analyze and consider each career cluster, decide which cluster is the best match for you. Then by exploring various careers within the cluster you have chosen, you will be able to select the career that best suits your unique qualities.

When he analyzes the career clusters, Matthew Nadro knows right away he can eliminate the ones that show a strong talent for math and science. Though Matthew does well in those subjects, he does not want to work with them every day. His music requires mathematical knowledge, but he uses it in a creative way.

Matthew's reserved personality, his preference for a solitary workplace, his creative writing talent, and his passion for music combine to point to a career in the Arts and Communication career cluster. Matthew uses a checklist, shown in Illustration 6-3, and his *P*A*T*H to Success* chart to be sure his cluster choice is right for him.

REAL PEOPLE
REAL CAREERS

Chef

When Jim Ridgeley began to think about a career, he decided to try cooking. He began his training by taking a class in Cajun cooking at a community college and was soon cooking the grits and stew popular in the Cajun/French areas of Louisiana. Jim continued taking more classes while he apprenticed with executive chefs.

What characteristics made Jim a good candidate for a career as a chef? Jim has always been a sensory person. He likes to touch the food, feel the steam rising from the stove, and smell the aroma of his creations. He also enjoys the excitement of continually keeping the orders moving. The pleasures he finds in his career outweigh the drawbacks. For example, a chef is likely to get burned—restaurant ranges can reach temperatures of 600°F. Other drawbacks are standing during long shifts and working with hazardous tools in busy kitchens.

Jim is now the grill chef at a restaurant in New Orleans. The restaurant industry is the second largest employer in the United States, so Jim will always be able to work in his career. To share his love of cooking with others, Jim teaches cooking at the community college that first inspired him and volunteers at a local soup kitchen.

For more information about:
- culinary careers, explore *www.acfchefs.org*, the web site of the American Culinary Federation, and *www.restaurant.org*, the site of the National Restaurant Association, where you can click on "Careers and Education."
- culinary schools, search *http://cookingcareer.shawguides.com*.

Source: Pouncey, Margaret. "This Might Pan Out." *My Generation*, May–June 2001, 30.

REAL PEOPLE—REAL CAREERS
Working in the Food Industry
Speak to an administrator at your local career/technical career center to arrange a visit for your class to observe a culinary arts class. Also try to arrange for your class to meet with the teacher after the regular class to learn more about culinary arts courses and careers in the food industry.

Illustration 6-3 Matthew Nadro's Checklist

Arts and Communication Career Cluster Checklist

	Answer *Yes* or *No*.
• Do you like to communicate ideas?	Yes
• Is sharing information one of your passions?	No
• Do your talents include creativity, imagination, and originality?	Yes
• Do you prefer expressing yourself in art, photography, graphic media, audio, or writing?	Yes
• Is performing your preference?	Yes

Passions (Interests)	Check *P*A*T*H* matches.
• Performing or writing	✓
• Being creative and original	✓
• Using imagination	✓
• Using music, art, drama, or writing	✓
• Sharing information and ideas	

Attitude (Personality)	
• Self-motivated	
• Sensitive	✓
• Persistent	✓
• Creative and enjoys being different	✓

Talents (Skills/Strengths)	
• Innovative style	✓
• Mechanical ability	
• Art, music, drama, or writing ability	✓
• Gift for recognizing details in surroundings, including colors and shapes	✓

Heart (Values)	
• Likes to create original ideas or objects	✓
• Likes to make beautiful things	✓
• Likes to work alone	✓
• Needs variety in activities	✓

ENRICH

Have students complete **Activity 6-B, "Imagine . . . .,"** found in the *Investigating Your Career Activities & Projects* book.

This activity encourages students to dream by having them create the workplace and tasks of their "dream" career. Describing their ideal work will help students set goals in Chapter 7 and will help them determine those aspects of their career they are unwilling to compromise. Encourage students to answer the questions as though they were really doing their "ideal" work.

You may choose to have students complete this form for a guest speaker or for an interview for job shadowing or an outside assignment. **Solution:** The solution for this activity appears in the *Teacher's Edition* of *Investigating Your Career Activities & Projects.*

INTEGRATED ACADEMICS
Arts and Communication

Invite a panel of speakers to your class. For the panel, choose people actively working in the arts community and in the field of communication. As a class, make a list of possible careers to include. Have different students write suggestions on the board. Next to each career, write a way to contact such a person. For example, next to *actor,* write *community theater;* next to *advertising copywriter,* write *business marketing department.* Have members of the panel discuss their careers.

Use **TM06-03**.
Students should realize that a career can span two career clusters by having characteristics of each of the clusters.

━━━ **APPLY** ━━━

Have students complete **Activity 6-5, "Choosing Your Career Cluster,"** on page 117. Teaching suggestions and the solution for this activity appear on page 117. An activity worksheet can be found on the Career Portfolio and Resource CD—**Text Activity 06-5.pdf**.

What do you think? Is it possible to choose a career that spans two career clusters? How?

You may find yourself strongly drawn to a career cluster that is only partially suitable. In that case, your best option may be to choose a career directly related to one career cluster but with some characteristics of another cluster.

Jo Ann's passions are working outdoors with plants and interacting with people. Her interest inventory and work values assessment confirmed her passions. Her personality assessment showed she is a person who is very thorough, and her ability assessment showed expertise in science and psychology, as well as language. Jo Ann, who also loves to solve problems, has analyzed all the career clusters. She believes the Environment and Agriculture career cluster may be the best fit for her *P*A*T*H to Success*.

Jo Ann knows she will not consider a career in farming or forestry, but she wants to explore landscape design. She plans to job shadow a landscape architect. She knows she would enjoy a career in landscaping, but she's concerned she would not be interacting with other people enough to satisfy her. So Jo Ann is also thinking about teaching landscaping. The Environment and Agriculture cluster would be her primary career cluster. To satisfy her need to work with others, she would share her passion for plants through the Human Resources/Services cluster. Together the two clusters match her *P*A*T*H to Success*.

Careers often cross two or more clusters by having some characteristics of each of the clusters. For example, a teaching career is included in the Human Resources/Services cluster. However, a teacher's subject may be in any of the other clusters. And the cluster that includes the subject may be the teacher's primary career cluster. An engineering career can also cross into most clusters. If your career seems to cross clusters, your primary career cluster will be the one that best matches your *P*A*T*H to Success*.

In Activity 6-5, "Choosing Your Career Cluster," you will use checklists similar to the one in Illustration 6-3 to determine the cluster that best matches your *P*A*T*H to Success*.

DIFFERENT LEARNING ABILITIES
Limited English Proficiency
Have students create a cartoon strip in their native language that illustrates how careers often cross two or more career clusters by having some characteristics of each of the clusters. All the words of the cartoon characters are to be written in the students' native language. Have the rest of the class try to guess by the illustrations what the cartoon characters are saying. Display the cartoons around the classroom.

Create a Plan

Deciding on the career cluster of your *Internal Career Design* marked the beginning of your career journey. Now you will research the various aspects of the cluster and choose one or two careers to explore further. Then you will need to evaluate the careers in terms of your research. When you are confident you have made the right decision, you will create a plan and goals to guide you on your career journey.

> What do you need to know about your future career before you can set goals and plan your career journey? **What do you think?**

The Next Step

The career cluster you have chosen is the best match to your *P*A*T*H to Success*—your passions, attitude, talents, and heart. Now you need to do some research within your career cluster on various careers that interest you. Your research will give you the information you need to narrow your choices and focus your education and training. You will need to:

- Research the workforce trends and demographics that can influence your career. An investigation into trends offers an outlook into the future, helping you predict how your chosen career may change and evolve. The last section of Chapter 4 provides numerous web sites you can use to conduct your research.
- Investigate the potential earnings and possibilities for advancement in your career area. Your lifestyle will be influenced by the amount of money you earn. Your satisfaction with your career will be affected by whether you can use and develop your talents. You will want to explore several careers within your career cluster.
- Look into the education and training needed for entry-level (or other) positions and for advancement. You need to know that the education and training you are planning will qualify you for the career you want.

CAREER SUCCESS TIP

When someone gives you career advice, especially about a career you know is not a fit for you, a good response is, "I appreciate your feedback and I'll consider your suggestions."

In addition to your research, you will want to begin an inventory of your transferable skills, the skills that are an asset to several careers and will transfer across career clusters. Identify the transferable skills you now have, and add to your inventory as you acquire new skills. Include documentation of situations in which you have effectively used your transferable skills.

Also, you will want to begin a list of your specialized skills, including the different equipment, technology, and talents you have that enable you to work and advance in specific careers. Your research into various careers should identify any specialized skills you need now and in the future for your chosen career.

CHAPTER 6 • • • • • *YOUR INTERNAL CAREER DESIGN*

What do you think?

Use **TM06-04**.
Students' answers will vary. Possible answers include educational requirements, physical requirements, potential earnings, and future employment opportunities.

TEACH

In this step of the decision-making process, students begin to create a career plan based on their cluster choice. Emphasize to students that their career goals may change but that they now have a foundation for their decision and can concentrate on exploring a specific career cluster. Explain that researching the trends, education and training, and career growth of various careers in their career cluster will allow them to narrow their career focus to one or two careers. Specific goal setting begins in Chapter 7.

 **CAREER SUCCESS TIP**

Discerning Advice from Others

Ask students to remember the last time someone gave them career advice. Once students have recalled such an occasion, have them write journal entries answering the following questions: In what ways did you find the advice helpful or unhelpful? How did you feel when the person was giving you the advice? Did you follow the advice? Why or why not? If you followed the advice, what was the result? Tell students that not all advice is good advice. They should listen graciously to all advice and then discern what works for them.

Matthew Nadro researched the Arts and Communication career cluster, looking especially at music and writing careers. He already knows music performance is not often a career in which people make a lot of money. However, he has music skills other than performance skills; he can write both music and lyrics. Matthew also knows that music composers are now using technology to write music. His research has verified that this trend will continue in the future. Although Matthew does not like this trend, he has studied how to compose music this way. He keeps records of the technology he knows how to use, plus samples of his compositions and lyrics.

In addition to researching a music career in writing lyrics and composing music, Matthew researched a career in writing copy for advertising. His career assessment showed that he could excel in advertising, and he has decided to pursue this career area. He researched the need for music composers and advertising writers in the Denver area, where he eventually wants to live. Because Matthew needs to begin planning his education and training, he also researched schools in Phoenix, in his hometown, and in Denver. Matthew hopes to be able to concentrate solely on his music some day, but for now, he is happy to have found a career path that will allow him to develop his passions.

Activity 6-6, "Career Cluster Research," gives you the opportunity to find in-depth information on your chosen career cluster.

Evaluate Your Career Decision

Your research will help you evaluate your career decision so you can be sure your career meets your expectations. Ask yourself the following questions about the career cluster and the careers you have chosen:

- Do you think of the problems you are likely to encounter in your career as challenges?
- Will you find pure enjoyment in the career?
- Is the product or service needed and respectable?
- Will you respect the kinds of people working in the career area?
- Will you respect the work your career involves?
- Will you have opportunities for personal and professional growth?
- Will you make enough money to support your desired lifestyle?

If you answered yes to the majority of these questions, you have chosen appropriately. If you have two or more no answers, you may want to investigate another career or even another career cluster.

Set Goals

After you have researched and evaluated your cluster and your chosen career to be sure you are on the right track, you can begin to set goals and create a plan to achieve your goals. You may already have some goals in place. If so, you are moving right along. If not, you can focus on the goals necessary to achieve your *Internal Career Design*.

By setting goals, you make sure your classes support your future career and meet your graduation requirements. Your goals may include choosing some electives in your career area to test whether the career is a good fit for you. Part-time and summer jobs are good ways to sample a career too. Classes and jobs may also help you develop skills that support your career goal.

Setting goals and creating a plan are the next steps along your career journey, the steps that will guide you toward making your dreams realities. In Chapter 7, you will use the information from this chapter and from your Career Journey Folder to set goals and figure out the time lines that will allow you to achieve your goals.

Use Activity 6-7, "Learning from Others," to observe a career that interests you.

> **" People may try to talk you out of your dream career, but you have to shut out those voices and go with your gut. "**
>
> —*Maria Shriver,
> Journalist and Author*

Monitor the Success of Your Decision

The career you choose now is likely to be just the first of five to eight careers during your life. Basing your first choice on your *P*A*T*H to Success* will build a firm foundation for all of your career choices. Evaluating your career plan periodically will also tell you whether you are on the right track.

Your Career Journey Folder

Your Career Journey Folder includes all the documents important to your career choice and your career path. Besides results from specific activities in *Investigating Your Career*, you should include:

- Records of accomplishments, certificates, badges, and so on.
- Newspaper articles, programs, brochures, or similar documents about your activities. If your name does not appear in the document, keep it anyway and make a note of your participation.
- Photos of projects and achievements.
- Letters concerning your activities and achievements.
- Copies of anything indicating outstanding results or your exceptional qualities.

Have students complete **Activity 6-7, "Learning from Others,"** on page 118. Teaching suggestions and the solution for this activity appear on page 118. An activity worksheet can be found on the Career Portfolio and Resource CD—**Text Activity 06-7.doc**.

ENRICH

Have students complete **Activity 6-D, "Career Customers,"** found in the *Investigating Your Career Activities & Projects* book.

Although similar to Activity 6-7, this activity allows students to consider other careers related to the ones they researched.
Solution: The solution for this activity appears in the *Teacher's Edition* of *Investigating Your Career Activities & Projects*.

TEACH

Discuss the contents and purpose of the Career Journey Folder. Be sure students are aware of all the items they need to include and why these items are important for their career journey. The Career Portfolio and Resource CD has a form that students can use to keep track of the contents of their folders.

INTEGRATED ACADEMICS
Social Studies
Have students work in small groups. Provide each group with a period of history, such as the Bronze Age, the Roaring Twenties, or the Industrial Age. Have groups write a skit that tells something about the working conditions during that time period. Have each group perform its skit before the whole class. Have the class vote on which time period they would prefer living in. Discuss their answer; ask why they prefer this time period.

What do you think?

Use **TM06-05**.
Students' answers will vary.

TEACH

Students need to realize that although they have realistically assessed their talents and correlated them with their passions to discover their *Internal Career Design,* they have taken only the first step on their career journey. Point out that they will need to monitor their career decision regularly.

APPLY

Have students complete **Activity 6-8, "Coming to Terms,"** on page 118. Teaching suggestions and the solution for this activity appear on page 118. An activity worksheet can be found on the Career Portfolio and Resource CD—**Text Activity 06-8.doc**.

CLOSE

Wrap up this chapter by having students complete **Project 2, "Career Storybook,"** found in the *Investigating Your Career Activities & Projects* book.

For this activity, students work as a team to create a storybook for primary grades. Each student designs a page based on one of the careers they researched in Activity 6-6. As an alternative, ask each student to create a poster of his or her career for children in primary classes.
Solution: The solution for this activity appears in the *Teacher's Edition* of *Investigating Your Career Activities & Projects.*

Why should you save these items in your Career Journey Folder? They are physical evidence of your achievements and will help you remember all that you have accomplished. Keep your folder up to date so you can use it during the job search and admissions processes—whenever you need to explain your talents to others. Your Career Journey Folder also reinforces your career decision. By reviewing its contents, you can see why you chose your career.

Check Your Progress

What do you think? How can you make sure your career journey is headed in the direction of your *P*A*T*H to Success?*

After you have made your career decision and created your plan, you need to monitor, or keep track of, the success of your decision. Checking your progress along your career journey helps you be sure you are headed in the right direction. Periodically review your progress by:

CAREER FACT

A myth about career decision making is that once you make a career choice, you are stuck in that career field. Not at all. Changing your decision does not necessarily limit your options.

1. Asking yourself the following questions:
   - Is my career choice working for me?
   - Are my goals incorporated in my plan?
   - Am I meeting the time lines of my goals?
   - Does my career decision still match my *P*A*T*H to Success?*

2. Analyzing your answers to the questions in #1. If you answer no to any of the questions, determine what you need to do to change your answer to yes.

If you discover that your career plan is not taking you in the right direction, make adjustments. You need to be flexible to adapt to new experiences and situations. You may also need courage to stay on track and pursue the career of your dreams. You may meet resistance from some of the people who have influence in your life (such as your friends, your family, or even an employer), but you need to make your own choice.

After years of experience on the job with extensive education/training, you will achieve **career maturity**. With career maturity, you use your expertise. By basing your *Internal Career Design* on your *P*A*T*H to Success,* your career journey will end with **career satisfaction**, the pleasure of working capably in an area that allows you to use your passions.

Activity 6-8, "Coming to Terms," will check your understanding of the important terms in this chapter.

CAREER TREND
A Change in Careers

Even famous actors may decide to make career changes. Early in his career, Ronald Reagan worked as an actor and appeared in movies and on television. He became interested in politics and ultimately was elected President of the United States. Students may change their careers more than once in their lifetime and their different careers may or may not be related to one another.

- **I can describe the decision-making process.**

  The decision-making process has six steps: (1) understand that I need to make a decision, (2) identify the benefits of making a good decision, (3) consider all possible decisions, (4) make a decision, (5) create a plan to carry out my decision, and (6) monitor the success of my decision.

- **I can explain why I need to make a career decision now.**

  Making a career decision now allows me to choose my courses, add to my transferable skills, and increase my specialized skills.

- **I can identify the benefits of making a good decision.**

  My career should be based on my *P*A*T*H to Success*—my passions, attitude, talents, and heart. If I make a career decision based on my *P*A*T*H*, I will benefit by having a satisfying and fulfilling career.

- **I can examine possible career decisions.**

  I can examine my career possibilities in the six career clusters in terms of self-understanding and formal and informal assessment results. The six career clusters—Arts and Communication; Business and Management; Environment and Agriculture; Health Services; Human Resources/Services; and Technology, Science, and Engineering—are groups of careers that have common interest and skill requirements.

- **I can choose my *Internal Career Design*.**

  After looking at the questions and characteristics of each career cluster, I can choose the cluster that best matches my *P*A*T*H to Success*. Though some careers seem to span two clusters, one cluster will dominate and be my primary career cluster.

- **I can create a plan to carry out my career decision.**

  I will research and evaluate possible careers in my chosen cluster to narrow my choices and focus my education and training. Then I will be able to set goals and create a plan for my career journey.

- **I can monitor the success of my career decision.**

  I can organize the contents of my Career Journey Folder so I have evidence of my achievements and am able to review my career path. I know how to check my career progress periodically to be sure I am headed in the right direction for career satisfaction.

> 66 Figuring out who you are is the whole point of the human experience. 99
>
> —Anna Quindlen, Author

Remind students about the objectives set forth at the beginning of the chapter and use this summary to reinforce the concepts presented in this chapter.

Career Journal

Ask students to spend 10 minutes writing Career Journal entries that answer the following questions:
1. How well did what you thought you knew match what the chapter presented?
2. What questions do you now have about the chapter topics, and where do you think you can find the answers to those questions?
3. How will the content of the chapter help you investigate *your* career?

ASSESS

Administer the printed objective test for Chapter 6, available with this package. Test solutions are found in the *Teacher's Edition* of *Investigating Your Career Chapter Tests*. Use the **Exam***View*® CD to create your own objective test for this chapter.

Suggestions for Parents and Family Members

Talking with Teens
Following are ways parents and family members can support their child's career discovery process:

1. Share your own passions, attitudes, talents, and heart and how these influenced your career decision.
2. Talk with your child about his or her personal passions, attitudes, talents, and heart. Help your child understand how his or her career decision matches these.

Activity 6-1: Decision-Making Process

This activity gives students practice using the decision-making process by requiring them to make common decisions.

For this activity, divide the class into groups of five or six students. You may choose to use other decision-making situations that your students face.

Solution: Answers will vary. Make sure students clearly delineate each step of the decision-making process.

Activity 6-2: Nine Boxes of Life

This activity helps students identify the things that are truly important to them and to realize how they actually spend their time. If you need to offer ideas, suggest activities, hobbies, pets, types of people (not names), possessions, and so on. Remind students that they need to be honest with their rankings to learn more about themselves.

Solution: Answers will vary. Many students will find that they do not spend most of their time on the most important things in their lives. Discuss the implications of such results and how students might want to adjust their priorities to spend more time on their passions. (Students will learn about goal setting and time management in Chapter 7.)

Activity 6-3: Charting the Course

This activity prepares students for comparing their *P*A*T*H to Success* to the six career clusters. Students use completed activities from Chapters 1–3 to organize their passions, attitude, talents, and heart and their descriptions of their ideal lifestyle and climate and community preferences in a chart they will use in Activity 6-5.

Refer students to Illustration 6-1 of their text for an example. Because students will be using specific activities from their Career Journey Folder, you may want to suggest they update the tracking and contents of their folders.

Solution: Students record individual data.

Decision-Making Process

In small groups, choose one of the following topics and make a decision about it. Use the decision-making process on page 100 to make your decision. Write down an explanation of each of the steps your group uses to make the decision. Be sure each group member agrees on each step of the process.

1. The class song

2. This year's graduation dance theme

3. The best way to save money for summer vacation

Nine Boxes of Life

Writing down the important parts of your life helps you understand why you need to make your career decision now. This activity will help you discover your priorities.

1. Print the form from your CD, or draw nine boxes on a separate sheet of paper.

2. Write the nine most important things in your life inside the nine boxes.

3. Number the boxes from 1 to 9 according to what is most important in your life. (Number 1 is the most important.)

4. Number the boxes from 1 to 9 again, this time according to how you currently spend most of your time. (Number 1 is how you spend the most time.)

What did you learn from this activity?

Charting the Course

Print the chart for this activity from your CD, or use the chart provided by your teacher. Use the appropriate activities from your Career Journey Folder, and record the following results on the chart.

- Passions (Interests): List the Interest results from Activity 3-2.
- Attitude (Personality): List the Personality results from Activity 3-3.
- Talents (Skills/Strengths): List the Strengths results from Activity 1-3 and the Ability results from Activity 3-2.
- Heart (Values): List the Values results from Activity 3-3 and the Motivation results from Activity 2-4.
- Ideal Lifestyle and Climate and Community Preferences: List the results from Activity 2-3.

When you have finished, attach the activities to the chart. You will use the results of the chart in Activity 6-5 to determine which career cluster fits you best.

Case Challenges

 Each of the following case studies describes a person's *P*A*T*H to Success*. In small groups, discuss each case study and decide which career cluster best fits each person. List at least three careers the person might choose. Also include the reasons for your decisions. There are no right or wrong answers.

1. Jason was a sensitive person. He observed his surroundings with great care so he could re-create the environment in his imagination. Being alone was an essential part of each day for Jason. He needed to be alone to absorb the impact of everything he had experienced. Jason felt driven to express his understanding of his observations in a creative and original way.

2. At a very young age, Maya began to follow her father around the garden as he trimmed the roses. When she was older, Maya learned that soils need certain additives to produce healthy plants. Maya's passion for gardening and plants led her to experiment with grafting different types of plants to see what the outcome would be.

3. When a group at school needed a hard worker, someone usually called Will, who was always able to help. In the midst of stress and chaos, he was calm and could find solutions to problems. No one was surprised to learn that Will was a member of the Explorer post and helped with the fire department's emergency team. In a group, Will always tried to work with people.

4. Lauren handpicked the members of the Graduation Dance Committee to make sure everyone would work together to organize the event. Lauren had everything planned down to the last name tag. The time line of activities was thorough and covered every last detail. She knew the school's graduation dance this year would be the best for many years to come.

5. As a child, Sameer's favorite birthday gift was a box of interconnecting building pieces. After he received his first box, he asked for more and more increasingly complex sets. Then Sameer began drawing his creations on paper before building them. Analyzing the curve of a bridge or the height of a tower tested Sameer's problem-solving abilities. To anyone who knew him, it was obvious why Sameer was so proficient in computer drawing.

6. Nieca seemed to get along with everyone; she could never be accused of any bias. Groups usually chose her as their leader or as an officer because she was able to get the members to work together. Nieca had the patience to listen to everyone's opinion and to inspire everyone to take all ideas into account before making a group decision.

Choosing Your Career Cluster

 Print the six career cluster charts for this activity from your CD, or use the charts provided by your teacher. Answer each of the questions by writing yes or no. Then put check marks by any of the *P*A*T*H* characteristics that match the results you charted in Activity 6-3. Use the results from the charts to evaluate which career cluster fits you the best.

1. Which cluster is your best match?

2. What other clusters are also good matches?

3. List two or three careers you want to explore from your primary career cluster.

CHAPTER 6 • • • • • *YOUR INTERNAL CAREER DESIGN*

 117

Activity 6-4: Case Challenges

This activity increases students' understanding of the characteristics of the different career clusters and of how their *P*A*T*H to Success* leads to the most appropriate cluster. The activity also helps students improve their analysis and team skills.

Divide the class into groups of four or five students. Remind students to give the reasons they had for matching the people in the case studies to the characteristics of the recommended career clusters. Explain that when choosing three possible careers for the person in each case study, students are not limited to the careers listed in the career cluster descriptions.

Solution: Answers will vary. Although each scenario fits a specific career cluster, some students may suggest an alternative cluster. Their answers will be correct if they can substantiate their decisions. Suggested answers are as follows:

1. Arts and Communication
2. Business and Management
3. Environment and Agriculture
4. Health Services
5. Human Resources/Services
6. Technology, Science, and Engineering

Activity 6-5: Choosing Your Career Cluster

In this pivotal activity, students choose their primary career cluster, any alternative clusters that are good matches, and two or three careers they want to explore. Their choices are based on the chart they created in Activity 6-3 and checklists for each career cluster.

You may wish to divide the class into groups of four or five students after students have chosen their career clusters. Students in each group should have chosen the same career cluster. By working together, students are likely to discover careers to investigate beyond those listed in Illustration 6-2 on pages 106–107.

Solution: Answers will vary. In a class discussion, explain that the nonprimary clusters that are good matches may lead to careers that span two or more clusters or to alternative career decisions. Also mention that eliminating career clusters helps students narrow their career focus.

Activity 6-6: Career Cluster Research

This activity provides students with information that will help them narrow their career choices and set their career and education/training goals. Encourage students to research more than the two careers required for this activity. Working with a partner who has chosen the same career cluster will increase the number of careers researched.

Note that O*NET, which is accessed through one of the web sites listed in the activity, is based on the knowledge, skills, abilities, interests, preparation, contexts, and tasks associated with careers. By clicking on "Snapshots" at the O*NET site, students can read brief information about various occupations before they conduct in-depth research.
Solution: Answers will vary.

Activity 6-7: Learning from Others

This activity helps students acquire firsthand knowledge about a career in their chosen career cluster through a job shadowing experience combined with an interview. If possible, students should allow at least a two-hour time period for the job shadowing experience and interview. They should plan this activity after school, on a weekend, or during a vacation. They could also take a career study tour.

All students should make an introductory call and present the person they are interviewing with a letter from you giving the background for the activity's assignment. After the experience, students should write thank-you notes to the people they observed.
Solution: Answers will vary. Students should share the results of their job shadowing experience and interview with the class.

Activity 6-8: Coming to Terms

The questions in this activity should help students understand the definitions of the terms.

Discuss the definitions of the terms before students begin answering the questions. Encourage students to provide examples of people they know well, such as family members or people they interact with in the community. Working with a partner

Research at least two careers in the career cluster you chose in Activity 6-5. Summarize the results of your research. Be sure to include the information below. Then present your research results to the class. Include the transferable skills from one career to the other.

- Description of the work
- Transferable skills among the careers researched
- Working conditions
- Training and education requirements
- Earnings, including starting salary
- Future outlook
- Workplace or workforce trends and how they might affect the careers you chose

Some starting points for your research could be the following resources:

- o*net OnLine at *http://online.onetcenter.org*
- America's CareerInfoNet at *www.acinet.org/acinet*
- Bureau of Labor Statistics at *www.bls.gov*
- The sites listed in Chapter 4, page 69

You will use this information to set your goals in Chapter 7.

ACTIVITY 6-7   **Learning from Others**

Visit someone who is working in the career cluster you chose. Job shadow the person, observing him or her for at least two hours during the working day. Your teacher, family members, or counselor can help you find someone.

1. Before you go, write a list of questions to ask the person about his or her daily career life. Include (a) questions that address the career goals of the person and (b) questions based on the questions on page 112 that you used to evaluate your career decision.

2. When you return from your observation, share your information with your class.

ACTIVITY 6-8   **Coming to Terms**

With a partner, answer each of the following questions on a separate piece of paper.

1. Why is self-understanding important when choosing a career? Describe someone who made a career decision based on self-understanding.

2. Describe someone who has achieved career maturity. How did he or she achieve career maturity?

3. What is career satisfaction? Why is it important? Describe someone who is satisfied with his or her career.

supports more thorough answers and often helps students supply more examples.
Solution: Answers will vary.

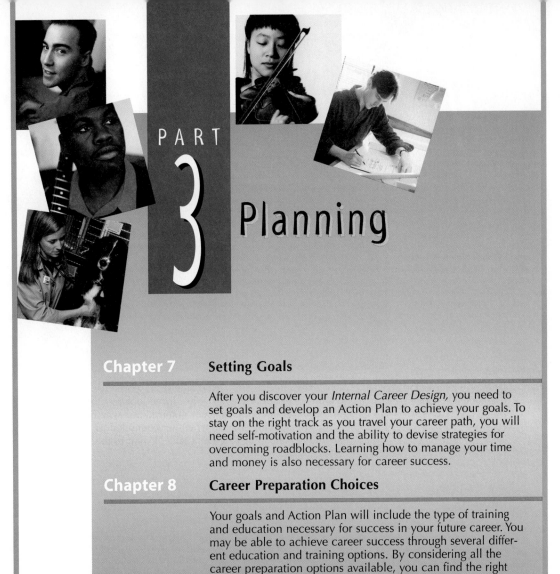

PART 3 Planning

PART 3

Focus

In Part 3, the student begins the career planning process from general goal setting and time management to plotting a hypothetical admissions time line.

Before beginning this part, have students interview a family member or family friend about their career planning time line, including goal setting, time management as a student in high school and later, and education and training decisions and time periods. Use this information for comparison at various points throughout Part 3.

FOCUS

In Chapter 7, students begin to develop the self-motivation and strategies they will need for planning their career and achieving their career goals. Students write the short-term, mid-term, and long-term goals they will need to accomplish their education, career, family, and lifestyle ambitions. Then they create Action Plans that include strategies for overcoming roadblocks to their success. To help achieve their goals, students learn how to budget their money and manage their time.

Use the **Objectives** and **Key Terms** printed in the margin to help students focus on the content of this chapter. Use the **video segment** for Chapter 7 to trigger discussion.

TEACH

Discuss the chapter's opening scenario with students. Have students explain what motivates *them*. Ask them how they will need to spend their time in order to achieve long-term satisfaction and their long-term goals.

What do you think?

Use **TM07-01**.
Students' answers will vary.

Career Journal

Ask students to spend 10 minutes writing Career Journal entries that answer the following questions:
1. What do you think this chapter will cover?
2. What do you already know about these topics?
3. What three things do you want to learn about these topics?

7 Setting Goals

OBJECTIVES

After completing this chapter, you will be able to:
- Motivate yourself.
- Understand the differences among long-term, mid-term, and short-term goals.
- Develop an Action Plan for a long-term goal.
- Develop strategies for overcoming roadblocks.
- Create a budget.
- Manage your time.

Key Terms:
- self-motivation
- procrastinate
- backup plan
- long-term goals
- mid-term goals
- short-term goals
- Action Plan
- mentors
- roadblocks
- budgeting

Lena's passion was cars—especially sleek sports cars. She really wasn't that interested in driving. She just loved looking at the flowing designs and beautiful lines of cars. Lena admired cars whether they were moving or just standing still. So when her counselor asked her what career she might want some day, Lena said, "I want to design cars."

"You're going to need a plan," said Lena's counselor. Soon Lena was doing research in several areas. First, she had to find out what skills were required for a career in auto design. Then she had to learn what education or training she would need and whether she should enroll in a bachelor's, associate, or technical program. Lena decided she would begin in auto bodywork at the career center and then transfer to a community college that had an excellent program in metal sculpture. Finally, she would take an industrial engineering course at one of the colleges that had a good reputation in that field.

With her counselor's help, Lena made a list of the goals she would need to reach over the next few years. One of her important goals was to improve her math and science grades. Lena knew she would need strong math and science skills to be admitted to an industrial engineering program. Lena reached one of her goals when she was able to get a summer job as an assistant in an auto body shop. Repairing auto bodies would give her hands-on experience in the types of paints and lacquers used on cars.

What do you think?
What are some of the goals you need to complete your career plan?

CHAPTER RESOURCES and MATERIALS

Activities & Projects book
Instructor's Resource CD
- Forms and Worksheets for Chapter Activities 7-1 through 7-8
- Internet Links for Chapter 7
- PowerPoint Presentation for Chapter 7
- Lesson Plans
- Teaching Masters for Chapter 7
- Video Discussion Guide for Chapter 7

Chapter Tests book
Exam*View®* CD
Video
Web Site

Self-Motivation

What strategies do you use to motivate yourself in school? **What do you think?**

After you discover your *Internal Career Design*, you need to plan how you will achieve this ideal career. What strategies should you follow? What goals should you set? How will you stay motivated to reach your goals if your plan is not working out as you had hoped?

Maria's career plan was to follow her sister Eliza into public relations. Eliza gave some advice to Maria as to how she should begin to plan now to reach her goal. Eliza recommended that Maria take all the writing classes offered at her school, volunteer to write for the school newspaper, and work hard to secure an internship in public relations. Maria took Eliza's advice, but sometimes she was not motivated to work hard, preferring instead to spend time with her friends. Whenever she felt discouraged, she would call Eliza, and Eliza would tell her about the satisfaction of a public relations career. Then in her senior year, Maria lost the public relations internship to another student. But by now, Maria was determined to succeed. She found a part-time job with a professional baseball team in her area and used her writing skills in the team's public relations office.

> **❝ I've always felt it was not up to anyone else to make me give my best. ❞**
> —*Akeem Olajuwon, Basketball Player*

Achieving the goals you set for your career and your life requires **self-motivation**—the determination to stay on track and avoid distractions. Self-motivation helps you take responsibility for managing your life. Instead of feeling as if events are controlling you, you can take charge and begin to feel good about each accomplishment that brings you closer to your goals.

People often need to be self-motivated to stick to career planning. Without self-motivation, you may tend to **procrastinate**, or delay planning. You may also find that events in your life sometimes distract you from thinking about your career plan. The following general guidelines can help you stay motivated and become an effective career planner.

Make time for career planning. Planning takes time in the beginning, but it's the only way to make sure you end up with the career you want. Build routine career planning into your school schedule so at the beginning of each school year, you know you are choosing the right courses and outside activities.

Research your ideal career. Research in this sense means gathering information—from books, magazines, the Internet, family, friends, teachers, counselors, and employers and employees in your career field.

What do you think?

Use **TM07-02**.
Students' answers will vary.

TEACH

Emphasize the general motivation and planning guidelines on pages 121–122 of the text. To be sure students understand the guidelines, have them give examples to explain each guideline.

ONLINE RESOURCES

Check out the web site **www.investigatingyourcareer.com** for teacher resources, student activities, and replacements for broken links for this chapter. To access the teacher resources:

Username: career
Password: investigate

Ask students what matters most to them, including what is essential or very important in their lives. Teenagers have indicated in surveys that being well-off financially and raising a family are far more important for their future happiness than anything else. Other categories, which were at least 20 percentage points behind, were being an authority in their field, developing a meaningful philosophy of life, becoming successful in their own business, and becoming a community leader. Discuss these results with students, encouraging them to express their opinions. Ask if the categories in the survey are the things that motivate them.

APPLY

Have students complete **Activity 7-1, "Long-Term Ambitions,"** that appears on page 134. Teaching suggestions and the solution for this activity appear on page 134. An activity worksheet can be found on the Career Portfolio and Resource CD— **Text Activity 07-1.doc.**

Identify the possible routes to your ideal career, and select the best one. Several routes may exist to your career choice, including an associate's or bachelor's degree, technical training, an apprenticeship, military service, an internship, on-the-job training, and others. Evaluate the alternatives and choose those that fit your needs.

Divide your career plan into small steps. Your task will seem much smaller if you divide your career plan into many small steps. Then you can see your accomplishments as you progress.

Decide whether any of the steps will be easier if you get help. One benefit of planning is that you can identify ways people can help you. For example, your counselor, teacher, or media center person can tell you about good web sites to visit to learn about your ideal career. Family members, friends, and other people may be able to help you by talking to you about your career choices.

Work backward from the date you want to reach your ideal career; then set intermediate deadlines. Planning works best when you do it backward. That isn't as odd as it sounds. If you know you want to start your career by age 21, ask yourself when you need to finish your training and what type of training you'll be able to obtain within your time frame.

Understand the order of the steps: put first things first. Following through in the right order is often a key to career planning. Figure out what stages are likely to produce results that will lead you to the other steps. Volunteer work, for instance, will provide experience for future employment.

Put your career plan in writing. Writing your plan helps you identify any gaps or problems and motivates you to take action. A written plan also helps you remember all the good ideas you had.

Periodically evaluate your progress and make revisions as needed. Even the best career planners can't foresee everything that may happen along the way. Schedule an annual review of your progress, and decide whether to modify your plan. Unexpected circumstances may also cause you to revise your plan. If, for instance, your family decides to move to another state, will your school offer the classes you need? Will you need to enroll in a different training program that requires more (or less) time to finish?

Maintain flexibility. The best career plans can be adapted to allow for unexpected events. Suppose you're offered an internship that provides great on-the-job training but lengthens your time in school. To take advantage of the internship opportunity, you can develop an alternative plan, called a **backup plan**. Your backup plan would add a semester or two to your continuing education plan.

Activity 7-1, "Long-Term Ambitions," will help you understand how to plan backward.

CAREER SUCCESS TIP

If you have a big project, break up the project into chunks to make it easier to complete.

CAREER SUCCESS TIP

Make a Time Line
Choosing a career and finding the right path to success in that career can seem overwhelming to young people. To help students with goal planning, have them make a visual time line. They should begin by making the big-picture list using the information on this page. At the beginning of the time line, they should set today's date. Next, they should set an end goal and a date for that goal and then fill in the middle. Suggest that students hang their time lines on their walls at home.

Reaching Your Goals

Goals can be grouped according to how long you think it will take for you to achieve them. **Long-term goals** are those you expect to achieve in five or more years. **Mid-term goals** are those you expect to achieve in one to two years. **Short-term goals** are those you expect to achieve in one to six months.

> What short-term and mid-term goals will you need to achieve to reach your long-term career goals? What are you doing now to achieve your short-term goals?
>
> **What do you think?**

Your long-term goal may be to become an executive in a company in your career field. But to reach this goal, you first must set and achieve several short-term and mid-term goals. One important mid-term goal may be to work as a sales representative in your career field. A short-term goal may be to take a job as an assistant or a technician in your career field.

Raniero wanted to be a lawyer for as long as he could remember. He took a stand on many issues, arguing his side with confidence. In his classes, he was first to volunteer to speak about the environment, politics, and other interests. He spent many hours researching his "cases" for papers and speeches—and to help him win arguments with friends. His excitement lasted long after the talking stopped. Raniero ran for office to gain experience as a student leader.

During his job shadowing, Raniero learned that many lawyers had participated in debate in school. So Raniero joined the debate and speech teams. When he was a sophomore, he began part-time work in his uncle's law office. The work was valuable, and it gave him a realistic picture of a lawyer's daily life. After his first summer of work, Raniero revised his school schedule to include more English classes to gain additional writing experience. Now Raniero is a senior in high school. He recently began a half-day internship in the district attorney's office. All of Raniero's research and experience has reinforced his desire to be a lawyer. He feels confident his career plan is on the right track.

Raniero's goals began early. He recognized that reaching his long-term goals would mean setting and revising short- and mid-term goals along the way.

Setting goals is an important part of your entire life, not just your career. You will also set goals for your personal life, goals that are based on your values and your habits. Examples of personal goals include becoming physically fit, being considered reliable and honest, and keeping your living space and workspace organized. The principles for setting and achieving goals are the same whether the goals are personal or career goals.

Activity 7-2, "Achieving Goals," will help you focus on the relationships among your short-term, mid-term, and long-term goals.

Strategies for Setting Goals

You can apply various techniques to help you set useful goals that will lead to success. Goals must be useful, or you will ignore them. When you set your goals, be sure each goal is:

- **Realistic.** Your goals should be things you know you can actually accomplish. If math is your weakest subject, should you plan a career as an accountant?

- **Challenging.** Your goals should require you to make an effort. Otherwise, you'll lose motivation.

- **Important.** Your goals should represent what you are most eager to achieve. You'll work harder to reach them.

- **Positive.** Your goals should be expressed in positive terms, such as "Take geometry," rather than "Don't take algebra." Positive statements motivate you to succeed.

CAREER SUCCESS TIP

A goal not written is only a wish.

Successful goal setting involves paying attention to all of your goals and working to see that they support one another. Identify those goals that have the highest priority for your career and your personal life. Make sure these major goals are compatible. For example, suppose you set two goals: "Learn to play the piano" and "Play an instrument in the school marching band." While you can achieve both of these goals, you will likely have to consider them as unrelated goals that require different strategies for success.

Putting your goals in writing will help you clearly identify what you want to achieve. Each goal should have a specific, measurable objective so you know when you have achieved the goal. Written goals also increase your personal commitment to your goals, which can provide motivation for working hard to reach them. The satisfaction of accomplishing even a minor goal can inspire you toward working on and achieving your next goal.

Plan to review and revise your goals periodically. You are growing as a person, and as you change, your goals will evolve and change too.

CAREER SUCCESS TIP

Writing Down Your Goals

Have students spend 20 minutes journal writing about their life goals. Ask students to choose one goal and write a short positive statement they can recite over and over to remind themselves they can obtain this goal. Tell students studies show it takes 21 days to form a habit, so they are to say their positive statement three times each day for 21 days. Suggest they write their positive statement on note cards and post them in different places.

Time Lines for Goals

To achieve most long-term goals, you must attain a number of short-term and mid-term goals. Each long-term goal consists of steps or activities you must accomplish before you can achieve the long-term goal. By setting target dates for completing each step or goal, you will be able to plan more effectively. The following guidelines describe how to develop a time line for a long-term goal:

- Determine how much time is required to meet each step or goal.
- Divide the time needed into smaller components. Are days, weeks, or months needed for reaching your short-term goals? How much time will it take to achieve each mid-term goal? How many months or years will it take until you can reach your long-term goal?
- Use a desk calendar, a planner, or an agenda to schedule the day, month, or year by which each step should be completed.
- Write down your time line, including all the steps necessary to reach your long-term goal.

> **Start by doing what is necessary, then what is possible, and suddenly you are doing the impossible.**
> —*St. Francis of Assisi*

Have you ever used a time line to try to meet a goal? Did it help you reach the goal? *What do you think?*

Kyle, an eighth-grade student, prepared the time line below. Although each of his intermediate goals is specific, some will require additional steps to complete them. For example, the goal of spending a summer working in Spain will probably require Kyle to research and investigate the types of jobs available, learn how to apply for work in a foreign country, earn money to pay for the trip to Spain, and so on. Thus, as the time to achieve this intermediate goal gets shorter, Kyle will have to revise his time line to include various short-term goals.

Kyle's Time Line

My Long-Term Goal:	Target Date:
Be a Spanish translator for Americans working in Spain.	10 years

Intermediate Goals:

Intern for the American consulate in Spain	9 years
Major in Spanish language in college	5–8 years
Spend a summer working in Spain	6 years
Volunteer in summers for a Spanish-speaking community project	1–2 years
Take four years of high school Spanish	1 year
Become involved with the local Spanish-speaking community	Now
Tutor a new Spanish-speaking immigrant	Now

Activity 7-3, "Case Challenges," will help you understand how to set goals effectively.

TEACH

Explain that time lines are essential for achieving goals. Time lines show all the short-term and mid-term goals—the intermediary steps and activities—needed to achieve long-term goals. Students can better appreciate the time needed to achieve long-term goals if they set specific target dates for all goals.

What do you think?

Use **TM07-04**.
Students' answers will vary.

APPLY

Have students complete **Activity 7-3, "Case Challenges,"** on page 134. Teaching suggestions and the solution for this activity appear on page 134. An activity worksheet can be found on the Career Portfolio and Resource CD—**Text Activity 07-3.doc**.

DIFFERENT LEARNING STYLES

Kinesthetic Learners

Have students work in small groups to write, edit, and direct videos that illustrate time lines for goals. For example, student actors might wear different costumes to represent different phases of growing up, going to college, and beginning a career. Each actor would say a few lines about his or her goal. Encourage students to be creative in making their videos. Videos must include at least three goals—a short-term goal, a mid-term goal, and a long-term goal.

> " It's not hard to make decisions when you know what your values are. "
>
> —Roy Disney,
> Walt Disney Company

Your Action Plans

Preparing Action Plans is key to achieving your goals. An **Action Plan** is a strategy that shows how to get from where you are to where you want to be. It is like a map of your future. An Action Plan details everything you need to know to reach a goal. An Action Plan has a starting point and a destination—a goal—and lists the skills and knowledge you need to reach your destination. In a way, an Action Plan allows you to look into the future. The following paragraphs describe some of the important points you should consider as you develop an Action Plan.

Use Your Strengths and Talents

Your *Internal Career Design* is based on your passion, talents, and strengths—your *P*A*T*H to Success*. Your Action Plan should describe how you plan to use your strengths and talents to fulfill your passion. For example, if music is your passion, your Action Plan might identify the steps needed to develop a career as a performance musician. Remember your talents and passion when you develop an Action Plan.

Remember Your Values

What do you think?
What happens when one value conflicts with another value?

Recall the inventory of your values that you developed in Chapter 3. Your values guide you through life and should be considered when you develop an Action Plan.

> Jeronda loved biology, especially studying animals. She knew her career focus should involve biology and research. Her biology teacher, Mr. Braun, sent her to interview for a job in the university's biology lab. After a successful interview, Jeronda toured the lab, where she discovered that the university used animals for testing. Even though the job seemed ideal and paid more than working for a veterinarian, Jeronda turned down the job offer. She loved animals. She didn't want a part in harming them, even for the purpose of research.

When life situations—such as career decisions—are at odds with your values, you experience conflict. Let your values guide you as you make decisions for your career and your future.

Look over the Horizon

The U.S. job market is in a constant state of change. Old industries fade and new ones take their place. Some career fields have too many workers for the number of available jobs, while others cannot find enough people to fill the openings. An Action Plan should look ahead and see if the career you are considering will be there—not only when you start your first job but also 10 or 15 years in the future.

INTEGRATED ACADEMICS
Social Studies
Ask students if their values are affected by the media—television, movies, video games, and music videos. Ask students to keep a log for one week of the media they are exposed to. Along the left side of the page, they should write the name of the media and the show, game, or video. Across from this, on the right side of the paper, they should jot down a few words about how they feel. At the end of the week, ask students again how their values are affected by the media.

Regardless of the career field you choose, be sure to look across the entire range of careers in that field. For example, suppose your passion is healing and helping others and you are planning a medical career. Many people automatically think "doctor" when they imagine a career in the healthcare field. But medicine also includes medical researchers, nurses, pharmaceutical salespeople, designers of medical equipment, acupuncturists, technicians, and many more. The wider the career choices within your field of interest, the better off you will be.

Role of People

Your Action Plan is likely to include people in different roles. Some people will have already helped you. You are responsible for acknowledging the help you have received. If your Action Plan calls for a financial commitment from your family so you can get a good education, then you have a responsibility to make the necessary effort to do well. If an internship employer gives you an opportunity to gain job experience, then you have a responsibility to provide high-quality work.

You may also turn to others for information, advice, or assistance in getting a job or an internship in your field. Your Action Plan should include a list of people you can rely on for advice and assistance. Include their phone numbers and e-mail addresses so you know how to contact them when you need to talk or meet with them.

One of the important steps for success is finding a mentor. **Mentors** are experienced people you can turn to when you have a complex decision to make or a problem to solve on the job. Mentors make themselves available to suggest positive approaches, point out pitfalls, and make suggestions. Sometimes they work where you do, but not always. As you advance in your career, you will meet men and women you respect and who listen to you and help you. Successful people know that mentors make a difference. You would be smart to find a mentor for every job you take.

Do you know anyone who might serve as your mentor? What questions would you like to ask this person?

What do you think?

Use Activity 7-4, "Coming to Terms," to understand some of the important terms in this chapter more thoroughly.

TEACH

Discuss how mentors can help students at every stage of their career journey, and encourage them to find a mentor if they don't have one. Explain what defines a positive relationship with a mentor, and ask students who have a mentor to discuss the relationship. Encourage students to model the behavior of their mentor and to ask their mentor's advice in setting and achieving goals.

What do you think?

Use **TM07-06**.
Students' answers will vary.

APPLY

Have students complete **Activity 7-4, "Coming to Terms,"** on page 135. Teaching suggestions and the solution for this activity appear on page 135. An activity worksheet can be found on the Career Portfolio and Resource CD—**Text Activity 07-4.doc**.

DIFFERENT LEARNING ABILITIES
Attention Deficit Disorder
Have students work in pairs to create flash cards of key information from this chapter. On one side of the card, have students write a question taken from the material in the chapter. On the back, they should write the answer. Students should read the text and then use the flash cards to review the key information. Instruct students to put cards for incorrectly answered questions in one stack and cards for correctly answered questions in another. Have pairs talk about any questions that were answered incorrectly.

Remind students that part-time work is not for everyone. Even though part-time work generally teaches responsibility and economics, students who work more than 20 hours a week often have lower grades and insufficient interaction with family members. Students should discuss with their families the pluses and minuses of working part-time jobs. If they or their families notice any negative effects, students should be prepared to quit working.

Part-time work may include babysitting, mowing grass, and other work that doesn't involve students getting a paycheck. Internships for younger students may include working for a teacher, being a teacher's helper or aide, or assisting a group of campers or a Sunday school class. In other words, internships may be informal arrangements, especially for younger students.

Have students complete **Activity 7-B, "Should You Work Part-Time?,"** found in the *Investigating Your Career Activities & Projects* book.

This activity helps students assess whether part-time work is an appropriate option for them at this time or in the near future. The quiz also helps them analyze their attitudes toward money and work. If time permits, discuss the results as a class. **Solution:** The solution for this activity appears in the *Teacher's Edition* of *Investigating Your Career Activities & Projects*.

Have students complete **Activity 7-5, "Plan of Action,"** on page 135. Teaching suggestions and the solution for this activity appear on page 135. An activity worksheet can be found on the Career Portfolio and Resource CD—**Text Activity 07-5.doc**.

Part-Time Jobs

If you can find a paid internship or a summer job in your field, do it. While such jobs are most likely entry level, you get a feel for the day-to-day responsibilities and career possibilities. Several positive benefits may result from part-time work experience:

- You may become passionate about the work and even more committed to sticking with your Action Plan.
- You may decide this is not the field for you. Great! You now have the opportunity to search for a more compatible career.
- You may have the opportunity to develop a mentor.
- You will gain experience in working with others in a job situation. Good interpersonal skills are as important to your long-term success as the hands-on job skills you develop.
- If you receive a salary, you can begin to learn how to budget your resources. The sooner you learn how to manage your money, the better your chances of reaching your personal and career goals.

REAL PEOPLE
REAL CAREERS

Toy Photographer

When Sharon Estano was a child, she did what most children did. She played with toys. But that wasn't all. She loved scenery, the beautiful pictures that nature offered. Her family noticed her fascination and bought Sharon her first camera when she was in the seventh grade. The camera was easy for Sharon to use; she could just point and shoot. The camera opened up a new world for Sharon. Taking pictures of nature was her passion. Wherever she went, her camera was with her.

With her family's encouragement, Sharon developed the confidence to experiment on her own, learning what worked and what didn't. Sharon's passion for photography and videos inspired her to enroll in the Electronic Media program at the local university. She became fascinated with the power and flexibility of taking still pictures with digital cameras. With the help of her mentor, Professor Sanders, Sharon extended her creativity by learning to use computer software to process photographs, correct color, and alter images. When she received her associate degree, she was hired by Hasbro. Hasbro makes Milton Bradley, Tonka, Parker Brothers, Playskool, and other brands of toys and games.

Now Sharon shoots photographs of action toys for use in e-commerce. Designers use her shots for paint approval, design changes, and packaging options. She is a vital part of Hasbro's marketing effort, she loves what she does, and she still gets to play with toys.

To learn more about photography as a career:
- explore *http://stats.bls.gov*. Go to the *Occupational Outlook Handbook*. Using the A-Z Index, choose "Photographers" and "Camera Operators."
- check out *http://photography.about.com/cs/businessmatters*.

Source: Estano, Sharon. "Life Beyond the Program or My Personal Toy Story." *E-Media Tech Trends*, Summer 2000, 1.

REAL PEOPLE—REAL CAREER
Photography
Provide students with several different magazines on photography. Arrange students into groups. Give each group a few magazines. Have groups use the magazines, the Internet, and the library to research careers in photography. Have each group choose one field of photography, such as commercial photography or fashion photography. Ask each group to give an oral report on its findings. Each member of the group is to take part in researching, writing, and presenting the report.

Use Activity 7-5, "Plan of Action," to practice developing Action Plans for two of your long-term goals.

Roadblocks

Roadblocks are obstacles that slow or stop progress. Some of the common roadblocks to career success are the following:

- Difficult school courses
- Inability to concentrate
- Indecision
- Distractions
- Procrastination
- Lack of money for education
- Strong competition for jobs

What roadblocks have you faced in the past as you tried to reach a goal? In looking back, how did you—or how could you have—overcome the roadblock?

What do you think?

Andrew knew he wanted to be a doctor. And Andrew knew where he wanted to attend college—at the state university a few hours from his home. When Andrew was in the seventh grade, his counselor, Mrs. Christos, met Andrew and his parents for a scheduling conference. Mrs. Christos urged Andrew to begin a foreign language in the eighth grade. By starting a language early, Andrew could get four years of a language completed before his senior year. Many universities required four years of a foreign language for admission. Andrew insisted he would need only two years, which is all the state university required. So Andrew set up a five-year schedule that included starting a foreign language in the eleventh grade.

The summer after ninth grade Andrew won a scholarship to attend a science camp at Webster Hall, a prestigious university. The professors admired Andrew's work at the camp so much that they offered him an assistant's position for the next summer. With that summer job, Andrew would be eligible for a large tuition scholarship to attend Webster.

When Andrew returned to school, he told Mrs. Christos about his plan to go to Webster Hall instead of the state university. She looked up Webster Hall's admission requirements. The school required four years of a foreign language. Unfortunately, Andrew would be beginning a foreign language his junior year. Andrew had created his own roadblock. Now he had to decide how to overcome it. He knew he would be accepted at the state university with his schedule as planned. Or he could try to take distance learning foreign language courses during his vacations and summer break to increase his number of foreign language

CAREER SUCCESS TIP

Study successful people in your chosen career field. What characteristics do they have that make them successful? Do you possess some of these characteristics?

TEACH

Explain that because they are evolving and changing, students may need to revise or change some of their goals. Reviewing goals periodically allows students to revise the goals and helps avoid unexpected roadblocks. Students should have a backup plan for each of their major goals in case a goal needs to be changed.

What do you think?

Use **TM07-07**.
Students' answers will vary.

TEACH

Explain that one backup plan may be to pursue a dream part-time instead of full-time. If plans to achieve a dream fall apart, perhaps because the person is unable to earn enough money to live the dream, the dream can become a secondary career that is financed by a full-time job.

ENRICH

Have students complete **Activity 7-C, "Reaching Short-Term Goals,"** found in the *Investigating Your Career Activities & Projects* book.
Although similar to Activity 6-7, this activity allows students to consider other careers related to the ones they researched. The interview may provide them with career possibilities that they had not considered.
Solution: The solution for this activity appears in the *Teacher's Edition* of *Investigating Your Career Activities & Projects*.

CAREER SUCCESS TIP

Successful people share common characteristics. Most successful people have an attitude of cooperation, a creative spirit, and a willingness to step out ahead of the norm. John Lennon and Paul McCartney, part of one of the world's most famous rock groups—The Beatles—certainly show all three of these characteristics. From 1962 to 1970, The Beatles recorded 214 songs, many of them written by Lennon or McCartney. By studying successful people, students can learn which positive characteristics to develop.

—Source: www.aboutfamouspeople.com

> 66 **Procrastination is the art of keeping up with yesterday.** 99
>
> —*Don Marquis, Philosopher*

credits. However, to take four years of a language in two years would be very stressful. A backup plan would be to take a foreign language at the local university and enter Webster Hall one semester late. Andrew decided he preferred to attend Webster Hall and didn't want to delay his start there, so he signed up for the distance learning courses. He redid his time lines and Action Plans for his goals, creating a backup plan. Then Andrew promised himself he would not delay anything that could affect his future.

You can anticipate some roadblocks—based on your Action Plans and your knowledge of the goals you have chosen. Other roadblocks, such as an illness in the family that causes you to interrupt your education, cannot be anticipated.

If you can anticipate a roadblock, you can prepare for it. When you develop your Action Plans, look for possible roadblocks to reaching your goals. Develop backup plans for overcoming these roadblocks.

The following strategies can help you overcome roadblocks:

- Ask for guidance from someone who understands your situation. For example, if your family does not have the financial resources to send you to college, discuss your options with your guidance counselor.
- Break a roadblock into smaller problems, and try to find a solution to each problem.

Activity 7-6, "Learning from Others," helps you learn how to identify roadblocks and develop strategies for overcoming them.

Budgeting

Budgeting is simply a realistic look at your income compared to your expenses. While this does not seem like a difficult idea, the inability to prepare and follow a budget is a roadblock to success for many people. Many men and women have reached or exceeded their career goals, only to be undone financially by their failure to control spending.

While teens have learned how to spend money—an astounding $153 billion annually—they don't know how to budget or save money. Such ignorance can lead to real financial problems. A survey of recent college graduates found that 35 percent had debt payments of more than $1,000 a month unrelated to their education.

Credit card companies contribute to the financial problems of students. An 18-year-old college freshman often has little trouble securing a credit card in his or her name—and, unfortunately, has little trouble getting into debt with it. The average undergraduate leaves college with almost $3,000 in credit card debt.

Without a budget and the ability to follow it, you could have all the talent in the world and still be financially unsuccessful. A budget is an essential part of your Action Plan. It gives you the information you need to make wise decisions, to know what is realistic and what is not.

Here are sources of income to consider as you work toward a career:

- Scholarships
- Support from family members
- Part-time work
- Student loans

Here are expenses to consider:

- Cost of food at home
- Cost of food away from home
- Housing (home and away)
- Clothing, including dry cleaning and laundry
- Transportation (travel to and from college or work; car costs, including insurance, fuel, and maintenance; mass transit or cab fare)
- Health and personal care
- Entertainment
- Education and training costs
- Paycheck deductions (taxes, retirement, dues)
- Miscellaneous expenditures

Everyone practices some degree of budgeting every day, probably without thinking about it. Suppose you have $5.25 with you, and you want to buy a magazine that costs $4.00. If you are hungry too, you know you cannot spend more than $1.25 on food if you are going to buy the magazine. That's budgeting—making decisions about your expenses based on the money you have available. Of course, budgeting for your education and life is more complicated than that—but it is not overwhelming. Budgeting is a way of maintaining control over your finances, whether they are large or small.

Activity 7-7, "Budgeting," will help you complete a budget that identifies your sources of income and your expenditures.

CAREER FACT

A credit check is standard for employees in the finance industry or any industry where workers handle a firm's money. Companies are unlikely to hire you to take care of their money if you can't manage your own.

ENRICH

Have students complete **Activity 7-D, "Potential Earnings,"** found in the *Investigating Your Career Activities & Projects* book.

This activity helps students gain a more realistic picture of potential earnings for common careers. Students also begin to see the relationship between education and income earned, including the relationship between skills in math, science, and technology and earning power.
Solution: The solution for this activity appears in the *Teacher's Edition* of *Investigating Your Career Activities & Projects.*

ENRICH

Have students complete **Activity 7-E, "The Good Life,"** found in the *Investigating Your Career Activities & Projects* book.

Students examine and evaluate their personal attitudes toward credit by analyzing appropriate and inappropriate use of credit cards. By examining the aspects of what they perceive to be the "good life," students should discover more stability in their thinking about material goods and the use of credit.
Solution: The solution for this activity appears in the *Teacher's Edition* of *Investigating Your Career Activities & Projects.*

CAREER TREND

Maintain Good Credit

Unless students are majoring in business or finance, they may never take an accounting or business math course. Suggest that students take a beginning accounting or business math course to help them with their personal finances and in their careers. If students miss this important step in their high school and college education, they can enroll in a course later through a community college, the Internet, or an adult education program.

TEACH

In your discussion of the bulleted list on page 132 of the student text, emphasize the importance of time management to students. Time management helps them plan their work and work their plan. They will be able to manage interruptions rather than letting interruptions control them. Ask students if they have learned any other tips that help them manage their time.

Remind students that they should schedule time each week, daily if possible, for activities they enjoy. By managing their time effectively, they can take part in these activities.

APPLY

Have students complete **Activity 7-8, "Managing Your Time,"** on page 136. Teaching suggestions and the solution for this activity appear on page 136. An activity worksheet can be found on the Career Portfolio and Resource CD—**Text Activity 07-8.pdf**.

CLOSE

Wrap up this chapter by having students complete **Activity 7-F, "Priorities,"** found in the *Investigating Your Career Activities & Projects* book.

In this activity, students create and prioritize their tasks for a week using information from Activity 7-8, Part 2. They analyze why they have chosen their priorities.

Solution: The solution for this activity appears in the *Teacher's Edition* of *Investigating Your Career Activities & Projects*.

> **66** Decide what your priorities are and how much time you'll spend on them. If you don't, someone else will.**99**
>
> —Harvey Mackay,
> *SAM's Club Source*

How often do you find there are not enough hours in the day to complete everything you need to do? How often are you late in finishing an extracurricular project or a homework assignment? Have you ever wondered whether there might be a better way to use your time?

It's the week before the Harvest Dance when Miss Hopper assigns a research paper—due the Monday after Harvest Weekend. The dance is Friday, so Mercedes knows she must finish her English paper *before* Monday's deadline. Finishing a paper early is something she's never done before, but she already has much of her research done. Anyway, in this case, she has no choice; she must finish by Friday. Mercedes decides to write down her schedule. She thinks she will be more likely to accomplish her goals by committing to a time line on paper.

Mercedes' plan is to finish her research and outline the paper tonight. Then she'll be able to write the rough draft on Tuesday. She sets aside Wednesday to meet with Gregor, who can help her edit the rough draft. After her session with Gregor on Wednesday, she might have time to begin writing the final draft. That leaves Thursday to finish her rewrite of the final draft and to key it on her computer. Then Mercedes can enjoy a worry-free Harvest Weekend!

Before you can manage your time effectively, you need to find out how you are spending it. By keeping track of how you spend your time for a week, you will have a good idea of where your time wasters are and how you can save time. After you know how you spend your time, the following tips can help you manage your time more effectively:

- **Learn to say no.** You really don't have to do what everyone asks of you.
- **Learn to set priorities.** Make sure you spend time on the things that are most important to you.
- **Don't be a perfectionist.** You can spend more time than necessary on trying to make something perfect. Know when to quit working on a project.
- **Learn how to schedule.** Taking time to make a schedule will often save you time in the long run.
- **Avoid procrastination.** Delaying finishing a task does not make it any easier to complete, and you waste time in rescheduling the task.
- **Set deadlines.** Setting a date when a task must be finished forces you to manage your time in order to meet the deadline.

Activity 7-8, "Managing Your Time," will help you analyze how well you manage your time.

INTEGRATED ACADEMICS
Business Basics

Time management is an important part of being successful in business. Have students keep a log of how they spend their time every day for one week. At the end of the week, have students make up a schedule and try this schedule for one week. At the end of this week, have students revise their schedules. Ask them to continue this exercise until they have a good idea of how they are spending their time and can make a realistic schedule that fits their lives.

- **I know that to be successful, I need to motivate myself.**

  Self-motivation is the determination to stay on track and avoid distractions. Self-motivation helps me take charge of my life and feel good about each accomplishment that brings me closer to my goals. I need to be self-motivated to stick to career planning.

- **I understand the differences among long-term, mid-term, and short-term goals.**

  Long-term goals are those I expect to achieve in five or more years. Mid-term goals are those I expect to achieve in one to two years. Short-term goals are those I expect to achieve in one to six months. To achieve most long-term goals, I will need to achieve a number of short-term and mid-term goals.

- **I can develop an Action Plan for a long-term goal.**

  An Action Plan details everything I need to know to reach a goal. An Action Plan should describe (1) how I plan to use my strengths and talents to fulfill my passion, (2) how my values will affect my decisions, (3) available careers in the future and the range of careers in a field, (4) people who have already helped me or who I think can assist me in the future, and (5) part-time work experience.

- **I can develop strategies for overcoming roadblocks.**

  If I can anticipate a roadblock, I can prepare for it. My Action Plan should include possible roadblocks and my back-up plans for overcoming these roadblocks. One strategy for overcoming a roadblock is to break it down into smaller parts and then try to find a solution for each part.

- **I can create a budget.**

  Budgeting is a realistic look at my income compared to my expenses. By creating a budget, I can maintain control over my finances. A budget gives me the information I need to make wise decisions.

- **I can manage my time.**

  Before I can manage my time effectively, I need to find out how I am spending it. Some tips for managing my time effectively include learning to say no, setting priorities, not trying to be a perfectionist, learning how to schedule, avoiding procrastination, and setting deadlines.

IN A NUTSHELL

Remind students about the objectives set forth at the beginning of the chapter, and use this summary to reinforce the concepts presented in this chapter.

Career Journal

Ask students to spend 10 minutes writing Career Journal entries that answer the following questions:
1. How well did what you thought you knew match what the chapter presented?
2. What questions do you now have about the chapter topics, and where do you think you can find the answers to those questions?
3. How will the content of the chapter help you investigate *your* career?

ASSESS

Administer the printed objective test for Chapter 7, available with this package. Test solutions are found in the *Teacher's Edition* of *Investigating Your Career Chapter Tests*. Use the **Exam**View® CD to create your own objective test for this chapter.

Suggestions for Parents and Family Members

Supporting Goals and Action Plans
Parents and family members need to support the career discovery process of teens. Ways they can assist teens with the topics in this chapter include:

1. Help your child to select courses that explore career options or support career goals.
2. Ask periodically to see your teen's Career Journey Folders; discuss how the contents of the folder can help your child create goals and Action Plans.
3. Encourage your child to set goals and make Action Plans.

Activity 7-1: Long-Term Ambitions

This activity encourages students to dream about what their life will be like when they are 30 years old. It also provides a dash of realism by having them describe the events that must occur for them to have their dream life. Often students are either too ambitious and imagine much more than they could accomplish or they are not ambitious enough and do not give themselves enough credit for what they can accomplish. The only limitations are that their ambitions must be legal and their career must produce income. Students may be able to visualize their ambitions better if they use a time line or label each event by years. If necessary, refer students to the sample time line in Activity 1-2.

Encourage students to complete this activity by themselves, perhaps as an overnight assignment. Students tend to "borrow" others' ideas rather than create the life *they* want to have. However, you may want to allow them to edit their answers after the class has shared some of its goals. **Solution:** Answers will vary. Be sure students include all the categories suggested in the activity and the events are as concrete as possible.

Activity 7-2: Achieving Goals

In this activity, students write long-term, mid-term, and short-term goals for the four major categories of their future—education, career, family, and home. Goals are based on the ambitions students described in Activity 7-1. Emphasize that students' career goals must produce income and must be legal. Explain that students who want to be homemakers should always have an income-producing career as a backup plan. Encourage students to complete this activity by themselves or with a partner.
Solution: Answers will vary. Students should write at least one long-term, one mid-term, and one short-term goal for each category. You may want to have students write more goals, especially mid-term and short-term goals, but writing even one goal gives students practice and a concrete beginning. If you grade this

Imagine where you want to be when you are 30 years old. Think about what education you will have, what your career will be, what your family will be like, and where you will live.

1. On a separate sheet of paper, write a brief description of each of these characteristics of your life at age 30.

2. Working backward, write down the events or steps that will need to occur for you to have the life you described in Question 1.

You will use these long-term ambitions in Activity 7-2.

Think about the long-term goals you want to achieve by age 30. These goals are likely to be the same as the long-term ambitions you described in Activity 7-1. You will use these goals in Activity 7-5.

1. Write at least one long-term goal in each of the following categories. Use a separate sheet of paper for each category.
   - Education
   - Career
   - Family
   - Home

2. Write one or more mid-term goals for each of the categories in Question 1.

3. Write one or more short-term goals for each of the categories in Question 1.

With a partner, develop strategies to meet the short-term, mid-term, and long-term goals listed below. Write the first step for each.

1. You want to get your homework finished on time.

2. You want to make new friends.

3. You want to break a bad habit. (List the habit.)

4. You want to arrive at school or work on time.

5. You want to improve your appearance. (List the feature you want to change.)

6. You want to save money for something special. (List the special item.)

7. You want to get a part-time job in the career field you chose in Chapter 6.

assignment, do not correct the goals. However, you may suggest ways to make the goals more tangible.

Activity 7-3: Case Challenges

This activity helps students understand how to achieve goals by having them describe ways to meet goals that are common in their everyday lives. Working with a partner will help students devise more approaches to solving the problems by setting goals. Although students are required to write only one step for each situation, encourage them to write more.
Solution: Answers will vary. However, answers should be as concrete as possible, with students incorporating action verbs and time lines for the completion of each step.

ACTIVITY 7-4	**Coming to Terms**

On a separate sheet of paper, describe the importance of each of the following to your career.

1. Self-motivation

2. Backup plan

3. Long-term goals

4. Mid-term goals

5. Short-term goals

6. Action Plan

7. Mentors

ACTIVITY 7-5	**Plan of Action**

An Action Plan will help you determine all the steps and events needed to reach your long-term goals. It will detail everything you need to know to achieve a goal.

1. Select one long-term career goal and one long-term education goal from the goals you listed in Activity 7-2.

2. Write an Action Plan for each of the goals you selected in Question 1. Be sure to include all necessary details.

3. Write down two things you can do immediately to work on your education goal. Examples include completing an assignment, improving your grade in a class, and searching for a college.

4. Write down three specific skills you need for the career area you chose in Chapter 6. Include how you can obtain them. For example, if your career area is programming, skills could include learning advanced business applications or passing the math proficiency test.

ACTIVITY 7-6	**Learning from Others**

With a family member or another adult, brainstorm several roadblocks that stand between you and your career goal. Consider all sources of roadblocks—financial, educational, personal, and anything else that could stand in your way. List the roadblocks on a separate sheet of paper.

Working with the same person, devise a plan to overcome each of the roadblocks you identified. For example, if finances present a problem, list potential sources of income to pay for your education (scholarship, loan, work, and family). Or if moving away from home presents a problem because of an illness in the family, list options for remaining nearby.

CHAPTER 7 · · · · · SETTING GOALS

135

Activity 7-4: Coming to Terms

This activity checks students' understanding of how some of the terms in this chapter apply to students' careers. Discuss the definitions of the terms before students begin answering the questions. Encourage students to be specific in their answers.
Solution: Answers will vary.

Activity 7-5: Plan of Action

This activity guides students in developing a strategy and lets them begin to take the steps necessary for achieving two of the goals written in Activity 7-2. Emphasize that students must write steps they can begin immediately. Review with students the benefits of starting their Action Plans now.
Solution: Answers will vary. Action Plans should be as specific as possible.

Activity 7-6: Learning from Others

This activity helps students identify and develop strategies for overcoming roadblocks that might impede their career journey. Working with a family member, a mentor (such as a teacher or an employer), or another adult, students can learn firsthand about roadblocks they may encounter in achieving their goals. Students may want to ask the adults about roadblocks they have encountered and the changes the adults made in their career goals. The adults can help students understand that in the real world, things do not always work out as planned.

Explain to students that they should work with an adult with whom they can talk openly. Encourage them to be specific in the strategies they identify to overcome roadblocks. Some of the roadblocks students identify may involve common fears, such as fear of failing, being rejected, enduring pain and sacrifice, making the wrong choice, not being in control, or being successful.
Solution: Answers will vary. You may want to discuss some of the roadblocks identified to expand students' awareness of types of possible roadblocks.

Activity 7-7: Budgeting

This activity gives students practice in writing a budget. It also forces students to face the reality that their incomes may not always be enough to allow them to purchase everything they want. Emphasize that for a budget to provide information, students must list all expenditures. Also point out that as their lives change, they should update their budgets to help them plan their expenditures.

Solution: Answers will vary. Your class discussion after students complete their budgets should focus on the questions at the end of the activity. Help students realize both the short-term and long-term consequences of not living within their budgets.

Activity 7-8: Managing Your Time

Part 1—Time Management Quiz: This quiz gives students insight into their time management skills and helps them realize why they don't seem to have time to do the things they enjoy doing.

Solution: Answers and scores will vary. After students score their quizzes, discuss the quiz in class. Point out how each statement reflects effective time management.

Part 2—Weekly Time Planner: This activity provides students with a method to help manage their time effectively. Have students use a blank form to record their activities for a week. Then using the information from this form, have them plan their next week's activities on a blank form. Tell them to be sure to allow time for the things they enjoy. Explain that they need to determine:

• The best time and place to do each activity.

• The amount of time needed to do each activity.

• Whether an activity is worth doing or is a time waster.

Many schools provide students with planners, or agendas, for recording their assignments and activities. If your school provides these books, use them for the planning portion of this assignment. Encourage students to use their planner at the beginning of the week to schedule their time for the entire week.

136

Print the budget outline from your CD, or use the handout from your teacher. Log on to _www.jumpstart.org_ to learn of typical budget needs and the amount of money needed to cover a budget. Create a personal budget based on your current income (part-time job, allowance, the amount your family spends on you each week) and your current expenditures. Is your income more than your expenditures? What adjustments do you need to make?

ACTIVITY 7-8   **Managing Your Time**

Part 1—Time Management Quiz

The following quiz will help you determine how well you manage your time. Answer the questions on a separate sheet of paper. You may answer "yes," "no," or "sometimes."

1. I have a specific place where I always study.

2. I have a regular schedule for studying every day.

3. I plan my social life around my required assignments and tests.

4. When I study, I avoid distractions by turning off the television, not answering the telephone, and eliminating other distractions.

5. I use an agenda or a planner to plan my school, work, and social life.

6. I write my assignments and tests in my agenda or planner.

7. I start assignments when they are assigned, not just before they are due.

8. I review for my classes continuously, rather than just before a test.

9. I make time for fun (and household chores) every day.

10. I spend at least 20 minutes a day talking to family members.

Assign a point value to each of your answers: 3 points for "yes," 2 points for "sometimes," and 1 point for "no." Total the points and compare the total to the ranges below.

27–30 points	Excellent time management
20–26 points	Time management skills need improvement
10–19 points	Time management skills need immediate help

Part 2—Weekly Time Planner

Print the blank **Weekly Time Planner** from your CD, or use the handout from your teacher. Review the time management tips from this chapter, and then design a schedule using the blank **Weekly Time Planner.** Your schedule should allow you time to meet your commitments for a week and leave you time to relax.

136

Solution: Students' time plans will vary. Have students compare what they needed to do and what they wanted to do with what they actually completed when they recorded their activities. They should correct any discrepancies in their projected plans.

Career Preparation Choices

Will's passion was writing plays. He wanted to be able to earn a living as a playwright, so he looked for information that might help him achieve his goal. Will learned that knowing how the theater operated would help him become a playwright, so he joined the school drama club. He became involved in every aspect of producing a play—from building the set to directing lighting changes to acting.

In the fall semester of his junior year, he selected introductory courses in creative writing and audio engineering and won a role as a supporting actor in the high school production of *Anne Frank*. Later in his junior year, Will was able to job shadow a lighting technician at a downtown professional theater. He also set up a week's job shadowing experience with the managing director of the community playhouse.

Will looked for a part-time job and found one at the professional theater where he had job shadowed. The job allowed him to interact with the actors and stage crew and to learn more about theater operations. When the managing director asked if he would like to serve as a lighting intern for a major performance, Will was overjoyed. His theater experiences both at school and in the community reinforced his goal to be a playwright. Will followed his passion by majoring in performance writing in college and continuing to work in local productions.

How can your extracurricular activities at school and in the community help in your career planning?

What do you think?

OBJECTIVES

After completing this chapter, you will be able to:
- Explain how your goals influence your choice of education and training.
- Describe the education and training options available to you.
- Describe several ways to research your career area.

Key Terms:
- tech prep programs
- applied academics
- certificate
- cooperative (co-op) programs
- apprenticeship
- on-the-job training
- associate degree
- bachelor's degree

Chapter Overview

Chapter 8
Career Preparation Choices

FOCUS

In Chapter 8, students examine the various education and training options that prepare them for their career. By exploring all the options available, students can choose the path that best fits them and their career and lifestyle goals. Students learn about high school options, specialized high school alternatives, and postsecondary possibilities. Researching their career areas also helps them analyze the options.

Use the **Objectives** and **Key Terms** printed in the margin to help students focus on the content of this chapter. Use the **video segment** for Chapter 8 to trigger discussion.

What do you think?

Use **TM08-01**.
Students' answers will vary.

Career Journal

Ask students to spend 10 minutes writing Career Journal entries that answer the following questions:
1. What do you think this chapter will cover?
2. What do you already know about these topics?
3. What three things do you want to learn about these topics?

CHAPTER RESOURCES and MATERIALS

Activities & Projects book
Instructor's Resource CD
- Forms and Worksheets for Chapter Activities 8-1 through 8-4
- Internet Links for Chapter 8
- PowerPoint Presentation for Chapter 8
- Lesson Plans
- Teaching Masters for Chapter 8
- Video Discussion Guide for Chapter 8

Chapter Tests book
ExamView® CD
Video
Web Site

What do you think?

Use **TM08-02**.
Students' answers will vary.

APPLY

Have students complete **Activity 8-1, "Learning from Others,"** that appears on page 151. Teaching suggestions and the solution for this activity appear on page 151. An activity worksheet can be found on the Career Portfolio and Resource CD— **Text Activity 08-1.doc**.

Finding the Right Path

After you have determined your ideal career and set goals for achieving it, examine the possible training and education options available. By considering all your options, you can find the right path for you. Although some professional careers require at least four years at a college or university, other careers may have several different education and training options. Also, alternative education options are becoming more common, even for careers that used to require traditional attendance at a college or university.

> **If we all did the things we are capable of doing, we would literally astound ourselves.**
> —Thomas Edison, Inventor

Dajuan has worked part-time at Rakowski's Greenhouse since he was fourteen. Next year he hopes to have a summer job with this large florist and greenhouse company. Then he can begin the tech prep program in horticulture, where he will earn college credits two years before graduation. Dajuan is considering working full-time in Rakowski's nursery after he graduates from high school. He has learned that entry-level technicians start at a high hourly rate. Dajuan is sure he would start at an even higher salary because of his experience with the company.

Dajuan knows another alternative is to delay full-time work for Benken's until after he finishes an associate degree in landscape horticulture technology. He can continue to work part-time while attending college full-time. The college program is also a co-op program that pays him while he works and gains college credit. After earning his degree, he would be eligible for higher pay and more responsibility at Rakowski's. Another alternative is to use Rakowski's tuition reimbursement program. The company would pay for his college tuition while he worked full-time. Earning a college degree would take Dajuan longer, but he wouldn't have any tuition costs.

What do you think?
How can your goals and your budget help you decide which education and training option to choose for your career path?

As you look at the education and training options available for your career path, ask yourself the following questions:

- When do I want to start working?
- When should I begin the education and training necessary for my career choice?
- How long will my education and training take?
- How much money do I want to make to meet my lifestyle goals?
- How will I pay for my education and training?
- Do I want to combine work with education?
- Can I continue my education and training after I begin working?

In Activity 8-1, "Learning from Others," you can learn about a career in your career cluster from a person successful in your career field.

138

PART 3 • • • • • • PLANNING

ONLINE RESOURCES

Check out the web site **www.investigatingyourcareer.com** for teacher resources, student activities, and replacements for broken links for this chapter. To access the teacher resources:

Username: career
Password: investigate

Education and Training Options

Before you can determine your future training and education path, you need to know all the options available to you. Although your education and training path will depend partly on your career choice, you may find that you have several options you had not considered. By being aware of all the different paths, you can choose the best way for you to reach your career and lifestyle goals.

Often more than one education and training path will allow you to reach your goal. For instance, you might move directly from high school to your career. While you work in your career, you might receive on-the-job training or take courses on the Internet. Ultimately you may receive the same education and training as if you had gone from high school to a postsecondary school or formal training program.

Some options you should consider for your education and training are available in high school. Other options become available after you graduate from high school.

High School Options

What are some of the different education and training options for your career area at your high school? **What do you think?**

Different types of high schools have different options for planning your career path. You need to consider all of these options before you decide which training and education path best meets your career, lifestyle, and budget goals.

Traditional High School

Most traditional high schools have programs, or tracks, that can give you a head start on the education and training you will need for your career. A series of courses may be available for careers in areas such as business, agriculture, technology, and health. In addition, your high school will probably have an advanced placement track and a college prep track. These tracks include the courses you will need for entry into a college or university.

Career/Technical School

Attending a career/technical school or other specialized school can be an option for part of your high school education. Career/technical education is offered in a variety of ways and at many places. During high school, you may enroll at a career center; at a high school academy within a comprehensive high school; or at a magnet, or specialized, school. In a career/technical school, you focus on one career area. Career/technical schools offer courses of study for numerous career areas, and their offerings are expanding almost daily.

CAREER SUCCESS TIP

The biggest roadblock to your career success is procrastination. Set your goals, plan for deadlines, and stay on top of things.

CAREER SUCCESS TIP

Set Goals for Success

Provide students with poster board and art materials. Cut the poster board in half the long way to create a size that will fit on the inside doors of students' lockers. Have students create a road map to their goals that includes deadlines for each step along the way. Ask students to tape their road maps in a location they see every day, such as the inside of their school lockers. Tell students visual reminders will help keep them on track to their goals.

TEACH

If tech prep is an option in your school system, find out the requirements. Invite a local tech prep representative to discuss the requirements and the different career pathways your tech prep consortium provides through its articulation agreements with its postsecondary partners.

> **Everyone needs to be valued. Everyone has the potential to give something back.**
> —Diana,
> Princess of Wales

The Tech Prep Approach

Tech prep programs, sometimes called 2+2 programs, link the last two years of high school with two years of community college or technical school. Some students pursue the 2+2+2 option, which leads from high school to an associate degree to a bachelor's degree.

When her family and friends wanted to find Tara, they looked outdoors. She thrived on working with plants—experimenting with seeds, hybrids, and soils. In her sophomore year in high school, Tara talked to her biology teacher, Mr. Svoboda, about turning her passion for plants into a career. Mr. Svoboda suggested that Tara enroll as a tech prep student in horticulture. She had the prerequisite courses in math and science, nearly perfect attendance, and a high grade point average.

Tara's counselor explained that tech prep is different from the basic career/technical landscaping course. In tech prep, Tara would be taking higher level math and science courses. She could continue her experiments with plants, expanding her research to work with soil acidity levels and hydroponics (growing plants in a liquid nutrient solution). When Tara completes the tech prep program, she will have earned more than one semester of advance credits toward an associate degree at a branch of the university. Tara was sold on the idea—she enrolled in the tech prep program and began her college education while still in high school.

Tech prep is a new and different preparatory course for students who have the following characteristics:

* Interest in technology and science
* Mechanical inclination
* Average or better-than-average math skills and successful completion of a minimum of first-year algebra
* Preference for hands-on learning

A tech prep program is a partnership consisting of a secondary school; a postsecondary school; and business, industry, and labor. Students can complete the program in high school. Or they can continue in the program after high school and earn an associate degree or a bachelor's degree. Through the tech prep approach, students can find employment or can advance in their career fields.

One of the most important aspects of the tech prep approach is referred to as applied academics. **Applied academics** means that traditional school courses are used in practical real-life situations. Materials and instructional techniques give students hands-on experience in applying the theory of a subject, which often makes learning easier and more appealing.

DIFFERENT LEARNING ABILITIES
At-Risk and Reluctant-Reader Students
Pair at-risk and reluctant-reader students with other students, and have student pairs discuss applied academics. Suggest the following questions for their discussion: *What courses might at-risk and reluctant-reader students want to take that they are not currently taking? How will these courses benefit them now? How will these courses help them in the future?* Ask students to identify hands-on courses. Hands-on courses include any course where students learn primarily by doing, such as culinary arts, mechanical work, computer graphics, cosmetology, and so on.

Specialized Options for High School

Several specialized education and training options may be available to you while you are in high school. Certification programs, internships, cooperative programs, and apprenticeships all combine education and work experience. However, each emphasizes the roles of work and education in different ways, and the results of your experience will be different for each.

What skills can you acquire by working in your career field while you are in high school? **What do you think?**

Certification Course or Program

The skills required for some careers can be learned in a certification course or program. When you complete the program, you receive a **certificate**, an official document that proves you have successfully completed specific courses, have acquired necessary skills, and are qualified to perform a certain job. Certificates may be earned in many career areas, such as cosmetology, culinary arts, welding, and childcare.

Helen is passionate about technology, particularly computers, and knows her career will be in the Business and Management career cluster. She is drawn to courses that expand her knowledge, and the nearby career/technical school offers an entire career major in various facets of information technology. However, attending the career/technical school would limit Helen's high school activities, which are also important to her. She enjoys being a cheerleader and a member of her school's service learning organization. Practices and meetings for these activities often take place during the school day, either during study hall or lunch. She would be unable to participate fully in these activities if she attended the career/technical school.

Helen's counselor, Mr. Irvine, suggested an alternative. Helen could take Microsoft Office User Specialist (MOUS) and A+ computer service technician certification courses at her high school in her junior year and possibly during her senior year. Helen can complete the course work in one year and transfer to the career/technical school for additional specialization.

What do you think?

Use **TM08-04**.
Students' answers will vary.

TEACH

Explain to students that they have many choices about where they can receive the type of education and training they need for their career. Their options include many places for learning besides a traditional classroom. Also remind students that 85 percent of careers will require additional education and training and that education and training is almost always a lifelong process. Many of the options discussed in this chapter apply to lifelong learning. To be successful in their careers, students cannot stop learning.

ENRICH

Have students complete **Activity 8-B, "Am I Prepared?,"** found in the *Investigating Your Career Activities & Projects* book.

In this activity, students analyze the challenges necessary for education and training both during and after high school. After students score their quizzes, discuss the questions with the class. They can incorporate the results into an improvement plan, as they did for their Action Plan in Activity 7-5.

Solution: The solution for this activity appears in the *Teacher's Edition* of *Investigating Your Career Activities & Projects*.

DIFFERENT LEARNING STYLES

Print Learners

Instruct students to create a chart with the following three headings: Certification Programs, Internship, and Cooperative Programs. Ask students to research each heading in their career area. Then ask students to fill in the chart with information in each category. Next, have students choose one option within one category and investigate it more fully. Finally, have students write a report on their option of choice.

TEACH

Compare an internship to a three-month job interview that benefits employers and interns. If interns perform their jobs well, companies often want to hire them after the internship ends because the employers know and appreciate the abilities of the interns. In turn, the interns have more information about companies and careers and can make better career decisions.

> **It's good to have an end to journey toward, but it is the journey that matters in the end.**
>
> —Ursula K. LeGuin,
> Author

Or she can remain at her high school and complete the course work over two years. The course options would allow Helen to pursue her activities. In addition, if she wants to start her career by working either full-time or part-time after high school graduation, she would be qualified to start higher than an entry-level position.

Certification programs are offered through high schools and post-secondary schools, and classes may be in a traditional setting or online. All require you to take a standardized test for admission. Check on the quality of the school giving the certificate. If you want to receive an industry-accepted certification, find out what percentage of students actually earn the certification. (Some students may enter but then drop out, which is a sign that the school may not be highly regarded.)

Internship

As described in Chapter 3, an internship is a course that provides practical experience working in a specific career. As an intern, you may work after school or during the summer. Although you may receive a small amount of pay or none at all, an internship provides you with the experience of working in your career field.

In addition, an internship gives you the opportunity to "interview" the company and career before you commit to further education or training. As an intern, you learn about the work environment, the equipment used, the relationships between workers and supervisors, and the dress code. An internship may also lead to a full-time job after you graduate. People who have interned are usually more satisfied with their career choice, and many are in the same career and company five years later.

Internships are usually arranged through a high school in partnership with a local company. If an internship is not available in your career field or if you do not qualify for the program at your school, you can try to set up an internship on your own. Talk to the owner or manager of a business in your field, and see if you will be able to work for no pay in exchange for acquiring experience in your field. If the business owner is unfamiliar with internships, you may have to convince him or her that you will work hard and that the internship will benefit the business.

Cooperative Program

Cooperative (co-op) programs combine studies with paid work experiences in a specific career field. Co-op programs are available in high schools, colleges, and universities. In many college programs, students alternate work with school by working full-time for one term and attending school the next term. In most high school programs, students attend classes at their schools for part of the day and work at their co-op employers for the rest of the day. Students receive school credit for participating in a co-op program and are also paid for their work at the co-op employer.

INTEGRATED ACADEMICS
Language Arts

Have students work in small groups to create a questionnaire about student interns. Ask a school counselor about companies that provide internships to students in your school system. Provide each group with the name of one or two companies. Have students make a list of questions they want to ask to create their questionnaire. Then have students contact the companies and explain their assignment. After questionnaires are completed, have students compare their answers.

Work experience in a co-op program is related to your career field and goals. You apply the skills you learn in the classroom to an actual job in your career area. Offices, hospitals, and stores are some of the many co-op employers for high school students.

Lauren wasn't sure whether she wanted to teach preschool or elementary grades. She had to decide because she would soon be enrolling in college and would have to plan her course schedule. Lauren's parents suggested she participate in her high school's cooperative program in early childhood education. Lauren learned that the co-op program would give her experience in working with children of different ages and could help her determine her career focus.

Lauren began the co-op program her next semester. She went to English and her other classes in the morning and worked in her co-op course in the afternoon. The program was set up so Lauren spent one-fourth of her time in child development classes and three-fourths of her time in co-op work experiences. Each student worked as a preschool aide, assisted in an elementary after-school latchkey program, and provided help with young special-needs children. Lauren enjoyed the course and is now convinced her career will be teaching elementary school.

Co-op programs involve a formal relationship among the student, the school, and the employer. Usually, these three parties sign an agreement that outlines the responsibilities of each participant. The agreement may include the following:

• The job description and the work hours
• The methods used by the school, the employer, and the student to monitor and evaluate the student's progress
• The payment the student will receive

All three parties may also develop a training plan that outlines the skills, knowledge, and goals the student is expected to acquire. Co-op programs enhance your classroom learning, improve your career opportunities, and provide insight into a prospective career while you earn money.

Do you think a co-op program would benefit you? Why or why not?

What do you think?

TEACH

Some students may be pressured by peers or families to focus on college rather than other career preparation options. Emphasize to students that they should choose the career preparation option that is most appropriate for their career and lifestyle goals. Often the social and economic levels of the community have too great an influence on students' education and training after high school.

What do you think?

Use **TM08-05**.
Students' answers will vary.

DIFFERENT LEARNING ABILITIES
Gifted
Have students investigate cooperative programs in careers of interest to them. Students can work with their school counselor to find companies that offer cooperative programs. Ask students to create an advertising campaign that promotes the cooperative programs. Ad campaigns are to contain at least two pieces of literature, such as a script or a storyboard for a television ad, a brochure using computer graphics, a flyer, or a poster. Display the print pieces in the classroom.

Ask students for their opinions about virtual learning and what students consider the advantages and disadvantages to be. Some advantages are as follows:
- The variety of learning situations
- The convenience of using hand-held devices and cell phones
- The comfortable environment for reluctant or shy students
- The convenience of time and location
- The ability to take responsibility for learning
- The global sharing of experiences
- A safe environment for failure.

Some disadvantages are as follows:
- Too much text work
- A lack of variety of learning situations
- Less personal contact with other students and teachers
- The need to schedule in-person time
- Insufficient hands-on experiences

Some advantages may also be disadvantages, such as time and space separating students from each other and the teacher and students taking responsibility for their own learning. Emphasize that students must check the credentials of the institution offering the online courses.

Apprenticeship

An **apprenticeship** is a program in which a person works for a skilled worker in order to learn a trade. For centuries, people have worked as apprentices in order to learn the skills of a trade. At one time, an apprenticeship was the only way a person could learn some trades. You can work as an apprentice in many different types of industries, not only the construction and manufacturing industries often associated with apprenticeships. For example, training for a career as a childcare development specialist or an x-ray equipment tester can be accomplished through an apprenticeship program.

CAREER SUCCESS TIP

Think long-term. Career options are limited if you do not have education and training beyond high school.

Some apprenticeship programs are informal arrangements between a worker and an employer. However, most apprenticeship programs are registered with the federal government and with state agencies. Registered programs must meet federal and state standards, and they issue certificates of completion to apprentices. Because the government oversees the programs, the safety of apprentices is protected and programs provide high-quality training.

For some trades, you can begin apprenticeship training while you are still in high school in a program that leads to a journey-worker program after high school. This type of apprenticeship usually requires two years in high school and up to four years after high school. Some trades require completion of high school. These programs can take up to six years. As an apprentice, you take classes as part of your training. You are paid while you work, and as you learn the trade and require less supervision, your pay gradually increases.

Virtual and Distance Learning

In distance learning, time and space separate the learners from each other and from the teacher. Today distance learning is usually accomplished via the Internet and is often referred to as virtual learning. In the past, students participated by sending and receiving learning materials via mail. Distance learning via the Internet makes education and training available to people without the restrictions of time and space. You can work at a computer at your home, school, or workplace while the teacher and other students taking the course may be thousands of miles away.

Distance learning is gaining in popularity as an alternative for traditional postsecondary schools because students can balance the demands of work and family with their pursuit of additional education. A survey by the U.S. Department of Education predicts that, by 2025, 10 percent of public colleges and 50 percent of independent colleges will close as students turn to distance learning and bypass the traditional classroom. High school students are also taking advantage of virtual learning as an option for acquiring skills and training while still in high school.

CAREER SUCCESS TIP

Think Long-Term

American Indian communities recognize the role of education in achieving success. The Native American Tribal Colleges integrate cultural values and traditions while filling the need for long-term education. Curricula include traditional subjects and classes such as tribal languages, tribal stories, and the economic history of the reservation. Even the more traditional courses are geared to reflect tribal philosophies of education. The colleges also serve their local communities by providing childcare and counseling in substance abuse prevention and recovery and in nutrition. Thinking ahead promotes success.

—*Source: www.aihec.org*

Virtual learning is not for everyone, as little personal contact exists between the teacher and students. If you are good at time management and can work independently, virtual learning may be an appropriate option for you. Always check the quality of the course or school that offers virtual learning opportunities.

In Activity 8-2, "Education and Training Research," you can use the Internet to explore some education and training options.

Options beyond High School

After you graduate from high school, many education and training options are available to you. You must analyze your options in terms of your chosen career, your lifestyle goals, and your budget requirements. In addition to the options described in the following paragraphs, some of the high school options discussed earlier in this chapter are applicable after you graduate. Co-op programs are available in colleges and universities. Career/technical schools have one- or two-year postsecondary training courses and certification programs. In addition, distance learning or an apprenticeship program may provide the training you want.

How might your choice of an education or training option after you graduate influence the courses you take in high school? **What do you think?**

Straight to Career

Are you impatient to be finished with your schooling? Do you want to begin working right after you graduate from high school so you can start earning money and become independent? Do you think additional education or training will be a waste of time?

Many high school students would answer yes to these questions. And many companies are encouraging them along this path. These companies need bright, trainable, entry-level technical workers because of the explosive growth of information technology. So these companies are recruiting recent high school graduates. The high salaries available within two or three years of leaving high school are appealing, and many high school graduates who would otherwise have pursued postsecondary education are joining the workforce.

However, if you follow this path, you will likely eventually learn that the disadvantages of going straight to a career outweigh the benefits. Without additional education, the opportunities for career growth are severely limited. Technical skills alone do not determine career success. Communication skills, business knowledge, and an understanding of global economic issues are vital to career advancement.

Employers look for employees who know how to continue to learn and are able to adapt to change. Education beyond high school helps you develop these skills. Employers know this and, given a choice,

145

APPLY

Have students complete **Activity 8-2, "Education and Training Research,"** on page 151. Teaching suggestions and the solution for this activity appear on page 151. An activity worksheet can be found on the Career Portfolio and Resource CD— **Text Activity 08-2.doc**.

What do you think?

Use **TM08-06**.
Students' answers will vary.

TEACH

Mention that an advantage of working immediately after high school is that employers may pay for students' further education. A student often may receive partial or full tuition reimbursement from an employer, providing the student achieves a minimum grade requirement. Sometimes an employer will even pay for books and supplies.

DIFFERENT LEARNING STYLES

Auditory Learners

Hold a class discussion on students' options beyond high school. Then have students meet in small groups to continue the discussion. Have students ask each other questions about what options best fit their long-term career goals. In the discussion groups, mix students who are planning on continuing their education with students who plan on beginning their careers immediately after high school. After the group discussions, have a member of each group report on the group's discussion.

Explain some of the possible options in the military, such as the option of delaying entry until after high school graduation to ensure the occupational training wanted or the buddy option guaranteeing that two friends can enter and train at the same time and place. Also, depending on the area of training, students can extend their education to an associate, bachelor's, or graduate degree. Some branches of the military allow legal immigrants to join.

What do you think?

Use **TM08-07**.
Students' answers will vary.

will hire the better-educated person. Some form of education or training after high school is essential if you are to achieve career success and reach your lifestyle goals.

Military Service

For many people, joining a branch of the military after high school is an option worth considering. In addition to receiving technical training while in the service, you may be eligible for government college tuition assistance after you leave the service.

When Ethan began his career planning, he knew exactly what his career direction would be. He wanted to be an engineer, specifically a chemical engineer. He had always enjoyed research and especially liked the problem-solving aspects of science and math. Ethan knew his career choice required at least a bachelor's degree, and he realized he would have to work while he was in school to pay for his tuition and school expenses. He also realized it would be difficult for him to work in his career field and attend school at the same time.

So Ethan talked to an Army recruiter. He found that the Army would pay for his schooling while he worked in areas similar to his future career. In exchange, Ethan would agree to work for the Army for several years. Ethan liked the idea of serving his country while working toward his career goal. The military was a good option for Ethan because his goal was to be a chemical engineer with the U.S. government, possibly working for the Occupational Safety & Health Administration or the National Institute of Occupational Safety and Health. The Army would give him experience that would help him start a career with one of those agencies.

Several options are available for military service. In addition to the various branches of the military—Army, Navy, Air Force, Marines, and Coast Guard—you could investigate the National Guard and the Reserves. Generally, to enlist, you need to be a high school graduate, 18 years old, in good health, and a U.S. citizen. Of course, military service is not simply an education option. You may decide you want to pursue a career in the military.

On-the-Job Training

What do you think?
Will you need on-the-job training for a job in your career area? Why or why not?

On-the-job training (OJT) is one way to continue your education while you work. In **on-the-job training**, skills for a specific job are

INTEGRATED ACADEMICS
Language Arts/Computer Sciences
Have students work in small groups to create a booklet entitled "Options after High School." The booklet should be based on the information in this chapter. Students are to design, format, and print their booklets using computer desktop publishing and art programs. Encourage students to have fun creating their booklets. Have students vote on the booklet they think does the best job of conveying the information. Display the booklets around the room.

learned under the supervision of a skilled worker. Often OJT combines some type of classroom training with hands-on instruction. On-the-job training may take only a few days or may take a year or more, but it usually requires less time than an apprenticeship.

Some form of on-the-job training is necessary for almost all jobs. An employer hires you because he or she believes you have the skills and ability to learn how to perform the job. Regardless of your training and education background, employers do not expect you to be able to perform a job expertly on your first day. Take advantage of any OJT opportunity. Additional training and education in any form will help you achieve success.

Associate Degree

An **associate degree** is an academic title earned on completion of a program that usually requires the equivalent of two or more years of full-time study. The following education and training options can lead to earning an associate degree:

- Tech prep programs begin in high school and continue at a community college.
- Some career/technical schools offer both certificate and associate degree programs. One or two years of study are required, depending on the career area.
- Some apprenticeship programs grant an associate degree upon completion of the apprenticeship. Depending on the apprenticeship area, the degree may require up to six years of a combination of training and paid work.
- A community college or university grants an associate degree upon graduation. The degree usually requires two years of full-time study.

An associate degree is sufficient postsecondary education and training for many careers. For example, medical and veterinary technicians, computer service technicians, drafters, welders, construction managers, and auto mechanics may need only an associate degree.

An associate degree is a way to prepare for a specific career. Also, if you decide you want additional education after you have earned an associate degree, a college or university will often give you credit for courses you have taken in earning your degree. Most colleges have partnering arrangements with other colleges or universities, allowing for easy transfer of credits.

Bachelor's Degree and Beyond

A **bachelor's degree** is an academic title awarded by a college or university to a person who has completed undergraduate studies. Many careers require a bachelor's degree, which often takes between four and six years to earn. Some professions require graduate work after obtaining a bachelor's degree.

> 66 The will to win is important, but the will to prepare is vital. 99
>
> —*Joe Paterno, Football Coach*

TEACH

Ask students what they think are additional advantages of earning an associate degree versus pursuing a bachelor's degree. One advantage is the ability to begin working and earning money at a chosen career in a shorter period of time. Another advantage is that total tuition generally is lower, even for an associate degree from a branch of a university. Also, students who are less prepared socially or academically for a large university may find an institution offering an associate degree to be the answer. However, students need to be aware of the transfer requirements if they decide to change to a school that offers a bachelor's degree.

TEACH

Explain to students that only 15 percent of careers in the next ten years will *require* a bachelor's degree. Ask students for examples of professions that require such education. Then mention that alternative education options are becoming more and more prevalent, such as becoming a certified teacher.

DIFFERENT LEARNING ABILITIES
Dyslexia
Have students work together to create a board game. Title the game "Options after High School." Ask students to use the game to address the concepts and information in this chapter—and to make the game fun to play. Students are to provide written instructions for their game. Instructions should include how to score, play, and win the game. Students are to create the board and all the game pieces. Have different students play the games.

TEACH

Most students who plan to earn a bachelor's degree view a college education as essential for success and expect to find a high-paying job because of their degree. However, without a career focus, a college degree does not necessarily lead to career success. For example, 50 percent of full-time community college students already have a bachelor's degree or higher.

APPLY

Have students complete **Activity 8-3, "Case Challenges,"** on page 152. Teaching suggestions and the solution for this activity appear on page 152. An activity worksheet can be found on the Career Portfolio and Resource CD—**Text Activity 08-3.doc**.

Colleges and universities vary in the types of education and training they provide. Some colleges offer students a general education rather than training for a specific career. Other colleges provide specialized education in some career fields. Most large universities offer both alternatives—a general education and training in certain career areas. Keep in mind that college is not a career. You need to have a definite career goal that will be furthered by a college or university education.

In financial terms, the value of a college degree is clear. Starting salaries are significantly higher and lifetime earning potential is much greater for people with a bachelor's degree than for high school graduates. In addition, employers often prefer to hire candidates with well-rounded backgrounds and college degrees, even if the degree does not apply to a specific job. Teenagers are often not an employer's first choice because they lack life experience and sophisticated technical skills.

In Activity 8-3, "Case Challenges," you will have an opportunity to analyze situations and determine appropriate education plans.

REAL PEOPLE

REAL CAREERS

CEO

The same skills that Betsy Holden learned as a high school cheerleader have helped her in her career as a CEO (Chief Executive Officer). As a cheerleader, Betsy learned how to work on a team, how to plan and train for competition, and how to succeed through competition. She needs the enthusiasm, organization, and creativity she showed as a cheerleader in her job as the head of Kraft Foods, the company that owns Oscar Mayer, Maxwell House, and Jell-O.

After she graduated from high school, Betsy majored in education in college. Education was a natural choice because high school had been a great experience for her. She wanted to help other students the same way her teachers had helped her. Marketing was an easy decision for graduate school because of her ambitious personality, her ability to plan and organize, and her creativity. There Betsy was named Outstanding Marketing Student. After working for a Kraft rival, Betsy went to Kraft Foods. At Kraft, her marketing skills and her determination were highly valued and led to her present position as CEO. Today Betsy has a motto displayed outside her office that is reminiscent of her high school cheerleading days. Her motto is "Every day and every way, grow Kraft cheese, hey! hey! hey!"

For more information about careers in marketing:
- explore *www.nyama.org/cq.htm*.
- explore *www.careers-in-marketing.com*.

Source: "Career Shorts." *Career Opportunity News*, February 2001, 16.

REAL PEOPLE—REAL CAREERS

Video Interviews

Have students work in small groups to conduct video interviews with adults who work in marketing. As a class, make a list of companies with marketing departments in your area. Assign each student group a company. Have groups contact the company marketing departments to request an interview. Groups must include an interviewer and a cameraperson. If groups cannot travel to the company, ask the marketing person to travel to the school for the interview. Show the videos in class.

Planning Your Path

After you have analyzed all your education and training options, you can begin to think about the path to take to achieve your career and lifestyle goals. Before you make any final decisions about your choice of career, you should research your career area in various ways. Begin your research by:

- Finding out the traditional and nontraditional ways people prepare for a career in your field. Check publications from the industry, and use specialized resources such as career information systems.
- Checking with employers in your career area to find out what they look for when evaluating job candidates.
- Asking successful people in your career field which parts of their education and training were most helpful and which parts they would change.

> Do the traditional ways people prepare for a career in your chosen field apply to you? Why or why not? **What do you think?**

You should also take advantage of the opportunities offered by your school to explore your career area. For example, your school may sponsor a career day in which you can listen to one or two speakers who are knowledgeable about your career area. Or you may be able to attend a career fair. At a career fair, booths representing different careers are set up and you can ask questions at the career booths that interest you. Career days and career fairs can provide you with information about the education and training needed in your career area.

As discussed in Chapter 3, job shadowing and service learning can also provide you with valuable information about your choice of career. Job shadowing can often be arranged through your school. By job shadowing an employee in your career area, you will get to see what the person does and decide whether you would find the career satisfying. Take advantage of every job shadowing opportunity that comes your way.

If your school has service learning projects, you should take advantage of the experience. Service learning allows you to give to your community as you learn from the people you help. A service learning project in your career area can also help you explore the various careers in your career cluster.

A final way to help you research your career area is to find a part-time job related to your career cluster. You will not only earn money but also gain experience in your career field. However, be careful that your part-time job doesn't cause your grades or time with your family to suffer. Don't take on a job that requires you to work more than 20 hours a week.

Activity 8-4, "Coming to Terms," helps you relate the various education and learning options to a career.

CAREER FACT

Charles Carlson developed the process of photocopying in 1938, but he had to persevere for 21 years before the first Xerox copier was finally manufactured. The lesson to be learned from Carlson is never to give up.

CAREER TREND
Believe in Yourself

Successful people believe in themselves. To be successful takes hard work, dedication, and a deep belief that what you are doing is right. Along the road to success are many obstacles that will stop you if you don't believe in yourself and what you are doing. Ask students if they think Charles Carlson ever got discouraged. Ask them what they think kept him going. The right career for you begins with believing in yourself enough to choose a career that allows you to do what you want with your life.

Remind students about the objectives set forth at the beginning of the chapter, and use this summary to reinforce the concepts presented in this chapter.

Career Journal

Ask students to spend 10 minutes writing Career Journal entries that answer the following questions:
1. How well did what you thought you knew match what the chapter presented?
2. What questions do you now have about the chapter topics, and where do you think you can find the answers to those questions?
3. How will the content of the chapter help you investigate *your* career?

ASSESS

Administer the printed objective test for Chapter 8, available with this package. Test solutions are found in the *Teacher's Edition* of *Investigating Your Career Chapter Tests*. Use the **Exam***View*® CD to create your own objective test for this chapter.

> 66 If you don't know where you want to go, any road will take you there. 99
>
> —*Anonymous*

IN A NUTSHELL

- **I can explain how my goals influence my choice of education and training.**

  My career and lifestyle goals and my budget requirements will influence my education and training options. As I consider my education and training options, I need to determine when I want to start working, when I need to begin the education and training necessary for my career choice, how much money I want to make, whether I want to combine work with education, and whether I will be able to continue my education and training after I begin working.

- **I can describe the education and training options available to me.**

  High school options include a traditional high school, a career/technical school, and a tech prep program. Specialized options for high school include a certification course or program, an internship, a cooperative program, an apprenticeship, and distance learning. Options beyond high school include a cooperative program, a career/technical school, an apprenticeship program, distance learning, a direct step to a career, military service, on-the-job training, an associate degree, and a bachelor's degree and beyond.

- **I can describe several ways to research my career area.**

  I can research my career area by checking publications and career information systems, by talking with employers to find out how they evaluate job candidates, and by talking to successful people in my career field. I can also take advantage of opportunities offered by my school, such as career days, career fairs, job shadowing experiences, and service learning programs. Finally, I can find a part-time job related to my career field.

Suggestions for Parents and Family Members

Career Focus

Following are ways parents and family members can assist teens in increasing awareness of career options:

1. Reinforce that career planning now will make it easier for your child to reach goals.
2. Explain that attending college is not a career goal; it is a preparation. The No. 1 reason students drop out of college is lack of career focus.
2. Work with your child and counselors to plan the right course of study.

Learning from Others

Interview a person in the career cluster you chose in Chapter 6, someone who works in one of the careers in which you are interested. Your teacher, counselor, or family can help you find a person to interview either in person or over the telephone. Use the following questions for the basis of your interview:

- What is your job title? Describe your job.
- How did you start in this career?
- In what ways do you find your career satisfying?
- What frustrations do you experience in your career?
- What personal characteristics do people need to be successful in your career?
- What are the most important skills needed for success in your work?
- What types of additional learning do you expect to need to remain successful and to advance in your field?
- If you could do it over again, would you change your career? If so, how? Why?
- If you could do it over again, would you change your preparation for your career? If so, how? Why?
- What advice would you give to a person considering this career?
- What other advice would you offer students to help them make good career choices?
- What do you do on a typical workday?
- How do you see your field changing over the next ten years?

What conclusions can you draw from your interview?

Education and Training Research

Investigate at least one or two categories of education and/or training in two of the sites listed below. (If Acrobat Reader is not on your computer, you may have to download the free plug-in to read information on some of the sites. See your teacher if the plug-in is not on your school's computer network.)

Write down answers to the following questions for the sites you investigate. Keep your career choices from Chapter 6 in mind when you answer these questions.

1. What are the benefits of the education/training?
2. What are some drawbacks to this type of education/training?
3. How can this education/training give you a start for your career?
   - Apprenticeship sites:
     www.state.oh.us/odjfs/apprenticeship (Click on the box "Apprenticeship: What Is It? The Other 4-Year Degree!")
     www.doleta.gov/atels_bat
     www.njatc.org
   - Virtual and distance learning site:
     www.detc.org
   - Co-op education site:
     www.co-op.edu

Activity 8-1: Learning from Others

This activity, which provides students with information similar to what they would obtain in a job shadowing experience, helps students learn about the career preparation of a person working in their career cluster.

Encourage students to focus their questions on the career preparation path the person took, especially any changes he or she would have made.

As an extension to the activity, you may wish to divide students who have the same career clusters into groups so they can discuss their interview results. The discussions should focus on the similarities and differences in the career preparation options for different careers within the cluster. Also, students should discuss how career preparation options have changed since the person they interviewed trained for his or her career. **Solution:** Answers will vary.

Activity 8-2: Education and Training Research

This activity helps students explore career education/training options, including the benefits and drawbacks of each option.

Emphasize that students should consider their career choices and their personal situations when exploring the sites. Their learning styles, personality types, and attitudes toward different types of learning need to be taken into account when doing their research. Also remind students to think about their answers to the questions in the bulleted list on page 138 of their text when they investigate the sites.
Solution: Answers will vary. Encourage students to relate the benefits and drawbacks to their personalities and their career choices.

Activity 8-3: Case Challenges

This activity increases students' understanding of various career preparation options and the circumstances when the options are appropriate. Encourage students to explore the entire career path for the person in each case study, including the various options the person could choose at each stage in his or her career journey.

Solution: Answers may vary. Groups may consider more than one option for the case studies. Suggested answers are as follows:

1. Tech prep program or career/technical school now with an eventual bachelor's degree
2. Internship for career exploration and then perhaps a co-op program or a career/technical school; eventually, José may go to school to earn an associate degree
3. Internship for career exploration
4. Career/technical school, either during or after high school
5. Bachelor's degree

Activity 8-4: Coming to Terms

This activity checks students' understanding of some of the terms in this chapter and allows students to explore career preparation options for careers within their career cluster. Discuss the definitions of the terms before students begin the activity. They may want to refer to their research for activities in Chapters 6 and 7. Encourage students to be specific in their answers.

Solution: Answers will vary.

Work in a small group to analyze the type of education you believe would be helpful for the student in each of the following cases. Choose the type of education from the list below. (More than one answer may apply.) Explain the reasons for your choices.

- bachelor's degree
- tech prep program
- associate degree
- military service
- internship
- career/technical school
- apprenticeship program
- co-op program

1. Sasha plans to become a graphic artist as soon as possible. She currently has experience in creating small projects for her family and friends. She wants the technical expertise to start her career now, even before high school graduation. Ultimately Sasha hopes to become a high school art teacher.

2. José believes a career as a bookkeeper would be perfect for him. He doesn't expect he will ever want to become an accountant. However, he is not exactly sure what the difference is in the careers. He also has heard that the term *bookkeeper* is not the current job title.

3. Danielle expects to become a veterinarian. Science is her best subject. However, she knows there are many types of veterinarian careers, including working with small and/or large animals; being a veterinarian with one type of animal, such as at a racetrack; working at an emergency vet clinic, zoo, or animal shelter; or even choosing to be a veterinarian technician.

4. Tresa has always dreamed of being a hairstylist. When she creates hairstyles for her friends before school dances, they tell her she has a creative flair. She knows that ultimately she wants to own her own hairstyle shop, but she needs the cosmetology training first.

5. Seida has always liked babysitting. Her summer job is as a nanny for a set of triplets, plus she teaches children's beginning swimming classes in the evenings. She hopes to become an elementary school teacher.

The terms listed below relate to education and training options. For each term, describe a career in the career cluster you chose in Chapter 6 for which the education or training option is suitable.

1. Tech prep program
2. Cooperative program
3. On-the-job training
4. Apprenticeship
5. Certificate program
6. Associate degree
7. Bachelor's degree

From Here to Your Career

9

OBJECTIVES

After completing this chapter, you will be able to:
- List the requirements and preparation options for your career.
- Analyze career preparation providers.
- Begin implementing your career plan.
- Describe how to apply for admission.

Key Terms:
- career preparation provider
- accreditation
- scholarship
- grant
- loan
- cosigner
- work-study program
- Free Application for Financial Student Aid (FAFSA)
- Student Aid Report (SAR)
- expected family contribution (EFC)
- campus culture
- official transcript
- resume
- letter of recommendation

Music has always been a part of JJ Henri's life. His entire family enjoys singing in the church choir. They attend concerts together too. His mother plays the cello in the community orchestra. JJ plays the violin, but he does not want to be a performance musician. Instead, JJ wants to teach music. He wants to share his enjoyment of music with children. JJ's counselor, Mrs. Rohrig, suggested the related music careers of music therapist, librarian, or storeowner. However, teaching music to children is JJ's first career choice.

JJ researched the admission requirements and scholarship opportunities of several colleges to decide his high school schedule. He also investigated the state requirements for a music education license. Then JJ planned appropriate classes with Mrs. Rohrig's assistance. He knows he needs to take orchestra, choir, and advanced academic classes. Good grades in those classes will help him be accepted into a college with an excellent music education department.

Mrs. Rohrig also gave JJ some good ideas for extracurricular activities and part-time jobs. JJ continues to take violin lessons and to play in the state youth orchestra. Last summer he found a job as an assistant counselor and song leader in a camp for children. JJ found that his sense of humor and patience helped in working with the children. He is on his way toward his goal of a career in music education.

What steps can you take now to further the chances of success in your chosen career?

What do you think?

Chapter Overview

Chapter 9 From Here to Your Career

FOCUS

Chapter 9 focuses on practical steps students can take to integrate their career plans with their education and training choices. Students determine the requirements for their career fields, select appropriate career preparation providers, and learn about admission processes. Students begin implementing their career plans by choosing high school classes, activities, and jobs that further their career goals.

Use the **Objectives** and **Key Terms** printed in the margin to help students focus on the content of this chapter. Use the **video segment** for Chapter 9 to trigger discussion.

What do you think?

Use **TM09-01**.
Students' answers will vary.

Career Journal

Ask students to spend 10 minutes writing Career Journal entries that answer the following questions:
1. What do you think this chapter will cover?
2. What do you already know about these topics?
3. What three things do you want to learn about these topics?

CHAPTER RESOURCES and MATERIALS

Activities & Projects book
Instructor's Resource CD
- Forms and Worksheets for Chapter Activities 9-1 through 9-8
- Internet Links for Chapter 9
- PowerPoint Presentation for Chapter 9
- Lesson Plans
- Teaching Masters for Chapter 9
- Video Discussion Guide for Chapter 9

Chapter Tests book
ExamView® CD
Video
Web Site

Obtain job descriptions from school, city, county, state, or private companies. Group students into teams and give each team one of the job descriptions. Explain that the team is an employer with an opening for the job explained in the description. Ask students to write an advertisement listing the skills, abilities, and training that they, as employers, would look for in an applicant for the job. Also have students write an explanation of how they would determine whether applicants meet the criteria.

What do you think?

Use **TM09-02**.
Students' answers will vary.

> 66 Life is what
> we make it.
> Always has been,
> always will be. 99
> —*Grandma Moses,
> American Artist*

Through determining the influences on your career choice, taking assessments to understand yourself, futurecasting, and developing an awareness of various careers, you have discovered your *Internal Career Design*—the ideal career for you. You have also set goals and explored various career preparation options. Now you can use all the information you have acquired to begin planning the path you will take to reach your chosen career. Before you proceed, check to be sure your career plan:

- Is based on the four steps of your *P*A*T*H to Success*.
- Will prepare you for various employment options.
- Allows you to develop a wide range of transferable skills.
- Will help you adapt to changing employment markets.
- Includes plans for lifelong learning.

What do you think?
Will the career plan you have now be the same one you have all your life? Why or why not?

Requirements of Your Career

Begin planning your career preparation path by analyzing the skills, experience, abilities and personality, and education and training requirements of your career field. The results of your analysis will provide the starting point for implementing your career plan. You will be able to choose the career preparation path most appealing to you and most appropriate for your situation.

Cassidy, whose favorite activity is building web pages for family and friends, has decided on a career in the information technology (IT) career field. Specifically, Cassidy wants to pursue a career in web page management. She currently has set two career goals: (1) to obtain marketable skills within two years of high school graduation and (2) to gain enough experience within five years to offer web site design and maintenance services to small businesses.

To reach these goals, Cassidy researched and analyzed the requirements of the information technology career field. She learned about general training and advancement expectations. To examine the qualifications employers require for web developers, Cassidy did some online research. Finally, she acquired course catalogs from career/technical schools and colleges to review the education and training programs available.

After completing her research, Cassidy summarized entry-level requirements for would-be web page developers. She used the headings of skills, experience, abilities and personality, and education/training. Illustration 9-1 shows Cassidy's summary.

ONLINE RESOURCES

Check out the web site **www.investigatingyourcareer.com** for teacher resources, student activities, and replacements for broken links for this chapter. To access the teacher resources:

Username: career
Password: investigate

Illustration 9-1 Entry-Level Requirements for Web Page Manager

Entry-Level Requirements

Skills

- Keyboard skills
- Clear and correct written and spoken communication
- Team leadership and participation skills
- Project coordination and problem-solving skills
- Competency in word processing, spreadsheet, database, and presentation application software
- Basic understanding of major stand-alone and network operating systems
- Visual design theory as applied to web page graphic design
- Proficiency in several web software languages across several operating system platforms
- Principles of database design and implementation
- Web ethics
- Web server administration and security management
- Marketing principles

Experience

- One to two years web page development
- Important, even from hobbies and school projects

Abilities and Personality

- Curious
- Creative
- Committed to lifelong learning
- Demonstrated passion for technology
- Adapts well to constant change

Education/Training

- Bachelor's degree preferred
- Associate degree often accepted

Skills

Each career field involves certain skills. For example, all landscaping jobs require the ability to operate and maintain hand and power tools. A music education career requires skills in reading music, playing instruments, conducting, and rearranging musical scores.

In addition, different careers in each career field require different levels of skills. For instance, landscape designers must be able to identify various plants, analyze soil conditions, and understand the needs of specific plants. Entry-level landscaping jobs do not require such extensive knowledge and skills. Similarly, preschool music specialists do not need the same level of expertise as music teachers.

Reinforce in students' minds the link between what they learn in school and what they need to know in the workplace. Ask students to study Illustration 9-1 and list the transferable skills shown in the entry-level requirements for Web Page Manager. Then have students identify ways their past and current experiences in school classrooms and extra-curricular activities are helping them develop some of the transferable skills they identified.

DIFFERENT LEARNING ABILITIES

Attention Deficit Disorder

Have students think about a career they might be interested in. Then have students make a list of the entry-level requirements for that career. Have students use the model on page 155. If any student believes the entry-level requirements are unattainable, have the student choose a different career and begin making another list of the entry-level requirements.

Experience

The different career levels in each field may call for different levels of experience. In the landscaping career area, entry-level laborers may need previous experience in using power tools. In contrast, aspiring landscape contractors usually need several years of progressively responsible landscaping experience. Sometimes, as in music education, advanced training or education may substitute for experience.

Abilities and Personality

Success in your career field may require specific abilities and personality. For example, people in service careers, such as landscaping and music education, are most successful when they are responsible, self-motivated, and able to work well with people. In addition, landscaping professionals must enjoy working outdoors in a variety of weather conditions, and music education professionals must enjoy making and teaching music.

Education/Training

Jobs within career fields require candidates for entry-level positions to complete various types of education or training. For instance, someone without a high school diploma may get a job as a landscape laborer; however, a landscape designer usually needs to complete specialized training or obtain an associate degree. In the music education field, preschool music specialists usually need an associate degree while teachers generally must have at least a bachelor's degree.

In Activity 9-1, "Requirements of Your Career," you summarize the requirements for success in your career field.

Match Options to Requirements

After identifying the requirements needed for your career field, you must decide how you will meet those requirements. Research and the career preparation options described in Chapter 8 will help you find the best path for you. Some careers (such as medical doctors, certified public accountants, and beauticians) have clearly defined, set preparation steps. Other careers have more flexibility in the way people can become qualified. For example, successful fiction writers have an amazing variety of backgrounds, but they all share a vivid imagination and a mastery of writing techniques.

JJ Henri analyzed the entry-level requirements and the preparation options for a career in music education. Illustration 9-2 shows how JJ identified the preparation possibilities for each point under skills, experience, abilities and personality, and education/training. Note that JJ included ways to prepare during high school as well as after high school.

In Activity 9-2, "Your Career Preparation Path," you match preparation options to entry-level requirements in your career field.

> ### CAREER FACT
>
> According to the Employment Policies Institute, minimum-wage workers with less than a high school education average wage increases of 8.06 percent in the first year, while high school graduates see an 11.75 percent increase. Those with some college education average gains of 14.47 percent, and college graduates see gains of 20 percent or more.

CAREER TREND
Living on Minimum Wage

Studies by the Employment Institute show that when the female head of the household has not finished high school, her income potential is more limited than that of women with a high school diploma. Women who do not graduate often are forced into entry-level jobs, which still require the same commitment that obtaining a diploma requires—a willingness to learn, discipline, and some basic skills. Hold a class discussion on the realities of living on a minimum-wage income, regardless of gender.

—*Source: **www.epionline.org** and **www.epionline.org/study_yelowitz_12-2000_10.html***

Entry-Level Requirements	Preparation Options
Skills	
• Play several musical instruments (The voice is considered an instrument.)	Courses in high school and college, private lessons
• Lead groups	School projects, community service, part-time/summer jobs, military service
• Teach various age groups	Community service, summer jobs, student teaching in college
• Work with diverse personalities	Community service, part-time/summer jobs, school projects, military service
• Conduct musical groups	School recitals and programs, community service, musical groups, formal training in college
• Read music	Classes in high school, private lessons, college courses
• Rearrange musical scores	School productions, join small musical group, formal training in college
Experience	
• Completion of student-teaching program	College student-teaching program
• Participation in musical recitals, groups, and/or plays	School- and/or privately sponsored recitals, music groups, and/or musicals
Abilities and Personality	
• Musical talent	Training and practice
• Creativity	Techniques for developing creativity
• Poise	Performance training and practice
• High level of self-discipline	Time management techniques
• Flexibility	Coping techniques
Education/Training	
• Music education and training beginning in high school or earlier	Classes in elementary through high school, private lessons, musical groups
• Bachelor's degree in music education	College

TEACH

Emphasize to students how helpful the Internet can be. Counselors have found that students who research career preparation providers via the Internet make more informed choices and have fewer undergraduate transfers.

DIFFERENT LEARNING STYLES

Visual Learners

Provide students with poster board and art supplies. Ask students to use the Internet, the library, and interviews to research a career in which they are interested. Their research is to include the entry-level requirements and preparation options. If two students are interested in the same career, allow them to work together. Have students create a poster board-sized chart that is modeled after the chart on this page. Encourage students to make their charts colorful and interesting.

Your Education/Training Path

After you have determined the requirements and preparation options for your career, you will need to investigate career preparation providers. A **career preparation provider** is any training program, school, institution, individual, or business that offers career preparation instruction. Your counselor can help you identify career preparation providers that offer the education/training you will need. Also, your school or community library may have a special section devoted to career preparation. Other information sources include government web pages, online search sites, and the National Joint Apprenticeship and Training Committee.

Selecting a Career Preparation Provider

What do you think? What criteria do you think you should use to select a career preparation provider?

When you are ready to choose a career preparation provider, your research should identify several whose courses meet the education/training requirements of your career. Which provider should you choose? Checking different aspects of each provider (including reputation, accreditation, offerings, cost, and campus culture) will help you make a good choice.

CAREER SUCCESS TIP

Employers in your field of interest may recommend or send their employees to education or training programs. Find out what programs employers use.

Reputation

The reputation of your career preparation provider will influence your future employers. A good reputation will reflect favorably on you, while a poor reputation may negatively affect an employer's opinion of your qualifications. Ask former students for their opinion of the education/training provider and the course of study you are considering. Check with the people you talked to while you were developing your career plan. Call employers in your career field, introduce yourself, and ask for their opinion.

Accreditation

In the early part of the twentieth century, education professionals began working together to develop a process, called **accreditation**, that would ensure a basic level of quality in postsecondary schools and programs. In the same spirit, many professions have established state and national associations, councils, or agencies to evaluate education and training programs related to their professions.

Any program or institution you are considering for your education and training should be accredited by a reliable authority. Accreditation will help you determine the quality of the education/training you will

158

receive. Just as the reputation of a school or program will influence a future employer, so will whether the school or program is accredited. Career preparation providers should be able to tell you who accredits their school or program and when they were last accredited. Schools and programs must renew their accreditation regularly.

Offerings

Different career preparation providers offer different levels of education and training, such as a certificate, an associate degree, a bachelor's degree, and so on. In addition, many providers offer more than one level. Before you select a provider, make sure you understand the different options offered. Confirm that the available levels of education or training match your career goals.

Cassidy planned to enroll in a career/technical school and earn an associate degree in web page management. Cassidy believed an associate degree would provide sufficient education and training, allowing her to offer web site design and maintenance services to small businesses. While researching schools, Cassidy interviewed Brianna Charon, who currently has a thriving small business designing web sites. Cassidy wanted to learn about Brianna's background and education/training path and whether she could recommend any career/technical schools. During the interview, Brianna mentioned that her bachelor's degree provides a competitive advantage when she bids for contracts. She recommended that Cassidy continue school to earn a bachelor's degree.

Cassidy checked with several colleges to see if they would accept credits from an accredited career/technical school. Most would accept Cassidy's credits, but they limited the number of credits that could be applied toward a bachelor's degree. Finally, Cassidy found a college that offered a bachelor's degree in applied science. The school would allow Cassidy to transfer and apply all the credits from a career/technical school toward a bachelor's degree if Cassidy began working toward a degree within the next two years. By investigating options early, Cassidy was able to make choices that would lead to a better chance for career success.

> **66** Once the 'what' is decided, the 'how' always follows. **99**
>
> —*Pearl Buck, Author*

═ TEACH ═

Emphasize to students that they should check out internships and cooperative job programs *before* choosing a career preparation provider. Internships and cooperative job programs may provide course credit, student pay, or grants for working at unpaid internships.

═ TEACH ═

Attending college/education and training fairs is a good way for students to research career preparation providers. Students may obtain books, view videos, and talk to representatives at fairs. The National Association of College Admission Counseling (NACAC) sponsors a web site at **www.nacac.com/fair.html** that provides schedules for the National College Fair and the Performing and Visual Arts circuits. NACAC also sponsors ongoing online college fairs at **www.onlinecollegefair.com** that address the educational needs of many types of students.

INTEGRATED ACADEMICS
Language Arts
Have each student research a specific career preparation provider to learn about the education or training offered by the institution. Have students write a report that answers the following questions: Is the institution accredited? What classes are required? What degrees or certificates are offered? How long it will take to get the degree or certificate? Is on-the-job training offered? Are placement counselors available?

Have students complete **Activity 9-3, "Learning from Others,"** that appears on page 174. Teaching suggestions and the solution for this activity appear on page 174. An activity worksheet can be found on the Career Portfolio and Resource CD— **Text Activity 09-3.doc.**

What do you think?

Use **TM09-05**.
Students' answers will vary.

Students who obtain scholarships generally must report them to the career preparation provider's financial aid office. Providers typically trim a student's aid package by the amount of the scholarship, although each school has a different policy about how it does the trimming. Some providers apply scholarships against school-awarded grants rather than against loan awards. As a result, a student may have just as many loans to repay as he or she had before earning a scholarship.

Because students often have no idea of postsecondary education/training costs, lead a class discussion about the different items students need to plan for, such as testing fees, application fees, travel costs, and moving expenses. Also have different groups of students research the costs for attending different types of career preparation providers. Possible costs include tuition, room and board, tools, books, and school supplies. Ask students to report their findings to the class.

Review your career plan and your research to determine whether the career preparation providers you are considering offer the education or training you will need for your chosen career path. For example, if you want to get a certificate, then work in the field, and then study for an associate degree, find out if the institution will apply the credits earned at the certificate level toward an associate degree. Also find out if the credits are transferable to other schools or programs.

In Activity 9-3, "Learning from Others," you discover how a successful person in your career field chose a career preparation provider.

Cost

Education/training costs vary widely and range from inexpensive fees to very expensive tuition charges. Therefore, you want to think ahead about what costs you will have. Keep in mind that accredited schools and programs often offer financial aid to qualified applicants.

What do you think? Do you think you will be eligible for financial aid to pay for your additional education/training? Why or why not?

Aid is also available from other sources, such as government agencies, private donors, and professional associations. Financial aid can be in the form of scholarships, grants, loans, or work-study programs.

CAREER SUCCESS TIP

Don't try to do everything yourself. Your counselor can help you find and apply for many sources of financial aid.

- A **scholarship** is money provided for your education that you do not have to repay. Scholarships may be awarded on the basis of need, academic achievement, or a combination of the two. If a scholarship is renewable from year to year, you must meet specific academic or other standards in order to continue to receive it. Scholarships are available from many sources, not just career preparation providers. For example, a professional organization may fund a scholarship for a qualified student who plans a career in that profession.

- A **grant** is money provided by government, schools, or private donors. For example, the Federal Pell Grant is a need-based grant for undergraduate students. You do not have to repay grant money, but you must meet the standards and qualifications set by the provider of the grant.

- A **loan** is money that must be repaid. Loans are available from the federal government, some state governments, and financial institutions. Government-sponsored loan programs offer lower interest rates and more flexible repayment options than commercial lenders. Although some federal programs loan money directly to students, most other loan programs require you to have an adult family member cosign a loan. The **cosigner** is the person responsible for paying back the loan if you fail to make payments.

- A **work-study program** provides money to pay students for qualified on- or off-campus jobs. Work-study programs are funded through a school and are awarded as part of a financial aid package. You must show financial need and find and apply for job openings approved by the school.

 CAREER SUCCESS TIP

Financial Aid

Contact a financial aid adviser at a local education provider to see if he or she will speak to your class. Have the speaker explain the different types of financial aid available. Ask the speaker to bring the different forms that people must fill out when applying for financial aid so students can have hands-on experience. Tell students that most career preparation providers for higher education have counselors to help students obtain the financial aid that best suits their individual situation.

To apply for need-based scholarships, grants, loans, or work-study programs, you and your family must complete a form called the **Free Application for Financial Student Aid (FAFSA)**. The FAFSA uses information from the income tax returns of your parent(s). Check the FAFSA web site for additional information. Schools usually give priority funding to students who submit their completed FAFSA by a specific date. This date varies depending on the school; some schools have a priority date as early as February 1.

The results of the FAFSA process are provided to you in a report called the **Student Aid Report (SAR)**. The amount you and your family should contribute to your education or training is shown on the SAR as the **expected family contribution (EFC)**. Almost all need-based financial-aid programs use the EFC as the basis for the amount and type of financial aid they offer students. Therefore, you should review the SAR carefully with your family. If you have any concerns or find any errors in the SAR, talk to a financial-aid representative of the school. Based on unusual circumstances (such as high medical bills or unemployment) or the school's award criteria, the school may adjust the results of the FAFSA process.

Campus Culture

The characteristics that give each school or training program its unique personality can be referred to as its **campus culture**. When the time comes, you can help yourself by visiting each possible career preparation provider to find out if its campus culture matches your needs.

> After growing up in a western city (population 150,000) bordered by mountains and surrounded by sagebrush and farms, JJ Henri wanted to explore life in a large metropolitan area in another part of the country. So he kept location in mind when researching career preparation providers. Several schools in the Minneapolis-St. Paul area had accredited music education programs, and the location seemed perfect to JJ. Minnesota, with its many lakes and parks, was very different from home, and JJ could hardly wait to explore downtown Minneapolis.
>
> Fortunately, the three schools that interested JJ were hosting open campuses for visiting students during the same week. JJ would have the expense of only one long-distance trip. By calling ahead, he was also able to arrange free overnight stays as well as campus tours at the schools. The admissions counselors also scheduled several activities, including attending classes.
>
> During the school visits, JJ discovered that culture shock is not limited to stays in foreign countries. Everything in Minnesota was different—no mountains, high humidity, and people everywhere. Even the differences JJ thought would be exciting—traveling around the city by bus, taking classes at more than one school, going to fantastic music programs and performances, and mingling with people from all over the world—were a little overwhelming. JJ began to wonder if Minnesota was the right choice after all.

> ### CAREER SUCCESS TIP
>
> Tax returns and the FAFSA should be prepared as early in the year as possible. Early applicants for financial aid have the best chance of getting favorable aid packages.

☛ CAREER SUCCESS TIP

FAFSA

Encourage students to learn more about the FAFSA process by visiting *FAFSA on the Web* at **www.fafsa.ed.gov**. Encourage students to print the Pre-Application Worksheet and share it with their parents. The worksheet provides a preview of the kinds of questions students will need to answer when completing the FAFSA. The worksheet also identifies information parents are required to supply. In addition, the worksheet outlines the documents applicants need to have available when they fill out the application.

▬ TEACH ▬

Help students understand the "real" cost of loans. The College Board web site at **www.collegeboard.com** offers a free "Student Loan Calculator" that helps students determine monthly loan payments. Suggest that students review their budgets from Chapter 7 and estimate how they would manage a loan payment each month.

▬ ENRICH ▬

Have students complete **Activity 9-A, "Campus Culture,"** found in the *Investigating Your Career Activities & Projects* book.

This activity helps students identify, think about, and discuss the aspects of campus culture that are important to them on a personal level or that will support their career goals. The activity also provides an opportunity for dialogue with family members. Class or team discussions may help students identify additional factors of campus culture.

Solution: The solution for this activity appears in the *Teacher's Edition* of *Investigating Your Career Activities & Projects*.

Use **TM09-06**.
Students' answers will vary.

APPLY

Have students complete **Activity 9-4,
"Analysis of Career Preparation
Providers,"** that appears on pages
174–175. Teaching suggestions and
the solution for this activity appear on
page 174. An activity worksheet can
be found on the Career Portfolio
and Resource CD—**Text Activity
09-4.doc**.

ENRICH

Have students complete **Activity
9-B, "Similarities and Differences,"**
found in the *Investigating Your
Career Activities & Projects* book.

This activity helps students learn
how to narrow choices by evaluating
the offerings of education/training
providers.
Solution: The solution for this activity
appears in the *Teacher's Edition* of
*Investigating Your Career Activities &
Projects*.

However, JJ felt more
comfortable after visiting
all the colleges and talking to counselors and
other students about the
differences between the
two cultures. After
returning home and
reliving all the new experiences of the trip, JJ
began to look forward to
going back to Minnesota.
In the end, the visit reinforced JJ's decision about
a music education
school. With the help of
family members and the
counselor at school, JJ
continued to plan to
attend one of the schools
in Minnesota.

What do you think?

What do you think an on-site visit can tell you about the employer,
school, or program you are considering for your education/training?

As you narrow your choice of a career preparation provider, be sure to
consider all aspects of the provider's campus culture. A variety of factors influence the campus culture of programs or schools, including
the following:

- The mix and ages of resident, day, and/or night students
- The type of provider (public school, private school, or workplace)
- The geographic origins of the students
- The geographic location, including the climate, of the school
  or workplace
- The number of students attending the school or training program
  and the size of the classes

All of these factors can affect the success of your education/training,
and you will need to think about each when you visit the possible
providers you have selected. During your visit, you may find that the
cultures of some providers are not at all what you expected. You may
find that a school or program you were not seriously considering has
just the culture you want, or you may find that a provider you thought
would be perfect is not.

In Activity 9-4, "Analysis of Career Preparation Providers," you will
use the Internet to evaluate education/training providers.

DIFFERENT LEARNING ABILITIES
Visually Impaired
Team visually impaired students with a partner. Provide art supplies to the teams, and
have them create a large print advertisement that encourages students to make on-site
visits to campuses. Have each team present its work to the class, and encourage other
students to provide feedback. Hold a class discussion on why students should visit the
campus of a school they are considering attending. Post the advertisements around the
classroom.

Determine Entrance Requirements

Regardless of the education/training path you finally select, you can increase your chances of being accepted by a career preparation provider by making sure your qualifications meet the provider's admission requirements. Even though you may not have decided yet on a specific school or program, you probably have an idea of your career preparation needs. For example, you are probably aware that most postsecondary schools or programs will require a high school diploma or its equivalent for admission.

Determining the entrance requirements of the programs or schools you are considering for your education/training will again require research. You can begin by sending for brochures and viewbooks from all the programs or schools you are considering and by reviewing the web site of each provider. Then talk to your counselor about the programs or schools.

Carefully study all the information you collect until you have a clear understanding of admission requirements. Finally, summarize them. Your summary will help you determine how you can benefit most from the education options you have right now. You can use the summary to plan your remaining classes, extracurricular activities, and part-time and/or summer jobs.

For example, JJ Henri discovered that the three music education schools in Minnesota had similar entrance requirements. JJ summarized the entrance requirements as shown below. He will use the summary as a reference while planning remaining high school classes.

JJ Henri's Summary of Entrance Requirements

Required for Admission:

English	4 years
Foreign Languages	4 years
Natural Sciences	3 years (includes 1 year of a laboratory science)
Social Studies	2 years
Mathematics	3 years
Performing Arts	2 years

Additional Requirements:

Proficiency on a musical instrument or in vocal performance as determined from an unedited audition tape. Audition tapes must be certified as unedited by a qualified music teacher.

Activity 9-5, "Summarize Entrance Requirements," helps you list the entrance requirements you will need to meet to reach your goals.

CAREER TREND
GED

Every year more than 860,000 adults who have not graduated from high school take the GED test. These three men received GEDs: Bill Cosby, comedian; Dave Thomas, founder of Wendy's restaurants; and Ben Nighthorse Campbell, U.S. senator from Colorado. To receive a GED credential requires study and discipline, the same requirements for successfully completing high school.

—*Source: **www.acenet.edu/calec/ged***

What do you think?

Use **TM09-07**.
Students' answers will vary.

APPLY

Have students complete **Activity 9-6, "Plan Classes,"** that appears on page 175. Teaching suggestions and the solution for this activity appear on page 175. An activity worksheet can be found on the Career Portfolio and Resource CD—**Text Activity 09-6.pdf**.

Begin Implementing Your Career Plan

> 66 It takes just as much energy to wish as it does to plan. 99
>
> —*Eleanor Roosevelt*

Developing your career plan has given you the chance to learn more about yourself, explore your career possibilities, and investigate your education/training needs. In the process you have:

- Followed your *P*A*T*H to Success*.
- Researched career fields.
- Interviewed successful people who work in fields that interest you.
- Examined programs and schools that can help you succeed.

With a clearer idea of what is important to you and what you want your future to be like, you can begin implementing your career plan.

Choose High School Classes

Many high schools offer a wide range of elective courses. Some also offer separate curriculums based on general differences in career goals. Your summary of entrance requirements can help you choose your remaining high school courses.

What do you think? How do you decide which courses to take? Will the courses you have chosen help you reach your career goals? Why or why not?

Although each state sets its own standards, states require credits in specific subjects for high school graduation. Students may also be required to take additional credits in electives. Plus, the average high school schedule allows students to take even more credits. With such a variety of courses and large number of credits available, you have the opportunity to gain practical workplace skills as well as to meet basic requirements for advanced training programs or for college.

As you choose your classes, try not to overspecialize. Rather than focusing all your electives in one area, choose courses that will provide you with a varied background. In particular, consider more math, science, and/or technology classes. Also resist the temptation to take easy electives. All the courses you take should make a positive statement about you and your goals. Your counselor can help you choose those classes that will be most useful for your future career. Counselors are trained to see how high school courses are linked to education/training requirements for career preparation providers.

A form called a High School Credits Tracker can help you plan and track four years of classes on one sheet of paper. The tracking method is flexible and will allow you to know when you have completed graduation requirements. Using the form, you can easily determine what entrance requirements you have already met and when you can take the additional courses you need. Illustration 9-3 shows JJ Henri's credits tracker and provides an example of how to use the tracking form.

In Activity 9-6, "Plan Classes," you will use a High School Credits Tracker to plan the classes that support your career goals.

164

Print Learners

Have students write a short essay entitled "What Classes Should Be Offered in High School." In their essays, students are to tell what courses they think should be offered and describe why each course would be a good one. Call on several students to read their essays in class. Remind students that their essays must be grammatically correct and use correct spelling and punctuation. Essays are to be double-spaced and computer-generated with 12-point type.

Illustration 9-3 JJ Henri's High School Credits Tracker

High School Credits Tracker

Name: JJ Henri

Black = Ink (Use for completed courses) **Blue = Pencil** (Use for courses not yet completed)

Required Subjects	Required Credits*	Sem. 1	Sem. 2	Sem. 3	Sem. 4	Sem. 5	Sem. 6	Sem. 7	Sem. 8	Totals
		Credits Planned								
American Government	2							AP¹ AG	AP¹ AG	2
Economics	1						Econ**			1
English	8	Eng 9	Eng 9	Engl 10	Engl 10	Engl 11	Engl 11	Engl 12	Engl 12	8
Health	1					Health				1
History	4	US	US			AP¹ US	AP¹ US			4
Academic Humanities	2			Latin 1	Latin 1					2
Performance Humanities	2	Orch	Orch							2
Math	4	Alg 1	Alg 1	Geom	Geom					4
Physical Education	2			PE**	PE**					2
Reading	1	Reading								1
Science	4	Earth Science	Earth Science	Biol	Biol					4
Speech	1		Speech							1
Required Electives	12	Tech 1	Drama 1	Orch Choir	Orch Choir	Alg 2 Orch Choir Latin 2	Alg 2 Orch	0	0	12
Total Graduation Requirements	44	7	7	7	7	7	5	2	2	44
Optional Credits: Additional Electives (None Required for Graduation)		0	0	Keybrd Apps	0	0	Latin 2 Art 1	Chem Math Anal Choir Art 2	Chem Math Anal Choir Art 3	11
Total Credits Planned		7	7	8	7	7	7	6	6	55

*Each semester of a class is worth one (1) credit   ** Summer School   ¹Advanced Placement Class

Tell students their High School Credits Tracker form provides them with *one* place in which to plan and record all their high school courses. Advise students to use pencil to write in classes they plan to take. Once they have completed a course, students should use ink to permanently record the class on their tracking form. A current High School Credits Tracker will make it much easier for students to adjust their course plans or to compare the courses and credits they have completed with the requirements of career preparation providers.

INTEGRATED ACADEMICS
Art

For a few weeks, have students bring magazines to class. Provide students with art materials and poster board to create a large graphic organizer of their High School Credits Tracker. Students can use the model on this page or create their own. Using the art supplies and pictures from the magazines, have students decorate their charts. Encourage students to be creative as well as practical with their charts. Hold a class vote to determine which student has the most imaginatively decorated chart.

Plan Activities

Deciding among extracurricular activities, volunteer opportunities, and part-time jobs can be challenging. Many students have several strong interests and not enough time to do everything they would like. To help you decide whether to participate in an activity, answer the following five questions:

- Does the activity support my values?
- Why is the activity important to me?
- How does the activity help me develop experience, knowledge, and skills that will support my goals?
- What effect will participating in the activity have on my schedule?
- Who else will be affected by my participation in the activity? Will they support my participation?

Your activity choices should further your goals. Most training programs and colleges prefer students who have varied backgrounds and who have participated in extracurricular activities that develop leadership and cooperation skills. Students who have worked as volunteers or have had part-time jobs are also considered to be strong applicants.

REAL PEOPLE
REAL CAREERS

Radiological Technologist

Rose Branson knew early in life she wanted to work in the medical field. Today as the director of radiological services at Bryn Mawr Hospital in Pennsylvania, she has reached her career goal. Her department is in charge of taking ultrasound images of patients as well as x-rays and computer-assisted tomography (CAT) scans. This ability to see inside a patient's body without surgery is a basic of today's medicine.

How Rose got where she is, is almost as interesting as what she does. In high school, Rose concentrated on science courses—biology, chemistry, and physics. She did well in those courses and planned for a career in the field of radiology. She went to a community college and earned an associate degree in radiological technology. But she didn't stop there. Rose realized all of her education and training was in science, and she wanted to expand her knowledge to other fields. So she transferred her credits and earned a bachelor's degree in English literature. Although the degree did not further her career goal of working in medicine, Rose believed the experience enriched her life and helped her better understand people.

As Rose began working in radiology, she realized that to advance to a job with more responsibility, she would need additional education and training. So she went back to school and got a master's degree in health administration. Now as head of the department, Rose still takes courses and encourages everyone on her staff to do the same. She believes lifelong learning is essential for both career and personal development.

For more information about:
- radiologic technology careers, investigate *www.arrt.org*.
- careers in health administration, explore *www.aupha.org/student.htm*.

Source: Interview with Rose Branson.

REAL PEOPLE—REAL CAREERS
Radiology and Health Administration

Assign half the class to investigate radiology careers and half the class to investigate careers in health administration. Students can use the web sites provided in Real Careers on this page. Have each student use the research to write a fact sheet that identifies and describes at least three facts about a career in radiology or a career in health administration. Have students share their information to create one class fact sheet for each of the two careers. Post the fact sheets in the classroom.

Decide about Jobs

Like many students, you may have a part-time or summer job or be seriously thinking of finding one. Statistics show that part-time jobs help students develop characteristics employers value, such as responsibility, organization, and time management. Working also provides benefits that teens value, such as money and increased independence. However, as mentioned in Chapter 8, you must be sure that a part-time job doesn't interfere with your school work or your career goals.

JJ Henri appeared to be facing a dilemma. Last year JJ was on the swim team at the local Y and earned a lifeguard certificate. Although JJ enjoyed swimming, this year's schedule of classes and music activities left no time for team practice. Plus, JJ wanted to find a part-time job to earn money for clothes and leisure activities with friends. Also, music education college will be expensive, and JJ hoped to begin saving some money for college expenses.

JJ had not really started looking for a part-time job when the swim coach mentioned that a lifeguard was needed for four hours on Saturdays and wondered if JJ would be interested. On the same day, the Y's director of after-school care offered JJ a job working eight hours a week as a counselor. JJ would be working with children of various age groups and would probably be involved with planning and supervising activities as well. Then JJ's next door neighbor, who is a route manager for the local paper, asked if JJ wanted to take over the neighborhood paper route. Delivering papers would pay about 10 percent more than the combined pay for the two Y jobs and take about the same amount of time.

The dilemma? JJ had to decide which job or jobs to take. Then JJ remembered the list of requirements and preparation options for a music education career. Would the list help with his decision? After looking at the list, JJ realized there was no dilemma after all. Obviously, the counseling job at the Y would provide work experience related to JJ's career goals.

Part-time and summer jobs can provide valuable experience that directly supports your career goals. You have spent considerable time and energy developing your career plan and describing your personal goals. Doesn't it make sense to choose jobs that further your career aspirations or help you meet your goals?

TEACH

Help students realize that not all part-time jobs will be appropriate. Ask students to list the characteristics a part-time job must have to meet the scheduling needs of students in middle school or junior high school. Students' answers may include (1) the need for public transportation or company location close enough to walk or bike to, (2) scheduling flexibility to accommodate after-school and weekend work times, and (3) work that meets local, state, and/or federal restrictions for employing teenage or younger students.

DIFFERENT LEARNING ABILITIES
Dyslexia

Have students work in pairs to brainstorm and list five ways summer and part-time work experience can directly support their career goals. Have student pairs share their list with another group to make one list. This group of four is to eliminate duplicates from their individual lists. Use this list as a basis for a class discussion on part-time and summer jobs students have had and those they might have in the future. Also discuss how these jobs might provide valuable experience that directly supports their future careers.

Use **TM09-08**.
Students' answers will vary.

TEACH

When discussing **What do you think?** on page 168, ask students to make a list of part-time or summer jobs that would help them learn more about a career or start them in their career field. Examples include the following: (1) In the veterinary field, work as a pet store clerk, veterinarian's assistant, or pet groomer. (2) In the teaching field, work as a camp counselor or as an after-school tutor. (3) In the healthcare field, work as a pharmacy cashier or as an orderly in a hospital or skilled nursing facility.

APPLY

Have students complete **Activity 9-7, "Case Challenges,"** that appears on pages 175–176. Teaching suggestions and the solution for this activity appear on page 175. An activity worksheet can be found on the Career Portfolio and Resource CD—**Text Activity 09-7.doc**.

What part-time or summer jobs would help you meet your career goals?

Manage Your Time

You, like many of today's students, may be juggling family, school, work, social, and community commitments. Busy teens may leave the house to attend team practice at 6 a.m., return home after mowing yards, eat dinner, and then do homework until nearly midnight. No wonder WebMD, Inc., reported that nearly 15 percent of students fell asleep in class!

As you begin implementing your career plan, look at the Weekly Time Planner you prepared in Activity 7-8 and filed in your Career Journey Folder. Also review the time management tips in Chapter 7. Before taking on any new activities, consider how they will affect your schedule. Keep your planner current and use it to record your commitments. If you are organized, you will be able to use your available time more productively. For example, you may need less time in the evening for study if you work on your homework during the day between other commitments. Also consider untraditional approaches. For example, if you work during the evening but do not have early morning obligations, try switching your homework period from evening to morning.

Also keep in mind you will need some "down time" to recharge. Try planning breaks into your day when you can relax. If your schedule is so busy you have no time to relax, reevaluate your commitments.

Activity 9-7, "Case Challenges," provides an opportunity for you to analyze some case studies of people who are beginning their careers.

CAREER FACT

According to the National Sleep Foundation (NSF), one cause of mid-afternoon sleepiness is a drop in body temperature. The NSF recommends a 15- to 20-minute nap to restore alertness and memory and relieve stress and fatigue.

Apply for Admission

All education and training programs have an admission process. Your research and planning will prepare you to meet admission requirements when the time comes. Completing and tracking your application will be the final steps toward entering the career preparation program of your choice.

Completing Your Application

Fill out your application documents truthfully, completely, and neatly. Submit your application packet and the required fees in time to meet submission deadlines. Late applications may disqualify you for admittance or for financial aid. Dishonesty is an automatic disqualifier. In addition to neatness, completeness, and accuracy, admission counselors judge applications on the quality of the answers. You may find it helpful to complete a copy of the application as practice. Then you can review it with your counselor before filling out the final application. Finally, keep copies of your application packets in your personal files.

CAREER TREND
Afternoon Naps
With the cooperation of your administration, assign the following class project: Have students create a school schedule that allows them to take a 15- to 20-minute nap in the afternoon. Have students write a proposal to the administration. Proposals are to include the logistics of how an afternoon nap would work and logical arguments as to why the naps are necessary. Have students access the web site of the National Sleep Foundation **www.sleepfoundation.org**, for information and statistics for their proposal. Have student representatives deliver the completed proposal to the appropriate administrator at your school.

Besides an application form and fees, admission requirements typically include the following:

- **Official transcript.** An **official transcript** is one that contains the school seal and has an original signature of a school official. In addition to courses and grades, transcripts may include other information, such as the results of state graduation or proficiency tests, the results of college entrance exams, and copies of certifications earned. You will be able to obtain a transcript request form from your counselor. Find out how much time is needed to process your request so you can meet admission deadlines.

- **Resume.** A **resume** is a brief written account of personal, educational, and professional qualifications and experience. Chapter 14 will cover resumes in depth and discuss their use in applying for jobs. However, admissions counselors may use resumes to decide if applicants will be able to handle the work and make a positive contribution to the school or program. A resume is also helpful for filling out applications and assisting your counselor. As in JJ Henri's resume in Illustration 9-4 on page 170, your resume should highlight your school, job, and community accomplishments.

- **Letters of recommendation.** A **letter of recommendation** is written by someone who can provide information about your personal, school, or employment background. Ask people who will give you a *positive* recommendation to write letters. Most schools or programs will want letters from teachers, employers, school officials, and community leaders. You should not ask relatives for letters. Give people who agree to write a letter a copy of your resume and an envelope that is stamped and addressed to the admission office. Finally, send a thank-you note to every person who writes a letter for you.

- **Essay or letter.** In general, the school or program admission office will define the topic for an essay or a letter. Usually, admission counselors want to get a glimpse of your personality and to find out your motivation for attending their school or program. Outline what you want to say and list the items you want to include before you begin writing. Then write accurately, clearly, and precisely using correct grammar and spelling. Before writing your final essay or letter, have a teacher or family member proofread your draft.

Tracking Your Applications

Applications contain many parts, involve the participation of several people, and include several time frames. Your responsibility during the admission process includes following up to make sure the other people involved meet the application deadlines. Planning ahead, allowing ample time for people to do their part, and checking to make sure people are able to meet the deadlines will be easier if you use the Application Checklist shown in Illustration 9-5 on page 171.

Use Activity 9-8, "Coming to Terms," to understand some of the important terms in this chapter more thoroughly.

> ## CAREER★SUCCESS TIP
>
> Many schools and training programs allow you to complete and send your application online. Check with your career preparation providers to find out how they prefer to receive applications.

CAREER SUCCESS TIP

Online Applications

Have students go online to obtain information about a career preparation provider that interests them. Have students find out the procedure for applying online. If the chosen school or program does not offer online applications, have students choose another school or program that does provide this service.

Students sometimes have difficulty requesting letters of recommendation. In addition to the points covered in the student text, discuss with students the benefits of their doing the following:

• Asking politely, such as finding out whether the potential reference has time to talk when you call or visit or whether making an appointment would be more convenient

• Being prompt for appointments

• Giving the potential reference a copy of your resume and any other necessary material, including the return deadline

• Waiving your right to see the recommendation letter

Also emphasize the importance of sending a thank-you note to each reference.

Illustration 9-4 JJ Henri's Application Resume

JJ Henri
2401 Broadway Boulevard
Boise, Idaho 83706-4621
Telephone: (208) 555-0146
Email: jjhenri@cablenet.com

EDUCATION

Senator High School, Boise
Expected graduation, June 2006

HIGH SCHOOL HONORS AND AWARDS

State High School Orchestra (by audition), 2003-Present; Principal Chair, Second Violins
Idaho Law Foundation Mock Trial, Second Place at State Competition, 2004
National Honor Society, 2003-Present

ACTIVITIES

State Youth Orchestra, Violinist, 2004-Present
Senator High School Orchestra, Violinist, 2006-Present
Choirs: A Cappella Choir, 2002-2003; Classic Choir (by audition), 2003-Present
Key Club, 2004-Present
Y Leader's Club, 2002-Present: Teen Nights Coordinator, 2004-2005
Mock Trial Team, 2003-Present
St. Paul Church, Food Bank Volunteer, 2002-Present
Y Swim Team, 2003-2004

WORK EXPERIENCE

Y Family Center, Boise
Residence Camp Assistant Counselor and Song Leader, Summers 2002-Present
Coordinate the activities of five to eight campers in summer residence-camp sessions. Plan one cabin activity and lead two multicabin activities each day. Make sure campers clean the cabin every morning. Accompany campers to meals and evening activities. Plan and lead musical activities at evening campfire. Ensure campers know and follow safety and hygiene rules. Follow Y-approved leadership techniques and policies. Elected Outstanding Assistant Counselor by other camp staff.

Assistant After-School Counselor, part-time, 2004-Present
Organize and monitor activities for children aged six to ten years. Initiated music class twice a week to teach children basic rhythms on percussion instruments.

Basset Family, Boise
Baby-sitter, 2001-2003
Cared for three boys (ages two, four, and six) from 6:45 p.m. to 9:15 p.m. two nights a week and every Friday evening from October through May.

DIFFERENT LEARNING STYLES

Print Learners

Have students use the computer to compose an application resume for a career preparation provider of their choice. Hold a class discussion on the components of an application. Call on different students to speak about the different sections. Advise print learners to print out the application for editing and proofreading rather than proofread on the computer screen.

Illustration 9-5 Application Checklist

Application Checklist

School/Program Name:	
Street:	Mail Stop:
City, State, Zip:	
Telephone:	Fax:
Admission Counselor:	E-mail:
Date Application Requested:	Date Received:
Application Deadline:	Financial Aid Application Deadline/s:

Prepare Application Packet for H.S. Counselor to process.   Date Turned In:
Turn in a minimum of three (3) weeks **before** application deadline.

	Date		Date
1. H.S. transcripts requested Fee paid		6. If application essay/letter required:	
2. Test scores requested Fees paid		a. Essay/letter drafted	
SAT		b. Essay/letter edited	
ACT		c. Essay/letter finalized	
AP Exams			
Other			
3. Completed, signed application		7. Portfolio, if required	
4. Application fee check/money order		8. Addressed/stamped envelope	
5. Your resume		9. Filed copies of packet	

Application Follow-up Date application sent to school/program:
Date school/program received application:

Letters of Recommendation: Request **at least** *four* (4) weeks before application deadline.

First Author:	**Third Author:**
Date requested the letter:	Date requested the letter:
Date letter required:	Date letter required:
Date school/program-addressed/stamped envelope to author:	Date school/program-addressed/stamped envelope to author:
Date resume to author:	Date resume to author:
Date letter mailed to school/program:	Date letter mailed to school/program:
Date delivered thank-you note:	Date delivered thank-you note:
Second Author:	**Fourth Author:**
Date requested the letter:	Date requested the letter:
Date letter required:	Date letter required:
Date school/program-addressed/stamped envelope to author:	Date school/program-addressed/stamped envelope to author:
Date resume to author:	Date resume to author:
Date letter mailed to school/program:	Date letter mailed to school/program:
Date delivered thank-you note:	Date delivered thank-you note:

ENRICH

Have students complete **Activity 9-D, "Imagine . . . .,"** found in the *Investigating Your Career Activities & Projects* book.

This multipart activity gives students an appreciation for the thought, time, and coordination necessary to complete elements of the admissions process for postsecondary training/education. Students identify deadlines and develop a process timeline. Used together, Activity 9-D and Project 3 comprise a complete mock application process. The mock application process is especially appropriate for middle school students who may not receive additional information about the secondary admissions process before they must begin applying to career education providers.

Solution: The solution for this activity appears in the *Teacher's Edition* of *Investigating Your Career Activities & Projects.*

Career Journal

Ask students to spend 10 minutes writing Career Journal entries that answer the following questions:
1. How well did what you thought you knew match what the chapter presented?
2. What questions do you now have about the chapter topics, and where do you think you can find the answers to those questions?
3. How will the content of the chapter help you investigate *your* career?

INTEGRATED ACADEMICS
Computer Science
Have students use the computer to create an application checklist. Suggest that students use the model on this page to help them get started, but to create a checklist that fits their individual needs. Have students work with another student to proofread their checklists. As a class, talk about the components students chose to include on their checklists and why they chose these components. Have them add any missing components.

Remind students about the objectives set forth at the beginning of the chapter, and use this summary to reinforce the concepts presented in this chapter.

CLOSE

Wrap up this chapter by having students complete **Project 3, "Application, Resume, and Essay,"** found in the *Investigating Your Career Activities & Projects* book.

In Part 1, students complete a college or training program application. In Part 2, students plan and write a resume for their postsecondary training/education application. In Part 3, students plan and write an answer to an application essay question. Finally, in Part 4, students track their completion of each part of the application process.

This project lends itself well to team teaching. Perhaps the English/Language Arts teacher would work with students to develop answers to the essay question. School counselors may want to provide possible essay questions as well as explain to students the way admission teams rate essay answers. In addition, counselors may wish to explain to students what they should include in their application resume and how long their answers to the essay questions should be. The last page of this project reproduces Illustration 9-5, Application Checklist. If you elect to have students complete the full mock application process, the Application Checklist is an ideal tracking tool for each student. Have students change the deadlines for each item to reflect your time periods for the project.

Solution: The solution for this activity appears in the *Teacher's Edition* of *Investigating Your Career Activities & Projects.*

ASSESS

Administer the printed objective test for Chapter 9, available with this package. Test solutions are found in the *Teacher's Edition* of *Investigating Your Career Chapter Tests.* Use the **Exam**View® CD to create your own objective test for this chapter.

- **I have listed the requirements and preparations for my career.**

  I have summarized the requirements of my career in terms of the skills, experience, abilities and personality, and education and training needed for career success. I have also determined the preparation options necessary to meet the requirements of my career.

- **I have analyzed career preparation providers.**

  I have identified several career preparation providers that meet my education/training needs. I have analyzed each provider in terms of its reputation, accreditation, offerings, cost, and campus culture. I also determined the entrance requirements of each provider.

- **I can begin implementing my career plan.**

  Using my career plan and the entrance requirements of schools or programs I wish to attend, I can choose courses, plan activities, and decide about part-time and summer jobs that will help me reach my career goal. I have also reviewed my schedule and time management tips so I can manage my time productively.

- **I can describe how to apply for admission.**

  When the time comes, I know how to complete my school or program applications truthfully, completely, and neatly.

Suggestions for Parents and Family Members

Encourage Teenagers to Attend College

Ways to assist teenagers in selecting career preparation providers include:

1. Assisting teens in obtaining informational interviews.
2. Arranging for teens to visit any school or program in which they are interested.
3. Encouraging teens to attend college fairs or program open houses.
4. Investigating test preparation courses.
5. Creating a mutually agreeable list of career preparation providers in terms of offerings, cost, location, and campus culture.

ACTIVITY 9-1   Requirements of Your Career

Print the **Entry-Level Requirements and Preparation Options** form from your CD, or use the handout from your teacher if a computer is not available. In the *left column* of the form, summarize the skills, experience, abilities and personality, and education/training required for success in your career. Use information from your Career Journey Folder, research, and earlier chapters to identify the requirements. You will use the same form in Part 2 of Activity 9-2.

ACTIVITY 9-2   Your Career Preparation Path

Part 1—Career Preparation Options

Study the career preparation options shown on the wheel below. On a separate sheet of paper, write down the options that are appropriate for *your* career preparation path. Prepare a presentation to show the skills you will gain that are transferable among several careers. List these careers and explain how the transferable skills apply to each one.

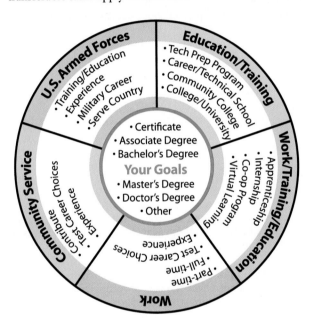

Part 2—Match Options to Requirements

Match the career preparation options you selected in Part 1 of this activity with the entry-level requirements you listed in Activity 9-1. Use the form from Activity 9-1 to record your findings.

CHAPTER 9 • • • • • FROM HERE TO YOUR CAREER

173

9-1 on page 155 as an example of the types of specific information students should provide. Students complete the Entry-Level Requirements in this activity and the Preparation Options in Activity 9-2.
Solution: Answers will vary, but students' statements should provide specifics about a particular attribute, such as "know word processing, database, spreadsheet, and presentation application software." Students should avoid general statements, such as "know computer software."

Activity 9-2: Your Career Preparation Path

Part 1—Career Preparation Options: Students envision which combination of career preparation options fits their lifestyle, goals (from Chapter 7), and career needs. Students use the Career Preparation Options wheel to summarize their education and training goals, review the broad spectrum of options, and make appropriate selections. Seeing the big picture helps students place their education/training and career decisions into the broader contexts of time and personal preferences.

Discussing the Career Preparation Options wheel (**TM09-03**) may help students review all their options before they begin the activity.
Solution: Students should list and explain their option choices.
Part 2—Match Options to Requirements: Students see how their education/training choices specifically relate to job requirements in their chosen field. Understanding the direct correlation helps students stay motivated throughout the education/training process.
Solution: Answers will vary, but students' statements should provide specifics about a particular preparation option, such as "take word processing application software classes," and avoid general statements, such as "take computer classes." Illustration 9-2 on page 157 shows the types of specific information students should provide.

Activity 9-1: Requirements of Your Career

The completed activity provides basic information students will need to begin making practical decisions about career preparation options.

Using information from their Career Journey Folder, their research, and earlier chapters, students identify the skills, experience, abilities and personality, and education/training required for success in their chosen career. Use Illustration

Activity 9-3:
Learning from Others

This activity reinforces students' understanding of the relationship between education/training and career success. Students discover how people in their career fields have chosen career preparation providers and learn how successful those choices were in promoting career growth.

Solution: Students should submit a completed questionnaire and a written summary of the results of their interview, including what they discovered about selecting a career preparation provider. You may wish to discuss and compare the results of the various interviews in class.

Activity 9-4:
Analysis of Career Preparation Providers

This activity gives students practice doing web research using keywords and teaches students how to check the accreditation of any school, program, or apprenticeship they are considering.

To help students find out about schools and programs that offer instruction in their field of interest, obtain viewbooks from various schools and programs to supplement the Internet research. Encourage students to research at least three or four career preparation providers. Consider asking students to answer the following questions: If you had to attend one of the career preparation providers you just analyzed, which one would you choose? Why?

Solution: Students should complete one sheet of the form on the Student Resource CD for each school, program, or apprenticeship they investigate.

Interview a successful person in your career field to find out how the person chose a career preparation provider. Use the following questions as the basis for your interview.

- What is your current job title? Describe your job.
- What education or training option did you choose?
- What type of career preparation provider did you use?
- How did you choose your career preparation provider?
- What was the provider's reputation? How did you determine its reputation?
- What was the provider's accreditation? How and when did you determine its accreditation?
- Did your career preparation provider offer the education/training you required? If not, how did you get the education/training you needed?
- Did you have any type of financial aid for your education/training? If so, what type and how did you get the aid?
- Did you visit your career preparation provider before applying? If so, what was your impression of the provider? If not, why not?
- If you could do it over again, would you use the same career preparation provider? If not, what would you do differently?
- What advice would you give a young person about selecting a career preparation provider?

Write a summary of the results of your interview and what you discovered about selecting a career preparation provider.

1. Locate and investigate providers of education and training. To search for and link to the schools you are considering, use the site of the National Center for Education Statistics, *http://nces.ed.gov/ipeds/cool/search.asp*. Also use Internet search engines. For colleges and universities, try keywords **college links, college search,** or **finding colleges.** For apprenticeship programs, try keywords **apprenticeship programs.**

2. To document the accreditation of a school or program, check the school viewbook, course catalog, or web site. Then check the lists of recognized accrediting agencies on the Department of Education web site at *www.ed.gov*. To document the registration of an apprenticeship program, check the Department of Labor Employment & Training Administration web site at *www.doleta.gov/atels_bat*. Click on "Finding a Program" under the heading "For Individuals." Then choose "U.S. Department of Labor Bureau of Apprenticeship and Training Office" to locate the state office nearest you. Call the State Apprenticeship Office, and find out if the apprenticeship program(s) you are considering is registered.

174

3. For each school or program, use the **Analysis of Career Preparation Providers** form from your CD or write down on a separate sheet of paper what you find out about the school or program in the categories listed below.

a. Provider name
b. Reputation
c. Accreditation/Registration
d. Offerings
e. Cost
f. Campus culture

ACTIVITY 9-5   Summarize Entrance Requirements

Determine the entrance requirements for each career preparation provider you investigated in Activity 9-4. On a separate sheet of paper, list recommended or required courses, skills, and experience preferred by the provider. Also include any other entrance requirements listed by the provider. Summarize your results using JJ's Summary of Entrance Requirements on page 163 as an example.

ACTIVITY 9-6   Plan Classes

Use your school's credit tracking form, the **High School Credits Tracker** form from your CD, or the **High School Credits Tracker** handout from your teacher to plan the classes you will complete before graduation. Also plan extracurricular, cocurricular, and community activities for high school that will support your career choice. Refer to Illustration 9-3 on page 165 as you complete the form.

ACTIVITY 9-7   Case Challenges

Each of the following case studies describes the beginning of a career journey. Discuss each case study in small groups, and analyze how each career journey might continue. There is no right or wrong answer; you only need to think in logical steps.

1. Shannon graduated from high school with an emphasis in business and technology courses. Because of her expertise with computers, she was hired as a salesperson in a local discount department store. Shannon learned about her department's merchandise quickly, received many compliments from customers, and led her section in sales. She was soon promoted to assistant manager of her department. Shannon enjoyed retailing and decided to make it her career. She wanted to take the next step and become a department manager, but she didn't have the knowledge in sales techniques, inventory management, and supervision that managers needed.

CHAPTER 9 • • • • • FROM HERE TO YOUR CAREER

 175

Activity 9-5: Summarize Entrance Requirements

This activity gives students practice in summarizing the specific entrance requirements of schools, programs, or apprenticeships in which they are interested.

The results of this activity set the framework for the decisions students will make in Activity

9-6. Direct students to JJ's Summary of Entrance Requirements, shown on page 163 of the student text, for an example of how their final summary of requirements should look.

Solution: Students' summaries should list academic- and skill-requirement levels. Be sure students investigate the requirements for all the career preparation providers they analyzed in Activity 9-4 before they create their summaries.

Activity 9-6: Plan Classes

This activity gives students the opportunity to plan for their high school classes. Remind students that the objective is to choose classes that directly support their career goals. Students are also asked to plan extracurricular, co-curricular, and community activities for high school that support their career choice. Remind students to use pencil to write in the classes they plan to take. Those students who have completed some high school courses through summer school or some or all of their freshman year should use ink to record the completed classes.

Solution: The High School Credits Tracker forms should show classes and credit totals that satisfy the graduation requirements of the high school that students will be or are attending.

Activity 9-7: Case Challenges

In addition to giving students practice in predicting the outcome of career preparation choices, this activity helps students develop critical thinking and team skills.

Solution: Answers will vary. Look for how well students understand the circumstances described in each case, the options open to the person in each case, and the consequences of the career preparation options selected. You may wish to discuss and compare the results of the various teams in class.

175

Activity 9-8: Coming to Terms

Part 1—The Free Application for Federal Student Aid: Students practice using FAFSA terms and exploring the FAFSA web site, **www.fafsa.ed.gov**.

Solution: Answers may vary slightly but should include the following:

1. Definitions

FAFSA—The Free Application of Federal Student Aid is used to apply for federal student financial aid (grants, loans, and work-study) and by most states and schools to award nonfederal financial aid.

SAR—The Student Aid Report shows all the student's information on file at FAFSA.

EFC—The expected family contribution is the amount the student's family is expected to contribute toward the cost of the student's education.

Financial need—This is the difference between the student's EFC and the cost of attendance (which can include living expenses) at the student's school.

2. (Access "Before Beginning a FAFSA" link.) If applicable to them, students need the following records: social security number; driver's license; W-2 forms/other records of money earned; previous year's federal income tax return for student, parents, and spouse; the previous year's records of untaxed income, bank statements, and any other financial records; and (non-U.S. citizens) alien registration card.

3. Understanding the FAFSA process helps you receive all the financial aid for which you qualify.

Part 2—Types of Financial Aid: This activity reinforces students' understanding of the differences among the major types of financial aid.

Solution: Answers should include the following:

1. Scholarship: Money provided for education that students do not have to repay.

2. Grant: Money provided by government, schools, or private donors that students do not need to repay. Students must meet grant requirements to receive a grant.

3. Loan: Money from federal/state governments and financial institutions that students must repay.

176

---

2. Basel worked part-time in a machine shop while taking manufacturing technology courses at the career center. After he earned his high school diploma, Basel joined a union apprenticeship program, working toward becoming a journeyworker. He worked full-time in the machine shop during the day and took classes sponsored by the union at night.

3. Marki expected to become a computer programmer after attending college and majoring in information technology. Because math was his favorite subject, he took advanced placement math courses each year. In addition, he took a number of science and computer courses. For the remainder of his schedule, he took the easiest courses his counselor would approve. As far as he was concerned, he didn't really care what else he took.

ACTIVITY 9-8   Coming to Terms

Part 1—The Free Application for Federal Student Aid

  The Free Application for Federal Student Aid (FAFSA) has a web site at **www.fafsa.ed.gov**. The FAFSA site is sponsored by the U.S. Department of Education.

1. Access the FAFSA web site. Use the site map to access general student aid information. On a separate sheet of paper, write down how the site defines the following terms:

   a. FAFSA

   b. SAR

   c. EFC

   d. Financial need

2. Use the back button to return to the home page, and then click on "Documents and Information." If you were explaining to a friend how to fill out the FAFSA form, what records would you tell your friend to gather before completing the form?

3. Why is it important that you thoroughly understand the FAFSA process?

Part 2—Types of Financial Aid

On a separate sheet of paper, explain the differences among the following types of financial aid:

1. Scholarship

2. Grant

3. Loan

4. Work-study program

---

4. Work-study program: A program that provides money to pay students to work at qualified on- or off-campus jobs.

PART
4 Preparing for
the Next Step

Part Overview

Part 4: Preparing for the Next Step

Part 4 explains what students need to know to achieve success in their first job in their career field. Career success depends on adjusting to the characteristics of the workplace, having the basic qualifications all employers want, and being able to overcome barriers to career growth. Students discover that many basic work skills are the same skills they need for success in school, including communicating effectively, accepting responsibility, and having a positive attitude. Students explore in depth how to work effectively as a member of a team, a vital skill for career success today and in the future. Finally, learning about areas of employment related to management of the workplace increases students' understanding of employers' perspectives.

PART 4
Focus

Part 4 brings the student into the workplace. Your students may not be working for pay now; however, they may experience many situations that are similar to a worksite.

Before beginning this part, have students brainstorm school situations that present conditions similar to a worksite. Examples include some of the following: attendance expectation, reward (compensation) received, supervisor evaluation, teamwork, rules/regulations, and so on. List the situations on the board. Use this information for comparison at various points throughout Part 4.

When students begin working, their career success and growth will depend on adjusting to the specific characteristics of the workplace and having the qualities and skills that employers want. Key skills include working well in a team, communicating effectively, and being able to overcome obstacles to career success.

Use the **Objectives** and **Key Terms** printed in the margin to help students focus on the content of this chapter. Use the **video segment** for Chapter 10 to trigger discussion.

What do you think?

Use **TM10-01**.
Students' answers will vary.

Career Journal

Ask students to spend 10 minutes writing Career Journal entries that answer the following questions:
1. What do you think this chapter will cover?
2. What do you already know about these topics?
3. What three things do you want to learn about these topics?

10 Succeeding in a Career

OBJECTIVES

After completing this chapter, you will be able to:

- Describe how to adjust to your workplace.
- Identify the skills and characteristics that employers look for in employees.
- Identify the skills that are key to a successful career.
- Analyze some of the barriers to career growth.

> ❝ Pleasure in the job puts perfection in the work. ❞
>
> —Aristotle,
> Greek Philosopher

Key Terms:

- corporate culture
- business etiquette
- competencies
- actual barrier
- perceived barrier

For the past year, Lisa has been working at The Diner as a server. She knows this part-time job is not a career; however, her earnings are paying for her school expenses. She has even managed to save some money because she has received two promotions and pay raises since she started working. Lisa is seriously considering working at The Diner full-time after she graduates so she can save money for design school.

Lisa's employer considers her a model employee. Why? She has never missed a day of work and has never even been late. Lisa always plans ahead and schedules her days off for times she knows she will need to study. Also, Lisa wears exactly what The Diner's dress code requires, and her outfits are clean and pressed. Lisa respects her fellow workers and displays a positive attitude every day at work. The professionalism she displays and her skills as a leader and team player confirmed the manager's decision to have Lisa help train new employees.

Lisa is also willing to act on her own. When she saw that all part-time employees were not working equal shifts, she created a sample work schedule on her computer. Her manager liked the chart and shared the innovation with the regional manager. As a result, Lisa received her second promotion and pay raise in six months!

What do you think?
How will your career choice influence other parts of your life? Will your job support the type of life you want outside of work? Why or why not?

PART 4 · · · · · · PREPARING FOR THE NEXT STEP

CHAPTER RESOURCES and MATERIALS

Activities & Projects book
Instructor's Resource CD
- Forms and Worksheets for Chapter Activities 10-1 through 10-5
- Internet Links for Chapter 10
- PowerPoint Presentation for Chapter 10
- Lesson Plans
- Teaching Masters for Chapter 10
- Video Discussion Guide for Chapter 10

Chapter Tests book
Exam*View*® CD
Video
Web Site

Adjusting to Your Workplace

When you begin working in your first entry-level position, you will have to adjust to your workplace. Just as you had to adjust to different situations and rules when you entered school, you will have to adjust to different situations and rules when you begin working full-time. Every career and every workplace has different characteristics.

In what type of workplace will you feel most comfortable?

- Youthful?
- Conservative?
- Creative?
- Traditional?
- Team-oriented?
- Individual-oriented?
- Formal?
- Informal?

What do you think?

What do you think?

Use **TM10-02**.
Students' answers will vary. Have students give workplace examples of each term to be sure they understand and can distinguish between these different types of workplaces.

During the summers while he was in high school, Theo worked for his Aunt Eva, a civil attorney with an old established law firm. Theo learned about legal processes and procedures and even attended court proceedings once or twice a year. He enjoyed everything about his legal experiences except the workplace. He disliked having to wear a jacket and tie to work every day, and he was uncomfortable having to speak quietly in the hushed law offices. Theo knew he could not be happy working in such a formal and conservative workplace. He decided to research other legal careers where the workplace would fit his goals and lifestyle.

> ❝ What lies behind us and what lies before us are small matter to what lies within us. ❞
>
> —*Ralph Waldo Emerson, Philosopher and Writer*

To help you adjust and be successful in your workplace, you will need to find out the corporate culture of your new company. You will also need to learn how to dress appropriately and practice business etiquette.

Corporate Culture

As an individual, you have characteristics that make you unique, or different from every other individual. Similarly, each organization has characteristics that make it different from every other organization. These characteristics give each organization a unique personality, referred to as the organization's **corporate culture**.

The corporate culture of an organization defines how its employees behave, the way work gets done, and how coworkers interact with each other and with management. The corporate culture of a company is established through formal rules, unspoken rules, and expected behaviors. As a new employee, you will need to find out the corporate culture of your workplace quickly in order to be successful.

How can you find out a company's corporate culture quickly? What can you do to fit into a workplace smoothly?

What do you think?

TEACH

In your discussion of corporate culture, emphasize the importance of using the accepted form of communication, such as e-mail, face-to-face meeting, word of mouth, or printed memo. Mention to students that a supervisor's preferred method of communication may be different from that of coworkers or the company in general.

What do you think?

Use **TM10-03**.
Students' answers will vary.

ONLINE RESOURCES

Check out the web site **www.investigatingyourcareer.com** for teacher resources, student activities, and replacements for broken links for this chapter. To access the teacher resources:

Username: career
Password: investigate

Discuss workplace dress in depth, having students provide examples of appropriate dress for different types of businesses. Be sure students understand that an employee who has contact with someone outside the company, including suppliers and delivery people, is a representative of the company and must dress accordingly. Also emphasize that casual does not mean sloppy and that casual dress does not apply every day for every workplace occasion. For additional clarification, have students find examples in magazines of appropriate and inappropriate everyday and casual business dress.

Discuss visible tattoos and body piercings, emphasizing that both will reduce the chance of career success and growth. Explain that the average workplace tends to be conservative and is not the place to display such adornments. Mention that unusual hairstyles are also inappropriate in the workplace.

What do you think?

Use **TM10-04**.
Students' answers will vary.

To learn about a company's corporate culture:

- **Observe how people interact with each other.** Do they usually speak to one another quietly and professionally? Do they normally appear serious and formal? Are they serious about their work but relaxed with each other?

- **Try to determine who has the power to make decisions.** The individuals with the most important sounding titles may not be the actual decision makers. Assistants and technicians often are powerful because they have access to decision makers and can influence them.

- **Listen.** If someone offers a suggestion, take it seriously regardless of how unimportant the advice may seem. Ask questions of the speaker to make sure the message you heard was the one intended. Observe body language to identify hidden messages.

- **Ask questions.** Everyone you will work with, at one time, had a first day of work and probably had the same questions you will have. Don't be afraid to approach your coworkers and ask questions. Keep a running list of questions. Then ask several at a time to avoid interrupting others while they work. Continue asking follow-up questions until you are satisfied you understand.

CAREER ★ SUCCESS TIP

Choose to work for organizations and people that think as you do and that have values similar to yours.

When you have learned the written and unwritten rules and policies of the company, you will be able to determine where you and your job fit in the company's plans and structure. You will be able to decide whether you can advance to a higher position within the company or whether you will have to move to another company to advance your career. You will also find out what you must accomplish in order to succeed.

Appropriate Dress

One part of a company's corporate culture concerns the way employees dress at work. Some companies, particularly those that have daily contact with the public, require their employees to dress formally. Other companies allow casual dress. A recent Levi Strauss & Co. poll indicates that more than forty million American employees are allowed to dress casually at work every day. Many other companies have adopted one day a week, usually Friday, for casual dress.

What do you think?
What work situations require formal business clothes? When is casual dress appropriate?

Workplace dress can be classified as formal, business casual, or casual. Formal dress requires a shirt, jacket, and tie for men and a dress or a suit for women. Business casual calls for slacks, a collared shirt, and often a jacket; women also have the option of wearing a skirt and blouse. For either formal or business casual dress, athletic shoes are inappropriate. Workplaces with a casual dress code have few rules for dress, though even casual dress codes do not allow revealing clothes.

CAREER SUCCESS TIP

Investigate the Company
Tell students that when looking for employment, they need to investigate the company and its culture to see if they will be happy working there. Students should consider the following: Do the employees have a set work schedule, or does the schedule vary? Is the company locally owned? A family business? What are the values, or mission, of the company? By investing time in investigating the company, students can ensure they will be happy in their careers.

Cesar's company has a casual dress code, meaning his typical attire of jeans, a collared shirt, and running shoes is considered acceptable for work. After he arrives at work one day, he remembers that an important client is visiting for an all-day meeting. Without enough time to drive home and change, Cesar quickly looks in the mirror, combs his hair, and thinks, "Oh, no! How will I impress anyone when I'm dressed like this?"

Jeans and sneakers may have suited Cesar on typical workdays, but he should have worn a jacket and tie on the day the client visited. A simple solution would have been for him to keep a change of clothes at work so he would have appropriate dress when needed.

Different work situations require different forms of dress. For example, dress that is appropriate at the workplace may not be appropriate at a client's workplace. When attending a meeting at a client's workplace, employees should find out the client's dress code before the meeting so they can dress appropriately. People judge others by the way they look and will remember any inappropriate dress. Employees should dress according to the situation, making sure hair, skin, and nails are clean and well groomed.

Business Etiquette

While each workplace has its own unique corporate culture, certain professional standards are universal. These standards are often referred to as **business etiquette**. To show professionalism and business etiquette on the job:

- Adopt the basics of good manners.
- Show a positive attitude.
- Be dependable, honest, and trustworthy. Show up for work on time every day. Do what you say you will do.
- Treat others with respect and courtesy.
- Listen without interrupting.
- Be energetic and enthusiastic.
- Speak clearly and use good grammar.
- Avoid gossip.

In Activity 10-1, "Learning from Others," you will see how workplace expectations compare to your familiar school expectations.

Students' primary focus for business etiquette should be on courtesy and a positive attitude. Explain that it is important to acknowledge others for the work they do by expressing gratitude and praise. Ask students to practice business etiquette by complimenting five people a day for their good work.

Telephone skills are another important part of business etiquette. Discuss the proper way to answer a business telephone, including how to take a message, how to schedule an appointment, and so on. Prepare a list of additional calling situations so students can practice their telephone skills in small groups or in a whole class situation. At the end of each call, have students critique the telephone skills of the participant, pointing out positive and negative examples.

APPLY

Have students complete **Activity 10-1, "Learning from Others,"** that appears on page 192. Teaching suggestions and the solution for this activity appear on page 192. An activity worksheet can be found on the Career Portfolio and Resource CD—**Text Activity 10-1.doc**.

DIFFERENT LEARNING ABILITIES
Gifted
Using the information in the chapter, have students create crossword puzzles. Students are to use key words and concepts from the chapter. Clues are to be in definition form, and the key terms and concepts are to be used in the answers. Remind students to create answer keys. Make copies of the crossword puzzles for everyone else in the class. After the class has studied the chapter, pass out the crossword puzzles.

What Employers Want

To be successful in your career, you need to have the skills and characteristics that employers want. Certain characteristics are important to all employers, including honesty, integrity, responsibility, loyalty, cooperation, and a positive attitude. Arriving on time and putting in a full day of high-quality work, for example, demonstrate both integrity and responsibility. You cannot take classes to acquire these characteristics, and you will have to work hard to develop them.

Basic Qualifications

While different employers look for different characteristics and abilities in their potential employees, certain basic qualifications for employment are universal. The following qualifications show up on almost every interviewer's list.

- **Employees must be able to pass a drug test.** If your employer suspects you are a substance abuser, you will be viewed as unreliable and may ultimately lose your job.
- **Employees must observe work hours.** You will be expected to come to work every day and to do so punctually even if you do not feel your best or you have a personal problem. Oversleeping will not be seen as an acceptable reason for being late.
- **Employees must possess basic reading and math skills.** Without mastery of these skills, performing your work will be difficult.
- **Employees must be willing and able to learn.** Assuming you have little or no experience working in a particular field, one of your most marketable and attractive skills will be your ability and willingness to listen to coworkers and to learn from them. Be enthusiastic!
- **Employees must be able to get along with their coworkers and supervisors.** Your supervisors and colleagues will expect you to interact respectfully and pleasantly with them. Almost every career involves working with others on a daily basis.

What do you think? What characteristics and skills do you possess that employers want?

SCANS

Over the last decade, educational, business, and governmental organizations have made repeated attempts to pinpoint the workplace skills and abilities essential to keeping the United States competitive. One of the most important reports on this topic is known as SCANS, which was developed by the **S**ecretary's **C**ommission on **A**chieving **N**ecessary **S**kills.

The SCANS report, published by the U.S. Department of Labor, identified the competencies critical for every person's work success. **Competencies** are the skills you ought to possess to ensure a long and fulfilling career. If you are weak in any of the following

> 66 It is not because things are difficult that we do not dare, it is because we do not dare that things are difficult. 99
>
> —Seneca, Roman Philosopher

182

PART 4 · · · · · · PREPARING FOR THE NEXT STEP

TEACH

Discuss the bulleted list on student text page 182 from the employer's point of view. Ask students to explain why these basic qualifications of employees are important to the success of a business.

What do you think?

Use **TM10-06**.
Students' answers will vary.

TEACH

To help students understand the SCANS workplace competencies, in a class discussion, encourage them to provide additional explanations and specific examples. Assist them in seeing how the competencies apply to familiar skills such as the following:
Resources: Schedule time; budget funds; arrange space; assign people to specific tasks.
Interpersonal: Cooperate with others to provide customers with the best possible service; influence others to improve; manage conflict; assist in decision making; make positive suggestions for change.
Information: Assist with a survey; research; prepare a report; evaluate results; put information into a computer format; give a speech.
Systems: Understand your role as a student, an employee, or a committee member in the group as a whole; understand the consequences if your performance is not appropriate and realize how to correct your performance; understand how to use a computer and various computer programs.
Technology: Know how to choose equipment to use for a presentation; use a computer to manage a budget; repair complex equipment, such as a computer, car, or stereo.

DIFFERENT LEARNING STYLES
Kinesthetic Learners
Arrange student into five groups. Have groups read the section "Basic Qualifications." Assign each group one of the basic qualifications. Have each group create a skit that demonstrates what happens when the basic qualification is not followed and what happens when it is. Encourage students to have fun with their skits, yet to make sure they communicate the basic lesson. Provide class time for the skits to be performed.

182

categories, try to acquire that skill or ability before seeking a job. The categories are divided into two groups: (1) foundation skills and personal qualities and (2) workplace competencies.

Foundation Skills and Personal Qualities:

- **Basic Skills.** Reads, writes, performs arithmetic and mathematical operations, listens, and speaks.
- **Thinking Skills.** Thinks creatively, makes decisions, solves problems, visualizes, knows how to learn, and analyzes.
- **Personal Qualities.** Displays responsibility, self-esteem, sociability, self-management, integrity, and honesty.

Workplace Competencies:

- **Resources.** Identifies, organizes, plans, and allocates resources. The resource categories are time, money, material and facilities, and human resources. You should be able to (1) explain how to set goals, such as preparation for a project; (2) identify and explain the needs for the project, such as materials, time, budget, human resources; and (3) identify the steps needed to reach the goal or complete the project.
- **Interpersonal.** Work with others. The interpersonal categories are participates as a team member, teaches others new skills, serves clients/customers, exercises leadership, negotiates, and works with diversity. You should be able to (1) explain experiences of working with others as a member of a team, (2) lead a team, (3) teach others, (4) work with people of various backgrounds, and (5) manage conflicts.
- **Information.** Acquires and uses information. The information categories are acquires and evaluates information, organizes and maintains information, interprets and communicates information, and uses computers to process information. You should be able to (1) explain who to consult and where to go to find information necessary to set and reach goals or complete projects and (2) describe how the information you find would be used.
- **Systems.** Understands complex interrelationships. The systems categories are understands systems, monitors and corrects performance, and improves or designs systems. You should be able to explain how things relate to each other, such as how the departments in a large organization are related to each other and to the organization. You should also be able to explain how making policy changes within a system might have either a positive or a negative effect on the system's operation or the people within it.
- **Technology.** Works with a variety of technologies. The technology categories are selects technology, applies technology to tasks, and maintains and troubleshoots equipment. You should be able to select, use, and explain various types of technology, such as computers, the Internet, and video or audio equipment.

CAREER FACT

Fifty-two percent of Americans say they sometimes must work more than 12 hours a day to get their jobs done.

183

In a class discussion, compare a traditional classroom and a SCANS classroom. Topics to consider include the role of the teacher; how students work together; the organization of the classroom; classroom interaction, including all learning styles; expectations of students; and so on.

ENRICH

Have students complete **Activity 10-A, "SCANS Experiences,"** found in the *Investigating Your Career Activities & Projects* book.

In this activity, students examine their lives in school, home, and community to identify experiences, such as projects or assignments, when they have used each of the five SCANS workplace competencies. Then students indicate how they can gain more experience with each SCANS skill. Students may share experiences and suggestions as a class if time permits.

Solution: The solution for this activity appears in the *Teacher's Edition* of *Investigating Your Career Activities & Projects*.

CAREER TREND

What Is a Normal Workweek?

In America, the trend is to expect more work from fewer employees, which means many employees must work longer hours. The 40-hour workweek may be a thing of the past. Discuss with students how they feel about longer hours in the workplace. Ask if they think this is a healthy lifestyle. Ask them to explain their answers. Have students organize into small groups to talk about long working hours and their effect on society. Have each group give an oral report of their discussion.

APPLY

Have students complete **Activity 10-2, "SCANS on the Internet,"** that appears on page 192. Teaching suggestions and the solution for this activity appear on page 192. An activity worksheet can be found on the Career Portfolio and Resource CD— **Text Activity 10-2.doc**.

TEACH

Attendance is a habit; students who have problems attending class will be adults who have problems attending work. Help students learn to accept responsibility for their actions by making them accountable for their tardiness and absence in your class. The importance of attendance and punctuality cannot be overemphasized.

ENRICH

Have students complete **Activity 10-B, "Career Satisfaction,"** found in the *Investigating Your Career Activities & Projects* book.

This activity helps students identify the importance of specific items related to career satisfaction. Students rank the items in order of importance to their own career satisfaction. Students can compare their results with *The Wall Street Journal* national survey results on **TM10-05**. **Solution:** The solution for this activity appears in the *Teacher's Edition* of *Investigating Your Career Activities & Projects*.

The competencies identified by the SCANS report may seem complex when you first read them. However, you probably already possess many of these competencies. Many are simply phrased in unfamiliar ways.

Basically, employers seek intelligent employees who can master the technical demands of their jobs, work without constant supervision, adapt to new technologies, teach themselves how to use complex equipment, and have a positive attitude toward work. Being book smart is rarely enough. Skills in problem solving, communication, and teamwork are most important.

In Activity 10-2, "SCANS on the Internet," you will work in a group to solve a project based on SCANS competencies.

Key Characteristics and Skills

> ❝ Whatever your life's work is, do it well. A man should do his job so well that the living, the dead, and the unborn could do it no better. ❞
>
> —Martin Luther King, Jr.

Certain characteristics and skills can help you become an outstanding employee in any employment situation. Many basic work skills are the same as the skills you need to be successful in school. The following skills apply to both school and work:

- Attend every day
- Be on time
- Work cooperatively with others
- Be able to read, write, and compute
- Be able to choose workable solutions to resolve issues
- Set goals and be organized
- Motivate others toward goals

In addition, having a positive attitude, accepting responsibility for your actions, communicating effectively, and working competently in a team are necessary skills for a successful career.

Attitude

Every employer throughout your career will expect you to arrive for work each day with a positive attitude and to maintain this attitude throughout the workday. A good attitude will increase your personal productivity and creativity and will raise the morale of your coworkers. Conversely, a bad attitude acts like a virus, spreading throughout the workplace and adversely affecting others and their productivity.

While employers realize your private life will not always be perfect, they expect you to prevent personal problems from interfering with your work activities. Sometimes you will wish to be anywhere else but at work; however, you will need to control your negative mood. While hiding sad or angry feelings is at times difficult, do your best to handle them in the privacy of the employee lounge or another secluded area. If you are overwhelmed by personal problems, talk to your supervisor about taking vacation time to work them out.

INTEGRATED ACADEMICS
Communication
Have students work in small groups to develop an advertising campaign for SCANS. Advertising campaigns may include a poster, a brochure, or other literature. Students may use computer graphics or art materials to create their advertising pieces. Remind students that their work is to be visibly appealing, easy to read, and informative. Display the advertising pieces in the classroom.

When Tim's mother woke him early Saturday morning for his landscaping job, he knew he shouldn't have stayed out so late the night before. He was grumpy and took out his lack of sleep on his mother. Tim missed meeting the company truck to take him to the jobs for the day, so he had to drive himself, which cost him gas and caused him to be late. Because of his lateness, Tim missed the choice job of riding on the lawnmowers; instead he was left with running the weed trimmer and the leaf blower.

While thinking of the argument with his mother, Tim nicked Ms. Asher's new sapling so deeply it had to be replaced. Then not concentrating again, Tim blew grass into the swimming pool. It took Tim a half hour to fish the grass clippings out of the pool, and his supervisor didn't let him put the extra time on his timesheet. If Tim had just had more sleep and gone to work with a better attitude, he probably would have enjoyed his job the way he usually did every Saturday.

Here are some things you can do to help you overcome a bad attitude:

* Smile—if you act as though you're in a good mood, chances are you soon will be.
* Think pleasant thoughts.
* Change negative thoughts to positive ones. Instead of thinking "I can't,"
  think "That'll be tough, but I'll do the best I can."
* Surround yourself with positive, upbeat people as much as possible.

How does your attitude about your work influence:
• How much money you make?
• The people with whom you associate each day?
• Your sense of self-esteem?
• Your status in the community?
What other things are influenced by your work attitude?

What do you think?

Activity 10-3, "Successful Student/Successful Worker," will give you an opportunity to explore the similarities between the characteristics needed for success in school and in work.

TEACH

Have students suggest ways to control a bad attitude, to work effectively with a difficult coworker, to cope with a difficult customer, and so on.

Though teams and team behavior are discussed thoroughly in Chapter 11, emphasize getting along with coworkers when discussing this chapter. Students may mimic their peers' poor behavior, such as bullying and forming cliques. You *must* emphasize positive behavior.

What do you think?

Use **TM10-07**.
Students' answers will vary.

APPLY

Have students complete **Activity 10-3, "Successful Student/ Successful Worker,"** that appears on page 193. Teaching suggestions and the solution for this activity appear on page 193. An activity worksheet can be found on the Career Portfolio and Resource CD— **Text Activity 10-3.doc**.

DIFFERENT LEARNING ABILITIES
Limited English Proficiency
Have students write a positive affirmation statement that will help them overcome a bad attitude. Students with limited English proficiency are to write the statement in their native language and then translate the statement into English. Suggest to these students that they say the statement first in their native language and then in English. All students should repeat their positive statement until their attitude has shifted into a more positive, uplifting, and life-affirming place. Suggest that students use their positive statements whenever they have a bad attitude.

TEACH

Ask students why an employee would use the excuse "It's not my job." Ask what that excuse conveys to the employer about a person's work attitude. Encourage students to express their opinions about the statement.

Accepting Responsibility

Everyone makes mistakes. However, everyone is not able to accept responsibility for a mistake by saying "I'm wrong" or "It was my fault." An employer or a teacher will want to see whether you assume responsibility for your mistakes or whether you try to shift the blame to someone or something else. Employers will expect you to be responsible for your mistakes and to correct them swiftly and smoothly.

Accountability and responsibility do not involve just mistakes. You are also responsible for completing your work tasks on time and keeping your supervisor informed of your progress. In addition, you are responsible for the quality of your work.

If your supervisor or teacher criticizes your work, do not take the criticism as a personal attack. View the comments as a sign of your potential. Receiving feedback is actually to your advantage. If your supervisor takes the time to explain a situation to you, he or she is taking an active interest in your growth and development. Critical feedback allows you to learn from your mistakes, to avoid making the same mistake twice, and to impress your supervisor with your positive attitude.

REAL PEOPLE
REAL CAREERS

Photo Restorer—Reconstructing History

Baby Boomers are becoming more interested in their family history. However, the photos in the attic or basement often are of poor quality. The solution is to find a professional photo restorer to return the photographs to their original quality. Cherie Yannone is the president of A Stroke of Genius Photographic Restoration in Phoenix. Customers' interest in tracing their family roots helps her business grow. Her company is able to satisfy nearly every customer.

How did Cherie Yannone begin this unique career? Cherie always knew she had artistic talent. She took art and photography classes in high school. After graduation, she worked in graphic arts and design. She took college classes in art and technology. Photo restoration began as a hobby using photographs of her own family. Cherie's attention to detail and her patience to perfect her skills led her to develop new software. This technology corrected problems that commercial software couldn't repair. Cherie's interest in computers caused A Stroke of Genius to expand into the global market. As webmaster, Cherie created a web site that showed the difference that photo restoration could make. Cherie Yannone "listens to what the customer really wants, not what you believe they want."

For more information about:
- a photoprocessing career, explore *www.bls.gov*. Search for photographic process workers.
- Cherie Yannone's company and the business of photo restoration, explore *www.photorestoration.org*.

Source: *A Stroke of Genius. www.photorestoration.org.*

186

REAL PEOPLE—REAL CAREERS
Photo Restoration Careers
Organize students into two groups. Assign photo processing careers to one group and photo restoration careers to the other group. Students may use the web sites listed on this page for their research. Have student groups create a pamphlet that describes their findings. Pamphlets should include a description of photo processing or photo restoration and at least five interesting facts about the subject. Display the pamphlets in the classroom.

Accepting responsibility demonstrates your honesty, willingness to learn, and concern for the needs of the business—all characteristics employers value and reward.

Communication

Good communication occurs when all participants in a conversation or meeting—and all readers of the same letter or report—come away with the same understanding.

> Miss Jenny didn't know whether her kindergarten students had learned their colors yet. So she decided to test them. Miss Jenny pointed to a color. Then she asked a student what the color was.
>
> Miss Jenny tested the students every Tuesday and Wednesday. The students were nearly always correct. One day as Miss Jenny began to test the students again, Bart tried to stop her. When Miss Jenny asked Bart why he was interrupting, he replied quietly, "Miss Jenny, we think you should try to figure out some of these colors for yourself."

Communication is one of the most important factors in whether a business succeeds or fails. Employers and employees, workers and customers, and sellers and buyers must all communicate with each other. A breakdown in communication, such as the one in the story above, can be extremely costly for everyone involved.

When you communicate with supervisors and coworkers in your workplace, you want them to receive the message you intended. Otherwise, misunderstandings will occur. The following guidelines will help you communicate effectively:

- Plan what you want to say so you don't have to think it out as you speak.
- State the purpose of your communication so your listener or reader doesn't have to figure it out.
- Use words the listener or reader understands.
- Don't preach, ramble, or talk down to your listener or reader.
- Keep your message clear and to the point.

Working Effectively in Teams

Chapter 4 discussed that managers of companies are depending more and more on the team concept. Teamwork is essential in today's highly technical, fast-changing, global environment. Many of the problems and challenges companies face are simply too complex for any one person to address. By pooling talents, expertise, experience, and creativity, teams are often able to find solutions to complex problems. The ability to work effectively in a team is one of the important skills employers expect from their employees.

CAREER FACT

Ninety-one percent of people will stop doing business with a person or an organization that has offended them.

ENRICH

Have students complete **Activity 10-C, "School and Work,"** found in the *Investigating Your Career Activities & Projects* book.

This activity is a follow-up to Activity 10-3 in the textbook. Students will link school habits to work skills valued by employers. This activity involves personal work skills that could correct bad school habits. Students can discuss how to correct the bad habits and what positive benefits could result from changing the bad habits.

Solution: The solution for this activity appears in the *Teacher's Edition* of *Investigating Your Career Activities & Projects.*

CAREER TREND
Being Offensive to Others Hurts You

Ask for student volunteers to tell a story about a time they were offended by an organization. The story should answer the following questions: Why was the student offended? What did the organization do to offend the student? How did the student react? How did the organization react? Does the student still frequent that organization? Remind students to remember these stories when they are tempted to offend someone else.

APPLY

Have students complete **Activity 10-4, "Case Challenges,"** that appears on pages 193–194. Teaching suggestions and the solution for this activity appear on pages 193–194. An activity worksheet can be found on the Career Portfolio and Resource CD—**Text Activity 10-4.doc.**

TEACH

To be sure students realize the difference between actual and perceived barriers, have them provide examples of each type. You may want to begin the discussion with barriers that exist in students' present lives and then lead the discussion to potential barriers they may experience in their future careers.

ENRICH

Have students complete **Activity 10-D, "Transferable Skills,"** found in the *Investigating Your Career Activities & Projects* book.

This activity lists skills that can be used in both career and school situations. Students write down situations where transferable skills are used at school and at work. This activity can be done with small groups of four or five or with students working individually.

Solution: The solution for this activity appears in the *Teacher's Edition* of *Investigating Your Career Activities & Projects.*

CAREER SUCCESS TIP

Personally recognize the efforts of others with a handwritten thank-you note. Be specific and avoid "gushing" praise in your note.

In middle school, Lily was named the assistant editor of the school yearbook. While a member of the yearbook team, Lily first discovered she had effective team skills. She was able to organize and assign tasks easily to just the right team members. The yearbook advisor commented several times that Lily's yearbook team worked more smoothly together than any other team in recent years.

After college, Lily's effective team skills helped her land a job with a top-notch publishing company, one that insisted upon all work being done in teams. Lily loved her job and enjoyed bouncing ideas off her coworkers. The managers of the publishing company noticed her exceptional team skills and increased her work responsibilities and her pay. Lily was on the path to a successful career.

Building an effective team can be a difficult process. For example, misunderstandings among team members can hinder group harmony. As a team member, you can help prevent misunderstandings by (1) asking a lot of questions and (2) making sure each detail of the project or assignment is thoroughly understood by all team members.

Because team members rely so heavily on each other, more than one person should be trained to complete each task. Teams accomplish this goal by cross training each member to handle multiple tasks. If an individual member departs, the team can still act effectively. Working in teams will be discussed in depth in the next chapter.

In Activity 10-4, "Case Challenges," you will work in a group to analyze employee behaviors.

Barriers to Career Growth

Regardless of your career goal, you are likely to run into barriers and will have to overcome them. Barriers are things that can inhibit your career growth and prevent you from achieving the success you envision. Being aware of barriers will help you find ways to skillfully avoid them.

Lavon was the strongest starting forward on the Eagles soccer team, and the players expected him to be captain. But then Coach Barnes named Miguel, the youngest team member, as co-captain. Miguel, an outstanding goalie, had been part of the Eagles for only a year. He didn't have the team "history" that a captain usually had. At a recent team meeting, some parents stood up and asked that only Lavon be team captain. The parents said they were shocked by Coach Barnes' decision. They said they could not support a team that had an inexperienced captain who, they thought, didn't have the necessary seniority to represent the team. Some parents even wanted Coach Barnes fired.

188

PART 4 • • • • • • PREPARING FOR THE NEXT STEP

CAREER SUCCESS TIP

Thank-You Notes

Ask students how they feel when someone takes the time to write them a thank-you note. An e-mail thank-you note is a nice gesture; however, a handwritten note is even more meaningful. Tell students to keep their notes simple and to the point and to keep the purpose of their note in mind—to thank someone for something. Their notes need only say thank you and mention the specific act for which they are grateful. To practice, have students write thank-you notes to others. Read several aloud in class. Students may wish to use stationery or printed thank-you notes.

188

Actual and Perceived Barriers

An **actual barrier** is an obstacle that prohibits you from being able to do your job, such as not meeting the height requirement to be a law enforcement officer or not having sufficient riding experience to be a jockey. Actual barriers have the potential to prevent you from achieving your career goals.

A **perceived barrier** is an obstacle that exists in people's minds—your mind or an employer's mind or a potential customer's mind. Perceived barriers to career growth (such as age, experience level, gender, or cultural background) can slow your progress.

Alisha was excited—and honored. Abdul, the team captain, had asked her to be on Clark's Quiz Bowl team. It was one of the best teams in the region, having gone to state the past two years. However, the other team members held a meeting with Abdul and the team adviser, Miss Kirker. Alisha was hurt when she heard they had requested that she be an assistant to Miss Kirker, not a team member. The team knew Alisha was hearing-impaired, and they believed she wouldn't be able to react quickly enough to quiz questions because she used an interpreter. When Alisha discovered the team member's comments, she knew she had to find a way to overcome this barrier of prejudice.

Alisha and her interpreter set up a rehearsal schedule. They practiced quiz questions for several hours a day the week before team practice started. Alisha's father made a buzzer system so she could practice her reaction time. When the team began practice, Alisha, with her interpreter, asked to be part of the first practice round. She ended up answering 75 percent of the questions! Alisha's team members apologized and extended their congratulations. They wanted her on the team.

What are some other perceived barriers to career growth? What barriers might exist in your career field? **What do you think?**

DIFFERENT LEARNING STYLES

Hearing Impaired and Visually Impaired

Invite speakers who can discuss hearing impairment, visual impairment, or any other medical or physical disability to talk to your class. Ask speakers to talk about the disability and how the class members can help and hinder a student with the disability. Encourage students to ask questions. Be sure to let students with disabilities know the speakers are coming. If any students with disabilities want to speak to the class, provide class time to them.

What do you think?

Use **TM10-08**.
Students' answers will vary.

TEACH

Discuss the terms *actual barrier* and *perceived barrier* with students. Use examples from students' current situations; for example, a person cannot get a driver's license until he or she turns the legal age (actual barrier) and certain careers are only for men or only for women (perceived barrier).

Some barriers to career success involve various forms of workplace theft. Ask students why employers worry about stolen pens, personal photocopies, or falsified expense reports. Emphasize to students that stealing time is a form of employee theft. Employers pay employees for actual work done on the job. When employees use work time to take care of personal business, such as phone calls, e-mails, and Internet searches, the employer suffers. Encourage students to suggest ways employees can avoid stealing time from an employer.

What do you think?

Use **TM10-09**.
Students' answers will vary.

ENRICH

Have students complete **Activity 10-E, "What's the Problem?"** found in the *Investigating Your Career Activities & Projects* book.

In this activity, students analyze real-life cases, stating the problem and proposing a solution to the employee's dilemma. Students should be realistic and creative with their answers. The activity can be done in groups of four or five or with students working individually.
Solution: The solution for this activity appears in the *Teacher's Edition* of *Investigating Your Career Activities & Projects*.

Use **TM10-10**.
Students' answers will vary.

TEACH

Ask students how employees can be positive when airing their issues and frustrations to a supervisor. Examples include

• discussing issues in private
• calming down before voicing frustrations
• thinking of the worst-case scenario that could happen by airing grievances
• listening as well as demanding
• choosing the right time
• picking one or two major issues rather than airing a long list
• offering practical suggestions to resolve issues

Most importantly, emphasize that employees should attack issues, not people. (Chapter 11 addresses conflict management.)

CLOSE

Have students complete **Activity 10-5, "Coming to Terms,"** that appears on page 194. Teaching suggestions and the solution for this activity appear on page 194. An activity worksheet can be found on the Career Portfolio and Resource CD— **Text Activity 10-5.doc**.

Your Relationship with Your Supervisor

What do you think? What things might you do to develop a good relationship with a supervisor?

At some point during your working years, you may have a supervisor who is not supportive. Although the situation may not be your fault, you are still responsible for creating a solid working relationship with your supervisor.

> Rosangela is a nurse's assistant at a large hospital. Her supervisor, Mrs. Catrone, a head nurse, is irritable, ill-tempered, and critical. Rosangela, who has worked at the hospital for several months, is used to Mrs. Catrone and avoids her bad moods as much as possible. By taking a lot of notes at staff meetings, paying careful attention to the details of her job, and staying after hours to complete her work, Rosangela has earned Mrs. Catrone's respect. Although the two of them are not friends, Rosangela manages the relationship well and has earned her upcoming raise.

Developing a positive relationship with your supervisor is crucial. Your supervisor is the one person who can (or cannot) recommend you for promotions, grant your requests, and help you progress (or ensure that you do not). Below are a few helpful tips for developing a good relationship with your supervisor.

66 Coming together is a beginning, keeping together is progress, working together is success. **99**

—Henry Ford, Automobile Manufacturer

Do:

• Begin work on time.
• Respect your supervisor's time.
• Be honest in all your dealings with your supervisor.
• Become a finisher of projects, someone who can be depended on when the team is up against a tough deadline.
• Turn in accurate work.
• Organize your thoughts before approaching your supervisor so as not to waste his or her time.
• Respect your supervisor's authority.
• Suggest a solution when you bring up a problem.

Do not:

• Disturb your supervisor with problems you can resolve yourself.
• Complain about your supervisor to others.
• Bring personal problems to work.
• Waste time.
• Take every harsh reply or unfriendly action personally.

Use Activity 10-5, "Coming to Terms," to understand some of the important terms in this chapter more thoroughly.

INTEGRATED ACADEMICS
Language Arts
Have each student interview an adult to learn what values this person uses for good relationships with coworkers, including supervisors. Ask students to write an article about their interviews, using the question-and-answer format. Each article should begin with a few introductory paragraphs that explain who the person is and why the student chose this person. The remainder of the article should be in the question-and-answer format.

- **I can describe how to adjust to the workplace.**

  Every workplace has different characteristics. To adjust to my workplace, I need to find out the corporate culture of the company, to dress appropriately for different work situations, and to practice business etiquette.

- **I can identify the skills and characteristics that employers look for in employees.**

  Basic qualifications that employers look for in employees include being able to pass a drug test, observing work hours, possessing basic reading and math skills, being willing and able to learn, and being able to get along with coworkers and supervisors. In addition, the competencies identified in the SCANS report are critical for work success.

- **I can identify the skills that are key to a successful career.**

  Many important work skills are the same skills I need to be successful in school. These include attending every day, being on time, being able to set goals, and being organized. In addition, having a positive attitude, accepting responsibility for my actions, communicating effectively, and working competently in a team are necessary skills for a successful career.

- **I can analyze some of the barriers to career growth.**

  An actual barrier is an obstacle that prohibits me from being able to do my job, such as not meeting the height requirement to be a police officer. Actual barriers can prevent me from achieving my career goals. A perceived barrier is an obstacle that exists in a person's mind—my mind or an employer's mind or a potential customer's mind. Perceived barriers can slow my progress, and I should try to find ways to avoid them. I need to develop a good relationship with my supervisor because a poor relationship will be a barrier to my career success.

IN A NUTSHELL

Remind students about the objectives set forth at the beginning of the chapter, and use this summary to reinforce the concepts presented in this chapter.

Career Journal

Ask students to spend 10 minutes writing Career Journal entries that answer the following questions:
1. How well did what you thought you knew match what the chapter presented?
2. What questions do you now have about the chapter topics, and where do you think you can find the answers to those questions?
3. How will the content of the chapter help you investigate *your* career?

ASSESS

Administer the printed objective test for Chapter 10, available with this package. Test solutions are found in the *Teacher's Edition* of *Investigating Your Career Chapter Tests*. Use the **Exam***View*® CD to create your own objective test for this chapter.

Suggestions for Parents and Family Members

Encourage Career Opportunities

Parents and family members can support the career discovery process of their children in the following ways:

1. Encourage your teenager to work part-time. If your child's schedule does not permit part-time work, support regularly scheduled service learning activities so your teen can explore career possibilities and experience the sense of pride and accomplishment part-time work brings.
2. Discuss skills used in household projects that relate to possible career choices.

Activity 10-1:
Learning from Others

This activity increases students' recognition of the direct relationship between work and school expectations and students' awareness of the rewards for fulfilling work and school responsibilities.

Solution: Interviews will vary. The discussion should directly correlate workplace expectations to school expectations and reveal the resulting rewards. Emphasize to students that school expectations mirror those of the workplace and that the bases for school success are similar to the bases for career success.

Activity 10-2:
SCANS on the Internet

By applying SCANS skills to real-world projects and problems, students increase their understanding of the SCANS skills and competencies.

The web site in the student text has a variety of programs that include projects and problems ranging from the simple to the complex. Some projects involve plans that require two or more weeks of study and/or activities. Although some projects have actually been completed, students could replicate them in your area. Help students choose projects that fit your time schedule and pique their interests.

The projects involve other subject areas, so you may want to team with another teacher, allowing students to use their projects in both classes.
Solution: Answers will vary.

Though workplaces are different, employers often have similar expectations. Expectations of work and school are also frequently related. Work habits learned in school will often help you be successful on the job.

1. Interview a family member about his or her employer's expectations. What are the expectations at work concerning each of the following?

   - Attendance
   - Punctuality
   - Completing assignments
   - Dependability
   - Teamwork
   - Follow-through
   - Cooperation
   - Respect for authority
   - Honesty

2. What are the rewards for fulfilling your work responsibilities?

3. Now answer the same questions about your school's expectations. What are the expectations at school concerning each of the following?

   - Attendance
   - Punctuality
   - Completing assignments
   - Dependability
   - Teamwork
   - Follow-through
   - Cooperation
   - Respect for authority
   - Honesty

4. What are the rewards for fulfilling your school responsibilities?

5. How are the work and school expectations similar?

6. Compare your interviews and answers with your class after everyone has completed the assignment.

Explore the web site *SCANS 2000: The Workforce Skills Website*, at **www.scans.jhu.edu/default.htm**. Click on "Programs." Click on "Publications." With a partner or a small group, choose one of the CD-ROM modules. Your teacher will help your group adapt the module to fit the class time and needs. Use the Internet as your primary research resource.

Successful Student/ Successful Worker

Working in a small group, study the list below of characteristics of a good student. As a group, select the three *most important* characteristics of a successful student. Write down the characteristics and rank them 1, 2, and 3. Then select the three *least important* characteristics. Write down these characteristics and rank them 13, 14, and 15. The group must agree on the characteristics chosen.

Characteristics:

Is honest
Respects others
Maintains a neat and clean appearance
Completes work on time
Speaks clearly
Is a good listener
Shares ideas
Follows directions
Is friendly
Helps others
Is punctual
Has good behavior
Has no absences
Has a positive attitude
Uses free time wisely

Share your group's results with the class. Compare the qualities of a good student to those needed for a good employee. Are they similar? Do school skills equal work skills? How?

Case Challenges

Each of the following cases presents a workplace situation in which an employee's actions are questionable. Working in a small group, discuss each situation. Consider the following questions in your discussion:

- What is the problem with the employee's action?
- How should the problem be resolved by the employer?
- How do you think a good employee would have acted?

After your group has analyzed each situation, share your group's analyses with the rest of the class.

1. Ernesto's job at Giraffalo's Ice Cream Parlor was making cones and ice cream desserts. When he was working, he usually was the server for the drive-through window. Ernesto's friends, Walker and Ryan, visited the drive-through window with a carload of people at least once a week when Ernesto was working. Ernesto charged them for only one dessert, letting everyone else in the car have free desserts.

CHAPTER 10 · · · · · SUCCEEDING IN A CAREER

193

Activity 10-3:
Successful Student/
Successful Worker

This activity emphasizes to students that school success equals work success and helps them identify the qualities that are most and least important to school success.

Students often believe that the way they act in school is not how they will act after they are working in the "real world." However, studies show that work behavior often mirrors school behavior.

Solution: Answers will vary. The discussion should focus on equating school success with work success. However, also discuss students' choices for most important and least important qualities.

Activity 10-4:
Case Challenges

In this activity, students analyze real-world situations in which an employee has made an error in judgment.

Divide the class into groups of four or five students each. Encourage students to use concrete analyses and to be creative.

Solution: Answers will vary. If students have seen similar situations in their workplaces, before they answer the questions, ask them to describe what was done or should have been done. Suggested answers are as follows:

Case 1:
Problem: Theft—giving free desserts to friends.
Resolution: Take Ernesto off the drive-through and away from direct customer contact. In fact, many employers would fire Ernesto immediately.
Good action: Ernesto should have charged his friends for all the desserts and told them they must pay, as other customers do.

Case 2:
Problem: Unexcused absences from work and poor work attitude.
Resolution: Fire Ken for five unexcused absences.
Good action: Ken should have discussed the interruption problems with Mr. Poe. He also could have asked for alternative assignments during inventory week.

Case 3:
Problem: Procrastination, laziness, and hiding the truth.
Resolution: Ms. Lopez may not find out about April's actions. If she does find out, she will need to supervise April's actions more closely. Many employers would fire April because she hid a work-related problem from her supervisor, thereby jeopardizing the success of the company.
Good action: April should have told Ms. Lopez what happened.

Case 4:
Problem: Laziness and causing the store to lose time and money.
Resolution: Supervise Sarin more closely. Perhaps create a tag to identify the lower-priced sweaters more clearly. Again, some employers might fire Sarin because she willfully disobeyed a supervisor's instruction and

caused the store to lose money and/or annoy customers.

Good action: When Sarin realized what had happened, she should have apologized to Jack, sorted the sweaters, and put correct price tags on all the new sweaters.

Activity 10-5: Coming to Terms

In this activity, students expand their understanding of some of the important terms in the chapter by relating them to their current work or school situation.

Discuss the definitions before students begin the activity, and discuss students' answers after they have completed the activity.

Solution: Answers will vary.

2. Ken disliked inventory time at Poe's Hardware. To complete an inventory, he had to count every nut and bolt in a bin and write down the quantity for each item. After he finished one bin, he had to go to the next bin and repeat the process, counting and sorting each size. He often lost count and had to start over—either because he was distracted by a customer or because Mr. Poe would interrupt him with something trivial, such as asking how he was doing. So Ken decided to show Mr. Poe he didn't like to take inventory. He decided not to come to work during inventory week. And to avoid an argument, he decided not to tell Mr. Poe he wasn't coming in.

3. April's supervisor, Ms. Lopez, asked her to go to the post office to mail the pizza coupons. They were being sent out ten days before the holiday weekend. Because of the promotion, Ms. Lopez needed to order extra supplies ten days in advance. She based her order on last year's sales, but with an increase because the restaurant was growing in popularity. April said she would mail the coupons the next day, but she forgot to go to the post office, leaving them in her boyfriend's car. April didn't see her boyfriend all week. Finally, she discovered the coupons and mailed them over a week late. April decided not to tell Ms. Lopez. After all, April figured, she was only a few days late in sending them. When the holiday weekend arrived and only a few people redeemed the pizza coupons, Ms. Lopez was left with extra supplies, many of them quickly spoiling.

4. Jack, the owner of Chez Paul, told Sarin to put price stickers on the new shipment of sweaters in the junior department. Sarin decided that pricing all the sweaters was a waste of time because she would have to refold each sweater after putting on the price tag. Instead, she put the sweaters on a separate table with a sign indicating the sweaters' price. During the day, several customers picked up sweaters from the table and considered buying them. Then they changed their minds and put them down, often on a different table. These sweaters became mixed with other lower-priced sweaters. Other customers picked up the new unmarked sweaters from these displays, thinking the price of the sweaters should be the same as the other sweaters in the display. The checkout clerks had to run price checks on the unmarked sweaters or take the customers' word for the price. Either way Chez Paul lost time and money.

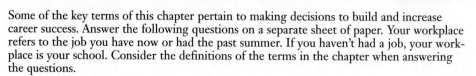

ACTIVITY 10-5   **Coming to Terms**

Some of the key terms of this chapter pertain to making decisions to build and increase career success. Answer the following questions on a separate sheet of paper. Your workplace refers to the job you have now or had the past summer. If you haven't had a job, your workplace is your school. Consider the definitions of the terms in the chapter when answering the questions.

1. **corporate culture**
   a. What ten words would you use to describe your company?
   b. What is really important to your company?
   c. What are your company's goals?

2. **business etiquette**
   a. How common is gossip in your company? Who starts rumors?
   b. What behaviors get rewarded in your company? Why?

3. **perceived barriers, actual barriers**
   a. Who fits in and who doesn't? Why?
   b. Who gets promoted or rewarded? Why?

Teamwork

11

Jonathan had been involved in a variety of activities in school and during the summers, including athletic trainer, camp counselor-in-training, and teacher's aide. While he never intended any of these activities to be his career, Jonathan found all the experiences valuable. He learned new skills at each job, but more importantly, he began to discover things about work life that appealed to him.

The biggest surprise to Jonathan was how much he enjoyed working in a team instead of doing tasks by himself. At camp, he worked on a team with four other counselors. They were responsible for creating different sports and arts programs for the campers. By the end of the summer, the team members had become close friends. After this experience, Jonathan realized he wanted teamwork to be a part of his career.

Jonathan's assessment of his abilities and interests helped him make his career decision. He had often thought about being a teacher, so he chose teaching middle school science. Many middle schools use the team approach to learning, something Jonathan believes will help his students and his career. He is looking forward to his future education and has the satisfaction of knowing he will be a valuable part of a team.

What teams have you been a part of?
How do you feel about the experience?

What do you think?

OBJECTIVES

After completing this chapter, you will be able to:

- Explain the concept of teams.
- Describe the process of team building.
- Explain how teams function in the workplace.
- Describe some ways to manage conflict within a team.

66 One Team, One Purpose. 99

—Starbucks,
The coffee company

Key Terms:

- team
- collaborate
- empowerment
- leader
- brainstorming
- consensus
- conflict management

In the world of work, a **team** is a group of employees working together to achieve a specific goal. Companies have found that teams can often accomplish tasks and solve problems more efficiently than can individuals working alone. Being able to work effectively in a team is an essential skill for employees in most organizations today.

What do you think? What skills do you have that will help you work effectively as a member of a team?

In school and at work, you will probably be asked to **collaborate**, or work with others, to complete an assignment. You may collaborate on a short-term basis (for example, to complete a project with fellow students), or you may be a member of a more permanent team. In any case, you must be able to get along with your classmates and coworkers to be successful. You may recall from Chapter 10 that the SCANS report lists good interpersonal skills as one of the eight critical competencies needed to build a successful career. In fact, the No. 1 reason people are fired in the United States today is that they are not able to get along with coworkers.

In the workplace, a team may be formed to complete a particular task or to carry out an ongoing function. Permanent teams, such as factory-worker teams, may stay together for several years. When an individual member leaves a permanent team, another employee is selected as a replacement. On the other hand, temporary teams may be together for only a short time. For example, a team set up to plan and coordinate a company event, such as a sales meeting, stays together only until the event follow-up details are complete.

CAREER FACT

As technology progresses, more and more teams include people who work in different cities, states, and countries. The members of these "virtual" teams meet via teleconferences, e-mail, online forums, and video-conferences.

Rise of Teams

During the 1980s, American manufacturers were being outproduced by manufacturers in foreign countries, particularly in Japan. Analysts in the United States determined that Japanese firms had a competitive advantage because they used work teams to increase their productivity. Two popular approaches to teamwork, Total Quality Management (TQM) and Quality Circles (QC), resulted from the study of the Japanese model of business management.

TQM encourages team members to look for ways to reduce errors and improve product quality. In addition, TQM teaches team members to measure the effect of their improvements and to check the accuracy of their work at the most effective point in the process. Quality Circles brings team members together on a regular basis to discuss how the flow of work might be improved. Typically, suggestions resulting from the QCs are submitted to a supervisory board. Often QCs who submit suggestions chosen by the board are awarded bonuses.

ONLINE RESOURCES

Check out the web site **www.investigatingyourcareer.com** for teacher resources, student activities, and replacements for broken links for this chapter. To access the teacher resources:

Username: career
Password: investigate

Betty, Ricardo, and Patrick work the lunch shift at the local drive-in. Ricardo takes and delivers the orders, Betty cooks and assembles the hamburgers, and Patrick wraps the hamburgers and cooks and bags the fries. Different wrapping papers are used for different kinds of hamburgers. So hamburgers with standard ingredients and special-order hamburgers are wrapped in different papers. The team was having problems processing the special orders. Patrick had to open each hamburger to see if it contained something other than the standard ingredients. Then he wrapped the burger in the appropriate paper. The extra step was slowing down the order flow during the busy lunch hour, and customers sometimes got the wrong hamburger wrapped in the wrong paper.

The team decided to move the wrapping papers to Betty's work area to see if the special orders could be processed more efficiently. Betty placed each burger on the proper type of paper, and Patrick wrapped it. Then Ricardo assembled the order for delivery. The team tracked the results of the new process and found it saved 30 seconds in completing an average order and reduced the number of incorrect deliveries by 95 percent. The process helped the team be selected Team of the Month, and each member received a bonus.

Benefits of Teamwork

How might having good team skills help you advance in your career?

What do you think?

Teamwork benefits both the organization and the team members. For example, no one member of a football team can win a championship for its school. Team members must work together to win games. Companies that use teams to develop, produce, and market their products reduce the number of people involved in decisions. As a result, they can get their products to market more efficiently.

Teams also encourage members to think creatively and to take pride in their efforts. Team members who are proud of what they do tend to make fewer errors. For a company, fewer errors means saving money. In the workplace, team members who are happy with their jobs tend to stay with the company longer, resulting in a lower employee turnover rate.

Hewlett-Packard, a company that attracts skilled workers from around the world, began using teams before many other U.S. companies did. Because of the high productivity of its teams, the company has been able to capture and retain a large part of the worldwide printer market.

> **When what we are is what we want to be . . . that's happiness.**
>
> —Malcolm Forbes, Publisher

TEACH

Emphasize that teams are not a fad, but are a fixture in the workplace of today and the future. Employers named teamwork as one of the five SCANS skills essential for the workplace.

What do you think?

Use **TM11-03**.
Students' answers will vary. Answers should include comparing teamwork in school to team skills in the workplace.

TEACH

Mention to students that they are cooperating members when they are part of a club, team, or small group. Have them elaborate on the benefits of being on a team, rather than acting as an individual, in those groups. Ask students what happens when one or more students in a small group do not do their part of a group project. Have students tell how it feels to be on such a team. Summarize their answers on the board under the heading "Uncooperative." Then ask students how it feels to be in a small group where everyone pitches in to make the project a success. Summarize their answers on the board under the heading "Cooperative." Lead a class discussion on the consequences of poor group performance and the rewards of good group performance.

DIFFERENT LEARNING ABILITIES
Gifted
Tell students that the American workforce is becoming increasingly culturally diverse. Have students work in small groups to discuss how this affects the workplace. Provide students with the following questions to discuss: Should companies provide employees with flexible holidays to accommodate different religious and cultural beliefs? How should companies deal with cafeteria menus, dress codes, and meditation or prayer time? Have the group give a report to the class, with each member contributing.

APPLY

Have students complete **Activity 11-1, "Teamwork,"** that appears on page 209. Teaching suggestions and the solution for this activity appear on page 209. An activity worksheet can be found on the Career Portfolio and Resource CD—**Text Activity 11-1.doc**.

TEACH

Discuss *empowerment* with students. Use examples from school, such as the satisfaction that comes from getting and maintaining good grades.

To help students practice teamwork skills, many teachers divide classes into small groups, use tables instead of desks in the classroom, encourage peer editing, and so on. Ask students for other ways they have seen teachers use teams in schools.

Team members, too, benefit from teamwork. One reward is the sense of empowerment that comes from working on a successful team. **Empowerment** is the feeling of satisfaction that comes with managing and controlling your own work. Being on a workplace team can improve your position within the company. Team success reflects positively on each member, and recognition of your contributions may increase your chance of being promoted.

Activity 11-1, "Teamwork," helps you judge how ready you are for being a member of a workplace team.

Building a Team

While any group of individuals can be considered a team, the group is an effective team only when it works together to reach its defined goals. Building an effective team requires carefully selecting team members, setting the goals of the team, developing a plan for achieving the goals, and determining the roles and responsibilities of team members.

Selecting Team Members

Businesses have found that teams are especially productive when members come from a variety of backgrounds and have different areas of expertise. Research has shown that diversity can improve group creativity and decision making. In addition to gender, cultural, and ethnic diversity of members, managers select team members with different talents, skills, attitudes, knowledge, and experience. Managers look for people who have the skills and imagination to find creative solutions that also support the goals of the company.

Mrs. Hockenberry's information technology class had to create group projects using new presentation software. She chose the group leaders and then asked each leader to choose two other team members. Mrs. Hockenberry chose Enrique to be the leader of his group. Enrique chose Mary and Daniel to join his team. He believed their strengths would add to the success of the team.

Mary held a part-time job with the community newspaper and worked on the yearbook staff. She had written many articles and could help with the wording of the presentation. Daniel was experienced with computers. He had completed several outstanding assignments and had solved some technical problems for Mrs. Hockenberry. Mary wasn't knowledgeable about the new software, and Daniel didn't have strong writing skills. However, Enrique believed their abilities would contribute to the success of the presentation.

DIFFERENT LEARNING STYLES
Kinesthetic Learners
Explain to students that all people have a unique talent that allows them to add to the effectiveness of a group or team. Some people's talents are easier to see than others, yet everyone has special talents and gifts. Then choose four group leaders. The leaders in turn choose members of their groups to create a song and a dance that celebrates how different people can come together and make one team. Provide class time for each group to perform.

With Mary and Daniel's help, Enrique's team was chosen to participate in the regional Business Professionals competition. Mary's creative writing and Daniel's hands-on understanding of the new software attracted the judges' attention. In addition, Mary has gained a basic understanding of the presentation software and Daniel has improved his writing skills. Combined with Enrique's leadership, the team went on to compete nationally.

Why do you think diversity in the members of a team makes a team more effective?

What do you think?

Setting Team Goals

A team's goals are the reasons why the team exists. Setting goals may take just a few minutes or may involve a series of meetings. Defining the team's purpose may involve a group discussion with everyone's input. Or the team's purpose may be defined in a simple order from a supervisor.

Team members may enter the group with certain ideas of their own about what the team should do. Setting team goals helps individual members come together and aim for specific goals. Writing down the team goals helps keep the team focused.

To be effective, team goals must be clear and measurable. In addition, achievement of the goals should have value for the group—the group should benefit when the goals are reached. For example, a team goal of a school choir might be "Sell 1,000 Thanksgiving pies during the fund-raiser for the out-of-state trip." The sale of the 1,000 pies will have value because it will allow the choir—the group—to compete in an important music festival.

Answering the following four questions will help a team identify and set its goals and determine the value to the group of achieving the goals:

1. What are we trying to do?
2. How will we know when we have succeeded?
3. What are the rewards for us and the organization if we succeed?
4. What are the consequences for us and the organization if we fail?

The answers to these questions will lead the team to a final statement of its goals.

How is setting team goals similar to setting personal goals? How is it different?

What do you think?

CAREER SUCCESS TIP

Integrity still counts in the career world. Dishonesty might be the fast track to temporary success, but in the long run, it can permanently damage a reputation.

Side column

What do you think?

Use **TM11-04**.
Students' answers will vary. Answers should include the fact that diversity results in different opinions and possibly more creativity. (Refer to Chapter 5 for more information on diversity.)

TEACH

Ask students why teams need to set goals and develop a plan. Discuss the four questions in the list on page 199, asking students to explain how each question helps define the purpose of the team and focus the team's efforts. Then discuss the bulleted list at the top of page 200, asking students what the results are likely to be if the team does not include actions, resources, and measurements in its plan.

What do you think?

Use **TM11-05**.
Students' answers will vary. Answers should include the fact that the goal-setting steps are similar. However team goals are set with all team members in mind. (Refer to Chapter 7 for more information on goal setting.)

CAREER SUCCESS TIP

Honesty Is the Best Policy

Have students define cheating and describe different scenarios they think constitute cheating. Ask students why someone might cheat—not enough time to study, lack of interest, pressure to get good grades. Ask students if they believe cheating damages them. Ask if it is damaging even if they don't get caught? Encourage students to explain their answers. Remind students that cheating does damage by depriving the cheater of personal integrity, of learning valuable skills, of the trust and respect of others, and by stealing rewards and opportunities from those who do not cheat.

What do you think?

Use **TM11-06**.
Students' answers will vary.

66 **You can observe a lot just by watching.** 99

—*Yogi Berra, Baseball Coach*

Developing a Plan

To be successful, a team must develop a plan for reaching its goals. Most organizations require teams to develop written plans and budg-ets before putting their plans into action. A plan should include:

- **Actions.** The team plan should list the steps the team will take to reach its goals.
- **Resources.** The team will need resources to carry out its plan. The resource list usually includes estimates of how much the supplies will cost.
- **Measurements.** The team states what measurements it will use to determine whether it is on track to achieve its goals. If a goal is not met, the team must evaluate the probable effectiveness of the remaining planned actions. The team may also decide to modify portions of the original plan.

For example, suppose the goal of a sports team is to win the state championship. It could plan to take the following *actions:* develop game skills; create game strategies; research the strengths and weak-nesses of opposing teams; and practice, practice, practice. The *resources* it needs may include an area to practice and play, the equip-ment necessary for the sport, money to travel to and from games, video camera and player, and so on. To determine whether it is on track to achieve its goal, the sports team may use winning the first three games of the preseason as its *measure* of probable success.

Roles and Responsibilities of Team Members

Teams usually have formal and informal roles. Formal roles are clearly stated and clearly defined. They are often assigned before work begins and may be decided by management. Formal roles are:

- A leader or facilitator who directs the team's efforts and runs meetings.
- A scribe or reporter who records group decisions and takes other notes as necessary.

Informal roles, on the other hand, are roles that members choose voluntarily. Some informal roles you may encounter in your work-place are:

- An initiator who often proposes new ideas.
- A synthesizer who brings others' ideas together.
- A supporter who praises others' efforts and helps build group solidarity.

At various times, team members often fill several informal roles. For example, during one meeting, the same person may propose a new idea, praise someone else's efforts, and suggest a way to blend two ideas.

What do you think? What team role or roles do you play effectively?
What roles would you like to take on?

INTEGRATED ACADEMICS
Social Studies
Have students work in small groups to create a political cartoon that depicts the globalization of the workplace and how different cultures must interact as team members. Student groups may use computer-generated graphics or art materials to create their cartoons. Have each group present their cartoon to the class. Display the cartoons in the classroom.

As you might expect, being a good team member means more than simply showing up and performing your job. You must fully commit to the team's goals and purpose. If you disagree with some aspect of the team's effort or have a difficult time getting along with some of the members, you must overcome any negative feelings and work for the benefit of the team.

As a team member, you are responsible for keeping a positive attitude, communicating effectively, working hard, cooperating with others, and being honest. Your responsibilities also include:

- Participating fully in team discussions and activities.
- Volunteering for tasks you are qualified to perform.
- Completing your tasks on time.
- Safeguarding confidential information.
- Respecting diversity.

In Activity 11-2, "Case Challenges," you will become part of a team that works to solve problems.

Leadership of a Team

One of the most important roles in a team is that of the leader or facilitator. According to the dictionary, a **leader** is "a person who guides, directs, or commands." However, *how* the facilitator of a team guides, directs, or commands a team often determines whether the team succeeds or fails in achieving its goals.

Ling, who is recognized as the "whiz" of the technical assistance team at her school, was recently chosen to lead the team by the faculty adviser, Mrs. Santana. In her role, Ling, who is new to the school, is responsible for advising other members of the team about how to handle technical problems with the school network. She is also responsible for helping Mrs. Santana resolve conflicts with team members and between a team member and a student.

While Ling is excited about her new role, she worries about not having any prior leadership experience. She is concerned that the juniors and seniors on the team will resent her or ignore her advice. Ling decides to talk to Mrs. Santana about her concerns. Mrs. Santana points out that Ling is already advising other team members about technical problems. The juniors and seniors respect her technical knowledge and voluntarily ask her opinion. Mrs. Santana suggests that Ling talk to one of the counselors about ways to improve her skills at resolving conflicts. The counselor helps Ling find a video course and an Internet course on conflict resolution.

Although Ling is a little nervous in her new role, her sincerity, technical skills, and newly acquired conflict resolution skills help her be successful.

> ## CAREER FACT
> Leadership skills are 90 percent interpersonal skills. Excellent people skills separate the exceptional leaders from the average ones.

What do you think?

Use **TM11-07**.
Students' answers will vary. Answers should include the fact that team leadership is not confined to just sports and elected office.

TEACH

Apply the characteristics of leaders on page 202 of the text to two elected officials in regional, state, or national politics. Discuss whether the officials are effective leaders because of their characteristics.

APPLY

Have students complete **Activity 11-3, "Leadership,"** that appears on page 210. Teaching suggestions and the solution for this activity appear on page 210. An activity worksheet can be found on the Career Portfolio and Resource CD—**Text Activity 11-3.doc**.

What do you think?

Use **TM11-08**.
Students' answers will vary.

What do you think?

What are some situations in which you were a group leader? What leadership issues did you face?

Different leaders use different styles of leadership, but all leaders tend to have certain characteristics. Companies that successfully implement the team concept usually choose team leaders based on the following basic characteristics:

- **Ability to gain respect and trust.** Effective leaders inspire others to respect and trust them. They retain this respect and trust by finding ways to help team members feel good about themselves and by publicly recognizing the contributions of others.

- **Dependability.** Effective leaders do what they say they will do. They take responsibility for their decisions and actions and acknowledge their mistakes.

- **Ability to communicate effectively.** Effective leaders listen without prejudging; keep team members informed; encourage participation in discussions; and give clear, honest feedback.

- **Flexibility.** Effective leaders consider unusual ideas or approaches without prejudice. They adapt quickly to changing circumstances.

- **Good judgment.** Effective leaders can gather and analyze appropriate information, accurately identify and weigh the consequences of risks, and use their experience to make sound decisions in a timely manner.

- **Courage.** Effective leaders are willing to stand up for unpopular ideas, resist inappropriate pressure, and manage stressful conflicts. They are also willing to take intelligent risks in order to reach team goals.

- **Honesty.** Effective leaders are truthful in their dealings with others.

In Activity 11-3, "Leadership," you will have an opportunity to analyze someone you know in terms of leadership abilities.

How Teams Function

After team members are selected, goals are set, a plan is developed, and the roles of various team members are determined, the team is ready to begin its tasks. The function of a team is to find solutions to specific problems that have been determined by the organization.

Problem Solving

What do you think?

What methods have you used to solve a problem? How successful were your methods in solving the problem?

People who study problem solving have identified six key steps in the process. Skipping any of these steps will reduce a team's chance of reaching the best solution.

DIFFERENT LEARNING ABILITIES
At-Risk and Reluctant-Reader Students
Have students interview each other about their leadership abilities. Students are to use the list of basic characteristics on this page. Interviewers ask their partners a question pertaining to each bulleted item. For example, *How do you inspire others to respect and trust you? How do you demonstrate dependability?* Every student must come up with an answer for each category. If at-risk and reluctant-reader students are having difficulty answering the questions, work with them individually to help them understand their own worth as a leader or potential leader.

Step 1: Define the Problem. The team must understand what the problem is. For example, suppose you are on a team set up by a retail clothing store whose sales are down from last year. Step 1 will involve determining what caused the decrease in sales. The decrease is a symptom of the problem, but the problem could be economic troubles, outdated merchandise, poor customer service, road construction in front of the store, or a variety of other factors. Your team will need to research the differences between last year and this year to define the problem.

Step 2: Set the Criteria. The team should determine the characteristics of a good solution. The criteria should address the real problem for the clothing store, not just the symptom of the problem. A good solution is one that will raise revenue for the short term and also provide a basis for future marketing. Thus, if the real problem is poor customer service, slashing prices during a sale won't solve the problem.

Step 3: Explore Alternatives. Instead of settling quickly on the most obvious solution, the team identifies a number of possible alternatives. The alternatives for the store could include having more promotional events, cutting regular prices to attract more shoppers, revamping product displays to increase merchandise appeal, or changing store policies and training salespeople to provide better customer service.

Step 4: Evaluate Alternatives. At this stage, the team studies the various solutions proposed in step 3 using the criteria chosen in step 2. Part of the evaluation process for the store is to determine how much each proposed solution will cost and to estimate how much revenue each solution will bring in. Having more promotions is a quick fix, as more shoppers will be attracted in the short term. However, improving customer service may be a more cost-effective solution in the long run.

Step 5: Choose and Implement the Best Option. After thoroughly discussing the alternatives, the team chooses the best alternative based on the analysis in step 4. This alternative is then put into action. The option chosen in step 5 should solve the underlying problem of the clothing store and produce steady results over time. The best option for the clothing store may be to lower prices, or it may be to improve customer service.

Step 6: Review the Effects of the Solution. In some cases, the problem-solving team will dissolve after it has proposed a solution. If it does not, the team should meet to evaluate the results of its decision. The team should determine whether its solution is successful or whether an alternative should be considered and used. The clothing store's revenue numbers should be reviewed periodically to see if they are better than last year's numbers. If sales have not increased, the team should consider implementing an alternative solution.

CAREER ★
SUCCESS
TIP

Remember that a person's name is to that person the most important sound in any language. You can never say someone's name too much.

Have students complete **Activity 11-A, "Problems Teams Face,"** found in the *Investigating Your Career Activities & Projects* book.

The cases in this activity suggest problems that many teams face. Students find solutions to the problems by using the problem-solving steps in the activity, explained on page 203 of the textbook. In discussing the solutions, ask students to relate the case problems to work situations. Have students do this activity individually or in groups of four or five. Discuss the results as a class if time permits. **Solution:** The solution for this activity appears in the *Teacher's Edition* of *Investigating Your Career Activities & Projects*.

Brainstorming

In step 3 of the problem-solving process, teams often use a technique called brainstorming to identify alternatives. **Brainstorming** occurs when team members meet and toss out as many ideas as possible—without evaluating them. Quantity, not quality, is the goal of brainstorming.

> The software design team of a company that designs video games was charged with the task of creating a game that will appeal to both girls and boys. Lindsay, the company's design manager and team leader, began the team meeting by stating, "We need to create a game that will appeal to both girls and boys." She went on to ask, "Should we duplicate aspects of other games to make this one, which will take less time, or should we start totally fresh, building from the ground up?"
>
> Steve, the team's artist, replied, "Let's just create a few female characters and add them to an existing game."
>
> Jia, from marketing, responded, "Market research has shown that girls do not buy a game simply because of the presence of a few female characters." She went on to explain the characteristics of the games that girls buy.
>
> After Jia's explanation, some of the team thought modifying existing games would still be the way to go. Others believed the team needed to create an entirely new game. The discussion went round and round for several more minutes, with all the members glancing at Lindsay for help. Knowing her team would benefit from talking through all the issues, she suggested they first brainstorm ways existing games could be adapted and then brainstorm ideas for a new game. The team agreed that seeing all possible alternatives would help them decide the most effective approach.

Many teams use brainstorming as a means of coming up with multiple alternative solutions to a given problem. Brainstorming has the following characteristics:

- The discussion is free-flowing and fast-paced.
- All members blurt out their thoughts, with no one holding back.
- Even wild, seemingly crazy ideas are accepted and noted.
- Nobody criticizes any of the ideas offered.
- Team members build on their coworkers' ideas when they can, adding changes and improvements.
- Every idea is written down for future analysis.

DIFFERENT LEARNING STYLES
Kinesthetic Learners

Tell students that in the Native American tradition, people come together in a circle to talk about important subjects. In the circle, a talking stick is used. The person holding the talking stick is the only person who speaks. He or she passes the talking stick to the next person, who then speaks, and so on. Have students make a talking stick and hold a circle in the Native American tradition to discuss a topic. Students can make a talking stick by attaching items from nature to a small tree branch.

Assigning Tasks

The process of dividing up tasks among team members and assigning responsibility for them can be difficult. Teams will likely use one of the following methods of assigning tasks:

* The team leader makes the assignments.
* Team members agree to task assignments by **consensus**, by arriving at an agreement within the group.
* Team members, after considering their expertise and available time, volunteer for assignments.
* Team members, by company policy, are responsible for all tasks in their area of expertise.

Occasionally individual team members may be unhappy with the task assignments. However, the facilitator's priority is to have the team succeed, and equal workloads may not be possible. For example, if team members are from different departments, they may have varying amounts of time available for the team project. Also, certain tasks may require the skills of specific team members. If a construction team is building a bridge, only the civil engineer is qualified to determine how the bridge should be built to withstand various stresses. No matter how the task assignments are made on your team, make a point of doing your best work and meeting your commitments to the team.

ENRICH

Have students complete **Activity 11-B, "Imagine . . . .,"** found in the *Investigating Your Career Activities & Projects* book.

The cases in this activity relate to team problems in the workplace. Students may use the steps for problem solving on page 203 in the textbook to find solutions for the workplace scenarios. Have students do this activity individually or in groups of four or five. Discuss the results with the class.

Solution: The solution for this activity appears in the *Teacher's Edition* of *Investigating Your Career Activities & Projects*.

REAL PEOPLE
REAL CAREERS

Forensic Scientist

Manuel Perry is a real CSI, crime scene investigator, officially known as a forensic scientist. Manuel and his team work to unravel mysteries in such crimes as arson, murder, and chemical spills. Although Manuel is a detective, he does not work for a law enforcement agency. He is a scientist who works at a government laboratory. His job begins with uncovering the chemical makeup of various types of samples collected at crime scenes, including hair, water, and soil. Next, he and his team of investigators link the evidence to the crime to assist in the solution. Finally, Manuel testifies about his findings as an expert witness in court.

Two important characteristics of a forensic scientist are curiosity and perseverance. Until the answer is found, investigators need to keep searching to find out *why* something happens. Science and math courses, which are full of problem solving, help to develop these traits. Also, skills learned in writing and speaking courses help with evidence reports and testimony at trials. A forensic science team's analysis of the messy details of a crime helps identify criminals and prepare evidence against them.

For more information about forensic scientists:
* explore *www.deakin.edu.au/forensic*. Click on "The Chemical Detective Forensic Science Website."
* explore *www.realscience.org*. Click on "Forensic Scientist."

Source: "Forensic Scientist." *Real Science. www.realscience.org.*

REAL PEOPLE—REAL CAREERS
Forensic Scientist

Arrange the class into two groups. Have each group investigate one of the web sites on this page. Ask groups to create a fact sheet from the information they obtain from their assigned web site. Next, have the groups create a graphic organizer of the facts obtained. Have members of each group explain their graphic organizers to the whole class and give a short report on the facts they obtained. Display the fact sheets and the graphic organizers in the classroom.

What do you think?

Use **TM11-09**.
Students' answers will vary.

APPLY

Have students complete **Activity 11-4, "Learning from Others,"** that appears on page 211. Teaching suggestions and the solution for this activity appear on page 211. An activity worksheet can be found on the Career Portfolio and Resource CD— **Text Activity 11-4.doc.**

TEACH

Ask students how they would resolve a conflict with their friends or fellow students. Then ask how they could use the same skills in a workplace situation.

Mention that conflicts can be resolved by winning, yielding, delaying, or finding a middle ground through compromise. Students tend to think that a conflict is always aggressive and involves bad feelings, which may be the case if the conflict is not resolved. But resolving a conflict usually leads to an improved relationship between the people involved.

ENRICH

Have students complete **Activity 11-C, "Handling Difficulties,"** found in the *Investigating Your Career Activities & Projects* book.

Problems with team members often happen when a team member's behavior needs changing. Students provide solutions to help the team members so the team can function more effectively. Have students refer to the rules to manage conflict on page 206 in the textbook. Have students do this activity individually or in groups.
Solution: The solution for this activity appears in the *Teacher's Edition* of *Investigating Your Career Activities & Projects.*

What do you think?

What individual strengths would you want on a team whose goal is to plan an event to honor a customer? If these strengths weren't available, what would you do?

Activity 11-4, "Learning from Others," helps you analyze a team in your community.

Managing Conflict

Even if you communicate well with others, have a positive attitude, and are honest, conflicts with coworkers will arise and must be settled. **Conflict management** is the ability to resolve disagreements constructively. Conflict management techniques can help you resolve disagreements and prevent them from interfering with your ability to work effectively. Six key rules govern conflict management.

1. Invite the other person to a neutral meeting place that provides sufficient privacy.
2. Put yourself in the other person's position and listen carefully.
3. Ask the other person to consider your position and listen to you.
4. Look at the problem objectively and discuss the conflict. Encourage the other parties involved to do the same. Get the differences of opinion out in the open.
5. Create a climate of trust by speaking respectfully and in a nonthreatening manner.
6. Reach a solution that allows everyone to come away with something he or she wants.

Resolving conflicts is stressful but very rewarding. After two people have worked through a disagreement and found a solution both can accept, their relationship usually improves.

> Russell was disappointed when he was not chosen to attend the leadership training. Russell blamed his team leader, Trish, and was determined to do only what was necessary to keep his place on the team. Russell's negative attitude influenced his work on the team. His feelings were obvious in how he treated Trish. Trish asked the team's adviser, Mr. Wheeler, for a meeting with Russell. She told Mr. Wheeler the conflict couldn't continue because it was affecting the team.

> Trish used the six rules of conflict management in her effort to resolve the conflict with Russell. (1) To make sure they would not be interrupted and could speak freely, Trish reserved the conference room for her meeting with Russell. She also asked Mr. Wheeler to be present. (2) Trish began the meeting by asking Russell to explain why he was upset. Russell described his disappointment with not being able to attend the leadership training. After listening to his explanation, Trish described in her own words why she thought Russell was upset. (3) Trish

> **Getting good players is easy. Getting them to play together is the hard part.**
> —Casey Stengel, *Baseball Manager*

PART 4 • • • • • • PREPARING FOR THE NEXT STEP

INTEGRATED ACADEMICS
Communication
Have students work in groups of four or five. Ask each group to create a skit that illustrates a conflict and shows a way to resolve that conflict. Suggest to students that they use the information on this page to guide them. Have each group present its skit to the whole class. Choose a couple of the skits that best illustrate effective ways to resolve conflict, and have students present the skits to other classes.

explained to Russell how she saw the situation. She described her reasons for choosing the other team member instead of Russell, being careful to emphasize the other person's qualifications. She mentioned but did not emphasize that Russell's weak interpersonal skills were the main reason he was not selected. She asked if he understood her position. (4) Trish and Russell continued to speak openly and honestly, each listening as the other presented additional points. Although they still were not in complete agreement, the conversation did not become heated, and Trish saw no reason to take a break. (5) Trish continued to present her position in a nonthreatening manner and eventually created a climate of trust. (6) Trish explained to Russell how important he was to the team and suggested ways he could improve his skills so he would be ready for the next leadership training opportunity. Russell realized Trish was willing to help him succeed and agreed to work on improving his skills. Both were comfortable with the resolution of their disagreement.

In Activity 11-5, "Coming to Terms," you will check your understanding of some of the important terms in this chapter.

When conflicts between team members cannot be resolved, the success of the team is in jeopardy. When the team fails to perform for any reason, the careers of all the team members suffer setbacks. Every member of a team must work hard to help the team resolve differences and focus on the team goals.

A manager whose work team argued frequently tried to settle their differences by speaking to each member individually. When this didn't work, she called them together. First, she laid a bunch of sticks together and tied them into a bundle. Then she asked each team member to break the bundle of sticks. Each tried unsuccessfully. Next, the manager untied the bundle, separated the sticks, and asked the team members to break them one by one. They did so easily. The manager pointed out that when the group was united and worked together as a team, it was strong. However, divided and separate, each individual was weaker.

Think of a conflict you've experienced. How would following the six rules for conflict resolution have helped?

What do you think?

APPLY

Have students complete **Activity 11-5, "Coming to Terms,"** that appears on page 211. Teaching suggestions and the solution for this activity appear on page 211. An activity worksheet can be found on the Career Portfolio and Resource CD— **Text Activity 11-5.doc.**

TEACH

You cannot overemphasize to students the topic of conflict management. Not getting along with coworkers is the No. 1 reason for being fired in the United States. Discuss examples of conflict management at school, then relate the subject to the workplace.

Use the short scenario at the bottom of text page 207 to introduce a discussion about how a united team is stronger than any one of its individual members.

What do you think?

Use **TM11-10**.
Students' answers will vary.

ENRICH

Have students complete **Activity 11-D, "Predicting Group Behavior,"** found in the *Investigating Your Career Activities & Projects* book.

This activity helps increase students' awareness of how the typical behavior of males and females varies in different group situations. Students can use the results of the quiz to analyze their own behavior and to determine ways that they can overcome the typical, or stereotypical, behavior. The answers come directly from various research project observations. You may use the quiz questions to analyze students' group behavior.
Solution: The solution for this activity appears in the *Teacher's Edition* of *Investigating Your Career Activities & Projects.*

DIFFERENT LEARNING ABILITIES
Gifted
Have students write a one-act play that deals with the word *conflict*. Plays are to explain a conflict and then resolve it. Have students use the principles on page 206 to resolve the conflict. Have the playwrights choose other members of the class to act in the play and work on costumes, scenery, and lighting. Reserve the school auditorium or another large room and hold a "Play Day." Invite parents and the whole school.

APPLY

Have students complete **Activity 11-6, "Conflict Resolution,"** that appears on page 211. Teaching suggestions and the solution for this activity appear on page 211. An activity worksheet can be found on the Career Portfolio and Resource CD—**Text Activity 11-6.doc**.

CLOSE

Have students complete **Activity 11-E, "Teams' Terms,"** found in the *Investigating Your Career Activities & Projects* book.

This activity uses all of the chapter's Key Terms in a word search puzzle.

Solution: The solution for this activity appears in the *Teacher's Edition* of *Investigating Your Career Activities & Projects.*

IN A NUTSHELL

Remind students about the objectives set forth at the beginning of the chapter, and use this summary to reinforce the concepts presented in this chapter.

Career Journal

Ask students to spend 10 minutes writing Career Journal entries that answer the following questions:
1. How well did what you thought you knew match what the chapter presented?
2. What questions do you now have about the chapter topics, and where do you think you can find the answers to those questions?
3. How will the content of the chapter help you investigate *your* career?

ASSESS

Administer the printed objective test for Chapter 11, available with this package. Test solutions are found in the *Teacher's Edition* of *Investigating Your Career Chapter Tests*. Use the **Exam***View*® CD to create your own objective test for this chapter.

 Use Activity 11-6, "Conflict Resolution," to research articles on the Internet that can help you understand how to resolve conflicts.

IN A NUTSHELL

- **I can explain the concept of teams.**

  A team is a group of employees working together to achieve a common goal. Effective teamwork is an essential skill for employees in most organizations today. As a team member, I will benefit from being on a successful team because I will increase my chance of being promoted. I will also have a sense of empowerment—the feeling of satisfaction that comes from managing and controlling my own work.

- **I can describe the process of team building.**

  Building a team begins with selecting team members. Managers select people who have the skills and imagination to find creative solutions. Setting team goals is also part of the process of team building. Team goals should be clear and measurable and should have value for the organization. A team must develop a plan for reaching its goals. A plan includes actions, resources, and measurements. Teams have both formal and informal roles, and at various times, team members may fill several informal roles. As a team member, I will be responsible for working for the benefit of the team. Team leaders usually have the ability to gain respect and trust; demonstrate dependability; communicate effectively; and show flexibility, good judgment, and courage.

- **I can explain how teams function in the workplace.**

  The function of a team is to find solutions to specific problems. Problem solving involves six steps: defining the problem, setting the criteria, exploring alternatives, evaluating alternatives, choosing and applying the best option, and reviewing the effects of the solution. Brainstorming is a technique often used to identify alternatives.

- **I can describe ways to manage conflict within a team.**

  Conflict management is the ability to settle disagreements constructively. Conflict management techniques can help me settle disagreements and prevent them from interfering with my ability to work effectively. If conflicts between team members cannot be resolved, the team may not be successful in reaching its goals.

Suggestions for Parents and Family Members

Help Teenagers Understand Teams

Ways parents and family members can assist teens in understanding teams include:

1. Pointing out team situations while shopping, on vacation, and in other places.
2. Discussing how teams are part of your workplace.
3. Talking about conflict resolution and explaining how you managed to prevent a conflict and the strategies you used.

Evaluate yourself to see how ready you are for teamwork in an organization. On a separate sheet of paper, number from 1 to 10. Decide whether each of the following statements is true or false, and write your answers on the paper. Write *sometimes* if an item is sometimes true and sometimes false. Answer as honestly as you can.

1. I like solving problems with others in a group.

2. In a group, I often let others do the talking before I express my views.

3. I am a good listener.

4. If I have a problem to solve, I talk over my options with others before making my decision.

5. I see myself as a potential leader.

6. If someone contradicts me, I consider the other person's side before I answer.

7. I enjoy having debates and hearing others' viewpoints on issues.

8. When I work with others, I like to set specific goals.

9. When I set goals, I usually achieve them.

10. I am often the mediator in disputes between friends and family.

Score 1 point for each True answer. Use the information below to evaluate your score.

> Score of 8–10: Good leader and team member
> Score of 6–7: Good team member, but probably not a leader
> Score of 0–5: Need to work on team skills

What do you need to do to become a more effective team member?

Part 1—Problem Solving

Working as part of a team to solve problems will help you understand how a team functions. Form a small group and sit in a circle. Choose a leader and a spokesperson. For each of the cases that follow:

• Have one person in the group read the case aloud.
• Moving around the circle, have each person state his or her opinion about the problem identified in the case.
• Open the discussion to the entire group.
• Discuss the case until the entire group agrees on a solution. (Your teacher will give you a time limit for each case.)

Activity 11-1: Teamwork

This quiz gives students a preview of the characteristics of an effective team member and allows them to assess their assets as team members.

After students have scored their quizzes, discuss each statement and its implications for a team's success. **Solution:** Answers will vary. Based on their scores, students learn whether they need to work on certain behaviors to be better team members and leaders.

Activity 11-2: Case Challenges

This activity has two purposes. First, the activity helps students develop problem-solving skills by analyzing and finding solutions to real-world problems. Second, and more importantly, students are directed to work together as a team to solve the problem. Each team member has equal representation in stating his or her opinion and in agreeing to a solution.

After teams have agreed on solutions to the problems, ask each team to describe the team behavior, both positive and negative, to the class. Record their responses on a transparency or on the chalkboard. Ask how the team behavior changed as the case discussions progressed. Then have students compare their team's actions with the problem-solving steps on page 203. **Solution:** Answers will vary.

Analyzing the characteristics of a person they believe is a good leader helps students discover the attributes of leadership.

Emphasize that students should be specific in their answers and give examples that support their conclusions. They should base their conclusions on actual observations they have made, not on information they have received from others, unless students' own observations support the secondhand information. Discuss students' answers to the questions, and examine the characteristics these leaders have in common. Ask students how they could use the common characteristics of the leaders they observed to model their own behavior in school and work situations.

Solution: Answers will vary.

1. You are unhappy with your job in a retail store, but you need to earn money. Your negative attitude toward your job has begun to affect your performance. You are not paying attention to details and are often late for work. In addition, you made a sarcastic remark about a customer, and the customer overhead your remark and complained to your manager. What should you do? What should your manager do?

2. You have a job you enjoy and have been given several pay raises for your outstanding work. Your best friend wants to work where you do and has asked you several times about openings. You know your friend is not very responsible and would not be an asset to your company. You have just learned that there is a job opening at your company and your friend plans to apply. What should you do?

3. Dustin seems determined to undermine you at work every chance he gets. He has a bad attitude, especially with you. The situation is difficult because you are the only two cooks scheduled for weekday evenings. You know you will eventually react to his behavior and start an argument. What should you do?

4. When you picked up your sister's dry cleaning, you noticed that one of her dresses was in two pieces. The dry cleaners had separated the dress that had formerly been sewn together. You brought the problem to the clerk's attention and asked to have the dress sewn back together. The clerk said it was not the responsibility of the cleaners and yelled at you in front of the other customers. What should you do?

Part 2—Employee/Customer Relations

As a group, write two additional scenarios showing positive employee/ customer relations. Then write two scenarios showing negative employee/ customer relations.

ACTIVITY 11-3   **Leadership**

With a partner, choose an adult you both know who you believe is a good leader, such as a parent, church official, or community leader. The person should be someone outside of your school.

1. Determine whether the person has the following characteristics of leadership:

- Ability to gain respect and trust
- Dependability
- Ability to communicate effectively
- Flexibility

- Good judgment
- Courage
- Honesty

2. What are the person's strengths and weaknesses?

3. What sets this person apart from others in the same position?

4. Is the person someone of high integrity? Why or why not?

5. Is the person a great speaker? Why or why not?

Summarize your results and report them to your class.

Learning from Others

Choose a group to observe in your school or community. Analyze one of their meetings or projects by observing their work and interviewing some of the team members. Some suggestions for possible teams are athletic groups, school committees, student council, church groups, and town committees. Discuss the results with your class.

Possible observation and interview questions:

- Why was the group formed?
- What was the purpose of the group's meeting or the group project?
- How many people are in the group? Was the number adequate or were there too many members? Why?
- Who provided leadership for the group? In what ways did the leadership contribute?
- Did the leadership change during the project? How?
- How did the leaders respond to others in a leadership role?
- What examples of respect for others' abilities did you observe?
- What were the team members' contributions to the meeting or project?

ACTIVITY 11-5 **Coming to Terms**

With a partner, set up an imaginary team of five people and devise a problem for the team to solve. Write a description of a team meeting using the terms below. Indicate which team member is the leader and which is the reporter. Include comments indicating the roles that group members assume, such as a synthesizer. The activity is completed when the team has reached a satisfactory solution.

1. Team
2. Collaborate
3. Empowerment

4. Brainstorming
5. Consensus

ACTIVITY 11-6 **Conflict Resolution**

Think of a time when you had a conflict with another person at home or school. Then investigate the Internet site Southern Poverty Law Center at *www.splcenter.org*. Click on "Teaching Tolerance," and then click on "101 Tools for Tolerance."

1. Write down at least three ideas you could use personally at home or at school.

2. As you read "101 Tools for Tolerance," take notes about what you can apply to reduce your personal conflict situation. Answer the following questions based on your research: How could you have avoided the conflict? How could you have settled the conflict sooner or more smoothly?

Activity 11-4: Learning from Others

Observing behavior in a group meeting helps students understand common characteristics of groups and the roles different team members play.

Point out that a group leader is not always elected as such. Different leaders may emerge in different situations during meetings. Ask students to identify the people who fill the team member roles listed on page 200 of the text.

If students observe an athletic team, they should base their answers on interview questions and observation of a team meeting, not on the team in a practice or competition. **Solution:** Answers will vary. In a discussion of the results of students' observations, have students decide whether the group they observed was an effective team. Ask them whether the team worked together as a unit, whether all team members contributed, and whether the team was able to reach agreement by consensus.

Activity 11-5: Coming to Terms

This activity checks students' understanding not only of some of the terms in the chapter but also of how teams function and solve problems. Discuss the definitions of the terms before students begin the activity. Explain that students should agree about the team members, the problem, and how the team will solve the problem before they write their descriptions. Before students begin writing, they may also want to make notes about various events in their imaginary team meeting, how they will use the terms, and some of the members' roles.

Ask students to read their descriptions to the class. Use these questions to stimulate discussion: Was the problem-solving process applied correctly? Was the problem solved satisfactorily? Were the terms used correctly?
Solution: Descriptions will vary.

Activity 11-6: Conflict Resolution

This activity increases students' awareness of ways to resolve conflicts effectively and helps students learn how to apply research information to situations in their lives.

In a class discussion after students have completed their research, ask students what they learned in general about how to resolve conflicts. Then ask if any of the advice would have helped resolve their specific personal conflict situation with better results.
Solution: Answers will vary.

FOCUS

Chapter 12 describes areas of employment related to management of the workplace. The chapter explains the laws that regulate workers' hours, workers' safety on the job, and the amount of pay workers take home. Students learn that the different ways employers choose to have work done affects the roles of the people they hire. Students also learn that their success will require meeting their employers' expectations.

Use the **Objectives** and **Key Terms** printed in the margin to help students focus on the content of this chapter. Use the **video segment** for Chapter 12 to trigger discussion.

TEACH

Discuss the chapter's opening scenario with students. Ask what they already know about withholding.

What do you think?

Use **TM12-01**.
Students' answers will vary but should include specific services that the local, state, and federal government provides.

Career Journal

Ask students to spend 10 minutes writing Career Journal entries that answer the following questions:
1. What do you think this chapter will cover?
2. What do you already know about these topics?
3. What three things do you want to learn about these topics?

12 Understanding the Workplace

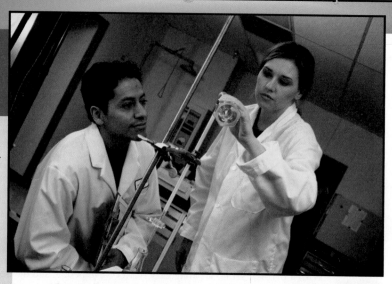

OBJECTIVES

After completing this chapter, you will be able to:
- Discuss federal, state, and local employment laws.
- Complete employment forms.
- Identify withholdings.
- Describe different types of employment.
- Explain employer expectations.

Key Terms:
- minimum wage
- overtime
- employment eligibility verification form (Form I-9)
- W-4 form
- gross pay
- net pay
- social security
- Medicare
- fringe benefits
- independent contractor
- contract workers
- ethics
- discretion
- performance evaluation

After graduation from a career/technical school, Sam quickly found a job as a medical laboratory technician. He worked two weeks before his first payday finally arrived. Sam was so excited he almost tore his paycheck as he ripped open the envelope. He stared at the amount of his check. The figure was too low! There had to be a mistake. Certain that a math error had been made, Sam went to the accounting department to find out what was wrong.

Sandra, the payroll manager, explained the numbers on the stub attached to Sam's paycheck. The top number was his gross salary. From that amount, federal income tax and Sam's social security and Medicare contributions were deducted. Additionally, their state had an income tax and their city had a payroll tax. Both of these taxes were deducted from each employee's paycheck. Usually, she concluded, all of the taxes amounted to about one-fourth of a person's salary.

As Sam walked to the parking lot, he still felt confused. He knew about income taxes and social security (both had often been in news reports), but somehow he hadn't connected them to his paycheck. Sam wasn't sure how the government used his money, but he would find out. In the meantime, he realized he would have to revise his budget. Sam lowered his expectations about a new car as he mentally considered the car payment he would be able to afford each month.

What do you think?
Why do various governments deduct taxes from your paycheck? How do they use your tax contributions?

212

CHAPTER RESOURCES and MATERIALS

Activities & Projects book
Instructor's Resource CD
- Forms and Worksheets for Chapter Activities 12-1 through 12-5
- Internet Links for Chapter 12
- PowerPoint Presentation for Chapter 12
- Lesson Plans
- Teaching Masters for Chapter 12
- Video Discussion Guide for Chapter 12

Chapter Tests book
Exam*View*® CD
Video
Web Site

Employment Laws

At what age can you legally work? What is the minimum wage you can earn? How much will you be paid if you work overtime? Should you join a union? How will you know if your workplace is safe?

To learn the answers to these questions, you need to know about employment laws. Federal, state, and local governments have all passed laws relating to employment. Knowing your and your employer's legal responsibilities will help you evaluate your employment opportunities.

Federal Laws

The federal government is responsible for most laws that cover workplace safety, the basic wage an employer must pay, and the circumstances in which teens younger than 18 years old may work. These laws were passed to improve conditions for workers.

Basic Labor Standards

Until near the end of the Great Depression of the 1930s, workers in the United States had few rights. Individual employers determined the rules regarding their workplaces and set worker wages as they chose. Many employers paid workers so little that the workers literally could not afford food and shelter.

An example of the conditions at that time involves Joseph Tipaldo, the manager of a laundry in Brooklyn, New York. Tipaldo had been paying nine women workers only $10 a week, an amount that was in violation of the New York state minimum wage law. When officials forced him to pay his workers $14.88, Tipaldo made the women workers give him back the difference. Tipaldo was jailed on various charges, including violating the state wage law. His lawyers' defense was that the New York wage law was unconstitutional. In 1936, the U.S. Supreme Court voided the New York law as a violation of liberty of contract, and Tipaldo was free to continue his practices until the law was changed in 1938.

In addition to their dissatisfaction over wages, many people were also upset over the exploitation of children in the labor market. Since the mid 1800s, children had been working at dangerous jobs instead of going to school. Employers paid children less than adults even though the children worked as much as 16 hours a day, 6 days a week. In addition, children were often injured or killed because of the brutal working conditions.

In response to incidents like the Tipaldo laundry case and the labor injustices to children, Congress passed the Fair Labor Standards Act (FLSA) in 1938. The FLSA applies to employers that do business in more than one state and meet certain annual sales requirements. The FLSA has been amended over the years and now regulates three areas that directly influence your career.

> **" Something has to be done about the elimination of child labor and long hours and starvation wages. "**
>
> —*Franklin D. Roosevelt, U.S. President 1933–1945*

ONLINE RESOURCES

Check out the web site **www.investigatingyourcareer.com** for teacher resources, student activities, and replacements for broken links for this chapter. To access the teacher resources:

Username: career
Password: investigate

Emphasize to students that the minimum wage and overtime laws are part of the FLSA and apply only to employees of businesses that do at least $500,000 in sales a year or that communicate with, buy from, or sell to people or businesses in other states. Refer students to the "Wages" link at www.dol.gov.

Make sure students understand why the various laws in this section were enacted. Ask if they think any of the laws are no longer necessary or should be changed in some way. Then discuss the reasons for their answers, making sure students realize the possible consequences of repealing or amending these laws. Ask if students think any areas of employment that are not regulated should be.

ENRICH

Have students complete **Activity 12-A, "Teen Safety,"** found in the *Investigating Your Career Activities & Projects* book.

This activity helps students discover why following workplace health and safety laws are important to working teens. Students also practice critical thinking by identifying safe and unsafe actions and analyzing why or how the actions impact safety. **Solution:** The solution for this activity appears in the *Teacher's Edition* of *Investigating Your Career Activities & Projects*.

In some states, employers do not have to pay the minimum wage to people who receive tips, such as restaurant servers, valet parking attendants, and bellhops. However, employers must pay a wage that, when added to average tips, is at least as much as the minimum wage.

Workers Younger Than 18 Years Old. People 16 and 17 years old, while not restricted in the number of hours they work, may not perform any hazardous job. Hazardous jobs include excavating, driving, and operating many types of power equipment. Exceptions are provided for career/technical students and apprentices under specified conditions. Students 14 and 15 years old may work in various nonhazardous jobs that are not in manufacturing or mining under the following conditions: no more than 3 hours on a school day, 18 hours in a school week, 8 hours on a nonschool day, or 40 hours in a nonschool week. Also, they may work only between 7 a.m. and 7 p.m. during the school year and until 9 p.m. in the summer. Exceptions are allowed in some circumstances, such as children working in the family business.

Wages and Hours. The **minimum wage** is the lowest hourly wage an employer can pay in the United States. It is set by Congress and changed periodically. In addition, employers must pay hourly employees overtime wages at a rate of 1½ times the regular rate of pay. **Overtime** is any time worked over 40 hours in a regularly scheduled seven-day workweek.

Equal Pay. An amendment to the FLSA, the Equal Pay Act of 1963, prohibits pay discrimination because of gender. Men and women who perform equal work must be paid equal wages. An employer may pay different wages if the wages are based on such things as seniority, skill level, or shifts worked.

Workplace Health and Safety

In addition to the safeguards established by the FLSA, Congress has enacted other laws to protect the health and safety of American workers. You will be expected to follow the policies that employers have developed to comply with these laws.

During high school, Holly spent summers working as a researcher in her town library. While she enjoyed the hours and interesting people, she was bothered by some aspects of her job. For example, her supervisor, Mr. Taylor, told her she had to stop wearing sandals to work. Holly thought Mr. Taylor was being unreasonable and considered quitting. After talking with her father, Holly decided to ask Mr. Taylor why the library had that particular regulation.

Mr. Taylor explained that the library required its employees to wear closed-toe shoes as a safety precaution. Carts filled with books could easily cause injuries if they ran over an unprotected foot. Even the books themselves could be dangerous if they fell from a high library shelf onto exposed toes. Holly had never heard of anyone being injured in these ways, but she decided to follow the rule.

CAREER TREND
Minimum Wage

In Ireland during 2002, the Union of Students protested the government's proposal to pay only £3 per hour to students for their work under the Students' Summer Job Scheme. Ireland's minimum wage is £4.40 per hour. The Union of Students said students should be paid the minimum wage. Have students research the minimum wages for adults and for young people in the United States. Is the minimum wage different for each group? Hold a class discussion on why adults should or should not be paid more than students.

—*Source: www.nuimsu.com*

What safety rules have you had to follow at school or work that you thought were unreasonable? How did you handle the situation?

What do you think?

The following paragraphs describe some health and safety issues and how their related laws affect the workplace.

OSHA. The Occupational Safety and Health Act of 1970 created an organization called OSHA to enforce health and safety standards in the workplace. Manufacturers and other types of companies must follow strict standards for the safety and health of their employees. For example, welders must wear safety goggles and healthcare workers must be provided with gloves for handling blood. OSHA is serious about enforcing the laws protecting workers. On October 25, 2001, a federal appeals court upheld the 17-year prison term of an Idaho employer who had ordered an employee to clean out a storage tank filled with hydrogen cyanide gas. The employee suffered severe brain damage and requires extensive care.

Drug Free Workplace Act. Random drug testing is common in many large companies today, primarily as a result of the Drug Free Workplace Act of 1988. When a company does more than $25,000 worth of business with the federal government, it is required to establish policies on drug awareness. Many organizations not covered by this act also follow its guidelines.

Family and Medical Leave Act. Employees who are new parents or new adoptive parents, employees with immediate family members who are seriously ill, and employees who have a serious health condition must be granted up to 12 weeks of unpaid leave each year if they work for a firm with 50 or more employees. In addition, many companies with less than 50 employees voluntarily follow the guidelines for leave set by the Family and Medical Leave Act of 1993.

Equal Employment Opportunity

The U.S. Civil Rights Act of 1964 and its amendments prohibit many forms of discrimination in the workplace. Specifically your race, color, national origin, religion, gender, disability, or pregnancy-related condition cannot keep you from being hired or promoted at a company that employs more than 15 people—as long as the factor doesn't interfere with your ability to do the work. For example, a person without

---

What do you think?

Use **TM12-02**.
Students' answers will vary.

TEACH

Discuss with students why these acts are important to know. Ask students to talk about what effect each act, especially OSHA and the Drug Free Workplace Act, could have on teens in the workplace.

Include affirmative action in your discussion of equal employment opportunity. The concept of affirmative action calls for minorities and women to be given special consideration in employment, education, and contracting decisions. Institutions with affirmative action policies generally set measurable goals and specific timetables for achieving increased diversity. Emphasize that modern affirmative action plans can direct hiring managers to choose a minority or woman from a pool of *equally qualified* candidates. Also, the U.S. government does *not* set quotas for affirmative action. Finally, affirmative action decisions are not supposed to give preference to unqualified candidates or to establish a pattern of "reverse discrimination." The Internet has information about the current status and history of affirmative action; search using the keywords *affirmative action*.

DIFFERENT LEARNING ABILITIES

At-Risk and Reluctant-Reader Students

Have at-risk and reluctant-reader students interview an adult who is working at a minimum-wage job. Coach students on ways they can respectfully ask how the people live and pay their expenses. Have students use a tape recorder for the interviews and turn the audiotape in for credit. To protect the privacy of interviewees, advise students to avoid recording real names. Tell students that even with a high school diploma, many people still earn only minimum wage. Point out that without a high school diploma, people have an even harder time earning more than minimum wage.

You may wish to invite one or more guest speakers to talk about various topics in this chapter. Consider asking people who work with one of the following topics: employment laws, OSHA regulations, labor unions, or contract workers. If you choose a speaker who represents a union, help the speaker prepare by providing ahead of time the questions listed in Activity 12-1.

What do you think?

Use **TM12-03**.
Students' answers will vary.

sight may be quite capable of keying recorded business correspondence by using listening devices and a keyboard. However, someone who is legally blind cannot safely drive delivery trucks. An employer who refused to hire a blind driver would not be violating the Civil Rights Act.

About 43 million Americans have one or more physical or mental disabilities. The employment opportunities of these Americans are protected mainly by the Americans with Disabilities Act (ADA), which took effect in 1992. As discussed in Chapter 5, employers are required to make reasonable accommodations for qualified applicants and must be able to show that an applicant's disabilities are not the reason the applicant was not hired.

What do you think?

Do you know anyone who is mentally or physically disabled, works productively, and earns a salary? How would that person's life be different if the ADA did not exist?

Whistleblowers

CAREER FACT

Seventy-eight percent of major U.S. companies actively check their employees on the job. Sixty-three percent monitor employees' Internet connection. Ten percent do not inform employees of surveillance.

Every year thousands of Americans witness wrongdoing on the job that endangers the health, safety, or lives of others. They may see managers at a nuclear facility who violate a safety code, workers at a chemical company who dump hazardous waste unlawfully, or owners of a food processing plant who attempt to sell contaminated meat to consumers.

Whistleblowers are workers who bring the wrongdoing of employers to the attention of the government, the press, or the public. Deciding when to speak out and when to remain silent is a choice each individual makes based on his or her personal values.

The Whistleblower Protection Act of 1998 defends an individual's right to blow the whistle and be protected. Whistleblowers need to be protected because what they do is brave and sometimes dangerous. Other employees who do not agree—or who fear their jobs will be lost if an employer is forced to change a practice—may try to cause physical harm or emotional and mental stress to the whistleblower.

Labor Unions

Because of the unfair working conditions in the United States in the 1930s, workers joined together in some occupational areas to form labor unions. The unions worked to improve wages, benefits, and working conditions by negotiating, picketing, and striking. Most employers resisted labor unions and fired workers who joined them. Violence often broke out among employers, union members, and nonunion workers.

CAREER TREND

Big Brother Is Watching

Organize students into two groups. Hold a class debate with one group representing employees and the other group representing employers. The debate is over whether employers have a right to monitor their employees on the job. Debate teams are to cover on-the-job surveillance and Internet connections. Suggest that students conduct an Internet search using the keywords *employee monitoring*, *employee privacy*, or *on-the-job surveillance*. Remind students that their arguments are to be logical and are to be backed up by research they cite in their answers. Each student on the team must take part in the debate.

In 1935, Congress passed the National Labor Relations Act (NLRA) to clarify the rights and obligations of unions and employers. By 1947, the unions had become so strong that Congress passed the Taft-Hartley amendments. These amendments added a "right-to-work" provision to the NLRA. This provision allowed states to pass laws that prohibited a union and an employer from agreeing to a union shop contract. Under a union shop contract, all employees of a company who are qualified to join the union are required to pay union dues, even those who do not choose to join the union. Today about half the states have upheld the practice of union shops and half have passed right-to-work laws.

As a child growing up in Idaho, Keith had always liked to construct buildings—model houses, stores, and even skyscrapers. His requests for birthday presents had always involved construction equipment and building kits. So no one in his family was surprised when he decided to pursue a career in construction management. To gain experience, Keith took construction skills courses during high school. The courses included building a three-bedroom house, which the school then raffled off to raise funds for various school-to-career experience programs. After high school graduation, Keith chose to attend a college in California for his bachelor's degree.

To earn money for college expenses, Keith returned home to Idaho to find a construction job during the summer after his freshman year. He had no trouble finding carpentry jobs in Boise. All he had to do was read the want ads in the paper. Because of the skills Keith had gained in high school, he was able to start working the week after he returned home.

After his sophomore year in college, Keith decided to find a construction job in California so he would have different work experiences. However, he found it difficult to find a job until he joined the carpenters' union. Everybody on his crew was a union member except Smitty, the contractor's nephew. Although Keith qualified for a special union program and understood how unions helped their members, he wasn't sure he liked the restriction of having to be a union member. He realized that after he got his degree and became a construction manager, he would have to decide whether he wanted to work in a union shop with right-to-work laws.

■ TEACH ■

Point out to students that Congress passed the National Labor Relations Act in 1935. Ask students what they know about 1935 from their history classes. Ask students if they think times have changed. Are labor unions still necessary? Why or why not? Organize students into two groups. Have one group argue for labor unions; the other, against. Remind students that their arguments must be logical and based on fact.

Discuss the impact of unions on job opportunities for students in your area. For example, in some areas, workers are not unionized; in other areas, younger workers must join a union if they work in grocery stores, retail stores, or some restaurants.

DIFFERENT LEARNING STYLES

Print Learners

Have students write a letter to a fictitious friend in another country to explain why labor unions are necessary or why labor unions should be abolished in this country. Students are to back up their arguments with information they obtain from Internet research. Their letters are to explain some history of labor unions and how unions work today. Post the letters around the room for the class to read.

━━━ **APPLY** ━━━

Have students complete **Activity 12-1, "Investigating Unions,"** that appears on page 232. Teaching suggestions and the solution for this activity appear on page 232. An activity worksheet can be found on the Career Portfolio and Resource CD— **Text Activity 12-1.doc**.

━━━ **TEACH** ━━━

Mention that some jobs may also require a health certificate, which is available from a doctor or the local health department.

What do you think?

How do you feel about union shops? Do you support right-to-work laws? Why or why not?

State and Local Employment Laws

The state and city where you live may also have laws and regulations that employers and employees must follow. Although most state laws protect workers on the same grounds as federal laws, some state laws are stricter than federal laws. For example, some states more strictly control the hours teens can work and the jobs teens can do. Some state and local laws also protect workers against discrimination for added reasons, such as marital status or sexual orientation or preference. States may also require employers to pay a higher minimum wage or require teens to obtain work permits.

In Activity 12-1, "Investigating Unions," you will use the Internet to explore the advantages and disadvantages of joining a union.

Employment Forms

In order for you to receive a wage from a company, you must be registered with the federal government as a legal employee. When you begin your first job, you must complete the forms described in the following paragraphs.

CAREER FACT

Identity theft is a fast-growing crime. Thieves who obtain social security and checking account or credit card numbers can ruin victims' credit. Bad credit can prevent people from obtaining jobs.

Social Security Card

Employment law requires employers to review your social security card and report your social security number as part of their payroll records. If you do not have a social security number, you may apply for one at a social security office. You will need to bring original documents, such as your birth certificate, that show your age, identity, and citizenship status.

Employment Eligibility Verification

Employers will ask you to complete an **employment eligibility verification form (Form I-9)**, which verifies that you are legally qualified to work in the United States. Form I-9 was developed by the Immigration and Naturalization Service (INS) and is distributed through the INS. Illustration 12.1 shows a completed Form I-9.

Your employer also will ask you to provide one or more pieces of identification that show your picture. Identification is required so your employer can be sure you are who you claim to be. Several types of photo IDs are acceptable, including a driver's license, school ID, and passport.

INTEGRATED ACADEMICS
Social Studies
Have students work in small groups to research their state and local employment laws. Groups are to make a graphic organizer of the laws to illustrate how they affect students, working conditions, and other information. Graphic organizers also should show how state laws and local laws interact with one another. Post the graphic organizers around the room. Have students compare and contrast their graphic organizers in a class discussion.

Illustration 12.1 Completed Form I-9

U.S. Department of Justice
Immigration and Naturalization Service

OMB No. 1115-0136
Employment Eligibility Verification

Please read instructions carefully before completing this form. The instructions must be available during completion of this form. **ANTI-DISCRIMINATION NOTICE.** It is illegal to discriminate against work eligible individuals. Employers **CANNOT** specify which document(s) they will accept from an employee. The refusal to hire an individual because of a future expiration date may also constitute illegal discrimination.

Section 1. Employee Information and Verification. To be completed and signed by employee at the time employment begins

Print Name: Last	First	Middle Initial	Maiden Name
Stendhal	**Robert**	**J**	

Address (Street Name and Number)	Apt. #	Date of Birth (month/day/year)
2700 Peerpoint Way		**7 / 31 / - -**

City	State	Zip Code	Social Security #
Hamilton	**Ohio**	**45011-2743**	**555-00-5000**

I am aware that federal law provides for imprisonment and/or fines for false statements or use of false documents in connection with the completion of this form.

I attest, under penalty of perjury, that I am (check one of the following):
☑ A citizen or national of the United States
☐ A Lawful Permanent Resident (Alien # A _____)
☐ An alien authorized to work until ____/____/____
(Alien # or Admission # _____)

Employee's Signature *Robert J. Stendhal*	Date (month/day/year) **10/11/20--**

Preparer and/or Translator Certification. (To be completed and signed if Section 1 is prepared by a person other than the employee.) I attest, under penalty of perjury, that I have assisted in the completion of this form and that to the best of my knowledge the information is true and correct.

Preparer's/Translator's Signature	Print Name

Address (Street Name and Number, City, State, Zip Code)	Date (month/day/year)

Section 2. Employer Review and Verification. To be completed and signed by employer. Examine one document from List A **OR** examine one document from List B **and** one from List C as listed on the reverse of this form and record the title, number and expiration date, if any, of the document(s)

	List A	OR	List B	AND	List C
Document title:	_____		_____		_____
Issuing authority:	_____		_____		_____
Document #:	_____		_____		_____
Expiration Date (if any):	__/__/__		__/__/__		__/__/__
Document #:	_____				
Expiration Date (if any):	__/__/__				

CERTIFICATION - I attest, under penalty of perjury, that I have examined the document(s) presented by the above-named employee, that the above-listed document(s) appear to be genuine and to relate to the employee named, that the employee began employment on (month/day/year) ____/____/____ and that to the best of my knowledge the employee is eligible to work in the United States. (State employment agencies may omit the date the employee began employment).

Signature of Employer or Authorized Representative	Print Name	Title

Business or Organization Name	Address (Street Name and Number, City, State, Zip Code)	Date (month/day/year)

Section 3. Updating and Reverification. To be completed and signed by employer

A. New Name (if applicable)	B. Date of rehire (month/day/year) (if applicable)

C. If employee's previous grant of work authorization has expired, provide the information below for the document that establishes current employment eligibility.

Document Title: _____ Document #: _____ Expiration Date (if any): __/__/__

I attest, under penalty of perjury, that to the best of my knowledge, this employee is eligible to work in the United States, and if the employee presented document(s), the document(s) I have examined appear to be genuine and to relate to the individual.

Signature of Employer or Authorized Representative	Date (month/day/year)

Form I-9 (Rev. 11-21-91) N

Tell students that this is a copy of an employment eligibility verification form. Ask students why they think employers would ask them to fill out the form. Ask students if they know what antidiscrimination means. Ask how antidiscrimination laws might affect their lives. Hold a class discussion on the need to have antidiscrimination laws that govern employment.

DIFFERENT LEARNING ABILITIES
Dyslexia

Have students create a bulletin board that uses different forms discussed in this chapter, including an employment eligibility verification form and a W-4 form. Have students obtain several forms for the bulletin board. Encourage them also to use art materials to make the bulletin board both informative and creative. Once the bulletin board is complete, have students explain to the rest of the class the purpose of each form.

Students may be surprised to discover that they may be responsible for paying federal income taxes. The Internal Revenue Service (IRS) maintains several web pages that provide tax information for high school and college students. Refer students to **www.irs.gov**. Direct them to select "Individuals," then "Students." You also may want to discuss with students how their tax dollars are used. Note that the IRS does not consider allowances from family members as earned income.

What do you think?

Use **TM12-05**.
Students' answers will vary.

APPLY

Have students complete **Activity 12-2, "Plenty of Paperwork,"** that appears on pages 232–233. Teaching suggestions and the solution for this activity appear on page 232. An activity worksheet can be found on the Career Portfolio and Resource CD— **Text Activity 12-2.pdf**.

W-4 Form

A **W-4 form** indicates to your employer how much money to take out of your paycheck for federal income tax. You are allowed at least one "personal allowance" that shelters a certain amount of your income from being taxed. Follow the instructions on the W-4 form to decide how many personal allowances you may claim. Illustration 12.2 below shows a completed W-4 form.

Illustration 12.2
Completed W-4 Form

---------------------- Cut here and give Form W-4 to your employer. Keep the top part for your records. ----------------------

Form W-4
Department of the Treasury
Internal Revenue Service

Employee's Withholding Allowance Certificate

▶ For Privacy Act and Paperwork Reduction Act Notice, see page 2.

OMB No. 1545-0010

20 - -

1 Type or print your first name and middle initial **Robert J.** | Last name **Stendhal** | 2 Your social security number **555 00 5000**

Home address (number and street or rural route) **2700 Peerpoint Way** | 3 ☑ Single ☐ Married ☐ Married, but withhold at higher Single rate.
Note: *If married, but legally separated, or spouse is a nonresident alien, check the Single box.*

City or town, state, and ZIP code **Hamilton, Ohio 45011-2743** | 4 If your last name differs from that on your social security card, check here. You must call 1-800-772-1213 for a new card. ▶ ☐

5 Total number of allowances you are claiming (from line H above **or** from the applicable worksheet on page 2) | 5 | **1**
6 Additional amount, if any, you want withheld from each paycheck . . . . | 6 | $
7 I claim exemption from withholding for 2001, and I certify that I meet **both** of the following conditions for exemption:
● Last year I had a right to a refund of **all** Federal income tax withheld because I had **no** tax liability **and**
● This year I expect a refund of **all** Federal income tax withheld because I expect to have **no** tax liability.
If you meet both conditions, write "Exempt" here . . . . ▶ | 7

Under penalties of perjury, I certify that I am entitled to the number of withholding allowances claimed on this certificate, or I am entitled to claim exempt status.
Employee's signature
(Form is not valid unless you sign it.) ▶ *Robert J. Stendhal* | Date ▶ *10/11/20--*

8 Employer's name and address (Employer: Complete lines 8 and 10 only if sending to the IRS.) | 9 Office code (optional) | 10 Employer identification number

Cat. No. 10220Q

What do you think?

Have you completed forms as part of an employment application process? What forms did the employer ask you to complete?

In Activity 12-2, "Plenty of Paperwork," you practice filling out the employment forms you will encounter when you begin your job.

Withholdings

On your job, you will be paid a specific pay rate expressed as an hourly, a monthly, or a yearly amount. In addition, you will be paid at the end of specific time periods, called payroll periods. Your payroll period may be once a week, every two weeks, once a month, or twice a month.

When you get your first paycheck, you—like Sam at the beginning of this chapter—may ask, "What happened to my paycheck?" You may think, "I'm supposed to earn $7 an hour and be paid every other Friday. I've worked 15 hours this payroll period, so my paycheck should be $105. Instead, the check is $78.75. Why?"

DIFFERENT LEARNING STYLES

Tactile Learners

After students have completed Activity 12-2, "Plenty of Paperwork," organize students into groups. Ask them to imagine they are reporters for a cable television show that teaches new citizens about W-4 forms. Have each group write a segment that explains what the W-4 form is, why it is used, and how to fill it out. Encourage groups to use visual aids to illustrate their main points. Each group member must play a role. Roles can include anchor, reporter, director, interviewer, and interviewee.

Part of what you earn on a job goes to taxes. By law, taxes are withheld, or subtracted, from your **gross pay**, the amount you earn based on your pay rate. You may also authorize an employer to withhold other amounts to pay for various programs. The amount left after all the withholdings is called your **net pay**.

Throughout the year, an employer sends the tax money withheld to the federal government and to the state and local governments. Your tax money is used to pay for services that benefit the entire population, such as court systems, highways, parks, schools, sanitation services, police and fire protection, and emergency medical services. The total of all your taxes is often a fourth or more of your yearly income.

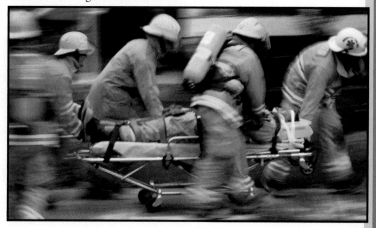

The stub attached to your paycheck shows your gross pay and all the deductions that resulted in your net pay. Employers are legally required to explain any deductions you do not understand.

Federal Taxes

Federal taxes that will be withheld from your paycheck include income taxes and social security taxes. The amounts withheld for both of these taxes depend on the amount of your pay.

Income Tax

All employees of all companies based in the United States are required to submit a completed tax form to the Internal Revenue Service (IRS) by April 15 each year. The IRS is the division of the U.S. Department of the Treasury that collects federal income taxes and enforces the federal tax laws. People who are self-employed or who do not have income tax withheld for other reasons pay an estimated tax to the IRS four times a year. People who owe more taxes than were paid or withheld send the additional amount with their tax return. Other people receive a refund because too much tax has been paid or withheld.

You can choose (1) to have a larger percentage of your pay withheld and owe less at the end of the tax year or (2) to have less money withheld and owe more at year's end. You make this choice when you fill out your W-4 form. The IRS would prefer that your withholdings be close to the amount of tax you owe. However, this may not always be possible if your income and personal circumstances vary from year to year.

After students complete the W-4 form in Activity 12-2, you may wish to hand out form 1040EZ and walk students through a simple tax return. You can print the form and its instructions from the IRS web site at **www.irs.gov**. This site also has information about filing a tax return using a telephone (Telefile) or a computer (e-file). This activity is especially appropriate during the first quarter of the year. If you decide to do this activity, you will need to discuss the W-2 form.

Explain that in addition to its special meaning related to taxes, the term *deduction* is also used as a general reference to any amount of money subtracted from employees' gross pay.

INTEGRATED ACADEMICS
Mathematics

Have students make a bulletin board-sized graphic organizer that illustrates and explains the different taxes that must be paid and how each tax is paid. Remind students to include federal, state, and local taxes in their graphic organizer. Assign roles to students. Have some students conduct the research, others design the graphic organizer, and still others create the graphic organizer.

In your discussion of social security and Medicare, explain that in recent years, Congress has not changed the tax percentages but has increased the maximum amount of wages to which the percentages apply. Point out that the combined employer and employee tax rates for social security and Medicare are equivalent to the self-employment tax rate. To find the most current information about social security and Medicare tax rates for employers, employees, and the self-employed, access **www.irs.gov**. Do searches using the keywords *social security tax rates, Medicare tax rates,* and *self-employment tax rates.*

What do you think?

Use **TM12-06**.
Students' answers will vary but should include the benefits—and drawbacks—of a higher tax rate.

> ❝ I see a good deal of talk from Washington about lowering taxes. I hope they do get 'em lowered enough so people can afford to pay 'em. ❞
>
> —Will Rogers,
> *Philosopher*

Social Security Tax

The Federal Insurance Contributions Act (FICA) is a federal social insurance program usually referred to as the Social Security Act. **Social security** provides income and health benefits for retirees, for underage survivors of employees who contributed to social security, and for employees who are disabled and cannot work. The funds for these payments come from taxes on workers' wages. Both the employee and employer contribute 7.65 percent of the employee's annual salary for social security taxes. The social security tax withheld from your paycheck may be indicated on the stub as FICA. Also, the tax may be separated into social security and Medicare. **Medicare** is the health benefits part of social security.

Not all employees have social security tax withheld from their paychecks. Government and school employees often have their own programs for providing the benefits paid for by social security taxes. In addition, self-employed people pay a 15.3 percent self-employment tax, which is comparable to the social security tax, and receive social security benefits.

State and Local Withholdings

Like the federal government, each state and local government may collect taxes. People who live in large cities typically pay more local taxes than do residents of small towns because large cities have higher costs for the services they provide, such as schools, street cleaners, and fire and police departments.

During one of Cory's visits home, he and Daryl, who had been friends since middle school, walked around the small town where they grew up. They talked about their high school years and how their lives had taken such different directions. Cory had left their hometown and worked as a welder for an automobile manufacturer in a different state. Daryl had stayed in the small town where they grew up and worked as an addiction counselor.

Eventually Cory told Daryl he was worried about not making enough money to support the lifestyle he wanted. After all, he said, he had moved from his hometown to the city so he could earn a good salary. They compared their wages and found that although they earned almost exactly the same amount of money, Daryl's net pay was considerably more than Cory's. At first, they couldn't figure out why Cory's biweekly paycheck was so much less than Daryl's. Then the two compared their taxes and realized that Cory paid 8 percent more in state and local taxes than Daryl did.

What do you think?
Will the amount of taxes you have to pay influence where you decide to live and work? Why or why not?

DIFFERENT LEARNING ABILITIES
Limited English Proficiency
Invite a representative of the Internal Revenue Service, a tax accountant, a tax preparer, or a tax attorney to address students with limited English proficiency. Ask the speaker to talk about taxes in students' native language. Allow students to use their native language to ask the speaker questions. After the speaker has left, ask students to paraphrase their learning in English. If there are not enough students with limited English proficiency in your class to invite a speaker, invite students from other classes to take part.

Other Withholdings

When you begin working, you may choose to have money withheld from your paycheck for a variety of reasons. For example, you may decide to purchase health insurance or deposit money to savings or retirement accounts. The following paragraphs describe some common withholdings.

Fringe Benefits. Your employer may offer **fringe benefits**, which are forms of compensation other than wages. The major fringe benefit offered by employers is participation in a group health insurance plan. Other examples are life insurance and pension plans. Often you must pay part of the cost of the benefit and have your share withheld from your paycheck. However, your cost will be less than if you purchase the benefit on your own.

Work-Related Deductions. If you decide to work in a union shop, your paycheck stub will show a deduction for union dues. Your stub may also show deductions for dues to other organizations, such as a health club you joined through your company's benefits plan. Another common work-related deduction is the cost of purchasing uniforms you must wear on the job. Some employers may also deduct the cost of cleaning the uniforms. Other employers will loan the uniforms and expect you to maintain them.

Garnishments. Although federal and state laws protect your earnings, they also protect the rights of your creditors, the people to whom you owe money. If you do not pay your bills, your creditors may get a court order that requires your employer to take, or garnish, a certain amount from your paycheck each pay period. This money goes through the court system and is paid to your creditor. Careful budgeting and good management of your credit will help you avoid garnishments.

Savings. The only sure way to guarantee having an income in the future is to start saving with your first job. Seriously consider saving even $5 a pay period; that $5 each pay period will be $50 in savings in ten pay periods. Many employers will deduct money for savings and deposit it directly into your savings account. If you are offered several types of employer savings plans, make sure you understand the costs and benefits of each. Talk to someone in your human resources department or to your family or friends before making your decision.

> For what reasons would you choose to have some of your salary withheld? What would you consider in making this decision? **What do you think?**

Activity 12-3, "Learning from Others," provides you an opportunity to learn about paycheck deductions from a person working full-time.

Employers may hire people specifically for short-term jobs, such as doing seasonal work harvesting crops or selling Christmas trees. When employers do their own hiring and pay the workers directly, the workers are called temporary employees.

Ask students to discuss what they have learned from parents or other family members about forms of employment. Encourage them to analyze the advantages and disadvantages of the various types of employment.

What do you think?

Use **TM12-08**.
Students' answers will vary but should include discussion of scheduling freedom and restrictions, overtime pay, and treatment by employers.

Although employers must follow employment and tax laws, they develop their own policies for everyday business operations. Employers decide how they choose to have work done and the roles of the people they hire.

Hourly versus Salaried Employees

If you are an hourly employee, you will be paid a wage for each hour worked, up to 40 hours per week. If you exceed this number of hours, you are eligible to receive overtime pay. As an hourly employee, your pay will be reduced for any time you are absent from work. Two exceptions are sick days and vacation days. Your employer may pay for a specific amount of time off if you are ill and may also provide paid vacation days. The number of paid vacation days is usually based on the length of time you have worked for the company and the length of your regular workweek.

If you are a salaried employee, you will earn a certain amount of money per year, divided into an established number of pay periods. Your workweek will usually be 37½ to 40 hours; however, you may be asked to work longer hours. You may know someone, for instance, who travels as a part of the job, often leaving or returning on weekends. Although salaried employees in management positions usually will have no limit on the number of hours they work, many salaried employees in nonmanagement positions have a set number of work hours per week. As a salaried employee, you will have a certain amount of paid time off for illness and will have paid vacation time. The length of your paid vacation is usually determined by how long you have worked for the company.

CAREER FACT

If a business must close temporarily due to flood or earthquake damage, the employer is not required to pay the employees during the temporary closure.

What do you think?

What are some of the benefits of working for a salary rather than an hourly wage? What are the disadvantages? Would you rather work for an hourly wage or a salary? Why?

Independent Contractors

Independent contractors are in business for themselves. They perform work for others, but they are not employees. Instead, the business that hires them is their client. Because clients do not provide employee-like benefits, such as insurance, pensions, or paid vacations, using independent contractors saves businesses money. Independent contractors are responsible for paying their taxes to the IRS four times a year. They also purchase their own insurance and invest in their own long-term savings programs for retirement.

In general, independent contractors make their own decisions about how, where, when, and by whom the contracted work will be done.

CAREER TREND
Insurance

Invite a couple of local insurance agents to speak to your class about business insurance. Have the class make up a list of questions to ask beforehand. Questions are to include some of the following: Is there a trend for small businesses or entrepreneurs to group together to buy insurance? With the rise in health insurance costs, what trends are you seeing in businesses supplying insurance for their employees? Why are floods and earthquakes not normally covered in policies?

Clients, however, have the right to say when the work must be completed and to set the quality level of the finished work. In addition, independent contractors usually use their own tools and equipment, can seek other clients, and can make a profit or loss on the jobs they do. Clients and independent contractors often have a written contract for a specific project. After the project is completed, the contractors are paid and the relationship ends.

Brent had chosen art for his high school major, and supplies for his art classes were expensive. He needed to earn money to pay for them, but he didn't really have time for a regular part-time job. The time of day he was free didn't match many businesses' needs for part-time workers. Brent decided to become an independent contractor. As an independent contractor, he could adjust his work hours to the time he had available. He could set a project deadline to fit his schedule. Brent decided to base his prices on the number of hours it took to complete a project.

Marketing his services turned out to be easier than Brent had anticipated. Teachers and friends recommended him to people they knew. He also advertised in the teacher's lounge and on the grocery store bulletin board. During his first six months, Brent painted a picture of a company truck for a company's first-anniversary celebration and designed logos for T-shirts and other promotional items. He earned enough money through his jobs to pay for art supplies and also put aside some savings. Brent also enjoyed teaching Saturday morning art classes to elementary-school children. Through this experience, he discovered a love of teaching, which he intends to pursue.

The IRS makes the final decision as to whether a person is an employee or an independent contractor. To make a determination in questionable cases, the IRS investigates how much control and independence the worker has. If the worker and the client have a permanent, open relationship or if the services performed by the worker are a key aspect of the regular business of the client, the IRS may classify the worker as an employee.

What roadblocks might you encounter as an independent contractor in your chosen career?

What do you think?

TEACH

On the board, create the following graphic organizer: On the left side, write *Independent Contractor*. To the right of this title, write *Employee*. Draw a vertical line between these two titles. Ask students to take turns adding information under each title that explains the similarities and the differences between the two. Have students copy the graphic organizer into their notebooks.

What do you think?

Use **TM12-09**.
Students' answers will vary.

DIFFERENT LEARNING STYLES
Print Learners
Have students imagine they are an independent contractor. The IRS has asked them to submit a document that justifies the independent contractor status. First, brainstorm with students about what type of careers might be considered independent contractors. Make a list on the board from which students may choose, or have them come up with their own. Have students write a letter to the IRS that explains their job and then justifies their status. Students can use the information on this and the preceding page.

You may find it necessary to clarify the distinction among temporary employees, independent contractors, and contract workers. Temporary employees work exclusively for the employer who hired them for a specific short-term job. Independent contractors are self-employed and may be doing jobs for more than one company at a time. Contract workers are employees of an employment agency that pays them and sends them out on jobs that match their skills. Discuss the advantages of being a contract worker for people who like variety in their workplace and work tasks and for people who want to try different types of employment or different companies before deciding on a specific career or type of company.

Contract Workers

Sometimes a company has a project to complete in which:

1. The company needs to control how workers complete the project.
2. The project is not well defined.
3. The workers need to use company resources.
4. The project requires a team approach.

In this situation, the business may decide to use the services of a contract employment agency. The employment agency hires and pays workers who meet the business's requirements. The agency is responsible for withholding the required deductions and meeting all the tax requirements.

The workers, known as **contract workers** or temporary workers or temps, report to the business that contracted with the agency and follow the directions of the managers of that business. Contract workers are employees; however, they are not employees of the business where they work. They are employees of the employment agency. Some people prefer to work as contract workers rather than find a regular hourly or salaried position with a company. They enjoy the change in work tasks and the different work experiences.

REAL PEOPLE
REAL CAREERS

Statistician

Did you count everything when you were a child? On vacations, did you play games with your brothers and sisters counting farm animals? Did you ever win a prize for most accurately counting the jelly beans in a jar? If you did, you probably naturally like math courses. Science also involves counting, as do many technology courses, so you probably enjoy them too.

Dr. Adam Martinsek is a statistician—he gets *paid* for counting. After receiving his bachelor's degree in economics, he completed his master's degree and doctorate in statistics. Advanced degrees are generally required for statisticians. In his career, Dr. Martinsek solves problems using a logical approach that makes sense of numerical data. "Statistics is a portable skill, something you can apply to every job you do in every industry imaginable," he says. For example, a statistician working in the environmental field may analyze toxicology data or pollution levels. Statisticians also work for advertisers, manufacturers, government agencies, medical companies, educational testing businesses, and sports organizations.

For more information about:
- statisticians, investigate **www.bls.gov/oco**. Click on "Professional and Technical"; then click on "Statisticians."
- sports statisticians, explore **www.amstat.org/sections/sis/career**.
- actuaries, who are statisticians for the insurance industry, search **www.beanactuary.org**.

Source: Matheson, Kate, and Kendra McLeisch. "The Need for Statisticians Is Soaring." *Careerpronews. www.careerpronews.com.*

REAL PEOPLE—REAL CAREERS

Statistician

Arrange students into three groups. Assign one of the web sites in "Real People—Real Careers" to each of the groups. Have each group investigate its web site to learn about a career as a statistician. Provide groups with art materials, or have students use computer-generated graphics to create a poster that is filled with information from the web site. Each member of the group is to contribute. Some members can be designers; others can be researchers.

Contract workers may do the same work in the same conditions as a business's own employees, but contract workers do not receive benefits from the business. However, some employment agencies provide benefits for their contract workers. If the business uses the same contract workers for a long time, the IRS sometimes rules that the contract workers actually work for the business. As a result, the business must pay back pay and benefits.

What do you think?

Would you be able to work as a contract worker in your career field? If not, why not? Would you want to work as a contract worker? Why or why not?

Use Activity 12-4, "Coming to Terms," to understand some of the important terms in this chapter more thoroughly.

Employer Expectations

Fulfilling your employer's expectations will help you advance along your *P*A*T*H to Success*. As discussed in Chapter 10, your employer will expect you to perform your job tasks skillfully, to have a positive attitude, to communicate effectively, and to cooperate with your coworkers. Meeting employer expectations requires good customer service, ethical behavior, and discretion. You will be evaluated by your employer to decide how well you perform your job and satisfy your employer's expectations. In addition, your employer will expect you to follow some guidelines if you decide to resign your position.

Customer Service

Regardless of whether you work in information technology, advertising, construction, or another career area, your employer will expect you to follow the old adage "The customer is always right." Customers, who may be referred to in your career area as clients or patients or patrons, are the reason your job and your company exist. If customers are dissatisfied with your service or product, they will take their business to one of your competitors. However, if you provide service that exceeds a customer's expectations, the customer will not only return to your company but also recommend it to other potential customers.

As a representative of your company, you will be expected to provide excellent customer service at all times. If an order is delayed, inform the customer and politely explain the reason for the delay. If a repair is done improperly, consult with your manager about offering to redo the job at no cost. Keep the customer's needs and wants in mind as you perform your job.

 I do not consider a sale complete until goods are worn out and the customer still satisfied.
—*L.L. Bean, Retail Sales Owner*

Ethical Behavior

Ethics are the standards of conduct that individuals, organizations, and societies believe to be right and moral. Your employer may have a

What do you think?

Use **TM12-10**.
Students' answers will vary.

APPLY

Have students complete **Activity 12-4, "Coming to Terms,"** that appears on page 234. Teaching suggestions and the solution for this activity appear on page 234. An activity worksheet can be found on the Career Portfolio and Resource CD—**Text Activity 12-4.doc**.

ENRICH

Have students complete **Activity 12-B, "Imagine . . . .,"** found in the *Investigating Your Career Activities & Projects* book.

In this activity, students work individually or in teams to evaluate the quality of customer service from the customer's viewpoint. Students are to complete this comparison shopping activity at a specialty store (such as a shoe store or a tool store) *and* at a department store *without* actually purchasing any products. Once students have completed the activity, ask them to imagine they own the stores. What would they look for in sales employees? Why?
Solution: The solution for this activity appears in the *Teacher's Edition* of *Investigating Your Career Activities & Projects*.

INTEGRATED ACADEMICS
Communications
Have students work in small groups to create skits that illustrate both poor and good customer service. Encourage students to use incidents from their own lives. They could choose a time when they had to return an item to a store. How were they treated? Provide class time for students to meet in their groups. Have each group submit their idea to avoid duplications. Encourage students to use props for their skits. Have students perform their skits for the class.

Point out to students that the same ethics that apply to Jasmine and Dennis's situation also apply in the workplace. In the workplace, Jasmine might learn some confidential information while doing her job that Dennis could use to get a promotion. Dennis could guess that Jasmine knows the information because of the nature of her job. If Jasmine behaves unethically and gives Dennis the information, the employer could write an unfavorable report that negatively affects Jasmine's chances of receiving a raise or promotion. Jasmine could even be fired for disclosing confidential information. Being fired for an ethics violation could prevent Jasmine from getting a new job. Ask students to list the consequences Dennis may face if he gets Jasmine to tell him confidential information and he uses that information.

Point out that companies lose more money to employee theft than to any other kind of theft. Emphasize that misuse of company assets is theft and that employers may protect their assets by monitoring employees on the job. In fact, surveys of employers have found that:
• Seventy-eight percent of major U.S. companies actively monitor their employees on the job.
• Sixty-three percent monitor employees' Internet connections.
• Forty-seven percent store and review employee e-mail.
• Twenty-seven percent have fired employees for misuse of the Internet or e-mail.
• Fifteen percent videotape employees at work.
• Ten percent do not inform employees of surveillance.
Use **TM12-13** (Think ETHICS) to discuss the Career Success Tip and how applying the steps represented by each letter of ETHICS can help students attain career success.

written code of ethics that employees are expected to practice. If so, be sure you understand the guidelines you should follow on your job. In addition, not every ethical rule will be in writing. In many cases, you must determine the ethical course of action. By emphasizing honesty, trustworthiness, and integrity in your personal system of values, you will be able to judge whether your conduct is ethical.

Jasmine and Dennis are taking Algebra II from Miss Stuckey. They are in different classes, but they study together. Jasmine gets along well with Miss Stuckey. Miss Stuckey often compliments Jasmine on her class work and her positive attitude. Dennis is not so fortunate. No matter how hard he tries, he cannot seem to please Miss Stuckey. She watches him often, especially when he is concentrating on a complicated problem. Then she questions him until he gets more confused. Although Dennis is unhappy about Miss Stuckey's attention, his grades are improving as a result.

This week Dennis has a dentist appointment scheduled during his algebra class. Miss Stuckey is giving a test but suggests that Dennis take it during Jasmine's class. When Dennis studies with Jasmine, he suggests that Jasmine help him with the word problems. Jasmine agrees, but Dennis interrupts her. He means that he wants her to help him with the word problems during the upcoming test. Jasmine doesn't want to help Dennis cheat, but she doesn't want to jeopardize their friendship either. Dennis becomes so upset when Jasmine starts to say no that she agrees on a set of hand signals to help him. During the test, Jasmine gives Dennis a signal when she sees him looking at her. Miss Stuckey sees what is happening. As a result, she brings the situation to the attention of the assistant principal. Both Jasmine and Dennis behaved unethically. Now neither of them has the trust of Miss Stuckey.

Your behavior and the decisions you make in the workplace and classroom should be ethical—they should be honest and moral. For example, taking supplies from your workplace for personal use or making personal long-distance calls at work is a form of stealing and is unethical. Your employer is unlikely to tolerate unethical behavior of any type, and you could lose both your job and your good reputation if you are unethical.

Discretion

Discretion involves being careful about what you say, especially with regard to confidential matters. In the workplace, your employer will expect you to be careful in your dealings with people outside the company and to refrain from gossip both inside and outside the company.

CAREER SUCCESS TIP

Think ETHICS
Examine the facts.
Think about the alternatives.
Hold back if your action could embarrass you or get you into trouble.
Investigate how company policy and the law apply.
Check your conscience.
Seek advice if you are unsure.

CAREER SUCCESS TIP

Ethics
Invite a local university professor or an attorney to speak to your class about ethics. Have each student prepare a question to ask the speaker. Go over the questions to make sure there are no duplicates. Ask the speaker to provide time for questions and answers. Make sure the class writes a thank-you note to the speaker. Remind students that ethical behavior is expected in school as well as in the workplace.

In many career areas, information about your company and your customers is confidential and should not be revealed to people outside the company. For example, in a doctor's office, information about patients is confidential. In a legal firm, clients and their cases should not be discussed outside the office. Obviously, contracts and financial information about your business should not be revealed to competitors. Perhaps not as obvious is the fact that this type of information should not be revealed to suppliers or anyone else outside the company. Any information you reveal about your company or your customers may be misunderstood and could affect the success of the business.

Some companies require employees to sign a confidentiality, or nondisclosure, agreement. By signing this document, you agree to keep everything you do and everything you learn at the company a secret after you leave the employer. If you leave a company and go to work at one of its competitors, you could damage your former company by revealing its processes, financial status, or future plans.

Under what circumstances might it be ethical to reveal information about your employer? **What do you think?**

Another aspect of discretion involves gossip, or talking about people and their private affairs. As you are probably aware from your school experience, preventing gossip and rumors is almost impossible. However, you do not have to contribute to the problem. Your employer will expect you to avoid gossiping about customers, coworkers, and supervisors and to make sure any rumors stop with you. Your career success will depend in part on respecting rather than gossiping about your customers, coworkers, and supervisors.

Satisfactory Job Performance

Periodically your employer will conduct a **performance evaluation**, an assessment of how well your job skills, attitude, and work habits are meeting expectations. The evaluation helps your employer decide whether you should receive a raise, be promoted, or be transferred to another department more appropriate to your skills and knowledge. An evaluation provides you with feedback about work areas in which you are especially strong or you need to improve. In addition, your employer may suggest ways to get training in areas in which you need to improve.

> 66 Weakness of attitude becomes weakness of character. 99
> —Albert Einstein, Scientist

The evaluation process may vary depending on the size of the company. In a small business, your evaluation is usually informal and constant. Your employer will observe and evaluate you daily. In a large company, performance evaluation often involves a formal meeting with your supervisor. Before the meeting, your supervisor will complete an evaluation form that includes various categories related to skills, attitude, and work habits. During the meeting, your supervisor will discuss how well you meet expectations in these categories.

═══ ENRICH ═══

Have students complete **Activity 12-D, "Courteous Resignation Letter,"** found in the *Investigating Your Career Activities & Projects* book.

In this activity, students consider different reasons for leaving a job and plan for and write a courteous resignation letter. This is an appropriate application for team teaching with the teacher of writing composition.
Solution: The solution for this activity appears in the *Teacher's Edition* of *Investigating Your Career Activities & Projects*.

═══ APPLY ═══

Have students complete **Activity 12-5, "Case Challenges,"** that appears on page 234. Teaching suggestions and the solution for this activity appear on page 234. An activity worksheet can be found on the Career Portfolio and Resource CD— **Text Activity 12-5.doc.**

═══ ENRICH ═══

Have students complete **Activity 12-E, "Understand Your Workplace,"** found in the *Investigating Your Career Activities & Projects* book.

Use this crossword puzzle to help students review most of the key terms as well as three other important terms from this chapter.
Solution: The solution for this activity appears in the *Teacher's Edition* of *Investigating Your Career Activities & Projects*.

❝ Keep away from people who try to belittle your ambitions. Small people do that, but the really great make you feel that you, too, can become great. ❞

—Mark Twain, Author

Marcos, a cook employed by Queen City Burgers, has a performance evaluation every six months. He is nervous during evaluations because he knows his cooking times and the quality of his food are assessed. His supervisor, Andrea, measures the length of time between when an order is taken and when it is delivered to the customer. Andrea also times how long it takes to cook every main menu item and checks the quality of each item. Then she compares all the cooks based on time and quality of food preparation. Marcos has a hard time working under the stress, but knows he cannot receive a pay increase without the evaluation.

During his evaluation, Andrea mentions that Marcos' hamburger cooking time is a little too long. Marcos is upset, but Andrea assures him he can easily shorten the time now that he is aware of the problem. As a result, the customers will enjoy their meals more because the burgers will be less dry. The evaluation also reveals that Marcos is an excellent, efficient cook with the majority of the menu items. He will receive not only his pay increase but also a promotion to lead cook on the second shift.

Responding positively to your evaluation is an important part of job success. Without constructive criticism, you will not know whether you are meeting your employer's expectations. For example, if your supervisor believes you have weak customer service skills but fails to tell you, you may not realize you need to improve. Try not to become anxious about evaluations. Take your supervisor's criticism as an opportunity to advance in your career, not as a personal attack.

Courteous Resignation

 What do you think?

Have you ever resigned from a job? If so, how did you present your resignation to your supervisor? How was it received?

If you decide to move to another job, protect your future employability by resigning the correct way. The correct way involves announcing your decision in a respectful and straightforward manner. Use the following three guidelines when you decide to leave your company:

- **Give at least two weeks' notice.** Show your employer that you respect the need to select and train your replacement.
- **Write a letter of resignation.** Tell your employer you are leaving, and give your supervisor your letter of resignation. The written notification will make your decision official and reflect positively on you. Make your letter short and professional. Say you are leaving and state the date of your last day at work. Avoid including negative opinions about your coworkers or the company. You don't know when or where you might meet any of these people again.
- **Continue to do your best work during your last two weeks on the job.** Make sure you leave files, projects, and work areas in excellent condition. After all, you may need to ask your supervisor or coworkers for references or job leads in the future.

DIFFERENT LEARNING STYLES
Print Learners

Have students work in pairs to outline this chapter. Suggest that students use headings and subheadings for the major points of their outlines. After student pairs have completed their outlines, have them trade outlines with another pair. Have the pairs edit each other's work, adding any missing information. Then have students return the outline to the original pair. Make sure both partners have copies of their outlines after revisions. Tell students they can use these outlines to study for the final exam.

Finally, if you have done a good job for the company, ask for a letter of recommendation. Most people change jobs several times during their careers, and employers expect people who resign to ask for a letter of reference.

Activity 12-5, "Case Challenges," allows you to analyze situations dealing with employer expectations.

IN A NUTSHELL

- **I can discuss federal, state, and local employment laws.**

  Federal laws regulate hours and jobs for workers younger than 18 years old, minimum and overtime wages, equal pay for men and women, workplace health and safety, discrimination, and labor unions. Some state and local employment laws are stricter than federal laws.

- **I can complete employment forms.**

  I can complete an employment eligibility verification form (Form I-9), which verifies that I can legally work in the United States, and a W-4 form, which tells my employer how much money to take out of my paycheck for federal income tax.

- **I can identify withholdings.**

  My net pay is the amount of money I receive after taxes and other withholdings are deducted from my gross pay. Federal income tax, social security tax, and state and local taxes may be withheld from my gross pay. I may also have money withheld for fringe benefits, work-related deductions, garnishments, and savings.

- **I can describe different types of employment.**

  Hourly employees are paid a wage for each hour worked. Salaried employees earn a certain amount of money per year. Independent contractors perform work for others but are not employees. Contract workers are employees of a contract employment agency. They report to the business that contracted with the agency and follow the directions of the managers of that business.

- **I can explain employer expectations.**

  Meeting employer expectations requires good customer service, ethical behavior, and discretion. I will be evaluated by my employer to determine how well I satisfy my employer's expectations. My employer will expect me to follow guidelines if I resign my position.

CLOSE

Wrap up this chapter by having students complete **Project 4, "Attendance Report,"** found in the *Investigating Your Career Activities & Projects* book.
Solution: The solution for this activity appears in the *Teacher's Edition* of *Investigating Your Career Activities & Projects.*

IN A NUTSHELL

Remind students about the objectives set forth at the beginning of the chapter, and use this summary to reinforce the concepts presented in this chapter.

Career Journal

Ask students to spend 10 minutes writing Career Journal entries that answer the following questions:
1. How well did what you thought you knew match what the chapter presented?
2. What questions do you now have about the chapter topics, and where do you think you can find the answers to those questions?
3. How will the content of the chapter help you investigate *your* career?

ASSESS

Administer the printed objective test for Chapter 12, available with this package. Test solutions are found in the *Teacher's Edition* of *Investigating Your Career Chapter Tests.* Use the **Exam***View*® CD to create your own objective test for this chapter.

Suggestions for Parents and Family Members

Help Teens with Workplace Information

Parents and family members need to support the career discovery process of their children. Ways they can help teens understand the workplace include:

1. Explaining the types and percentages of withholdings on their pay stubs.
2. Explaining the authority relationship between them and their managers.
3. Encouraging teens to support and follow safety practices on the job.

Activity 12-1: Investigating Unions

This activity introduces students to the organization and role of unions and promotes critical thinking and online research skills.

Students are directed to visit **www.igc.org**.
1. Access **www.igc.org**.
2. Click on "Job/Volunteer Opportunities."
3. Click on "Organizations."
4. Fill in the search fields as follows: Organization Name *union;* Mission *labor union;* Area of Focus *any area of focus;* Country *United States;* Sort results *alphabetically.* Leave other search fields blank. Click on "Search."

If **www.igc.org** is no longer available, have students use a search engine to search for the keywords *labor union.*

Solution: Answers will vary. Note that students may have different viewpoints and strong opinions about unions because of experiences of their parents or other family members. In a class discussion, ask students whether they had any opinions about labor unions before completing this activity and, if so, whether their opinions have changed. Have students give reasons for their answers.

Activity 12-2: Plenty of Paperwork

This activity gives students practice completing W-4 and I-9 forms. The directions for completing both forms are somewhat complex, and you may want to have students complete the forms as a class activity to ensure they do it correctly.

Solution: Answers will vary, but every student should complete both forms.

Use the keywords *labor union* to search the Internet for information about union organizations and resources. Using the following questions, compare two unions that are active in the career cluster you chose in Chapter 6.

1. What type of worker does the union represent?
2. What are the advantages to joining the union?
3. How is the union organized; for example, in the local plant, nationally, or internationally?
4. What is management's view of the union?
5. Why should a worker join the union or not join the union?

What is your opinion about being a union member? What are the advantages and disadvantages of joining a union?

Before you start to work with a new employer, you will be required to complete a W-4 form and an I-9 form. To give you practice, print the **W-4** and **I-9** forms and the **Personal Allowances Worksheet** from your Career Portfolio and Resources CD or use the forms provided by your teacher. Use the steps below to guide you. For both forms, use black or blue ink. Print the information requested.

W-4 Form:

1. Fill in your full name and address. Use no abbreviations.
2. Fill in your social security number.
3. Check your marital status. If you are not married, you are *single.*
4. Check the box *only* if your last name is different on your social security card. You will need to get a new card.
5. Determine the number of deductions to claim using the Personal Allowances Worksheet:
   A. Can anyone else claim you as a dependent? If yes, write *0.*
   B. Are you single and have only one job? Or if you have more than one job, does the second job pay less than $1,000? If yes, write *1.*
   C. Are you single? If yes, write *0.*
   D. How many dependents other than yourself will you claim on your tax return? Write the number.
   E-H. These questions are generally for those people who have a family and/or a full-time job. If they apply to you, ask your teacher for assistance.

   The majority of students will claim *0* or *1* deductions. If you claim *0,* you will have more money deducted from your paycheck. If you claim *1,* you will have less money deducted to pay your taxes.
6. If you want more money deducted from your paycheck than the standard amount, write the amount here. Some people need to pay more taxes than the amount of the taxes normally withheld.

7. Write *Exempt* if you were not required to pay taxes last year and do not expect to pay any this year. Otherwise, leave this line blank. Writing *Exempt* means no taxes will be withheld. However, you cannot be exempt under certain conditions. Your teacher can assist you.

Sign your name in cursive. Sign your full name, including your middle initial. Your signature must be legible. Write the date you signed the form. The date can be written either December 11, 20-- or 12/11/--. The employer completes the remaining sections.

I-9 Form:

1. Fill in your full name, including your middle initial.
2. Fill in your complete address with no abbreviations.
3. Write your date of birth in this format: *7/31/--*. Use the last two digits of the year only.
4. Write your social security number.
5. Check the correct box for your citizenship or alien status. If you are an alien or are in the United States on a visa, you will need the numbers for one of these certificates.
6. Sign your full name in cursive. (Sign your full name, including your middle initial.) Your signature must be legible.
7. Write the date you signed the form. The date can be written either December 11, 20-- or 12/11/--.
8. If you needed a translator to help you fill out the form, that person must complete the information in the next section, including signature, printed name, full address, and date the form was completed.
9. The employer completes the next section. However, you must provide certain forms for the employer:
   A. You can provide your U.S. Passport; Certificate of U.S. Citizenship; or Certificate of Naturalization, Alien Registration Card with photograph, or other immigration documents. Your teacher can assist you.
   B. *Or* you can provide at least:
      • One document that proves *Identity*. Some of these documents include driver's license, state or federal ID, school ID, and various other documents. Your teacher can assist you.
      • *And* one document that proves *Employment Eligibility*. Some of these documents include social security card, birth certificate, and various other documents. Your teacher can assist you.

After completing the forms, keep them in your Career Journey Folder. The samples will help when you fill out the forms for a new employer.

ACTIVITY 12-3   **Learning from Others**

Interview a person who is working full-time about the items deducted from his or her pay. The person will need a current pay stub and a calculator to assist him or her in answering some of the questions. Use the following questions as a guideline.

• In what state and city do you work?
• List each of the payroll deductions on your current pay stub. For each deduction, answer these questions: (1) Is the deduction a flat amount or a percentage? If it is a percentage, how much is the percentage? (2) For what purpose is the deduction used?
• What percentage of your gross pay are your deductions?

After completing the activity, compare your results with those of your classmates.

This activity allows students to discover for themselves the impact of withholdings from gross pay.

Discuss with students the sensitivity they must use when asking people to share pay stub information. Explain that people usually do not share payroll information, especially the amount of money they earn. Two reasons for this are (1) employers often require employees to maintain confidentiality about pay rates and (2) people consider pay rates to be their private business. Suggest that students explain that they are studying the various *types* of withholdings and the *percentages* of withholding deducted from gross pay. Tell students to reassure the person they are interviewing that they are not asking for dollar amounts.

Solution: Answers will vary. In a class discussion of students' results, you may want to list on a transparency or the chalkboard the types of optional withholdings and how many people interviewed had each type withheld.

Activity 12-4: Coming to Terms

This activity reinforces students' understanding of some of the key terms in the chapter and provides students with information about the different types of careers in their career cluster.

Solution: Answers will vary. Be sure the jobs that students select to illustrate the terms match the types of employment listed in the activity.

Activity 12-5: Case Challenges

This activity increases students' understanding of ethical behavior in workplace situations and of employers' expectations.

You may want to use **TM12-13** to introduce the activity and to discuss how to determine whether behavior is ethical.

Solution: Answers will vary. Class discussion of students' decisions should focus on how the employer could resolve the unethical situations and what a good employee would have done.

The terms listed below relate to different types of employment. For each term, describe an appropriate job in the career cluster you chose in Chapter 6. If you know an actual job that fits the term, describe it.

1. Minimum wage position

2. Position with overtime pay

3. Independent contractor

4. Contract worker

5. Job with a performance evaluation

ACTIVITY 12-5 **Case Challenges**

In a small group, read each of the case studies below. For each case, answer the following questions. Then share your group's decisions with the rest of the class.

- What is the problem?
- Is the situation ethical? Why or why not? Explain your answer.
- If the situation is unethical, how could the problem be resolved by the employer?
- If the situation is unethical, what should a good employee have done?
- If the situation is ethical, what could the employee have done to make sure his or her ethics were clearly in order?

1. Jacinta copies her essay for a college application on her employer's copy machine.

2. Elan delivers flowers for a local florist. He is told to fill the van with gas at the beginning of the shift and to use it for florist deliveries only. Because his girlfriend's birthday is this week, Elan uses the van to pick up the ring he had in layaway at a store in the mall.

3. Pechika works in a bakery making cinnamon buns. The manager has given the employees permission to take home the leftover cinnamon buns after the store closes. Another employee, who wants to make sure she has enough for her family's Thanksgiving breakfast, asks Pechika to make extras today.

4. Pio and Drew work for a landscape company on weekends. Yesterday their manager told them that a customer complained about the way a shrub was planted. Pio told the manager that Drew was the one who planted the shrub, but actually Pio and Drew planted it together.

5. To save money on school supplies, Adriana occasionally takes home a pen and writing paper from work.

6. The movie theater where Gene is an usher gives him four passes a week for his family to use. Last week Gene's parents and sisters did not want to see the movie, so he gave the complimentary tickets to his friends, Danilo and Mac and their girlfriends.

PART

5 Creating Tools for the Future

Part Overview

Part 5: Creating Tools for the Future

Part 5 provides the information students need to continue their career journey outside the classroom as employees or entrepreneurs. Students begin their journey by identifying their job search goals and developing the initial job search skills they need to reach those goals. Then students learn how to create an effective resume—one that highlights how their skills, education, and experience match the requirements of a specific job. The discussion of the job application process continues with essential information about references, cover letters, application forms, and pre-employment tests. Finally, students develop the skills needed for successful job interviews.

PART 5

Focus

Part 5 introduces students to the job search process. Even though many students may not be searching for a job, learning job search techniques prepares them for the future. Prepare students for Part 5 by asking them to brainstorm situations where they would complete an application, use a resume, or be interviewed. Use this information for comparison at various points in Part 5.

Chapter 13 focuses on the job search process. Students identify job search goals, learn techniques for planning and using effective job search strategies, and discover how research will help them find employers who best match their skills and job search goals. Students also explore some of the differences between working for an employer and working for themselves.

Use the **Objectives** and **Key Terms** printed in the margin to help students focus on the content of this chapter. Use the **video segment** for Chapter 13 to trigger discussion.

What do you think?

Use **TM13-01**.
Students' answers will vary.

Career Journal

Ask students to spend 10 minutes writing Career Journal entries that answer the following questions:
1. What do you think this chapter will cover?
2. What do you already know about these topics?
3. What three things do you want to learn about these topics?

13 Searching for a Job

OBJECTIVES

After completing this chapter, you will be able to:
- Identify your job search goals.
- Manage your job search.
- Research employers and industries.
- Identify the next step to take to reach your career goal.

Key Terms:
- career portfolio
- networking
- job fair
- business plan
- marketing plan
- operating plan
- financial management plan

Near the end of the school year, Bud Nolan began looking for a summer job. While he wanted to earn money to buy a car, he really hoped to get some experience that would support his goal of a career in auto mechanics. Bud already knew a lot about repairing cars. He had helped several friends and neighbors fix theirs. But he had not earned any money as a mechanic.

Bud knew that to be successful in his job search, he would have to be organized and develop a plan. He began by making a list of his skills, strengths, and experiences. Then he designed a resume emphasizing his qualifications for automotive work. Next, he listed the people he knew who might be able to lead him to available jobs. He also checked the Yellow Pages to find mechanics, parts dealers, and other related businesses in his part of town.

After talking to several friends and relatives, Bud mentioned to a neighbor that he was looking for a summer job in auto mechanics. The neighbor had a cousin, Toby, who managed a nearby automotive shop, so she gave Bud the phone number. When Bud called, Toby suggested that he stop by the next day to talk about a job that was available at the front desk. Even though the job wasn't exactly what Bud wanted, he readily agreed. He thought the job would give him the opportunity to learn the terminology used in the automotive repair field and to gain skills working with customers.

What do you think?
What kind of job will help you reach your personal and career goals?

CHAPTER RESOURCES and MATERIALS

Activities & Projects book
Instructor's Resource CD
- Forms and Worksheets for Chapter Activities 13-1 through 13-8
- Internet Links for Chapter 13
- PowerPoint Presentation for Chapter 13
- Lesson Plans
- Teaching Masters for Chapter 13
- Video Discussion Guide for Chapter 13

Chapter Tests book
Exam*View*® CD
Video
Web Site

Your Job Search Goals

Your reason for seeking a job may be to earn money for a specific purpose or to gain experience in a particular career field. Or you may have an entirely different goal. In any case, your job search goal will affect the type of job you want to get. For example, if you need a part-time after-school job, you won't be looking for work as an airline attendant. At this time of your life, your job search goal will generally fall into one of the following categories:

- **Meeting your budget.** Maybe you are saving for your future education or training or setting aside money for your grandparents' anniversary gift. Maybe you are planning a trip, buying a DVD player, or paying for guitar lessons. Regardless of your reason for seeking a job, you probably already have plans to spend your earnings in a particular way. You will want to search for a job that pays you enough to meet your budget.

- **Supporting your P*A*T*H to Success.** Now that you have developed your career plan, you may decide to look for a job that directly supports your interest in a certain career field. Being flexible in the types of jobs you consider, however, may allow you to develop your transferable skills, expand your talents, and gain work experience in an equally valuable way. The important question to ask yourself is "How might this job support my *P*A*T*H to Success?*"

> Jackie planned to pursue a career in hotel management, and she needed a part-time job. Her goals were to (1) work about 15 hours a week, (2) gain experience in hotel services, and (3) save money for her education.
>
> At first, Jackie thought a front-desk job in a hotel would be perfect. She researched the number of jobs available in the hospitality industry in her part of the city. Few openings were available, so she changed her plan. She decided to look for a part-time job bussing tables at banquets or at a first-class restaurant. If she couldn't find that type of job, she would consider working as a food server at a small restaurant. Jackie chose food service jobs because of the potential to earn tips, a flexible schedule, and the many jobs available. That type of job would also give her the opportunity to learn about the food-service aspect of the hospitality industry.

Reviewing the goals you made in Chapter 7 will help you clarify your job goals before you begin the job search process. Your job search will be faster because you won't waste time pursuing a job that doesn't meet your needs. Make a list of the characteristics you want your job to have—the characteristics that will help you reach your goals. Then use the strategies in this chapter to find job openings that support your goals.

What characteristics do you want a job to have in order to meet your current goals?

What do you think?

> 66 Things may come to those who wait, but only the things left by those who hustle. 99
>
> —Abraham Lincoln
> U.S. President, 1861–1865

ONLINE RESOURCES

Check out the web site **www.investigatingyourcareer.com** for teacher resources, student activities, and replacements for broken links for this chapter. To access the teacher resources:

Username: career
Password: investigate

In Activity 13-1, "Your Job Goals," you will use your Career Journey Folder to identify and analyze your current job search goal.

Managing Your Job Search

Although finding a job takes time, you are now better prepared than most people are when the time comes to begin your job search. Consider what you have accomplished already:

- You have an understanding of the people and circumstances that influence your career decisions.
- You have assessed your interests, talents, personality, and values and have investigated career clusters.
- You have set goals for achieving your education or training, your chosen career, and your ideal lifestyle.
- You have studied workplace issues and have a clearer understanding of employer expectations.
- You have identified your immediate job goals.

Finding and obtaining a job that meets your goals may take anywhere from one week to three months. Get the best results from your job hunting efforts by preparing your career portfolio, using proven job search strategies, planning your time, and tracking your activities.

Preparing Your Career Portfolio

CAREER SUCCESS TIP

You can create an "office" for yourself—even if it is just a desktop or shelf—where you keep all job search materials together. You will want to keep your "office" organized and use a daily planner or calendar.

Throughout *Investigating Your Career*, you have been saving items in your Career Journey Folder. These items relate to your passions, attitude, talents, and heart and helped guide you to discover your *Internal Career Design*. When you are ready to begin a job search, you will need a **career portfolio**, a collection of materials whose purpose is to show your ability to do a specific job. Even when you are looking for your first job, you can find appropriate materials for your portfolio.

Bud Nolan had no paid work experience in auto mechanics. So he asked for letters of reference from the friends and neighbors whose cars he had helped fix. He put the letters in his career portfolio. He also included a list of the auto repair courses he had taken and would be taking in school.

In addition, Bud's assessments indicated that he had the outgoing personality necessary for success in a sales career. In fact, Bud had received an award for being the top salesperson during a school fund-raiser. He included the award in his career portfolio because he thought sales ability might help him find a job in a retail auto parts store. When he visited the automotive shop to find out about the job at the front desk, he planned to point out that his sales ability could help increase the amount of the average customer's order.

CAREER SUCCESS TIP

Home Office
Tell students that to help them get organized, they might want to visit an office supply store or an office supply web site. Office supply stores have many items that will help students get ideas for their home "office." Instead of buying some of the items, encourage students to be inventive. For example, suggest they use boxes instead of file holders to hold papers.

Your career portfolio should include letters of reference, awards you have received, and any other documents that are relevant to the job you are seeking. In addition, your portfolio should contain the essentials of job hunting listed below. (You will develop your list of references, Personal Fact Sheet, and resume in Chapter 14.)

- Employment documents (discussed in Chapter 12)
- Copies of your list of references
- Your Personal Fact Sheet
- A few extra copies of your resume
- Blank notepaper and a pen and pencil

In Activity 13-2, "Your Career Portfolio," you will select the items from your Career Journey Folder that support your current job goal.

Using Proven Job Search Strategies

If you began looking for a job today, how would you start? Why? **What do you think?**

An effective job search uses several different strategies. If you use only one or two strategies—for example, searching only the Internet or the classified ads—you can miss many potential jobs that fit your goals well. The proven job search strategies in the following paragraphs are discussed in order of their effectiveness.

Networking

The most effective approach to finding a job is **networking**, spreading news of your job search among the people you know and asking for their help in finding a job. Using a network to find a job is similar to using the Internet to find information.

On the Internet, you can enter keywords into a search engine to look for information about a topic. When the search engine finds Internet sites that match your keywords, it displays a list of links—site names you can click on to see what each has to say about your keywords. Each link may lead you to other sites until, eventually, you obtain the information you want.

Telling people you know about your job search is like entering keywords into a search engine. Through the resulting leads, or links, you may find just the job to support your career plan. According to different studies, between 60 and 94 percent of jobs are found through networking.

> Marta knew she should finalize her plans soon because graduation was fast approaching. She was looking forward to getting her first full-time job and beginning her career in interior decorating. Marta's goal was to become certified in interior design and run her own design firm. She wanted to begin her career journey as a "gofer," running errands for one of the reputable interior decorators in town. However, she didn't know anyone at the firms and wasn't sure how to approach them to ask for a job.

> 66 Does he or she know you, like you, trust you? Want to see you succeed? If so, then you have yourself a 'personal walking ambassador.' 99
>
> —Bob Burg,
> Author and
> Motivational Speaker

TEACH

Explain that networking is by far the most effective way to find a job. Emphasize that networking is not about asking for a job. Networking is about building relationships, sharing information, and making long-term career connections.

So Marta began calling her relatives and friends for advice. Her uncle gave her the telephone number of his former neighbor, Mrs. Iverson, who had just moved to the next town. She had bought a house and just recently had it decorated. Marta called Mrs. Iverson, introduced herself, and explained her situation. Mrs. Iverson provided the phone number of her decorator. Gathering her courage, Marta called the decorator, Ms. O'Reilly, and asked for job search advice. Ms. O'Reilly offered to meet with Marta at her office, show her around, and answer her questions.

On the day of the meeting, Marta dressed professionally and brought a list of questions to ask. The tour went well. Marta not only had her questions answered but also met Mrs. Jeffers, Ms. O'Reilly's business partner. The partners were so impressed with Marta's job search plan that they invited her to join them and another guest for lunch. The other guest turned out to be the owner of another of the town's large interior decorating firms.

Benefits of networking for employers and job searchers.
Employers benefit from networking because referrals make an employer's job easier. Advertising a position brings in a huge pile of applications that employers must sort through to find qualified applicants. Many employers prefer getting referrals from people in their networks rather than advertising job openings formally. Employers believe their networks of associates, employees, and business groups will refer qualified applicants. Because choosing among qualified applicants saves time, employers usually prefer to fill job openings with people found through networking.

As a job searcher, you will benefit from networking in two ways. First, a networking connection will give you an edge. While a referral doesn't guarantee you'll get a particular job, an employer is more likely to look favorably at applicants who have been referred through the employer's network. Even if a job is advertised, your networking connection could mean that your resume goes to the top of the pile.

Second, you will be able to meet and talk to employers before they have official job openings. For example, you might talk to a friend of

CAREER FACT

According to *www.jobstar.org*, approximately 80 percent of all job openings are part of the "hidden job market"—job openings that are never advertised.

CAREER TREND
Job Searches
According to **jobstar.org**, you can go beyond the newspaper want ads by following these six steps in your job search: (1) Focus on your selling points, (2) focus on one position and one target industry, (3) develop a custom list of targeted employers, (4) use your network, (5) make contact with the employer, and (6) get help. Tell students if they persevere in their job search, they will find what they want. If they give up, they won't ever find what they want.

—*Source: http://jobstar.org/hidden/jobplan.cfm*

a friend who works for a company that interests you. Even if the company doesn't have any openings, you might obtain the name of the person who hires people with your qualifications. You can then take advantage of the referral by setting up an informational interview. When you meet with the person, you can gain additional information about the company and the career area. You can also ask that your resume be kept on file in case an appropriate job opening occurs. Then if a job that matches your qualifications becomes available in the future, that person will have met you and know how to contact you. In addition, you will be able to add a new person to your network.

With proper attention, the network you build will expand and improve as time goes on. In ten years, someone you meet now could be the person who refers you to your dream job!

Learning how to build a network. Building a job search network is not difficult, but it does require commitment. By asking people to help you, you are offering to return the favor at another time. This give-and-take strengthens your network and makes it a valuable asset on your *P*A*T*H to Success*. Below are four steps to successful networking:

1. Make a list of *everyone* you know.

2. Contact many of the people you listed, and talk about the kind of job you want. Ask if they know of any possible job leads or have any advice for your job search. Also ask for the name and phone number of someone who might be able to offer additional help.

3. Follow up on the leads by contacting the people or companies mentioned.

4. Send each person who helped you a handwritten thank-you note on quality stationery. When you get a job, notify all the people in your network and thank them again for their assistance.

Joining organizations, volunteering, and participating in service learning programs are other ways to expand your network. You will meet people with similar interests, and some of them may have a friend or relative who works in your career area.

You may think that your friends, neighbors, and relatives will not be able to help you in your job search because they don't work in your career area. But if you know 50 people and each of them knows 50 people, soon you'll have a huge network of people who may be able to provide information for your job search.

Your Counselor

As mentioned previously, employers favor methods of filling job openings that reduce the number of unqualified people who submit applications. Sometimes employers look for qualified people by working with counselors in a school or through a school's career section

---

CAREER ★ SUCCESS TIP

Consider the following people for your job search network:
• Family members
• Teachers
• Counselors
• Friends
• Neighbors
• People with whom you do business

TEACH

Use **TM13-04** to discuss how the following tips will help students build an effective network:

• Speak with confidence, energy, and commitment. An effective style of communication encourages people to help you, to refer you to others, and to remember you and the conversation.

• Do your homework. Spend 90 minutes preparing for every 10 minutes of conversation you plan to have with a contact. Find out what the person's job is and research his or her company before calling and asking for job search referrals.

• Know in advance what you want to accomplish. Be clear on what to ask and what you hope to learn. Listen carefully and keep good notes.

• Thank your contact. If you receive advice or a referral, also follow up with a thank-you note.

• Make a positive impression. Then when people hear of a job opportunity, they are more likely to remember you and call you with a referral.

• Support your network. Networking is a give-and-take relationship, so plan to assist your contacts in their career-building activities.

CAREER SUCCESS TIP

Networking

In his article "Networking Our Way to a New Job," Randall S. Hansen, Ph.D. lists seven steps for successful networking: (1) Develop a firm grasp of job search basics, (2) conduct a self-assessment, (3) prepare a strong resume, (4) decide how to organize your network, (5) communicate with your network, (6) initiate informational interviews, and (7) follow up with your network. Point out to students that they will have completed all seven steps by the time they complete *Investigating Your Career*.

—*Source: www.quintcareers.com/networking_resources.html*

of the media center. Often schools post job openings on special bulletin boards or open web sites. In addition, counselors can give you advice about ways to improve your job search.

State Employment Office

You may be able to check out job leads in your area through a state-run employment agency, such as Job Service. Many companies list all their job openings through state employment offices. Job seekers who register at a state employment office have access to all the job listings and usually do not have to pay any fees. In addition, many of these offices offer individual counseling and/or classes on resume preparation and interviewing techniques.

Job Ads

Reading want ads in newspapers, on the Internet, and on community bulletin boards is a quick way to get a feel for the availability of jobs in your area. Even though the majority of available jobs are never listed in want ads, you can learn about the qualifications employers require in your career area. If you respond to an ad, carefully follow the instructions for applying.

Telephone Directories and the Internet

If you know you want to work for a particular type of company in a specific area, the yellow pages of the phone book are a convenient place to find a list of those companies. You can then take your resume and a cover letter to the companies you select. Mailing your information to the companies does not usually work. Most companies simply ignore resumes that are not sent in response to an advertised job opening.

A more productive approach may be to use the information in telephone directories to help you locate web sites for the companies that interest you. Use the names of the companies as keywords, and search for their web sites on the Internet. Many companies, large and small, have web pages and a link to a listing of their job openings.

In Activity 13-3, "Learning from Others," you will review the Learning from Others activities from previous chapters and write a summary of the strategies people used to find their jobs. You will also attend a career or job fair.

Planning Your Time

By planning your time, you can be sure you will use your job search hours productively. Make a daily or weekly schedule that indicates exactly when and for how long you will work on a specific job search activity. You may need to adjust your schedule after the first few days. You may find that various job search activities take either more time or less time than you anticipated.

CAREER FACT

The America's Job Bank web site at *www.ajb.org* provides links to state employment services in every state and Guam.

Bud Nolan realized that summer jobs in auto mechanics would be scarce and tough to find. He was determined to start looking early and to be methodical and persistent. Although he had a job lead through his neighbor, Bud knew he couldn't count on getting that job. He needed to plan his job search. He decided to search for jobs on the three days a week he didn't have team practice. He planned the following schedule for his first day:

3:30–5:00	Homework
5:00–5:30	List on index cards all the people I know and their phone numbers
5:30–6:30	Write an index card for each auto mechanic shop or related business I find in my research
6:30–7:30	Dinner
7:30–9:00	Call the people in my network and ask for job information and/or referrals

On his next job search days, Bud planned to use his time to follow up on job leads, to update his index cards, and to call people he added to his network.

Of course, each person's schedule will look different. While you are still in school, you will have other commitments. Your job search time will be limited to after school and on weekends. However, by making a schedule and sticking to it, you will be able to organize your job search and use your available time productively.

Tracking Your Activities

> **What do you think?**
> How can keeping records of your job search help you? What problems can arise if you don't keep any records?

Keep a detailed record of your job search so you can follow up leads, applications, and interviews easily. Your records will also help you remember to send thank-you notes, make necessary phone calls, and keep track of who told you what information. One easy way to keep job search information is with index cards. Index cards work well because they are inexpensive and easy to carry, file, and update.

Network Tracking Card

Make up a separate index card for each person in your network. Write down the following information on each card:

- The person's name and contact information
- When you talked to the person
- The information the person gave to you

Write on the tracking card and your schedule when you will follow up on the job lead or other job search advice. Illustration 13-1 on page 244 is an example of a Network Tracking Card.

> **66** People often say that motivation doesn't last. Well, neither does bathing; that's why we recommend it daily. **99**
>
> —*Zig Ziglar, Author and Speaker*

TEACH

Knowing how to organize research results so they are accessible and useful during a job search is a valuable skill. Emphasize how excellent tracking will facilitate following up effectively, thereby increasing students' chances of receiving job offers.

What do you think?

Use **TM13-05**.
Students' answers will vary but should include the fact that the more education and training a person has, the more complicated the job search.

243

DIFFERENT LEARNING STYLES
Print Learners
Have students use the Weekly Time Planner from Chapter 7 or their school agenda/planner to help identify the times they could work on a job search. Ask students to make a separate schedule, modeled after the one shown on this page, for each day of the week. Encourage students to do something every day toward their job search.

Illustration 13-1 Network Tracking Card

APPLY

Have students complete **Activity 13-4, "Track Your Networking,"** that appears on page 253. Teaching suggestions and the solution for this activity appear on page 253. An activity worksheet can be found on the Career Portfolio and Resource CD— **Text Activity 13-4.doc**.

ENRICH

Have students complete **Activity 13-A, "Beginning a Job Search,"** found in the *Investigating Your Career Activities & Projects* book.

Part 1 of this activity helps students realize that they know many people who can contribute to their job search network. Part 2 reinforces the organizational skills students need for successful job searches and emphasizes the direct link between researching an industry and a company and selecting potential employers.

Solution: The solution for this activity appears in the *Teacher's Edition* of *Investigating Your Career Activities & Projects*.

> **66** All the so-called secrets of success will not work unless you do. **99**
> —*Author Unknown*

Name:	May Wang	Tel. #: (559) 555-0105
Address:	57 Poplar Dr	E-mail: Mwang@mail.com
	Fresno, CA 93722	Referred by: Dad

Date	Discussed	Follow up
4/14	Mrs. Wang's cousin works at Fairly Reliable Felix—combo mechanic/auto body shop and used car dealership— Looking for Shop Helper	Call Lee Soong (559) 555-0113 on 4/16 after 2 p.m.
4/18	Told Mrs. Wang I have interview with Mr. Soong next week	

Company Tracking Card

Also keep an index card for each company you contact. The front of this card should include the following information:

- The name of the company and contact information
- The names and titles of the people you spoke to at the company and when you spoke to them
- The name of the person who gave you the lead
- The job you applied for
- The dates you sent in your application, went for an interview, sent a thank-you note, and followed up

On the back of the index card, record the results of your research about the company. Illustration 13-2 shows a Company Tracking Card.

Support for Your Job Search

Searching for a job is hard work—work that has discouraging moments. Remember that employers are not judging your worth as a person. They are looking for someone to meet *their* needs. Be persistent and you will find a job that meets *your* needs. Keep your attitude positive and your spirits high. Ask those close to you for support during the sometimes-exciting, sometimes-frustrating process of looking for a job.

Activity 13-4, "Track Your Networking," gives you an opportunity to make your own Network Tracking Cards.

INTEGRATED ACADEMICS
Computer Science

Have students set up hypothetical databases for the company tracking card systems used for a job search. Their database is to include the name of the company and contact; names and titles of the people students spoke with at the company and when they spoke; the name of the person who gave them the lead; the job for which they applied; and the dates they sent in their application, went for an interview, sent a thank-you note, and followed up. Have students print out their databases and bring them to class.

244

Illustration 13-2 Company Tracking Card

Company Name:	Fairly Reliable Felix	Tel. #: (559) 555-0123
Address:	101 S. Main	E-mail:
	Fresno, CA 93726	Referred by: May Wang

Date	Spoke to	Results and Follow-up
4/16	Lee Soong	Job available 5/1. Work after school 3:30-5:30 p.m. until summer—then 8:30 a.m.-5:30 p.m. Pick up application tomorrow. Include ref. list with resume.

Application Record
Job Title: Shop Helper
Date Applied: 4/18
Confirmed Receipt: 4/18
Interview Date: 4/18
Sent T-U Note: 4/18
Interview Follow-up: call 4/25

Items Submitted:
Cover letter
Resume
Reference list
Application form

Researching Industries and Employers

Knowing about an industry and a company will give you a competitive edge in your job search. Research will help you learn about working conditions in the industry. You can also check specific companies to find out which ones best match your skills and your job search goals. When you know your qualifications match the requirements of a job, you are better able to convince an employer that you are the best person to hire.

Finding Background Information

When you research an industry, look for information on the products and services of potential employers. You'll want to review industry trends, paying particular attention to the predicted growth or decline of the industry. You'll want to research career opportunities and look for job descriptions that match the job you want. Finally, you'll want to learn the salary ranges for people in similar jobs at different companies. Helpful sources include the following:

- **The Internet.** The web sites of individual companies usually have useful information. You will be able to check company home pages for links to job opportunities, product information, management and business beliefs, and recent press releases.
- **Professional and trade organizations.** Many professional and trade organizations offer student memberships for free or for a small fee. Some professions sponsor separate student organizations that emphasize obtaining and practicing needed career skills. As a

> 66 **I'm a great believer in luck and I find the harder I work, the more of it I have.** 99
>
> —*Thomas Jefferson,*
> *U.S. President, 1801–1809*

Arrange for students to discover how companies use the Internet for recruiting and hiring. Group students into teams. Assign one set of teams to survey large companies, another set of teams to survey medium-sized companies, and a final set of teams to survey small companies. Have the teams ask the companies the following questions:

• How does your company use the Internet to recruit and/or hire employees?

• Do you select interview candidates more from online applications or from traditional paper applications?

Have the teams share the results of their surveys with the class. Then discuss what the findings mean to the particular students in your class.

APPLY

Have students complete **Activity 13-5, "Comparing Pay Rates,"** that appears on page 254. Teaching suggestions and the solution for this activity appear on page 254. An activity worksheet can be found on the Career Portfolio and Resource CD—**Text Activity 13-5.pdf**.

What do you think?

Use **TM13-06**.
Students' answers will vary but may include setting up job shadowing sites, career study tours, informational interviews, and possibly an internship.

---

member, you will have access to a wealth of information about trends, conditions, and breaking news in the industry. Your membership could also be a source of contacts for your network.

- **Information from companies.** If you will be looking for a job at a medium-sized or large company, call the public relations office and ask for information. Many companies will send you product brochures or an annual stockholders report. For companies without public relations offices, simply ask the receptionist to send you brochures, annual reports, or other information about the company.

- **Libraries.** The reference librarian in a public library will be able to help you find information about working conditions, salaries, and educational requirements for industries and jobs. Most libraries also have professional journals that include information about working in a particular field. You may also find the business sections of local and national newspapers and magazines helpful. Finally, business directories may have information about specific companies that interest you.

Remember to record your research results on the back of the appropriate Company Tracking Card.

In Activity 13-5, "Comparing Pay Rates," you will use the Internet to see how pay varies among different types of entry-level jobs in your career field.

Talking to People

What do you think? What benefits might you realize from talking to people who work in your field?

The results of your background research will prepare you for discussions with knowledgeable people. Seek out those who work in the field or have personal knowledge about the industry and the companies that interest you.

Adelina, a student investigating career choices, had always been interested in a career in pharmacy. She paid special attention when a pharmacist spoke at the Career Day her school sponsored in the fall. Later on, an informational interview helped her learn about the job duties of a pharmacist. However, Adelina was now considering a career as a pharmacy technician and hadn't asked questions about that type of job at the interview.

So Adelina stopped by the drugstore one day when it wasn't busy and introduced herself to Mr. Pratt, the pharmacist. She told him about her interest and asked if he could speak with her sometime, either in person or over the phone. He agreed to meet with her during his lunch break the following Saturday.

CAREER FACT
The U.S. Department of Labor has found that more than 75 percent of all new jobs are created by small businesses that have fewer than 500 employees.

CAREER TREND
Small Business
Invite three local small business owners to speak to your class about running a small business. Have students write down several questions they would like to ask the speakers. Provide the speakers with the list before they make their presentations. Ask speakers to address these questions and add other pertinent information. Remind students to write a thank-you note to each speaker.

Adelina brought a list of questions and was prepared to take notes at the lunch meeting. Mr. Pratt began the meeting by saying he was happy about her interest in a pharmacy career and was glad to provide any information she needed. Adelina explained that she wanted to find out about the qualifications and job duties of a pharmacy technician. She learned that when Mr. Pratt hired a pharmacy technician, he looked for someone who was interested in chemistry and healthcare, enjoyed interacting with people, and had excellent customer service skills.

At the end of the meeting, Adelina thanked Mr. Pratt and agreed to call if she had any further questions. She went home and, after writing a thank-you card, added her notes to her file of information about pharmacy. Now more than ever, she was sure this was the kind of work she wanted to do.

Summarizing what you learn from your research about an industry, job, or employer will help you clarify your understanding and identify questions you still need to have answered. Then you can get answers to the questions you identify by talking to people. Listed below are three ways to get valuable firsthand information from knowledgeable people:

- **Attend job fairs and career fairs.** At a **job fair**, employers set up booths, give out reading material about their companies, and talk to job applicants or students. Attending job and career fairs is a great way to gather employer and industry information quickly and easily. If the employers you meet don't have an opening for the type of job you want, ask if they know of any other firm that does.

- **Arrange informational interviews.** Set up an informational interview with someone who has the job you want or who supervises that job. In *Investigating Your Career*, you have completed several informational interviews as part of the Learning from Others activities. Use your interviewing skills to find out more about the job you want and what will make you competitive for that job.

- **Job shadow.** If you're interested in a specific company, ask permission to spend time job shadowing one of its employees. Job shadowing is an excellent way to learn about the working environment in an organization and the day-to-day responsibilities of a job that interests you.

CAREER SUCCESS TIP

Schools, companies, and organizations sponsor job fairs. Announcements in newspapers may list the participating companies. You can do your online research before attending the job fair.

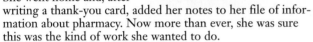

CAREER SUCCESS TIP

Job Fairs

After attending a job fair in your community, ask students to create a mock job fair in your classroom. Students can work in pairs to create booths similar to the ones they visited at the job fair. Have students visit each other's booths and ask questions. Invite other classes to visit your class's job fair, where your students can talk about the types of jobs their imaginary companies offer. Ask students to explain how job fairs can help them in their job search.

Follow up your discussions, interviews, and job shadowing experiences by writing thank-you notes. Add each of the people you spoke with to your network.

Activity 13-6, "Case Challenges," asks you to make recommendations about the type of research that would be helpful in each job search provided.

The Next Step

You have identified your job search goals. You know how to find out about industries, jobs that interest you, and companies where you might want to work. You have also learned ways to find job openings and to manage your job search. What do you do next? You must decide whether you want to find a job working for an employer or whether you want to explore the possibility of working for yourself.

Working for an Employer

Your job search goal will have identified the type of job you want to find. You may have decided you want to work for an employer in a part-time, summer, or full-time position. In that case, the next steps are to apply for positions and prepare for interviews.

Working for an employer provides you with steady income and valuable job experience. You have the opportunity to learn about the company and the type of work involved. You sharpen your skills and learn how to interact with coworkers and customers.

> 66 **Even if you're on the right track, you'll get run over if you just sit there.** 99
>
> —*Will Rogers, Philosopher*

Jake took a part-time job as an employee at a fast-food restaurant, working a couple evenings a week after school and on Saturdays. He enjoyed the job and working as a team with his coworkers to make the customers happy. He may or may not wish to pursue this work as a career. In either case, he would have acquired valuable work experience, expanded his skills, and learned something about himself too.

Or perhaps you want to investigate working for yourself. Does this mean you have wasted time and energy in learning how to search for a job? No, not at all. Many successful entrepreneurs have worked for other people in order to gain experience before starting their own businesses. In addition, you will likely need to search for part-time or summer employment before you take the steps necessary to start your own business. Your experiences with the job search process and your experiences working for an employer will teach you skills that every entrepreneur needs.

In Activity 13-7, "Coming to Terms," you confirm your understanding of the terms introduced in this chapter.

Working for Yourself

Are you considering self-employment? Do you think about starting a small business, perhaps house-sitting neighbors' pets while the owners are at work or on vacation? You may be successful working for yourself if you prepare well and if you share the six characteristics of successful entrepreneurs:

1. I can set goals and create the steps to achieve them.
2. I am willing to ask for advice.
3. I have good organizational skills.
4. I see problems as challenges and can develop alternative solutions.
5. I am enthusiastic, persistent, and optimistic.
6. I believe in myself and in the projects I tackle.

What are some advantages and disadvantages of working for yourself?

What do you think?

Starting your own business is more difficult than starting a new job working for an employer. Why? At the start of a new business, you must do all the jobs in the business yourself. Your first job will be

REAL PEOPLE
REAL CAREERS

Small Business Owner

Kim Almond never thought she'd be running her own business. But when she wanted to sell her old mountain bike and the local bike shop wouldn't take it, she had an idea. "I knew there had to be a lot of other people who wanted to sell—or buy—used sports equipment," she says.

Kim did some research to find out how much money people in her city spent on sports equipment, how many retail stores there were, and whether there were any stores selling used equipment. Kim found one used-equipment store, but it was very small and she thought she could do better. By talking to friends about her idea, she found someone who wanted to go into business with her and who could help with financing.

With a little bit of luck, a lot of hard work, a good business plan, and some old equipment from garage sales and friends, Kim and her partner opened their sports consignment store in just six months. Almost another year passed before the business started making a profit, but now the business has two locations and is very successful.

Kim enjoys managing the store, but she might want to try something else someday. "I'm interested in a lot of things," she states. Her advice to entrepreneurs: research thoroughly. "A lot of people think that if they enjoy doing something, they can turn it into a business," she says. "But you have to really do your research."

For more information about:
• the sporting goods industry, visit *www.nsga.org*.
• consignment and other resale stores, explore *www.narts.org*.

Source: Telephone interview with Kim Almond.

TEACH

You may wish to invite a member of the Service Corps of Retired Executives (SCORE) to discuss various aspects of owning a business. SCORE is a nonprofit association dedicated to entrepreneur education and the formation, growth, and success of small businesses nationwide. Working and retired executives and business owners donate their time and expertise as business counselors. SCORE provides confidential counseling and mentoring free of charge. Additional information about SCORE is available at **www.score.org**.

What do you think?

Use **TM13-08**.
Students' answers will vary. Answers may include the positives of being independent, being your own boss, and developing your passion and creativity. Drawbacks may include long working hours, the need to attend to all aspects of the business, the financial burden, and so on. Chapter 5 elaborates more on entrepreneurship.

REAL PEOPLE—REAL CAREERS
Small Business Owner

Organize students into groups of four or five. Have each group explore the web sites in the "Real People—Real Careers" section on this page and also do a search using the keywords *resale stores* and *resale industries*. Have students use magazine cutouts, computer graphics, and art materials to create a photo gallery bulletin board of visual information that identifies some of the types of things available in consignment and other resale stores.

Have students explore the potential for a service learning project in the community. They should choose a project that would improve the quality of life for a particular population or individual or group. Working in teams, students should then (1) develop a proposal for the project, (2) estimate the financial and human resources needed to make the project successful, (3) list possible sources for raising money and recruiting necessary volunteers, and (4) make a time line that shows the time required to accomplish the project.

APPLY

Have students complete **Activity 13-8, "Writing a Business Plan,"** that appears on pages 255–256. Teaching suggestions and the solution for this activity appear on pages 255–256. An activity worksheet can be found on the Career Portfolio and Resource CD—**Text Activity 13-8.doc**.

Career Journal

Ask students to spend 10 minutes writing Career Journal entries that answer the following questions:
1. How well did what you thought you knew match what the chapter presented?
2. What questions do you now have about the chapter topics, and where do you think you can find the answers to those questions?
3. How will the content of the chapter help you investigate *your* career?

> 66 **The nicest thing about not planning is that failure comes as a complete surprise, rather than being preceded by a period of worry and depression.** 99
>
> —*Sir John Harvey-Jones, Broadcaster and Author*

research. For example, if you are interested in lawn care, you need to find out how many residents in your area hire someone to mow and edge their lawns, trim their bushes, and rake their leaves. Second, you need to know what, if any, experience your clients would expect you to have. Third, you need to know how much competition you would have from others. Fourth, you need to figure out the best way to market your services to potential clients. Finally, you need to plan the financial side of your business.

If you decide you are ready, willing, and able to start your own business, your next step will be to write a business plan. A **business plan** is a detailed explanation of what you will do and how you will do it. You must prepare a well-written business plan before investors and lending institutions will consider financially supporting your new business. In addition, writing the plan encourages you to organize your thoughts about your business and its future. The body of a business plan can be divided into four distinct sections:

1. **Business Description.** What will you sell? Your product can be something tangible or physical, such as apple pie, or a service, such as cleaning gutters. In some cases, a business might sell both a product and a service. For example, a catering business provides a product—food—and a service—delivery. In the business description, you describe your product or service, explain the customer need your business fills, and explain what makes your product or service different and special from similar ones in the market.

2. **Marketing Plan.** Your **marketing plan** explains how you will (1) identify, attract, and keep customers; (2) identify, understand, and succeed against your competitors; and (3) identify and anticipate change in the marketplace. The types of questions you will answer in the marketing plan include the following: What specific groups of people will buy your product? Why will your product appeal to them? Who are your competitors? What strategies will you use to persuade people to buy your product or service instead of your competitors' products or services?

3. **Operating Plan.** Your **operating plan** explains how you will produce your product or service. Following are examples of the kinds of questions you will answer: How will you make or deliver your product or service? What materials will you need? Where and how will you get the materials? How many people will you need to hire, and what will they do? Where will you locate your business?

4. **Financial Management Plan.** Your **financial management plan** explains how you will finance your business and manage the income and expenses of your business. Following are examples of the questions you will answer in this part of the business plan: How much money do you need to start and operate your business? Where will the money come from? If you borrow the money, how will you repay your lender? How will you manage the income—the money you receive when customers pay you? How will you manage the expenses—the money you pay out for supplies, parts, and anything else you need to run your business?

INTEGRATED ACADEMICS
Music

Have students work in small groups to create a song that helps them remember the components of a business plan. Encourage groups to use traditional and nontraditional instruments with their songs. Have groups present their musical creations to the rest of the class.

Because starting a business is such a major commitment of time, money, and energy, you'll want to do everything you can to make your business a success. You will find it helpful to talk to other small business owners and potential customers. As you work out a plan for your career, concentrate on (1) gathering information, (2) building your network, (3) gaining related experience, and (4) getting the education you need.

Activity 13-8, "Writing a Business Plan," gives you an opportunity to plan a business.

IN A NUTSHELL

- **I can identify my job search goals.**

  I have identified my job search goals. My job search goals, which will probably be related either to meeting my budget or to supporting my *P*A*T*H to Success*, will affect the type of job I seek.

- **I know how to manage my job search.**

  I have prepared my career portfolio, a collection of materials that shows my ability to do a specific job. I know how to use proven job search strategies. In particular, I understand how to network, which is the most effective approach to finding a job. I can make a schedule to plan my job search time. I also know how to keep track of my job search activities by using index cards to record information about my network and the companies I contact.

- **I can research employers and industries.**

  Background information about employers and industries is available on the Internet, from professional and trade associations, from companies, and from libraries. Talking to people at job and career fairs, in informational interviews, and while job shadowing will provide me with firsthand information about industries, jobs, and employers.

- **I can identify the next step to take to reach my career goal.**

  If I decide to work for an employer, my next step is to prepare for the application process. If I decide to work for myself some day, I will have to research various aspects of my planned business. Then I will have to prepare a business plan that includes a description of my business, my marketing plan, my operating plan, and my financial management plan.

Suggestions for Parents and Family Members

Finding a Job

Send a note home with students to advise their parents and family members how they can support teens in their career discovery process in the following ways:

1. Assist teens in networking and obtaining informational interviews.
2. Encourage teens to attend job fairs.
3. Support teens in their effort to learn about business ownership.

Activity 13-1: Your Job Goals

Part 1—Comparing Your Job Goal to Your *P*A*T*H* This part of the activity helps students discover whether their *current* job goal reflects their *P*A*T*H to Success* and supports their career plan.

Use Illustration 9-1 on page 155 of the student text to point out the types of specific information students should provide in their answers to Question 1. After students have completed Question 1, you may wish to have them display their results by creating Venn diagrams with circles titled "Job-Required Skills and Abilities" and "Talents of Primary Career Cluster." Many students choose part-time and summer jobs without thinking about how those jobs could help or hinder their career journey plans. Students will be able to see from a Venn diagram how well their current job goal matches their career goals, helping them decide whether they could better support their career plan by changing their current job goal.

Solution: Answers will vary. A class discussion of the activity will help students realize how their current job goals will affect various aspects of their lives. Emphasize that because a job will impact achievement of students' career goals as well as their priorities and how they spend their time, they need to choose a job goal carefully.

Part 2—Updating Your Budget
Part 2 of the activity lays the groundwork for Activity 13-5, in which students discover how various pay rates for their current job goal and their career goal meet their present and future budget needs.

Emphasize to students that they should include an amount for each category on the budget forms, using a zero if the category does not apply. Explain that the amounts for their ideal lifestyle budget must be realistic; for example, students should find out through research how much the rent or mortgage will be for housing where they want to live. Also be sure students understand that the amount for each category must be a *monthly* amount.

Solution: Answers will vary.

252

Part 1—Comparing Your Job Goal to Your *P*A*T*H*

Temporary, part-time, or full-time jobs can support the career plan you've developed on your *P*A*T*H to Success*. Use the following activities to discover whether your current job goals reflect your *P*A*T*H to Success* and support your career plan.

1. Write down the skills and abilities you need to fulfill the requirements of the type of job you have chosen. Then look at the checklists from Activity 6-5 in your Career Journey Folder. Compare the skills and abilities you listed to the talents you checked in Activity 6-5 for your primary career cluster. What similarities do you find?

2. If you get the job you want, the amount of time you can devote to other activities will be affected.

   a. Print the **Nine Boxes of Life** form from your CD, or draw nine boxes on a separate sheet of paper.

   b. Write the nine most important things in your life inside the nine boxes. Include your job in one of the boxes.

   c. Number the boxes from 1 to 9 according to what is most important in your life. (Number 1 is the most important.)

   d. Number the boxes from 1 to 9 again, this time according to how you expect to spend most of your time after you begin working. (Number 1 is how you spend the most time.)

   e. Use Activity 6-2 from your Career Journey Folder. Compare the results of Activity 6-2 with the activity you just completed. Which areas have changed? How will having a job affect your priorities?

3. How well do you think your current job goal helps you meet the entry-level requirements and career preparation options you have identified? To find out:

   a. Print the **Meeting Requirements** form from your Career Portfolio and Resources CD or use the form provided by your teacher.

   b. Look at the form you completed in Activity 9-2. Transfer the Entry-Level Requirements you listed in Activity 9-2 to the left-hand column of the **Meeting Requirements** form. In the right-hand column of the **Meeting Requirements** form, list any characteristics of your current job goal that support or will improve your ability to meet the entry-level requirements in the left-hand column.

   c. Look at the right-hand column of the form from Activity 9-2. How well does your job goal fit your career preparation options? What is your main reason for selecting your current job goal?

Part 2—Updating Your Budget

1. Review the budget you made in Activity 7-7. Make any changes needed to reflect your current financial situation.

2. Print the **Monthly Budget for Ideal Lifestyle** form from your Career Portfolio and Resources CD, or use the handout from your teacher. Prepare a new budget that reflects your ideal lifestyle. Research on the Internet or elsewhere to find the information you need to complete the necessary amounts on the budget.

Save both budgets. You will use them in Activity 13-5.

Your Career Portfolio

Obtain a separate folder or other professional-looking holder to use as your career portfolio. Put the following items into your new portfolio:

- The completed W-4 and I-9 forms from Activity 12-2
- Blank notepaper, a pen that writes with black or dark blue ink, and a pencil with a good eraser
- One copy of the **Portfolio Checklist** form printed from your Career Portfolio and Resources CD or provided by your teacher

Keep your career portfolio where you can find it easily and where it will not get damaged.

Learning from Others

Part 1—Analyzing Job Search Strategies

1. Remove the following activities from your Career Journey Folder: Activities 1-2, 2-2, 3-4, 4-2, 6-7, and 8-1. Review your notes. Then write a summary of any information you have about how each person you talked to got his or her job.

2. Interview three people about how they got their current jobs. Change their names in your notes to protect their privacy because you will be working with a partner for the remainder of this activity. For each person you interview, list the following information about the person's job search:

- Any type of research each person did during the job search process
- The job search strategies each person used
- How long it took for each person to get the job
- How many applications each person completed
- How many job interviews each person attended
- Advice each person has about looking for a job

3. With a partner, analyze the job search techniques each person used. Then write down the ways you and your partner think each job search could have been better.

Part 2—Attending a Career or Job Fair

Attend a career or job fair. Talk to representatives of companies who offer jobs in your career cluster. Summarize the qualifications needed for one of the jobs you identified. Then explain how you can go about obtaining the necessary qualifications.

Track Your Networking

Make up at least five Network Tracking Cards using information for five people in your personal network. Use Illustration 13-1 as a guide.

Activity 13-2: Your Career Portfolio

In this activity, students begin building the career portfolio they will carry with them when filling out applications or participating in job interviews.

You may want to discuss in class the various types of folders students can use for their career portfolios, analyzing the positive and negative aspects of each type. Ask students for suggestions about how to prevent portfolios and their contents from being damaged.

Solution: Each student's portfolio should include neat copies of completed W-4 and I-9 forms from Activity 12-2, blank notepaper, a pen that contains blue or black ink, a pencil with a good eraser, and one copy of the Portfolio Checklist.

Activity 13-3: Learning from Others

This activity reinforces students' understanding of the relationship between research and job search success. Students develop their skills in writing summaries, interviewing, and analyzing information.

You may wish to check students' summaries before students conduct their interviews. Consider discussing some of the information from the summaries in class. The information from analyzing job search techniques may be more relevant for students if they are partnered with a student interested in the same career cluster.

Solution: Answers will vary. Be sure each team suggests ways the people interviewed could have improved their job search techniques. A class discussion of the techniques may help students realize the advantages and disadvantages of the various ways people can conduct a job search.

Activity 13-4: Track Your Networking

This activity gives students practice at making Network Tracking Cards.

Refer students to Illustration 13-1 for a sample of a completed Network Tracking Card. If any of your students are planning to conduct a job search in the next few months, you may want to recommend that they purchase a package of 4" × 6" index cards and begin preparing Network Tracking Cards for all the people in their network. Also suggest they develop a filing system for their cards.

Solution: Answers will vary.

Activity 13-5: Comparing Pay Rates

Part 1—Researching Wages or Salaries This part of the activity gives students practice at researching wages and salaries of potential jobs in the students' career field.

Discuss the form for this activity in class so students understand where they should record the information they acquire from their Internet research. Also be sure they realize that they should identify all three of the entry-level jobs listed in the activity even if they have already chosen a career preparation option. You may allow students who have chosen careers in the same cluster and who have picked similar preparation options to work together for this part of the activity. Point out to students that they should record *monthly* pay amounts and, if necessary, explain to students how to convert weekly or hourly pay amounts to monthly amounts.

Solution: Answers will vary.

Part 2—Comparing Wages or Salaries to Your Budgets This part of the activity helps students understand how the entry-level salary in their career cluster may affect their present budget and the budget for their ideal lifestyle.

Discuss how students should complete the form for this activity. Instruct students to work individually on this part of the activity so each student can realize the relationship between entry-level salary and lifestyle.

Solution: Answers will vary. In a class discussion, have students describe how their budgets compare to the entry-level compensation for the various careers they investigated.

Activity 13-6: Case Challenges

This activity helps develop critical-thinking skills and gives students practice in planning job search strategies.

Solution: Answers will vary. You may wish to record students' decisions on the chalkboard or a transparency. Then discuss the circumstances described in each case, the options open to the person in each case, and the consequences of the job search strategies selected.

254

Print the **Comparison of Pay Rates and Budgets** form from your Career Portfolio and Resources CD, or use the handout provided by your teacher. Use the information from Parts 1 and 2 below to fill in the form.

Part 1—Researching Wages or Salaries

1. Use the Internet to add to your research from Activity 6-6. Begin by identifying three types of entry-level jobs in your career cluster and recording the jobs on the form:
   - An entry-level job available to those without a high school diploma
   - An entry-level job available to those with a high school diploma
   - An entry-level job available to those with postsecondary education/training (certificate, associate degree, apprenticeship, bachelor's degree)

   Some starting points for your research could be these sites:
   - O*Net OnLine at *http://online.onetcenter.org*
   - America's Career InfoNet at *www.acinet.org/acinet*
   - Bureau of Labor Statistics at *www.bls.gov*

2. Visit online salary surveys and figure out the usual monthly pay for each of the entry-level jobs you chose in Question 1. Record the monthly pay for each entry-level job in each of the two places that are labeled "Entry-Level Pay" on the form. Some starting points for your research could be as follows:
   - *http://salary.com*
   - *http://jobstar.org/tools/salary/index.htm*

Part 2—Comparing Wages or Salaries to Your Budgets

Use the updated budgets from Activity 13-1. Copy the total amount of money you need from each budget to the appropriate lines on the **Comparison of Pay Rates and Budgets** form. Subtract the budgeted amounts from the pay amounts for each entry-level job. Record your answers in the appropriate "Difference" box on the form. What do the differences between the budgeted amounts and the pay amounts tell you?

In each of the following case studies, a person is about to start a job search. Which of the information sources listed below would you suggest to each person as good sources for researching his or her particular job market? Explain your answer. Then share your decision with the rest of the class.

Background Information	Information from People
Internet	Job fairs and career fairs
Organizations	Informational interviews
Companies	Job shadowing experiences
Libraries	Career study tour

254

1. After taking several career assessments and spending time with his art teacher, Tony believes photography is a career match for him. Because photography is a highly specialized career, Tony wants to be sure he will enjoy spending every working day as a photographer. His parents want him to stay at home and go to a local school in the Midwest, but Tony wants to go to school on the West Coast. However, he is unsure whether he will be comfortable with the climate and culture differences on the West Coast. So Tony decides to search for a summer job in California as a photographer's assistant.

2. Natalie has two loves—art and nature. As a freshman in high school, Natalie has already won several school and community awards for her paintings and sculpture. In fact, two of her sculptures were purchased during one show. While she was on vacation last summer, Natalie noticed many sculptures in yards and parks—not typical statues, but abstract, creative pieces like hers. Natalie would like a job with a landscape firm, one that offers design besides the usual landscape services. She thinks working for a company specializing in landscape design will give her the opportunity to sell her sculptures.

3. Danys needs to support himself. He is tired of earning money doing odd jobs around the house for his parents. Though they say they will have to pay someone else to do the work if he doesn't, Danys believes his parents create jobs for him just so he can have extra money. After reviewing his budget and his school schedule, Danys knows he needs to work ten hours a week at a job that pays at least $2 above minimum wage. At the present time, the wage is more important to Danys than the type of work.

ACTIVITY 13-7 **Coming to Terms**

Explain when and why the following terms are relevant during the job search process:

1. Career portfolio
2. Networking
3. Job or career fair

ACTIVITY 13-8 **Writing a Business Plan**

 Read the following case. Work with other students to develop a business plan for a school-based business that can be run by the student members of the service club.

The largest club at Clark School is a service organization. Many students join because of the help that the club gives to the community. The club has projects going on constantly; many of them year round. Typical projects include picking up trash in local neighborhoods, painting buildings, raking leaves and doing other yard work for senior citizens, and reading to young children.

The service club is self-supporting. It does not ask for money from the community or the school. The club only accepts donations of supplies; the club members don't directly ask for the donations. To continue giving help to the community, the club needs to raise money for additional supplies and other expenses. The club is a well-respected student service organization that both the students and the community trust.

Activity 13-7: Coming to Terms

This activity checks students' understanding of three key job search terms by having students explain the circumstances in which the three terms are relevant.
Solution: Answers may vary slightly. Be sure students' explanations indicate a thorough understanding of the role of each term in the job search process.

Activity 13-8: Writing a Business Plan

This activity helps develop critical-thinking skills by requiring students to extract and analyze pertinent information and develop an action plan. The activity also gives students an appreciation of the many aspects of running a business that a group of entrepreneurs must consider and helps students realize that employers must think about many variables besides employee hours and

wages. Ask students to form teams of four or five people. Have the teams complete the activity and make presentations to the class. Encourage students to incorporate visual and/or auditory aids into their presentation.
Solution: Answers will vary but should address the questions under each category of a business plan.
Business Description
1. The club should choose an ongoing fund-raiser that could easily be continued by future classes. Suggestions in the Activity include selling snacks or selling items that have the school logo.
2. The chosen product would be salable all year long because it meets a constant, identified customer need.
3. The chosen product is different and special because it is available on campus and (in the case of logo items) it is unique and not available any place else.
Marketing Plan
1. Buyers will be mainly students, staff, and parents.
2. The product will appeal to the customers because (a) it will fill a need not now met on campus, (b) customers like the convenience of buying at school, (c) customers want to support school spirit and community service.
3. The competitors identified will depend on the product chosen. Examples for a snack-based business are grocery and convenience stores or bake sales held throughout the year by other clubs. Examples for a logo-based business are department and sporting goods stores that offer clothing decorated with the school logo and parent associations selling logo items to support school sports teams, especially those in regional or state competition.
4. Answers will vary buy may suggest appealing to school spirit and the desire to support service projects. No answer is incorrect as long as the suggested strategies are ethical and legal.
5. Answers will vary but could include getting endorsements from teachers and students, talking to customers, visiting the competition, or offering special pricing.
6. Answers will vary but could include asking customers for suggestions, collecting and analyzing fluctuations in product sales, and watching for changes in tastes or styles.

Operating Plan

1. The business will operate at the school. With appropriate permission, club members could make snack products in the Life Styles kitchen or the cafeteria. With appropriate permission, club members would contract production of logo items with a specialty company or produce the product in the Life Styles classroom. Delivery options would depend on the product and school and student schedules.

2. Answers will vary depending on the products selected. Examples for a snack-based business may include snack ingredients and packaging materials. Examples for a logo-based business may include transfers of the school logo and items to put the logo on.

3. Materials needed and sources of materials will depend on the products chosen. Examples for a snack-based business include grocery stores and kitchen supply stores. Examples for a logo-based business include specialty advertising suppliers, clothing wholesalers, or local clothing or sporting goods store.

4. The club members and possibly parent volunteers will work at the business. Their duties will vary but could include ordering and picking up supplies, producing products, selling and distributing products, tracking costs and sales, banking and tracking money, and marketing the products.

5. The location depends on the chosen product. With permission, the Life Skills classroom at Clark School could be the home office of either type of business mentioned in the Activity.

Financial Management Plan

1. Startup costs will depend on the products chosen for the business. Encourage students to consider the following categories when determining the startup costs of the business: tools and equipment, materials to make the product, cash register and/or calculator, spreadsheet and/or business management software, office supplies, and initial marketing plans.

2. Sources of startup money will vary. Possibilities include fees from members, donations, a short-term fundraiser, a loan, seed money from another club or parent group, and general fund of the school.

Club members are tired of selling such things as candy, flowers, and t-shirts several times during the school year. The club officers meet with a committee of members to brainstorm fund-raising ideas. The committee believes the club needs an on-going fund-raiser that would bring in money regularly. This fund-raising project should be one that the club members can continue year-to-year, even with yearly changes in the student population. Since they are still in school, the club members want to be sure that the fund-raising business does not take all their time.

At Clark School, all students must take a Life Skills class to learn cooking, laundry, home repair, sewing, budgeting, money management, and career planning. The Life Skills teacher, Ms. Tyler, is also the service club adviser. She suggested that the members of the club create a business based on something they learned in the Life Skills class.

Some of the members of the committee think that Clark students need to be able to purchase snacks either before or after school. Others believe that Clark needs a school store that would sell some items with the school logo. The service club could use one of those ideas for their fundraiser or even another idea. But the committee agrees that the fund-raiser should be a school-based business. The students are already at school, so finding workers should not be a problem. Ms. Tyler would have to approve the fund-raiser. However, the club members would plan, manage, and run the fund-raiser and its budget.

You are a member of the fund-raising committee for the service club. Your committee must choose a fund-raising business and write a business plan that answers the questions listed below. Using the case text as background, create answers to any of the planning questions that aren't directly answered in the case text.

Business Description: What will you sell? What customer need do the products fill? How are the products different and special from similar ones being sold?

Marketing Plan: What specific groups of people will buy the products? Why will the products appeal to them? Who are your competitors? What strategies will you use to persuade people to buy your products instead of a competitor's products? What will you do to remain informed and competitive? How will you anticipate changes in customers?

Operating Plan: How will you make or deliver the products? What materials will you need? Where and how will you get the materials? How many people will you need to work for you, and what will they do? Where will you locate your business?

Financial Management Plan: How much money do you need to start and operate your business? Where will the money come from? If you borrow the money, how will you repay your lender? How will you manage the income—the money you receive when customers pay you? How will you manage the expenses—the money you pay for supplies, parts, and anything else you need to run your business?

3. Answers will vary. One possibility is to repay a startup loan in monthly payments from the club's profits.

4. Answers will vary but may include business operating software, spreadsheet software, or a manual bookkeeping system.

5. Answers will vary but may include business operating software, spreadsheet software, or a manual bookkeeping system.

Emphasize that a business plan is only the beginning stage of owning a business; actually operating the business requires a great deal of knowledge, ability, time, and commitment.

Applying for a Job

Marcela Gomez needs to find a good-paying job so she can add to her education fund. Her previous jobs as a servers' assistant and as a sales clerk don't pay as much as office work, which is what Marcela wants to do. She has office skills from her classes in applied business technology, and she interned in an office last summer. Now she is searching for a summer job that she hopes will continue into the school year. She knows she must prepare a resume to apply for jobs in her field, but she's not sure how to go about doing this. Her last job required only a completed application. She is nervous because she isn't sure she has enough information to include in a resume.

Marcela begins by reviewing her research about the type of job she is interested in. She wants to understand clearly what employers are looking for in potential employees. To have any chance of getting an interview, she knows her resume must show her to be a good job match.

Next, Marcela lists her education, skills, work experience, and related activities. As she writes, she realizes she has accomplished more than she originally thought—career/technical classes, service learning activities, a co-op internship, and several part-time jobs. Encouraged, Marcela decides that preparing an effective resume may not be as difficult as she thought.

Which of your activities and experiences might help you do a job well? Why?

What do you think?

OBJECTIVES

After completing this chapter, you will be able to:
- Complete a Personal Fact Sheet.
- Describe an effective resume.
- Write a resume.
- Select references.
- Write a cover letter.
- Complete a job application.
- Describe various pre-employment tests.

Key Terms:
- Personal Fact Sheet
- chronological resume
- functional resume
- combination resume
- references
- cover letter
- pre-employment test

Chapter Overview

Chapter 14
Applying for a Job

FOCUS

In Chapter 14, students begin their exploration of the job application process by preparing an inventory of their skills, education, and experience. They use this information to create an effective resume that highlights the ways their qualifications match specific job requirements. Students then learn how to select references, write cover letters, fill in application forms, and prepare for taking various types of pre-employment tests.

Use the **Objectives** and **Key Terms** printed in the margin to help students focus on the content of this chapter. Use the **video segment** for Chapter 14 to trigger discussion.

What do you think?

Use **TM14-01**.
Students' answers will vary.

Career Journal

Ask students to spend 10 minutes writing Career Journal entries that answer the following questions:
1. What do you think this chapter will cover?
2. What do you already know about these topics?
3. What three things do you want to learn about these topics?

CHAPTER RESOURCES and MATERIALS

Activities & Projects book
Instructor's Resource CD
- Forms and Worksheets for Chapter Activities 14-1 through 14-8
- Internet Links for Chapter 14
- PowerPoint Presentation for Chapter 14
- Lesson Plans
- Teaching Masters for Chapter 14
- Video Discussion Guide for Chapter 14

Chapter Tests book
Exam*View*® CD
Video
Web Site

- How long they worked on the accomplishment.
- How much money the accomplishment generated or saved.
- How much time the accomplishment saved at the time or in the future.

APPLY

Have students complete **Activity 14-1, "Personal Fact Sheet,"** that appears on page 281. Teaching suggestions and the solution for this activity appear on page 281. An activity worksheet can be found on the Career Portfolio and Resource CD— **Text Activity 14-1.pdf**.

TEACH

Before students read about Effective Resumes on this page of the student edition, ask them to explain the purpose of a resume. Then ask what they think an employer looks for in a resume. Many students erroneously think that their resume should reflect *their* needs and that employers will figure out what job would be best for an applicant. Students also often think their resume will land them a job.

After students read page 258, emphasize that to be effective, a resume must address the *employer's* concerns.

Personal Fact Sheet

> 66 A sloppy application says, 'This is who I am.' 99
>
> —*Fay Brown,*
> *College Development*
> *Director*

Your **Personal Fact Sheet** contains basic information about you and your education, experience, and qualifications. Employers may request this information at various stages of your job application and interview processes. You will use the information on your Personal Fact Sheet when you:

- Write resumes and cover letters.
- Complete job applications.
- Prepare for job interviews.
- Fill out forms after you get a job.

Be sure to spell out the complete names of your schools or employers and the street and city names of all addresses. Keep one copy of your Personal Fact Sheet in your career portfolio for filling out a job application or employment forms at a company. The Personal Fact Sheet Marcela Gomez prepared is shown in Illustration 14-1 on pages 259 and 260.

In Activity 14-1, "Personal Fact Sheet," you will fill out your own Personal Fact Sheet.

Effective Resumes

CAREER FACT

Several studies by human resources firms have found that more than one-third of job candidates commit "resume fraud" by lying on their resumes.

A resume is a summary of your qualifications and experience for a particular job. From your point of view, your resume will have one purpose: to persuade a potential employer to offer you a job interview. The kinds of questions employers will want your resume to answer include "Why should I hire this person? How can this person help the company succeed?" If your resume answers these questions well, you may be asked to come in for an interview. In an interview, you will be able to speak for yourself. Before an interview, you will have to rely on your resume to do the talking for you.

An honest resume will be critical to your success. Companies may be held legally responsible if an employee breaks the law and they did not do a pre-employment background check. As a result, most employers thoroughly check the statements and references provided by job candidates.

If a lie is discovered on an applicant's resume, the applicant will be rejected. For employers, even one hiring mistake is expensive. When lies are discovered on the employment documents of an employee, that employee is usually fired immediately. Protect yourself by being honest.

To develop an effective resume, you will need to learn what employers expect to see in a resume. The language, appearance, and format of your resume will be as important as the content.

PART 5 · · · · · · CREATING TOOLS FOR THE FUTURE

ONLINE RESOURCES

Check out the web site **www.investigatingyourcareer.com** for teacher resources, student activities, and replacements for broken links for this chapter. To access the teacher resources:

Username: career
Password: investigate

Illustration 14-1 Marcela Gomez's Personal Fact Sheet, page 1 of 2

TEACH

PERSONAL FACT SHEET

Personal Information

Full Name *Marcela Gomez*

Address *868 Fairmont Boulevard*
Street *Topeka*   *KS*   Apt. No. *66614-2253*
City   State   ZIP Code

Telephone Numbers (Home) *(785) 555-0189*   (Business) *( )*
E-mail Address *marcela.gomez@gomez.name*   Social Security Number *555-55-5555*

Educational Background

Name and Address of School
Oak Park High School
101 Campus Drive, Topeka, KS 66606-1555
Telephone Number *(785) 555-0144*
Program of Study *Business Technology*

Expected Date of Graduation   Dates of Attendance   GPA or Class Rank
5/2005   From *9/2001* To *present*   *3.8*

Major Subject Areas/Specific Course Titles
Computers and Technology, Introduction to Business, Keyboarding 1, Keyboarding 2,
Microsoft Office, Recordkeeping, Web Page Development, Computerized Accounting 1

Internships
Summer 2003; unpaid, Environmental Research Group, 898 Bridgeway Drive, Topeka KS
66606-1596 (785) 555-0102 Supervisor: Marlena Trent, Office Manager
Performed routine office duties, including filing, answering the telephone, greeting clients,
keying routine documents, and entering data into Access database

Certifications
Working toward Microsoft A+ certification

Bilingual Skills
English, Spanish

Computer Skills
Microsoft Windows XP, Word, Access, PowerPoint, Outlook, Excel, Internet Explorer,
Netscape Navigator; keyboarding at 50 wpm

Office Equipment Skills
Copy machine, fax, inkjet and laser printers, scanner

Point out that Marcela's e-mail address is a businesslike style that tells employers she is serious about her work. The e-mail address she uses in her personal life, **Jazz-Mar@hot-tracks.com**, is an accurate reflection of her interest in jazz but gives too much of an informal impression to employers looking for a responsible employee. Marcela also changed the greeting on her voice mail. Jazzy blues no longer play in the background, and callers are politely asked to leave their name and telephone number.

CAREER TREND
Resume Fraud

Ask one of the students to read the "Career Fact" on page 258; then hold a class discussion on "resume fraud" and how it hurts the applicant and the company. Ask students what they think people lie about when they commit "resume fraud." Grades? Work experience? Ask students why they think people commit "resume fraud." Tell students that most people who lie on their resumes are eventually caught and lose their jobs.

TEACH

Have students read what Marcela has written on the fact sheet for her responsibilities and accomplishments as a sales clerk. Ask students to identify her accomplishment. Tell students to imagine themselves as an employer: What would Marcela's accomplishment tell them about her abilities and attitude? Have students repeat this analysis process with Marcela's responsibilities and accomplishments entry for the server assistant position. Help students understand the positive answer that accomplishments will provide to the famous employer question "Why should I hire this person?"

Students who complete **Activity 14-1** in the student text, **Activities 14-A** and **14-B** in the *Investigating Your Career Activities & Projects* book, and **Activity 14-2** in the student text (in that sequence) will have an advantage. They will begin **Activity 14-3, "Writing a Resume,"** with the required personal information, a rough draft of their job objective, and confidence in their ability to write in "resume-ese." As a result, the students will be less intimidated when they are assigned to write their own resume.

Illustration 14-1 Marcela Gomez's Personal Fact Sheet, page 2 of 2

Special Skills and Knowledge

Filing, keying, answering the telephone, working with the public, operating a cash register, teaching Spanish to children, maintaining data in Access database

Honors and Awards

Attended service learning workshop sponsored by the Perlstein Foundation, 9/2002; Key Club Award for 100 hours of service

Club Memberships

National Honor Society, 9/2003–present; Ecology Club, 9/2001–present; Key Club, 9/2001–present; Business Professionals of America, 1/2002–present

Employment Background

Information for your current or most recent employment

Name of Employer   Trendy Apparel

Address of Employer   469 Main Street
Topeka KS 66604-1224

Telephone Number   (785) 555-0158   Dates of Employment   10/2003–present

Job Title   Sales Clerk

Name and Title of Supervisor   Ms. Mollye Couch, Assistant Manager

Was your employment part of an internship?   No   A work-study program?   No

Wages or Salary $7 per hour

Responsibilities and Accomplishments   Help customers, operate the cash register, oversee the dressing rooms, stock inventory. Most accurate at balancing the cash register for the last three months.

Information for your previous employment

Name of Employer   Burger Den

Address of Employer   2525 Entertainment Circle
Topeka KS 66606-1827

Telephone Number   (785) 555-0167   Dates of Employment   5/2002-5/2003

Job Title   Server Assistant

Name and Title of Supervisor   Waylin Estes, Manager

Was your employment part of an internship?   No   A work-study program?   No

Wages or Salary   Minimum wage

Responsibilities and Accomplishments   Bussed and set tables, served water, cleaned serving area and dining room, and assisted servers as needed. Increased my tips to 15 percent of servers' tips.

DIFFERENT LEARNING ABILITIES

Attention Deficit Disorder

Give extra time and attention to students with attention deficit disorder to help them write a Personal Fact Sheet. Pair attention deficit disorder students with a student mentor from a higher grade to work together, or ask the special needs coordinator or school counselor to devote some time to work with students. Help these students understand their value to prospective employers by telling each student individually of his or her worth. Pay special attention to the "Special Skills and Knowledge" section to make sure each student writes something.

Master "Resume-ese"

Before you can write a resume that convinces an employer to offer you an interview, you need to learn the basics of "resume-ese," the language of resume writing.

What do you think?

Why is the language you use in your resume important?

Employers appreciate resumes that present relevant information clearly and briefly. By learning the following basic guidelines, you can develop a winning resume.

Use only essential information. Employers recognize resumes by their formats, so you do not need to use the title *Resume*. Also, employers assume you will provide a list of references. Do not state "References available on request." Save resume space for essential information.

Omit *I*, *me*, and *my*. Your resume is obviously about you, so these words are unnecessary. Your phrases sound more active without them.

Use phrases instead of sentences. Rather than long, descriptive sentences, use brief phrases. Use simple, direct language and as few words as possible to get your information across.

Weak: I watched three grade-school children after school and made sure they did their homework. I also planned fun activities such as crafts.

Strong: Cared for three children, ages six to nine, after school. Scheduled homework time and planned and directed fun craft projects.

Begin each statement with a strong verb. Make your actions the main focus of the statement. Employers are interested in what you have accomplished.

Weak: My duties included walking home with the children; preparing, serving, and cleaning up after snacks; and helping the children set the table for dinner.

Strong: Walked the children home from school; prepared, served, and cleaned up after snacks; and helped the children in setting the table for dinner.

Use specific examples and numbers to show measurable accomplishments. Don't just say you accomplished something. Say what you did, how long you worked on it, how much money it brought in, or how much time or money it saved the company.

Weak: I helped the children learn their weekly spelling words and raise their grades.

Strong: Helped all three children raise their weekly spelling scores one full letter grade. The nine-year-old won the class spelling bee at the end of the year.

> **" Spectacular achievement is always preceded by spectacular preparation. "**
>
> —*Robert Schuller, Minister and Writer*

What do you think?

Use **TM14-02**.
Students' answers will vary.

TEACH

Explain that business writing emphasizes a concise, clear transmission of the main message. Describe "resume-ese" as the most succinct form of business writing. Emphasize that the information in a resume should be condensed as much as possible without losing the clarity of the message. Also stress the importance of making actions the main focus of statements.

Ask students to read and analyze the two examples under the header "Use phrases instead of sentences." Help students understand that the second example is strong because "cared for" is an active phrase that conveys energy and responsibility and the specific description "ages six to nine" emphasizes the accomplishment of working successfully with children in different age groups.

TEACH

Students in grades 6 through 9 may believe they do not have any skills or accomplishments to put on a resume. Help students identify how the examples on this page show employers the transferable skills of planning (scheduling homework and preparing crafts), fulfilling responsibilities (walking children home, fixing snacks, and setting the table), and being persistent (maintaining weekly spelling drills). Ask students to explain why a measurable accomplishment makes the resume content much stronger. To help identify their own skills and accomplishments, suggest that students brainstorm a list of chores they have done for neighbors or projects they have worked on for clubs, youth groups, school fund-raisers, community volunteer activities, or families' or friends' businesses; or favors they have done for friends that show job-related skills. For example, repairing bikes, building derby cars, or making jewelry all show hand-eye coordination, attention to detail, and persistence—qualities that employers value.

DIFFERENT LEARNING STYLES

Print Learners

Provide print learners with two sample resumes and two blank Personal Fact Sheets. Have the students work as a group to analyze the information on each resume and decide where that information should go on a Personal Fact Sheet.

Have students complete **Activity 14-A, "Master Resume-ese,"** found in the *Investigating Your Career Activities & Projects* book.

Part 1 of this activity requires students to think critically about several areas of a resume: resume-ese; grammar, spelling, and punctuation; content effectiveness; and visual attractiveness. Students may find resumes to critique and edit from library books or on the Internet, or you may provide copies of specific resumes you think most appropriate for your class. Part 2 gives students the opportunity to demonstrate that they have a clear understanding of resume-ese concepts and know how to apply them. Students are then able to tackle with confidence **Activity 14-2**, which is a more complex exercise. **Activity 14-2** may be done individually or in teams. The activity may be used to expand the number of resumes students evaluate and edit. **Solution:** The solution for this activity appears in the *Teacher's Edition* of *Investigating Your Career Activities & Projects*.

What do you think?

Use **TM14-03**.
Students' answers will vary but should include the fact that viewing photographs may lead to prejudice in hiring, whether intentional or unintentional.

Echo vocabulary used in your field. Know and use the vocabulary of your chosen career area. You can learn the keywords of your field by talking to knowledgeable people, reading ads and job descriptions for positions that interest you, and studying career publications.

Use correct grammar, spelling, and punctuation. Check, recheck, check again, and then have someone else check. Employers almost always throw out resumes containing errors. Impress potential employers with your attention to detail.

Use Attractive Visual Style

Although more and more companies use the Internet for the employment application process, many employers still require traditional resumes. These are the printed resumes you mail with a cover letter and bring to the job interview.

What do you think?
Do you think people should put their pictures on their resumes? Why or why not?

Marcela Gomez wanted her resume to make the best impression possible on potential employers. She knew employers could receive hundreds of resumes in response to job openings. She had heard that the best way to stand out was to use an unusual design on bright paper . . . or old-fashioned type on parchment paper . . . or colored ink . . . or white ink on black paper . . . or—the list seemed endless. She had even seen resumes where the applicant's photograph appeared next to the person's name. "Hmm," Marcela thought. "I can understand how these approaches would make an impression, but would it be the right impression?"

After researching resume writing on the Internet and at the library, Marcela attended a job fair and asked the representatives from the various companies what they looked for in a resume. Then she went home and used "resume-ese" while writing her one-page resume. She chose 12-point Times Roman for her font and used boldface, bullets, and white space in her layout. Finally, she decided she would print her resume on high-quality white paper using a laser printer and black ink.

INTEGRATED ACADEMICS
Communication
Have students work in groups to conduct a poll about resumes. Students should poll adults they know. Before conducting the poll, have students make up a list of questions they want to ask about resumes, such as the following: How important is a resume in finding a job? Should a photo of the applicant be included? Students are to poll at least five adults, including a minimum of one business owner or someone who works in a human resources department or with an employment agency. Have students compare their findings.

By using the guidelines in the following paragraphs, you will be able to design a traditional resume that is attractive and easy to read.

Keep your resume to one page. In general, employers will expect you to submit a one-page resume. After you have more than five years of experience and apply for a complex job, you may submit a two-page resume.

Print on light-colored, high-quality paper. Invest in special paper for your resume. Choose white or cream and matching envelopes. Avoid speckles and designs. Unless you are applying for a position in an artistic field, employers are most interested in the content of your resume. Also, if the employer scans your resume into a computer database, the plain, light-colored paper will help prevent scanning errors.

Use a standard font. Use a clear, common business font, such as 11- or 12-point Times Roman or Arial. Employers are used to reading these fonts. You want the employer to concentrate on your qualifications, not be distracted by an unusual font.

Use simple design elements. Boldface and plain bullets can help draw attention. However, any technique loses effectiveness through overuse. Avoid italics in resumes because italicized words are more difficult to read. *Never* put your picture on your resume. You will be protecting your personal safety *and* the employer's objectivity.

Use white space generously. White space, the areas of the page without text, makes your resume visually pleasing. Information is hard to find in crowded resumes, so employers are less likely to read them. Make your resume inviting by using 1-inch margins all around and generous spacing between sections.

Adapt Format for Computer Processing

Not too many years ago, job applicants always used traditional resumes. Although many companies today still prefer to receive traditional resumes, employers often request resumes in formats that can be processed by computers. The two formats requested are scannable resumes and electronic resumes.

- **Scannable resumes.** These resumes are paper resumes that become electronic when they are scanned into a computerized database. Scannable resumes need to be understandable to a computer. To adapt your traditional resume, you need to remove such formatting as underlining, italics, and columns. Scanners may have trouble translating the special font elements. The searching programs are usually unable to understand information presented in columns.
- **Electronic resumes.** These resumes are created, transmitted, and stored electronically on computers. Electronic resumes are rarely printed on paper. To prepare an electronic resume, remove formatting just as you would for a scannable resume.

CAREER SUCCESS TIP

An employer may discard a resume within a few seconds if the resume is not attractive and easy to read.

CAREER SUCCESS TIP

Attractive Resumes

Obtain several resumes in different styles. Make sure some are less attractive than others. Put them onto transparencies. Using the overhead projector, ask students their opinion of the appearance of each resume. Point out the resumes that are too busy as well as the ones that greet the eye with white space. Tell students that their resume is competing with several other resumes for the attention of the employer. To get the employer's attention, students need to make their resumes attractive and easy to read.

Suggest to students that they investigate the specific format an employer prefers for an electronic resume. For example, on their web site, some employers provide forms into which the applicants can paste the appropriate portions of their ASCII or Text Only resume. Other employers prefer that applicants include their resume in the body of an e-mail. Still other employers request that applicants send their resume and cover letter as an e-mail attachment to a Word or another program file.

What do you think?

Use **TM14-04**.
Students' answers will vary but should include the fact that resumes should vary according to the job.

APPLY

Have students complete **Activity 14-2, "Case Challenges,"** that appears on page 281. Teaching suggestions and the solution for this activity appear on page 281. An activity worksheet can be found on the Career Portfolio and Resource CD—**Text Activity 14-2.doc.**

TEACH

Explain to students that the best resume is rarely the result of the first writing effort. The best resume is the final result of a series of edits and rewrites.

> **66** Always bear in mind that your own resolution to succeed is more important than any other one thing. **99**
>
> —Abraham Lincoln, U.S. President, 1861–1865

An employer requests a scannable or an electronic format so a computer can be used to select applicants. The computer searches the resumes in a database for keywords that meet the requirements of the position. Even if you submit a scannable or an electronic resume, you will want to prepare a traditional resume as well. If you are invited for an interview, the interviewer will need a traditional resume for reference during the interview.

In Activity 14-2, "Case Challenges," you will replace weak resume segments with powerful ones.

Building Your Resume

On the average, employers take just ten seconds to glance through a resume and decide whether the applicant meets their hiring requirements. Employers are not interested in how a job will benefit you. They are interested in how hiring you will benefit *them*. They want to know how this person will make them more successful.

What do you think? Should you send exactly the same resume to every employer? Why or why not?

Use the basic elements of your resume to show what makes you an employer's best choice. Change the content of your resume based on the requirements of the specific job you are seeking. Tailoring your resume to a specific job shows how you would contribute to the company.

The most effective way to adapt your resume for a particular job is to highlight your qualifications that match the job requirements. If the job requires specific skills, education, or work experience that you possess, emphasize these in your resume. Focus on any experience you have in the company's field or any classes you have taken that directly relate to the position. Include keywords used in the job description to show you have the qualifications needed. Finally, choose the organizational style that best emphasizes your strongest qualifications for the job.

Elements of a Resume

Each resume will be different depending on where you are in your career and the type of job for which you are applying. Still, certain basic elements make up most resumes. You can combine, break up, add to, or even omit any of the following elements depending on which resume strategy you think will be most effective.

Personal Information

Your legal name, full address, telephone number(s), and e-mail address (if you have one) belong at the top of your resume. Exception: If you plan to post your resume on a web site, protect your privacy by providing *only* your e-mail address.

DIFFERENT LEARNING ABILITIES
Dyslexia
Have any student with dyslexia work with another student without this learning disability. Have the partners choose a television show they watch that has at least one character who has a career. Have the pair write resume-ese statements for the television character's performance on the job. The resume-ese statements are to be typed or computer-generated and must be grammatically correct. Have the class vote for the statements that best portray a television character.

Job Objective

The job objective comes immediately after your personal information and identifies the job for which you are applying. Keep the employer's interest by writing a clear objective that names a specific job. State the position title mentioned in the job description. You can emphasize your desire to work for a particular company by using the name of the company in your objective. Another good approach is to mirror the employer's concerns in your objective. Whichever approach you use, your strategy is the same: to convince the employer *you* are the right candidate to fill the position.

Weak: A job where I can use my skills to further my career.

Strong: Auto Body Technician with Quality Collision Repair Company

Strong: Pharmacy Technician position requiring a positive attitude and excellent customer service skills

Education, Internships, and Related Coursework

If your education is directly related to the job requirements, place your education section just under your job objective. If your work experience is more important to your job qualifications, place your education section near the end of your resume. Information about schools you have attended, degrees or diplomas you have earned, and fields you have studied belong in this section. You may also list internships and highlight how they relate to your ability to do the job well.

If you have little or no work experience directly related to the job you want, use the education section to focus on relevant classes you have taken. This technique is particularly useful if you don't have a certification or degree in your field of interest but have taken related classes.

Related Experience

List information about your work or other related experience. State each job title clearly, and describe your responsibilities and accomplishments. When writing about a current job, use the present tense; when writing about a previous job, use the past tense. This section can also include experience that is related to your field but not part of a job. For example, you could include extracurricular activities, volunteer work, and unpaid internships that are specifically related to the type of job you seek.

Workplace Skills

Highlight such things as computer knowledge; foreign language proficiency; skills with special tools or equipment; and notable time-management, organization, and communication skills. Be specific and honest—you might have to demonstrate these skills to an interviewer.

CAREER SUCCESS TIP

Your job objective is the opening line of your ten-second story—the average time an employer glances at a resume.

The spirit, the will to win, and the will to excel are the things that endure. These qualities are so much more important than the events that occur.

—Vince Lombardi, Football Coach

Honors and Activities

Use this section to list any honors and awards that demonstrate qualities that might be useful to an employer, such as productivity, responsibility, and perseverance. Show those extracurricular activities that relate to your qualifications as an applicant. Write about your hobby only if you have held a leadership position in a related association or if your hobby directly relates to the job for which you are applying.

Organizational Style

Employers expect resumes to be organized in one of three ways: chronological, functional, or combination. Each of the organizational styles calls attention to different aspects of your qualifications. Choose a style based on the information in your resume you want to highlight.

Chronological

The **chronological resume** style presents your information by date in reverse time, or chronological order. The most current information is shown first. You will want to avoid this style if you have gaps in your job record or if you lack experience directly related to your desired job.

Through her job search efforts, Marcela Gomez found an opening for a part-time office assistant position in an insurance company. Marcela is trying to decide how to organize her resume. She reviewed her education and experience carefully to decide which resume style would best show her qualifications.

Marcela has taken courses related to the duties of the available job. She also has worked as a summer intern in an office setting, which provides her with relevant experience. She is currently working in retail as a sales clerk at a clothing store. Her only other job was as a part-time cashier at her family's fast-food restaurant.

Although Marcela's work experience is varied, she does have office experience—through her summer internship position and through her applied business technology and keyboarding courses. She can show measurable accomplishments in her schoolwork and at each job. Marcela knows that environmental consulting firms work with sensitive information. As a result, these firms try to project confidence and competence by following conservative, traditional business practices. Marcela decides to use the chronological style resume. Illustration 14-2 shows Marcela's final resume.

Keep the following points in mind when using a chronological resume:

- The chronological style is effective if you want to show a record of steadily improving education, skills, and work experience.
- Some experts recommend the chronological style if you are applying for a job in a conservative industry, such as banking or government.

PART 5 • • • • • • CREATING TOOLS FOR THE FUTURE

Illustration 14-2 Chronological Resume of Marcela Gomez

TEACH

Using bullets draws employers' attention to the information the applicant thinks is most persuasive.

Marcela Gomez

868 Fairmont Boulevard
Topeka, KS 66614-2253

(785) 555-0189
marcela.gomez@gomez.name

OBJECTIVE Office Assistant with International Environmental Consulting

EDUCATION

Oak Park High School, Topeka, Kansas
Junior, Business Technology emphasis; will graduate May 2005

Relevant Qualifications
- General office experience in filing, answering multiline telephone, formatting business documents, and entering database updates
- Competent in Netscape Navigator and MS Windows, Office, and Internet Explorer
- Classes completed: Computers and Technology, Introduction to Business, Keyboarding 1 and 2, Microsoft Office, Recordkeeping, Web Page Development, and Computerized Accounting I
- Keyboarding at 50 wpm
- Operate scanners, inkjet and laser printers, faxes, and copy machines
- Bilingual in English and Spanish

Summer Internship   **May 2003 to September 2003**
Under supervision of the office manager at Environmental Research Group, performed duties as assigned. Organized and updated filing system for the working files of three engineers. Relieved the receptionist, greeting clients and routing telephone calls on five-line console. Used Word to create letters and memos. Entered field data for seven Kansas reservoirs into Access database.

EXPERIENCE

Trendy Apparel, Topeka, Kansas
Sales Clerk, Part-time   **October 2003 to Present**
Help customers make clothing selections, operate the cash register, oversee the dressing rooms, and stock inventory. Led all sales clerks in balancing the cash register over a three-month period. Was interviewed and quoted for a fashion article that appeared in *The Topeka Journal*. Received a bonus for demonstrating excellent customer service skills.

Burger Den, Topeka, Kansas
Server Assistant, Part-time   **May 2002 to May 2003**
Bussed and set tables, served water, cleaned serving area and dining room, and assisted servers as needed. Increased tips earned from 10 percent of servers' tips to 15 percent of servers' tips.

ASSOCIATIONS

National Honor Society	September 2003 to Present
Business Professionals of America, Student Chapter	January 2002 to Present
Ecology Club	September 2001 to Present
Key Club	September 2001 to Present

INTEGRATED ACADEMICS
Communication
Invite someone from the local community who works for an employment agency to speak to your class about creating resumes. Have students use the telephone book for leads, or ask if anyone knows someone who fits the criteria. Appoint a committee that will invite the speaker by phone or by letter. Have the class write several questions for the speaker to answer. Give these questions to the speaker ahead of time. After the speech, have the class write a thank-you note to the speaker.

For most students, a combination resume usually is the best style to showcase the match between the student's qualifications and the requirements of the available job. An exception is for students in the arts. Resumes for artists share similar categories:

• Performance History, which lists performances or shows by the artist and may include the name of the production or show, conductor or director, and/or stunt coordinator, as appropriate
• Awards (or Special Recognition)
• Commissioned (or Recorded or Published) Works, which may include the name of the commissioning person or organization, the production house, and/or the publisher
• Special Skills, which may include a list of specialized equipment or media the artist brings to the job
• Education/Training, which may include the names of well-known instructors

Assure students that any style of resume may be formatted as a traditional, scannable, or electronic resume.

Point out to students that the education section can be placed at the beginning or the end of a resume, depending on how the information in the section will influence employers' decisions about whom to interview. Discuss with students why Soo Lin placed her education section at the bottom of her resume:

• Her demonstrated skills are more pertinent to the job duties.
• She has not yet graduated from high school and has taken no classes directly related to the job duties.
• She does not want to emphasize the fact that she is not yet 18 years old.

268

Functional

The **functional resume** style matches your capabilities to the job tasks. Thus, this style of resume emphasizes your abilities rather than your career history.

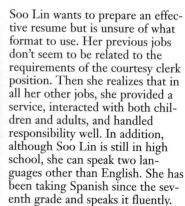

Soo Lin Lee is a senior in high school. She has had several part-time jobs in the past and is presently working part-time at a local diner. Now she has found out that the local grocery store has a job opening for a courtesy clerk. The grocery store offers better hours and the chance for advancement.

Soo Lin wants to prepare an effective resume but is unsure of what format to use. Her previous jobs don't seem to be related to the requirements of the courtesy clerk position. Then she realizes that in all her other jobs, she provided a service, interacted with both children and adults, and handled responsibility well. In addition, although Soo Lin is still in high school, she can speak two languages other than English. She has been taking Spanish since the seventh grade and speaks it fluently. Her parents have also taught her Korean. Soo Lin knows that both her service and her language skills will help her be an effective courtesy clerk.

Soo Lin decides to use a functional resume format. This format will allow her to emphasize how her abilities match the requirements of the courtesy clerk position. Illustration 14-3 shows Soo Lin's final resume.

Keep the following points in mind if you ever use a functional resume:

• The functional style is effective when you are making a career change or have gaps in your education or work experience.
• Employers are often cautious of functional resumes. Show measurable accomplishments to prove your ability in each skill.

Combination

A **combination resume** style uses features of both functional and chronological formats. Immediately after your job objective, highlight your skills that directly match the job requirements, as in a functional resume. Then show work experience in reverse chronological order, as in a chronological resume.

DIFFERENT LEARNING ABILITIES

Attention Deficit Disorder

Have students create a graphic organizer that helps them organize and remember the components of a resume. Suggest that students use different colors for different sections. Encourage students to use a computer to create their graphic organizer. To help students begin, supply them with several examples of graphic organizers. Make transparencies of the graphic organizers, and use the overhead projector to fill out a few of them with the class.

Illustration 14-3 Functional Resume of Soo Lin Lee

Soo Lin Lee

225 South Ash Street
Pittsburgh, PA 15207-3848

(412) 555-0196
soolinlee@zipmail.com

OBJECTIVE Courtesy Clerk at MegaMart

JOB-RELATED SKILLS

Customer Service
- Greeted regular customers of the Downhome Diner by name and welcomed others courteously; made sure customers were seated comfortably. Answered telephone; explained hours, menu selection, and take-out services. Handled customer payments at the cash register. Provided Spanish translation when necessary.
- Called 22 future campers of Eagle Camp and answered questions from parents and fifth-grade campers about what to bring to camp, camp rules and activities, and the camp bus schedule. Helped cabin counselor teach safety and hygiene rules to five campers whose first language was Spanish. Took sick camper to nurse's station, packed the camper's belongings, and sat with her until her parents arrived.
- Coordinated schedules with long-term regular babysitting client and arranged back-up sitter when necessary.
- Speak fluent Spanish, Korean, and English.

Sales
- Wrote up, packaged, and handled payment of take-out orders for Downhome Diner. Increased sales an average of $4 per ticket on 30 percent of take-out orders by describing the desserts menu.

Human Relations
- Got along well with adults of all ages at Downhome Diner. Won the monthly Customers' Choice award twice in six months.
- Helped three Eagle campers, ages 12 and 13, work out a major disagreement and heal hurt feelings. Coordinated the making and campwide signing of a 12" x 24" get-well card for a sick camper who had to leave camp.
- Babysat two young children for 15 hours per month for a year and a half. Played games, prepared meals, and made sure they did homework.

EXPERIENCE

Downhome Diner, Pittsburgh, Pennsylvania
Eagle Camp, Allegheny National Forest, Pennsylvania
The Jones Family, Pittsburgh, Pennsylvania

October 2002 to Present
Summer 2002
December 2000 to June 2002

EDUCATION

Central High School, Pittsburgh, Pennsylvania

Expect to graduate May 2004

DIFFERENT LEARNING STYLES

Visual Learners

Explain that some students think in pictures and symbols instead of words. To demonstrate this, have students create a chart on poster board that describes the components of a functional, chronological, and combination resume. Instead of using words, the chart is to be made up of symbols or pictures for each title and resume component. The chart creator must be able to read the chart. Display the charts in the classroom, and have the class guess what the symbols and pictures mean.

❝ **Never assume you understand. Ask the question.** ❞

—Brian Tracy,
Author and Motivational Speaker

Jack Harley will graduate from high school soon. He has worked for three summers with a small landscaping company as a general laborer, and he wants to make landscape design his career. Through his network, he has a lead on a job with a landscape company that would allow him to work full-time in the summer and part-time for the rest of the year. Year-long jobs for part-time employees are rare in this field, and Jack is anxious to get the job.

Jack believes his resume must immediately show the match between his qualifications and the job requirements. Jack does have some experience in the field and took several related classes in high school. To make the most of his limited experience and education, he decides to use the combination resume format. Illustration 14-4 shows Jack's final resume.

Keep the following points in mind when using a combination resume:

- Use a combination style to emphasize immediately the match between your skills and the position requirements.
- The combination style is effective if you have good skills but limited experience.

 In Activity 14-3, "Writing a Resume," you will write a resume using an appropriate organizational style.

References

CAREER SUCCESS TIP

If you have not talked to some of your references recently, write them letters to catch them up on your life, your interests, goals, and accomplishments. They'll be able to say more about you to impress an employer.

References are people unrelated to you who will give you a positive recommendation. Employers will expect you to supply a separate sheet with the names, job titles, addresses, and telephone numbers of your references. Illustration 14-5 on page 272 shows a portion of the reference sheet Marcela Gomez prepared.

Employers rely on references to give them an idea of the kind of employee you would make, so you should choose references carefully. After you select the people you want as references, you must ask them if they are willing to be your references. You will also need to keep them informed about your job search.

Select Your References

Use your Network Tracking Cards to help you select three references. Look for people who:

- Can vouch for the qualities that will make you a good employee.
- Have worked with you on a job or a project.
- Have known you well for a fairly long time.
- Write and speak well.
- Would be willing and able to spend time writing recommendation letters or talking to prospective employers.

Illustration 14-4 Combination Resume of Jack Harley

Jack Harley

438 Sunset Point Lane ■ Santa Rosa, CA 99120-4312 ■ (707) 555-0135

OBJECTIVE Landscaping Assistant with Landscaping Concepts, Inc.

QUALIFICATIONS

- Able to draft and read blueprints
- Experienced operating and maintaining hand and power tools used in landscaping
- Can analyze and treat soil conditions in the Santa Rosa area
- Familiar with planting requirements of a variety of perennials, shrubs, and trees
- Reliable, courteous worker who follows directions and asks appropriate questions

EDUCATION

Washington High School, Santa Rosa, California
Graduating class of 2004   GPA: 3.2

Related Classes

- Biology ■ Chemistry ■ Algebra ■ Intermediate Algebra ■ Geometry ■ Horticulture
- Geology ■ Introduction to Drafting Technology

WORK EXPERIENCE

Golden State Landscaping Company, Santa Rosa, California
Landscape Assistant in Training   Summer 2003
Under the direction of the landscape designer, planned the layout of ten 12-foot-long by 2-foot-wide planter boxes for the main parking lot at Super Grocery. Assisted with bid preparations by estimating installation time for planting the selected plants in beds on three large commercial jobs and eight residential contracts. Following the designer's sketches, drafted blueprints for follow-up conferences with customers and for 11 bid submissions.

Laborer   Summers of 2001 and 2002
Worked on five-member landscaping crew installing residential and commercial projects. Assisted in site preparation; laid sod; planted perennials, shrubs, and trees; laid walkways with wood, stone, brick, and cement pavers; and installed ponds and fountains.

Mission Nursery, Santa Rosa, California
Part-time Gardening Assistant   September 2002-June 2003
Assisted customers, tended plants, and maintained displays. Received quarterly raises.

Consumer Electronics, Santa Rosa, California
Part-time Customer Service Assistant   October 2000-May 2001
Assisted customers, unpacked and arranged stock, maintained displays.

ACTIVITIES

Fullback, Varsity football in junior and senior years
Varsity wrestling in sophomore year; second place in state championship

TEACH

Advise students that once they have earned an associate or bachelor's degree, they do not need to show their high school information on their resume.

Tell students that if they provide their GPA on their resume, many employers will use the GPA as an indicator of how hard the applicant will work on the job. As a general rule, employers are most impressed by GPAs of 3.5 or higher. However, if the applicant has worked part-time during the school year and still participated in school activities, a GPA over 3.0 usually gives employers a favorable impression of the applicant's work ethic and capabilities.

INTEGRATED ACADEMICS
Visual Arts
Provide each student with poster board on which to create a collage illustrating the information that goes into a resume. (For a few weeks before assigning the collage, you may want to have students bring magazines to class.) Provide the class with an instant camera to take photos of each other demonstrating some aspect of a skill that could appear on a resume, or have students scan photos they've already taken. Encourage students to use the photos in their collages. Display the collages around the room for a few days.

Illustration 14-5 Partial List of Marcela Gomez's References

Marcela Gomez
868 Fairmont Boulevard
Topeka, KS 66614-2253
785-555-0189
marcela.gomez@gomez.name

REFERENCES

Marlena Trent
Office Manager
Environmental Research Group
898 Bridgeway Drive
Topeka, KS 66606-1596
785-555-0102

Steve Rusinski
Chair, Business Technology Department
Oak Park High School

Ask Your References

Being a reference for someone can take a lot of work. Your references must write letters or be available to talk to potential employers on the phone. They also need to know you well and know about your career goals. Because of the effort involved, you need to ask people if they are willing to be references. Do not assume someone has the time or feels comfortable being your reference—always ask.

Asking your references can be as casual as talking to someone in person or as formal as writing a letter. Just be sure your references understand what they will have to do. Give all your references a copy of your resume so they have up-to-date information about your job plans.

Follow Up with Your References

Keep your references informed. Let them know if your plans change, if you find a job, or if you get an interview with one of their referrals. After your job search ends, thank your references for their time and energy. Write a thank-you letter to each reference that expresses your appreciation. Illustration 14-6 shows a thank-you letter Marcela Gomez wrote to one of her references.

In Activity 14-4, "Coming to Terms," you will demonstrate your understanding of some of the important terms in this chapter.

Marcela Gomez
868 Fairmont Boulevard
Topeka, KS 66614
(785) 555-0189
marcela.gomez@gomez.name

March 5, 2004

Mr. Steve Rusinski
Oak Park High School
100 Campus Drive
Topeka, KS 66606

Dear Mr. Rusinski:

Yesterday at a career fair, I met Dr. Alice Hranko of the State Hazardous
Materials Bureau. During our conversation, I happened to mention that you are
one of my references. Dr. Hranko looked thoughtful; then she told me about a
part-time entry-level administrative support position she believed was open at
International Environmental Consulting. She said Dr. Colleen Tomba, the field
office manager with the company, was the person to contact. Dr. Hranko even
suggested I use her name as a referral when I wrote to Dr. Tomba!

Mr. Rusinski, I am very grateful for your support. Thank you so much for all the
help you are giving me during my continuing job search. I'll let you know how
things go with International Environmental Consulting.

Sincerely,

Marcela Gomez

Marcela Gomez

TEACH

Tell students to print thank-you letters
on the same high-quality paper used
for the resume. Point out to students
how Marcela (Illustration 14-6) bal-
anced the look of the short letter by
using wider margins and a modified
block format.

Handwritten thank-you notes on
nice note cards or stationery are also
an effective, personal way to thank
references for their efforts.

DIFFERENT LEARNING STYLES

Print Learners

Have students work with a partner to write the following letters: (1) a letter that asks the partner
to be a reference, (2) a letter of reference for the partner or a letter that denies the request, and
(3) a thank-you letter for agreeing to be a reference or a letter of acknowledgment for the denial.
Have partners meet with another pair to exchange letters. Have the new partners read and edit
each other's work. Return all letters to the original partners after the editing is complete.

What do you think?

Use **TM14-05**.
Students' answers will vary.

TEACH

Encourage students to concentrate on generating ideas for their cover letter without thinking about clarity of expression, logic, grammar, punctuation, spelling, and format. Suggest that students use proven techniques such as brainstorming, webbing, nonstop writing, or tree maps to capture their creative ideas.

Cover Letters

A **cover letter** is an introduction to your resume and to you. Although it may sound like a routine document, a cover letter may be more powerful than your resume. A good cover letter can convince an employer to read your resume and possibly invite you for an interview. A bad cover letter will almost certainly get your resume discarded.

What do you think? What do you think should be included in a good cover letter—a letter that will convince an employer to read your resume?

Learning how to write a good cover letter is not difficult. The secrets are:

- To write about the employer's needs.
- To use a standard business format and correct grammar, spelling, and punctuation.

REAL PEOPLE
REAL CAREERS

Travel Booking Agent

When Matthew Chaifetz was thirteen, he was ill and could not attend school. After his homework was done, Matthew was not interested in playing video games. Instead, he decided to start a business that involved his two favorite passions: travel and flying. With his research, Matthew started booking travel for his relatives and friends. He was so successful that he decided to become a travel agent and receive a commission for what he enjoyed doing.

Travel agents must put up with increasing regulations and often lower or no commissions. Matthew eliminated that problem by creating his own company, Innovative Travel Concepts (ITC). ITC maintains records, files airline reports, makes commission payments, and offers travel agents access to reservation networks and travel organizations for a fee. ITC eliminates the headaches for the travel agents. Matthew's business was so successful that it was appraised at over $1 million while he was still a senior in high school. He continues to travel and is learning how to fly, his passion. Matthew Chaifetz's goal is to own an airline. With his growing resume of experiences, his dream should become a reality.

For more information about:
- Matthew Chaifetz, look under the *YoungBiz 100* at **www.youngbiz.com**.
- travel agents, explore **www.astanet.com** or search for *Travel Agent* at **www.bls.gov** under *Occupational Outlook Handbook*.

Source: Mayeu, Patty. "Let's Make a Deal." *Y&E: The Magazine for Teen Entrepreneurs.* http://ye.entreworld.org

REAL PEOPLE—REAL CAREERS
Travel Booking Agent

Arrange students into two groups. Assign one group to learn about the issues faced by the travel agents at the web site of the American Society of Travel Agents, **www.astanet.com**. Assign the other group the job of researching career information about travel agents in the *Occupational Outlook Handbook* at **www.bls.gov**. Provide each group 10 to 15 minutes to compose a fact sheet and share their findings with the class. Fact sheets should contain at least six facts of information taken from the web sites. Each member of the group is to take part in researching or teaching.

Think of a cover letter as an application for a job and a resume as evidence that you are qualified for that job. In the first paragraph of a cover letter, express your interest in the position and explain why you are interested. In the second paragraph, explain to the employer what you can bring to the company. Remember, employers want to know why they should hire you. Finally in the last paragraph, request an interview. Effective cover letters accomplish all these tasks in three paragraphs. Notice how Marcela Gomez's cover letter in Illustration 14-7 on page 276 makes use of the introductory, body, and concluding paragraphs.

Introduction

Use the introductory paragraph to explain your purpose for writing the letter—to apply for a job. Express your interest in the position, and be sure to use the title of the job from the job description. Explain why you are interested in the position. Does it sound like the ideal match for you? Why? Are you especially interested in this particular company? Again, why? Be specific and impress employers with your understanding of how your interest fits *their* needs.

Body

Use the body of your cover letter to present your skills and accomplishments. Make an organized argument for how you can benefit the company. Support this claim with strong points from your resume. For example, the two years you volunteered at the local food bank show hard work and commitment. Your high GPA shows intelligence and responsibility. Also, relate your characteristics to the specific job requirements. If the position needs someone who is good at motivating others, write about the fund-raiser you planned and how many people you recruited to help. By pointing out how you achieved positive results, you are showing the employer you are capable and self-confident. You are answering that famous employer question: "Why should I hire this person?"

Conclusion

In the concluding section, ask for an interview and indicate when and how you will follow up your cover letter. For example, you may state that you will call in a week. Then make sure you follow up as you say you will. If you do not, your chance of scheduling an interview and getting the job will be slim. Also, tell the employer how to contact you and say you look forward to hearing from him or her. Finally, use a standard closing, such as *Sincerely* or *Cordially*.

In Activity 14-5, "Writing a Cover Letter," you will have an opportunity to check your ability to write an effective cover letter.

CAREER SUCCESS TIP

Show the *you* attitude in your cover letters. Challenge yourself to make your points without using the word *I* more than once in a paragraph.

CAREER SUCCESS TIP

Cover Letter

Have students write rough drafts of a cover letter for their resumes. Then ask students to go back through the letter with a red pen and circle every *I*. Have students count the number of times they use the word *I*. Take a poll. Write the answers on the board. Ask students the following question: How many of you used the word *I* ten times or more? If anyone says he or she used it more than ten times, go to that number and begin there. If not, ask if anyone used the word *I* nine times, and so on. Have students rewrite their letters without so many uses of *I*.

Illustration 14-7 Marcela Gomez's Cover Letter (Block Style)

TEACH

Point out that Marcela Gomez addressed her letter to a specific person—Dr. Tomba. Tell students that in some cases, they will need to conduct research in order to identify the name of the person to whom they should address their cover letter. Normally that person has the authority to hire for the job. Students should avoid sending cover letters addressed "To Whom It May Concern."

TEACH

Explain that because employers often use a job application as a screening tool, students need to complete applications carefully. In your discussion of the list of tips on page 277 of the student edition, you may wish to add the following:

• If the application asks for the pay range you are willing to accept, write *negotiable*. If it asks what you were paid at a previous job, write *confidential*.

• If you have only unpaid work experience, such as in-service learning, internships, or community service, list these experiences in the Work History section of the application with the notation *Unpaid*. If you have both paid and unpaid work experience, list your paid experience in the Work History section and your unpaid experience on a separate sheet attached to the application.

• Consider your answer to the question "Do you know someone who works for our company?" The reputation of relatives or friends at the company may affect the employer's perception of you. A safe answer would be "I know several people who told me your company is a great place to work." Be prepared to answer more specifically during an interview.

(continued on next page)

Marcela Gomez
868 Fairmont Boulevard
Topeka, KS 66614-2253
(785) 555-0189
marcela.gomez@gomez.name

March 6, 2004

Dr. Colleen Tomba, Field Office Manager
International Environmental Consulting
239 Jefferson Street, Suite 401
Topeka, KS 66602-1756

Dear Dr. Tomba:

Dr. Alice Hranko of the State Hazardous Materials Bureau suggested writing to you about a possible environmental technician opening in your firm. Are you looking for someone with strong office skills and on-the-job experience? As a Business Technology student at Oak Park High School and a recent intern at Environmental Research Group, I meet those requirements.

My keyboarding speed is 50 wpm, and I formatted and proofread letters, memos, and research reports during my summer internship. The internship helped me become familiar with scientific terms as well as gave me practice answering and transferring calls on a multiline telephone, greeting clients, using Outlook, and working with a large Access database.

May we meet to discuss your specific requirements for an office assistant? My resume is enclosed for your convenience. I will call you Thursday morning to request an appointment. You may reach me before then at (785) 555-0819 or by e-mail at marcela.gomez@gomez.name. Thank you for your consideration of my application.

Sincerely,

Marcela Gomez

Marcela Gomez

Enclosure

CAREER SUCCESS TIP

Cover Letter

Tell students that a new cover letter should be written for each resume they send. Cover letters should be prepared with the prospective employer and the specific job in mind. Using a word processing program makes changing cover letters easy. Much of the letter may stay the same from employer to employer. By using merging capabilities, cover letters can be changed easily to target each employer. Remind students that for effective cover letters, they need to keep in mind the following: purpose, audience, content, and format.

—*Source: www.rpi.edu/web/writingcenter/cover_letter.html*

Job Applications

Some employers will require only a job application. Others will require an application in addition to a resume. Companies usually want you to fill out an application for two reasons:

- To give them a standard measure to compare applicants
- To protect them from charges of irresponsible or illegal hiring practices

Everyone's resume will include different information, but a job application includes the same information for every applicant. By requiring job applications, an employer can compare applicants to see whose qualifications best meet the requirements of the job.

Companies may also use job applications as a convenient way to get your legal permission for such things as drug tests and background checks. The application will clearly state that by signing the application, you give special permissions to the employer.

Before you begin to fill out a job application, study it to see what questions you are being asked. Most employers will allow you to take the application form home with you. However, some employers will require you to fill out the application at their offices. To be prepared for this situation, bring your Personal Fact Sheet with you when you go to pick up an application.

To have the best chance of getting an interview, follow these tips:

1. If possible, get an extra copy of the application. If you cannot get an extra copy, make a practice copy.
2. Read the *entire* application form before you start filling it out.
3. Follow the instructions carefully and exactly. Many employers use an applicant's ability to follow the directions on the application as a screening tool.
4. Answer every question. If a question does not apply to you, write *NA* (not applicable) in the space. You want the employer to know that you didn't overlook the question. For example, an application might ask you to supply any names you have used in the past. This question will apply to you only if you have legally changed your name.
5. Be honest, accurate, and thorough.
6. Print neatly in dark blue or black ink; type the answers on a typewriter; or scan the form into your computer, fill in the blanks, and print the completed version.
7. Whenever you can, answer questions using measurable statements. For example, instead of writing that you ranked high in your class, write that you ranked in the top 10 percent of your class.

In Activity 14-6, "Completing a Job Application," you will practice completing a job application.

> **❝ A professional is a person who can do his best at a time when he doesn't particularly feel like it. ❞**
>
> —*Alistair Cooke, Broadcaster and Author*

- If an application asks whether you have ever been fired and why, answer with a positive statement. For example, rather than writing "I was fired from XYZ Company for being tardy," write "My termination from XYZ Company led me to develop better communication and planning skills." Make only *positive* statements about former employers.
- When listing references on an application, choose only those people who will give you a good recommendation. If you know a previous supervisor will be a poor reference, ask another supervisor at the company to act as your reference.
- Some applications ask about criminal records. Learn what information your state allows employers to request. Be aware that most states provide more protection for juveniles' records. Then provide only the information requested that the law requires applicants to give employers. For example, if the application states "List any felony convictions on your record," do not supply information about arrests or misdemeanors. If you have any convictions, add a short statement referring the employer to a strong reference who has agreed to support your fitness for the job.

APPLY

Have students complete **Activity 14-6, "Completing a Job Application,"** that appears on page 282. Teaching suggestions and the solution for this activity appear on page 282. An activity worksheet can be found on the Career Portfolio and Resource CD—**Text Activity 14-6.pdf**.

DIFFERENT LEARNING ABILITIES

Dyslexia

Write key words about resumes and cover letters on note cards. Then organize the class into two groups. Give Team 1 a card. A student has one minute to draw images to help his or her teammates guess the word on the card. The student drawing may not speak, gesture, or use numbers or words. If the team guesses the word, give them a point. Then have a member of the other team draw a card and begin play with that team. The team with the most points wins.

Pre-Employment Tests

More and more companies are requiring potential employees to take **pre-employment tests** to determine everything from personality type to technical skills. Regardless of the kind of test, the employer has only one reason for wanting you to take it—to decide whether you are right for the job.

Marcela Gomez's hard work has paid off! She had a preliminary telephone interview with the environmental consulting company last week. The interviewer said the company was interested in setting up a formal interview. Before the interview, though, Marcela would need to take a pre-employment test to determine whether her ethical standards matched those of the company. Marcela understood how sensitive the work was that the firm did. So she could see the value of the test to the company.

However, Marcela was nervous. How could she prepare for the test? What types of questions would be on the test? She knew her chance of getting the position would depend on how well she did on the test.

Marcela gathered her courage and called her contact at the company. She asked the interviewer to describe the test and explain how the results would be evaluated. What type of score would Marcela need to pass the test? She was relieved when the interviewer offered to send Marcela a sheet that explained the test and included a few sample questions. Marcela knew she would do well on the test if she had a chance to prepare.

If you are asked to take a pre-employment test, find out what kind of test you will take. Knowing what the test measures will help you determine whether and how you can prepare. Employers test all sorts of things, but their tests usually fall into one of three categories: personality, ability, and integrity.

Personality Tests

Employers use personality tests to determine how you respond to authority, what motivates you, how well you work on a team, and so on. Personality tests help employers figure out whether your personality matches the characteristics needed for the job. For example, the job requirements of a librarian are not a good match for a person who

DIFFERENT LEARNING STYLES

Print Learners

Have students work in small groups to research and prepare a report on the different tests that employers give to prospective employees. Have students use the information in this chapter plus information they receive from interviews with people in employment agencies, human resources departments at local companies, and small local businesses. Each member of the group is to be responsible for helping to research or write the report. Ask groups to volunteer to give an oral report on their findings.

works best out of doors. You can't study for personality tests—just answer the questions honestly and accurately. Keep in mind that if your personality does not match a job's characteristics, you are unlikely to be satisfied with the job. So you should not "change" your personality to try to match a specific job.

In Activity 14-7, "Personality Tests," you will use the Internet to explore personality tests.

Ability Tests

Ability tests can be general or specific. General ability tests show employers whether you have the basic skills necessary for almost any job. These tests measure such skills as spelling, vocabulary, reading, and math. Specific ability tests measure your skills for a particular type of job. For example, if you're applying for an administrative support job, you might be required to take a word processing test.

You can study for both kinds of ability tests if you know the type of test and the score you will need to pass the test. If possible, ask the employer in advance about any ability tests you must take. Try to find out what will be covered on the tests and what level of accomplishment is considered acceptable. For example, ask the employer what level of math is measured in a general ability test. Also ask if you may see some sample questions.

> **"** Always do right! This will gratify some people and astonish the rest. **"**
>
> —*Mark Twain, Author*

Integrity Tests

> How would you feel about reporting a fellow employee for theft, drug abuse, or sleeping on the job?

What do you think?

Employers use integrity tests to try to find out how honest you are. An integrity test can be as simple as a true-false questionnaire or as complicated as a lie-detector test. Sometimes integrity tests present tricky situations. For example, you might be asked a question such as this:

> Tia's family income barely meets the family's expenses. They have no extra money. When each band member was asked to contribute toward new uniforms, Tia knew she could not ask her family for the money. One day you see Tia taking a twenty-dollar bill from the cash register. Do you report her?

In this case, the employer wants to know whether you sympathize with Tia or whether you will report the theft. You should be prepared for this type of question if you will be required to take an integrity test. You can't study for integrity tests. Just answer each question honestly.

In Activity 14-8, "Learning from Others," you will find out about pre-employment tests from an experienced professional.

Have students complete **Activity 14-7, "Personality Tests,"** that appears on page 282. Teaching suggestions and the solution for this activity appear on page 282. An activity worksheet can be found on the Career Portfolio and Resource CD— **Text Activity 14-7.doc**.

What do you think?

Use **TM14-06**.
Students' answers will vary. Answers could include a discussion of ethics (refer to Chapter 12) and the problem of a supervisor finding out that an employee did not report the problem.

CLOSE

Have students complete **Activity 14-8, "Learning from Others,"** that appears on page 282. Teaching suggestions and the solution for this activity appear on page 282. An activity worksheet can be found on the Career Portfolio and Resource CD— **Text Activity 14-8.doc**.

INTEGRATED ACADEMICS
Language Arts/Visual Arts
Have students continue in their groups from the activity for Print Learners on page 278. Have student groups create a flyer that explains the different tests that companies ask prospective employees to take. Groups may use computer graphics to enhance their flyers. Post the flyers around the room. Have students select a panel to critique the flyers.

279

Remind students about the objectives set forth at the beginning of the chapter, and use this summary to reinforce the concepts presented in this chapter.

Career Journal

Ask students to spend 10 minutes writing Career Journal entries that answer the following questions:
1. How well did what you thought you knew match what the chapter presented?
2. What questions do you now have about the chapter topics, and where do you think you can find the answers to those questions?
3. How will the content of the chapter help you investigate *your* career?

ASSESS

Administer the printed objective test for Chapter 14, available with this package. Test solutions are found in the *Teacher's Edition* of *Investigating Your Career Chapter Tests*. Use the **Exam***View®* CD to create your own objective test for this chapter.

IN A NUTSHELL

- **I can complete a Personal Fact Sheet.**

   My Personal Fact Sheet contains basic information about me. I will use the information on my Personal Fact Sheet when I write resumes and cover letters, complete job applications, prepare for job interviews, and fill out employment forms.

- **I can describe an effective resume.**

   An effective resume uses "resume-ese," an attractive visual style, and attractive formatting. In addition, an honest resume is critical to success.

- **I can write a resume.**

   I can adapt my resume by highlighting my skills, education, and work experience that match the requirements of a specific job. I can use the various elements of my resume to focus on my qualifications. A resume may be organized as a chronological, functional, or combination resume.

- **I know how to select references.**

   My references should be people who know me well and are familiar with my abilities and goals. I need to ask permission from my references and make sure they have up-to-date information about my job search. I also need to write a thank-you letter to each of my references.

- **I know how to write a cover letter.**

   My cover letter should convince an employer to read my resume and offer me an interview. In my cover letter, I should say what job I am interested in, why I am interested in it, and why I am a good candidate. I should also ask for an interview.

- **I know how to complete a job application.**

   I need to make sure I have all the necessary information when I fill out a job application. I should answer every question thoroughly and honestly or write *NA* if a question does not apply to me.

- **I can describe various pre-employment tests.**

   Pre-employment tests provide an employer with information about me. Personality tests help employers determine whether my personality matches the job. Ability tests measure my skills for a job. Integrity tests measure my honesty.

Suggestions for Parents and Family Members

Helping in the Job Search
Ways parents and family members can assist teenagers in their career discovery process and job search include:

1. Offering to proofread your teen's resumes, cover letters, and thank-you letters.
2. Recognizing the emotional toll job hunting takes (especially when the desired job goes to someone else) and consoling your teen and encouraging him or her to keep trying.
3. Expressing admiration for your teen's determination.

ACTIVITY 14-1   Personal Fact Sheet

Print the **Personal Fact Sheet** form from your Career Portfolio and Resources CD, or use the handout provided by your teacher. Fill in the information requested on the form. Attach a separate sheet of paper if you need additional space to fill in any section of the form.

ACTIVITY 14-2   Case Challenges

Review pages 261–264. Then working with a partner and using "resume-ese," rewrite each of the segments below. Use your imagination to provide needed information. Use your judgment to eliminate unneeded information.

1. Star Dry Cleaning, Counter Associate
   Receiving clothes, drapes, and so on, from customers. Counting and recording items for dry cleaning on the order ticket and giving the customer the numbered stub of the ticket. Inspecting items for stains or damage and pretreating stains. Using label gun to attach order number labels to each garment. Sorting garments by type of load into processing bins. After items have been cleaned, grouping items from each order and bagging and tying the order together. Hanging customers' completed orders by name on the automatic racks. Retrieving orders for customers and collecting payment. Calling customers if there is a problem with their order. I was named Associate of the Month in December, the busiest month of the year. I also received two raises in my first six months on the job.

2. Quality Body Shop, Paint Prepper
   Clean the vehicle: wash, wipe with tack cloth, and wipe with wax and grease remover. Prepare the vehicle for painting: mask off windows, mirrors, door handles, and trim. Prime salvaged fenders, doors, hoods, and trunk lids with spray gun and primer paint. Jam new parts (paint edges of new parts with final color). Set up prepared parts in paint booth for painter. After the painting is completed and dried, then I remove masking. Then prepare the vehicle for delivery to the customer: vacume vehicle, wash windows, and dust instrument panel and interior. Clean paint booth by vacuming to remove dust and particles. Primed, jammed, and masked 2-3 vehicles per day. Consistently competed preparation work 10 to 15 percent faster than scheduled.

ACTIVITY 14-3   Writing a Resume

Choose one of the organizational styles described on pages 266–271 and shown in Illustrations 14-2, 14-3, and 14-4. Write a resume for yourself in the style you chose. Use "resume-ese" to answer the important employer question "How can this person help the company succeed?"

Activity 14-2: Case Challenges

This activity gives students practice in selecting, organizing, and editing descriptive resume content, including correcting parallelism, punctuation, and/or spelling errors.

Solution: Although students' answers will vary, they should reflect the changes described below.

1. Students should condense the information; use past tense throughout; eliminate the use of *I*; correct the spelling of *retreiving*; and add some type of measurable accomplishment, such as "Served an average of 32 customers a day."

2. Students should condense the information, use present or present perfect tense as appropriate, eliminate the use of *I*, correct the spelling of *vacume* and its derivatives, and put the steps in sequential order.

Activity 14-3: Writing a Resume

In this activity, students prepare a traditional resume, applying all they have learned about resume writing.

Note that although students can prepare their resumes on a typewriter, using word processing software makes the project much easier. If students do not have access to a computer, suggest that they carefully and thoroughly edit their handwritten draft before typing a final copy.

Solution: Resumes will vary. You may wish to have students exchange resumes and critique each other's resumes using the checklist on the form for this activity. Students often will see things in another student's resume that they are unable to detect in their own. Emphasize that students should include positive as well as negative comments in their critiques. Students should then be given the opportunity to revise their resumes based on the comments they receive.

Activity 14-1: Personal Fact Sheet

In this activity, students complete a fact sheet that will be the basis for their resumes and that they will use to fill in job application forms.

Remind students that the information on their personal fact sheets will need to be updated regularly.

Solution: Answers will vary.

Activity 14-4:
Coming to Terms

This activity reinforces students' understanding of some of the key terms from this chapter. Instruct students to both define **and** explain the purpose and importance of each item.

Solution: Answers will vary but should reflect a correct understanding of how each item relates to the job application process.

Activity 14-5:
Writing a Cover Letter

In this activity, students apply what they have learned about writing cover letters.

You may wish to discuss the two formats of business letters shown in Illustration 14-6 (modified block style) and Illustration 14-7 (block style). Ask students to find the similarities and differences between the two styles.

Solution: Cover letters will vary. You may wish to have students exchange cover letters and critique each other's letters using the checklist on the form for this activity. Stress that students should include positive as well as negative critiques. Allow students the opportunity to revise their letters based on the comments they receive.

Activity 14-6:
Completing a Job Application

This activity gives students practice filling out a job application. Mention to students that using their Personal Fact Sheet will help them complete the activity. Also remind them to use the same job information they used to write the cover letter in Activity 14-5.

Solution: Answers will vary. Look for complete responses to each item, clear printing, and neat forms.

Activity 14-7:
Personality Tests

This activity increases students' understanding of different approaches to personality tests and why employers use these tests. If you prefer to use a site different from the one listed in the student text, try a search using the keywords *personality tests*.

Solution: Answers will vary. In a class discussion, encourage students

---

ACTIVITY 14-4   **Coming to Terms**

Describe the purpose and importance of each of the following terms to the job application process. Be sure to distinguish how terms 2–4 serve different purposes.

1. Personal Fact Sheet
2. Chronological resume
3. Functional resume
4. Combination resume
5. References

ACTIVITY 14-5   **Writing a Cover Letter**

Choose a job in your career field from an advertisement in the newspaper or on the Internet. If you cannot find an appropriate advertised job, use your imagination to supply any needed information, such as the company name. Write a cover letter applying for the job. Use a business format as shown in Illustrations 14-6 and 14-7.

ACTIVITY 14-6   **Completing a Job Application**

1. Print the **Job Application** forms from your Career Portfolio and Resources CD, or use the handouts provided by your teacher. Fill in the information requested on the forms as though you were applying for the job you used in your job objective on your resume.

2. What differences do you notice between the two job application forms?

ACTIVITY 14-7   **Personality Tests**

To take a personality test, go to the site recommended by your teacher or try *www.personalitypathways.com*.

ACTIVITY 14-8   **Learning from Others**

Take notes and summarize the presentation of the guest speaker from a contract employment agency that specializes in placing people in temporary jobs.

1. What types of pre-employment tests does the contract employment agency give to job applicants?

2. How does the contract employment agency recommend that job applicants prepare for those tests?

3. How does the contract employment agency use the results of the tests?

---

to express their opinions about the accuracy of personality tests and the usefulness of these tests to employers.

Activity 14-8:
Learning from Others

This activity gives students the opportunity to learn from a guest speaker about pre-employment tests used by a contract employment agency. At the time you arrange for the

speaker, provide an advance copy of the questions students will ask.

Solution: Answers will vary, but should accurately reflect the speaker's comments.

Interviewing for a Job

15

Michaela tried to relax as she sat in the front office of the local radio station. She had applied for several summer internships, and her first interview was with Susan Donnelly, the station manager of KAAZ. Michaela had practiced interviewing and had prepared a list of questions she thought she might be asked, but she was still nervous. Was she dressed appropriately? Would she know the right things to say? Would the manager ask the same questions Michaela had prepared, or would the interview include a lot of unexpected questions?

"Are you Michaela?" asked a woman smiling at her. "I'm Susan Donnelly." Ms. Donnelly was casually dressed, but Michaela was glad she had worn businesslike pants and a jacket. She wanted to show her interviewer she was serious about the job. Michaela stood up to shake hands and followed Ms. Donnelly into the manager's office.

"Tell me about yourself and why you're interested in radio," Ms. Donnelly instructed. Michaela was relieved—the first question was easy and was one she had practiced answering. As Michaela talked about her lifelong interest in music, she began to relax. The interview started to feel like a friendly conversation. By the time she stood up to shake hands and say good-bye, Michaela was positive that she had made a good impression. She went straight home to write a thank-you note to Ms. Donnelly. "Even if I don't get this job," she thought, "I'll be better prepared for the next interview."

How can you highlight your best qualities in an interview? What should you do to make a good impression?

> What do you think?

OBJECTIVES

After completing this chapter, you will be able to:

- Describe the purposes and styles of interviews.
- Explain how to prepare for interviews.
- Describe your preparations before an interview.
- Describe how to have a successful interview.
- Follow up after an interview.

Key Terms:

- unstructured interview
- structured interview
- behavioral interview
- performance interview
- stress interview
- group interview
- screening interview

Chapter Overview

Chapter 15
Interviewing for a Job

FOCUS

In Chapter 15, students explore the purposes of interviews and the different styles of interviews. Then they prepare for interviews by planning answers to questions, researching the company, and practicing interviewing. Students learn that interview success depends on preparation, practice, and competent follow-up.

Use the **Objectives** and **Key Terms** printed in the margin to help students focus on the content of this chapter. Use the **video segment** for Chapter 15 to trigger discussion.

> What do you think?

Use **TM15-01**.
Students' answers will vary but should emphasize the positive aspects of education, training, experience, and work habits.

Career Journal

Ask students to spend 10 minutes writing Career Journal entries that answer the following questions:
1. What do you think this chapter will cover?
2. What do you already know about these topics?
3. What three things do you want to learn about these topics?

CHAPTER RESOURCES and MATERIALS

Activities & Projects book
Instructor's Resource CD
- Forms and Worksheets for Chapter Activities 15-1 through 15-6
- Internet Links for Chapter 15
- PowerPoint Presentation for Chapter 15
- Lesson Plans
- Teaching Masters for Chapter 15
- Video Discussion Guide for Chapter 15

Chapter Tests book
ExamView® CD
Video
Web Site

TEACH

Students may think that their primary purpose in an interview is to convince the employer to hire them. Emphasize that students' primary purpose should be to determine whether they want the job. Students should not lose sight of this purpose in their anxiety to convince the employer to hire them.

Understanding the main purpose of employers during interviews allows students to plan effective interview responses. To help students appreciate the employer's purpose, you may want to base a class discussion on the following questions:
• How can an employer use an interview to determine your job skills?
• What does your appearance and attitude during an interview tell an employer about how well you will fit into the company?

What do you think?

Use **TM15-02**.
Students' answers will vary.

The Interview Process

What will happen at a job interview? Will all interviewers ask the same questions? What should you say, what should you wear, and how should you act? The interview process may seem overwhelming at first. However, if you know what to expect at an interview, you can prepare for it. You may even find that interviewing is a positive experience.

Purposes of Interviews

The purpose of an interview is not the same for you and for the employer. The employer's purpose is to find out whether you have the skills needed for a specific position. The interviewer will want to determine your job skills, appraise your appearance and attitude, and find out if you will fit into the company.

Your first purpose at an interview is to assess the position and the company to find out if you want the job. Use the interview process to determine exactly what the job entails and whether the company matches your goals and values. If you think the position is what you want and you believe you will fit the company's needs, then your second purpose is to convince the interviewer that you are the best applicant for the job.

What do you think?

What qualities of a company will you want to determine before you accept a job? How will you find out about these qualities?

As Darius approached the Step-Links administration building, he thought about his *P*A*T*H to Success*. He had based his career goals on his *P*A*T*H*, and as he walked, he looked at the list he had written from his goals. The list was qualities he strongly believed his workplace should have. Darius wanted to be sure all his jobs in special education matched his beliefs about education and his personal values.

Ms. Greenwald greeted Darius, and while giving him a tour of the camp for special needs children, she described the job duties of a teacher's aide. She emphasized that the main reason Step-Links hired aides was so each teacher could work with a small number of students. Darius mentally checked off one of his requirements for a

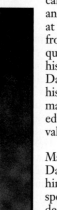

ONLINE RESOURCES

Check out the web site **www.investigatingyourcareer.com** for teacher resources, student activities, and replacements for broken links for this chapter. To access the teacher resources:

Username: career
Password: investigate

place where he would work. He asked if Step-Links thought special needs children should be treated as individuals or as a group. To his relief, Ms. Greenwald said that Step-Links believed each child should be treated as an individual but should also interact with other children.

Then Darius asked some specific questions about the duties of an aide. Would he be preparing for the activities and cleaning up, or would he be involved with the children, assisting the teacher? After Ms. Greenwald reassured him he would be assisting teachers, Darius thought that working at Step-Links would give him some valuable insight into special needs teaching. He hoped he would be offered the job. He was already looking forward to working at Step-Links.

Styles of Interviews

A typical job interview takes place at an employer's location and is a conversation or series of conversations with one or more people in the company. By the time you arrive for the interview, the interviewer will have reviewed your resume and cover letter and perhaps spoken with you briefly on the phone. However, paperwork and phone calls cannot tell an interviewer what makes you special, how you interact with people, and how you present yourself. An interviewer can find out these qualities about you only by talking to you and asking you questions. How the interviewer asks questions and the type of questions the interviewer asks identify the style of the interview.

Unstructured Interview

If you have an interview at a small company, the interviewer is likely to be the owner or manager of the business and the interview will probably be an unstructured interview. An **unstructured interview** is usually informal and conversational. The questions are often aimed at discovering whether you can and want to perform the job tasks. While an unstructured interview allows you to express your personality, you also need to emphasize your skills and experience.

Structured Interview

A **structured interview** is formal and frequently uses preplanned questions. The interviewer may use a form to rate your skills, attitude, appearance, education/training, and qualifications in order to compare you with other applicants for the position. Because this type of interview is based on factual information, you may need to find ways to show the interviewer your unique personality. A structured interview may include one or more of the following styles.

- In a **behavioral interview**, the interviewer asks you to provide specific examples of how you have successfully used the skills required for the available job. The interviewer may ask you to describe a situation where you resolved a conflict, showed leadership ability, or used problem-solving skills.

TEACH

Invite a human resources manager or someone who hires teens on a regular basis to speak to the class. Ask the speaker to discuss interview objectives from the employer's viewpoint.

> 66 The world stands aside to let anyone pass who knows where he is going. 99
>
> —David Starr Jordan, First President of Stanford University

DIFFERENT LEARNING ABILITIES
Gifted

Have students prepare role-play skits for unstructured interviews and the different types of structured interviews. Gifted students could act as interviewers. The remainder of the class should act as people being interviewed. Tell the interviewers to create the type of company they represent and the type of job students are applying for and to share this information with the class. Other students then come to the front of the class to be interviewed for the opening. Make sure students role-play different types of interviews.

• In a **performance interview**, you are asked to demonstrate a specific skill. For example, you may have to complete a task on a computer to show you can use a specific type of software competently.
• In a **stress interview**, the interviewer intentionally tries to upset you to determine how you react under pressure. Stress interviews are usually used only for high-pressure positions that involve stress on a daily basis.
• In a **group interview**, two or more employees of the company are present at the interview in order to get different people's opinions of you and your qualifications.
• A **screening interview** is a preliminary interview that an employer uses to determine whether you have the basic qualifications for a position. Screening interviews are usually conducted on the telephone or at a job fair.

 Use Activity 15-1, "Coming to Terms," to check your understanding of the different interview styles.

Preparing for Interviews

A successful interview does not just happen. Before any interviews are scheduled, you must prepare carefully and practice, practice, practice. Before you know where, when, and with whom you will interview, you need to review your resume, plan answers to questions you may be asked, and plan questions you will ask an interviewer.

Know Your Resume

An interviewer will often ask you questions about an activity or experience listed on your resume. For example, if you worked as a basketball coach for young children, the interviewer may ask you to describe the responsibilities you had, how you interacted with the children's parents, and how you dealt with safety issues. Be prepared to discuss in detail any part of your resume.

Plan Answers to Common Questions

Although interviews will be different, you can expect to be asked some of the same questions at every interview. By knowing in advance some of the common questions most interviewers ask, you can prepare your answers. Be especially careful how you answer questions that may reflect unfavorably on you, such as a question about your weaknesses. Answer such questions truthfully, but try to frame your answer in a positive way. For example, if you are uncomfortable speaking before a group, explain how you plan to overcome this weakness by taking a speech class.

CAREER SUCCESS TIP

Be prepared for a telephone screening interview. Keep a file containing your resume, Personal Fact Sheet, information about employers, and paper and pen next to the phone.

CAREER SUCCESS TIP

Phone Etiquette

Tell students that once they have applied for a job, they need to be on their best phone behavior. They never know when a prospective employer may call. If students have answering machines, they may want to ask a parent or guardian to make sure the message is appropriate. When speaking to a prospective employer, students should listen, be polite, and be ready to answer whatever questions they are asked.

Illustration 15-1 lists common questions asked by most interviewers. Note that some of the questions relate to an interview for a specific job while others are general questions. Think about how you should answer each question. Know what you want to say, but don't memorize your answers. In an interview, you should appear natural and self-confident.

Illustration 15-1 Common Interview Questions

Common Interview Questions

1. Tell me about yourself. How would you describe yourself?
2. What are your hobbies and interests?
3. What are your strengths? your weaknesses?
4. Why are you interested in this job, company, or career?
5. What did you learn from one of the experiences listed on your resume?
6. What rewards are you looking for in a job, workplace, or career?
7. Give an example of a conflict you've had with a coworker, and explain how you handled it.
8. What courses did you like best (or least) and why?
9. What extracurricular activities did you like best (or least) and why?
10. What type of supervisor or management style do you prefer?
11. Why should I hire you?
12. Have you ever been fired from a job? If so, please explain.
13. What do you see yourself doing five years from now?
14. What are your long-term career goals, and how do you plan to achieve them?

In Activity 15-2, "Your Answers to Common Questions," you will prepare answers to common interview questions.

Plan Answers to Illegal Questions

Employers cannot legally ask you about your religion, race, ethnicity or national origin, age, marital status, membership in certain organizations, or physical condition. How an interviewer phrases a question can determine whether the question is illegal. For example, an interviewer cannot ask the question "Do you have any disabilities?" However, "Do you have any physical conditions that might limit your ability to do the job?" is a legal question. Also, some questions are illegal during an interview but legal after you are hired for a position, such as whether you are a citizen of the United States.

Use **TM15-03**.
Students' answers will vary.

▬ TEACH ▬

When discussing Illustration 15-1, explain that promoting ability means reporting actual skill levels and showing how those skills resulted in real accomplishments. Employers look for applicants who can match personal abilities to job requirements.

Explain that the secret to successfully answering "Why should I hire you?" is to tell how your skills improve company results in money, image, or time.

▬ APPLY ▬

Have students complete **Activity 15-2, "Your Answers to Common Questions,"** that appears on page 301. Teaching suggestions and the solution for this activity appear on page 301. An activity worksheet can be found on the Career Portfolio and Resource CD—**Text Activity 15-2.doc**.

▬ ENRICH ▬

Have students complete **Activity 15-B, "One-Minute Summary,"** found in the *Investigating Your Career Activities & Projects* book.

This activity helps students answer the employer question "Why should I hire you?" Suggest that students incorporate the SCANS skills and competencies (page 183) into their one-minute summaries. Presenting their one-minute summaries to each other and receiving feedback will help students strengthen content and improve presentation skills.
Solution: The solution for this activity appears in the *Teacher's Edition* of *Investigating Your Career Activities & Projects.*

DIFFERENT LEARNING STYLES

Kinesthetic Learners

Create flash cards of important words from this chapter. Arrange the class into two teams. Have a student from one team draw a card and then use hand gestures and body language to act out the word's definition. The other students from this team try to guess the correct word within a two-minute time limit. Have the other team do the same. For every correct word, a team scores a point. The team with the most points at the end of the game wins.

What do you think?

Use **TM15-05**.
Students' answers will vary.

▬ TEACH ▬

The most effective way for students to achieve success in interviews is to practice interviewing. **Activity 15-3** is students' first practice interview. Evaluation forms provide students with a baseline against which to measure their upcoming improvement in interview skills. Two additional enrichment opportunities, described on pages 292 and 297, allow students to continue to practice interviewing skills and to measure their progress.

To ensure realism for the practice interviews, suggest that students dress in clothes appropriate to their interview situation. After the interviews, have students write a one-page summary describing interview skills they performed well, interview skills they need to improve, and a plan for improving their interview skills.

What do you think?

Use **TM15-06**.
Students' answers will vary.

▬ APPLY ▬

Have students complete **Activity 15-3, "Interview Practice,"** that appears on page 302. Teaching suggestions and the solution for this activity appear on page 302. An activity worksheet can be found on the Career Portfolio and Resource CD— **Text Activity 15-3.pdf**.

What do you think? What are some ways to answer an inappropriate question without mentioning the legality of the question?

CAREER FACT

In job interviews, two people with the same qualifications can be evaluated differently depending on the way they present themselves. One may show self-confidence, and the other may communicate self-doubt.

"What was that?" thought Steffi. She had applied for a job as a ski instructor, and in her interview, the owner of the ski lodge had said she might be asked to work during holidays. Then he asked her whether she celebrates Christmas. Steffi understands that the interviewer wants to know whether she can work on Christmas day, but she is uncomfortable discussing her religious beliefs. She also knows the question is illegal. Steffi thinks the question may have been an unintentional mistake and decides to give the lodge owner the benefit of the doubt. She ignores the reference to whether she celebrates Christmas and answers that she would be available to work on holidays.

Most employers understand the law and will not ask an illegal question, but you should be prepared just in case. Sometimes you might be able to sidestep the question gracefully. Other times you might not mind answering the question. But if you are uncomfortable, ask the interviewer how the question relates to your qualifications for the job. If you do not get a reasonable explanation, you can say you prefer not to answer the question. You may also decide you do not want to work for an organization where an interviewer asks such a question.

Plan Questions to Ask

An interview appears to emphasize the employer's need to decide whether you are appropriate for a job. However, equally important is for you to learn about the job and the company. In every interview, you need to analyze both the job and the company to be sure they will satisfy your values and career goals. Preparing questions before an interview will help you clarify what you hope to gain from a job and a company. In addition, asking intelligent and relevant questions will tell an interviewer you are serious about the job and are well prepared.

What do you think? What are some questions you might ask during an interview about a job in your career field?

Some or most of your questions may be answered before you ask them, when the interviewer explains the position and the job duties, so be sure to prepare a number of questions. Concentrate your questions on the requirements of the job, your qualifications, and the company. Do not ask questions about wages or benefits unless the interviewer brings up these subjects. Illustration 15-2 lists some questions you might ask.

In Activity 15-3, "Interview Practice," you will have an opportunity to practice how to ask and answer questions in an interview.

CAREER TREND

Self-Confidence

Tell students that when they are being interviewed, the prospective employer is watching how they sit, walk, speak, and act. Students want to appear self-confident, but not cocky. They want to be eager and enthusiastic, but not gushing with compliments. They want to convey an attitude of cooperation and a willingness to learn, as well as an attitude of self-assurance about their abilities. The biggest keys to a successful interview are to relax and to know they are fine just being themselves.

Illustration 15-2 Possible Questions to Ask in an Interview

Possible Interview Questions to Ask

1. What qualities would an ideal candidate have for this job?
2. How does this position relate to the rest of the company?
3. What type of training do you provide for this position?
4. May I have a copy of the written description for this job?
5. What would be your expectations of me during my first few months on the job?
6. What career growth opportunities might develop from my succeeding in this job?
7. What is the typical daily routine for this job?
8. Can you tell me about the people I would be working with in this job? Who would be my supervisor?
9. Do you have any more questions about my qualifications or experience?
10. What do you like about working for this company?

In your discussion of the questions applicants might ask in an interview, ask how each of the questions in Illustration 15-2 on page 289 will help students determine whether they want to work for an employer. In particular, ask students to explain how specific questions can help them find out whether the company matches their values and career goals. Also encourage students to use active listening during the interview so they can avoid asking questions the employer has already answered. Remind students to use an interested conversational tone while asking their questions rather than rattling off questions as quickly as they can.

Before the Interview

You have searched for jobs, identified the ones you want to pursue, practiced interviewing, and sent out resumes and cover letters. Now you are ready to follow up your resumes and arrange interviews. Sometimes an employer will call you as soon as your resume and cover letter arrive, but usually you must telephone the employer.

Claire is preparing to call Younger Brothers Dairy. The dairy is the premier producer of milk products in the Midwest, and Claire has applied for an internship in the farm manager's office. Claire sent her resume and cover letter to Younger Brothers last week, but she has not heard from the company.

When Claire calls Younger Brothers, she reaches Miss Dines, the assistant in human resources. Claire introduces herself and asks if she may speak to Mr. Marrero, the manager of the department. Because she can answer many applicants' questions, Miss Dines asks the nature of Claire's call. Claire replies that she mailed her resume ten days ago and asks if it has been received. Miss Dines checks the mail log and reassures Claire that her resume was received a week ago. Then Claire asks if the interviews for the internship are being scheduled. Miss Dines transfers Claire's call to Mr. Marrero, who is screening the internship candidates personally.

> **❝** Accept the challenges so that you may feel the exhilaration of victory. **❞**
> —*General George S. Patton*

INTEGRATED ACADEMICS
Visual Arts

Have students create a visual album of their emerging career selves. Students can use photos of themselves, drawings, magazine cutouts, and other art materials to make their albums interesting. Albums should show students at a younger age and then show them in the future. For example, a future business owner may include a photo of herself as a child running a lemonade stand, a photo of herself with a computer, and a magazine cutout of a woman (with the student's head superimposed) standing at the head of a boardroom table. Allow students to display their albums, but do not make it mandatory to do so.

Information about publicly held companies is more widely available than information about small local firms or privately held companies. Students looking for information about local firms should search for a company web site and check their local library. Many local newspapers publish special weekly business sections that feature stories about local firms. Students researching publicly held firms can check for company web sites or search the Internet using the keywords *company research*.

Claire introduces herself to Mr. Marrero, stating that Younger Brothers received her resume and cover letter a week ago. Then Claire mentions her interest in interviewing as the intern in the farm manager's office. She points out that her qualifications include an emphasis in production agriculture at Bartlett High School.

Mr. Marrero, who has several applicants for the internship, evades Claire's question about setting up an interview. Then Claire mentions that she has a letter of recommendation from her teacher, Mr. Sherman, and that he has offered to discuss Claire's suitability for the position. Mr. Sherman is well known in the farming community and has a reputation as an excellent teacher. Mr. Marrero schedules Claire's interview because he is impressed with her qualifications—and her persistence.

After you have arranged an interview, you must prepare for it. To prepare for a specific interview, you need to research the company, plan for a discussion about wages or salary, prepare your portfolio, practice interviewing for the specific job, and check last-minute details.

Research the Company

Learn everything you can about the company before your interview. The information you acquire from your research will not only allow you to create a positive impression in your interview, but also help you decide if you match the company's corporate culture. Try to have answers to the following questions before your interview:

CAREER SUCCESS TIP

Company web sites are good sources of information. You can also talk to your counselor and check magazines related to your career field.

- What products or services does the company provide?
- Who are the company's customers, and where are they located?
- Where are the company's offices or plants located?
- What is the company's corporate culture, including the dress code?
- What types of jobs exist in the company?
- How many employees does the company have?
- Who are the company's competitors?
- What is the company's reputation in the community?

As you conduct your research, you will likely find other useful information about the company. Analyze the information carefully. Remember, your career success will depend in part on whether the company's policies and culture match your personal and work values and your career and lifestyle goals.

CAREER SUCCESS TIP

Research the Company

Have students choose a company they might want to work for. The company does not have to be in your local area. Have students use the Internet to research the company. Brainstorm with students to help them make a list of questions they might have, such as information about benefits and advancement opportunities and whether the company is a good corporate citizen. Tell students that if a company is involved in something they disapprove of, that company is not the right one for them to work for.

Plan to Discuss Wage or Salary

Although an employer will usually not discuss pay with you until you receive a job offer, eventually you must decide the amount of money you want and believe you deserve. Before you interview for a specific job, know the standard pay range and decide the lowest pay you will accept. Analyzing your budget will help you identify the amount of money you need for your lifestyle goals. You should also consider any fringe benefits in determining your desired compensation.

Ms. Bando is interviewing Sonya for a landscape assistant's position with Clamara's Country Garden. Sonya knows she is well qualified because she is already two years into the agriculture career pathway at her high school. She has more skills than the average entry-level applicant. Sonya thinks the interview is going well. Ms. Bando seems especially impressed with Sonya's knowledge of the equipment and the latest trimming techniques. However, Sonya has one overwhelming concern. As much as she likes Clamara's, she cannot work there unless she earns the average pay for a landscape assistant. She knows what she needs to earn during the summer to be able to pay her school fees and to save for her education fund. Ms. Bando has not yet approached the subject of money. Should Sonya bring it up?

At last, Ms. Bando ends the interview. She offers Sonya the job and mentions an hourly rate that is $1 less than the amount Sonya had in mind. Sonya asks if there are periodic performance evaluations. When Ms. Bando says there are, Sonya asks if a positive evaluation means a pay raise. Ms. Bando explains that Sonya will have her first evaluation after a year on the job. If she receives a positive review, she can earn $1 more per hour. Sonya also learns she can work on weekends while in school, which will increase her savings more than she had planned. By waiting to ask the question about pay, Sonya seems eager to work, not greedy.

If an interviewer asks what salary or wage you expect, try to avoid naming an exact dollar amount. For example, ask what dollar range the company usually pays for the position and what benefits are provided.

Prepare Your Portfolio

Before you go to an interview, you will want to organize your portfolio to include only those materials you need for the specific job interview. Your interview portfolio—a small briefcase or a folder—should include the following items:

- **Your resume and reference list.** Include several copies of your resume. If you are planning to apply for different types of jobs and have prepared several different resumes, be sure to include the resume that is appropriate for the interview. If you have more than one interviewer, give a copy of your resume to each interviewer. Give the reference list to the interviewer when requested.

CHAPTER 15 · · · · · INTERVIEWING FOR A JOB

291

Have students complete **Activity 15-4, "Research Wages and Salaries,"** that appears on page 302. Teaching suggestions and the solution for this activity appear on page 302. An activity worksheet can be found on the Career Portfolio and Resource CD—**Text Activity 15-4.pdf**.

Have students complete **Activity 15-C, "Career Portfolio Preparation,"** found in the *Investigating Your Career Activities & Projects* book.

This activity helps students select documentation and work samples to include in their Career Portfolio. Remind students that portfolio materials may be items other than documents. Applicants in trucking firms, for example, may construct samples of the different types of knots they can tie.

Solution: The solution for this activity appears in the *Teacher's Edition* of *Investigating Your Career Activities & Projects.*

Help students become comfortable using their portfolio by having them practice interviewing using their portfolios. Divide the class into the same groups used for **Activity 15-3** (on page 302), and follow the instructions in the student text for that activity. Print **TM15-07** from the Instructor's Resource CD, and make enough copies for students to use in evaluating one practice interview for each person in their group. Encourage students to use their portfolio materials to demonstrate skills relevant to the job and to show samples of the type of work students could do for a specific employer. Also, instruct interviewers to ask for students' references. For classroom purposes, a sheet of paper labeled with the name of a portfolio item may be used for any "copy" left with the interviewer.

- **Your Personal Fact Sheet.** Your Personal Fact Sheet has all the information you will need to fill out an application or other employment forms.
- **Letters of reference.** Include copies of your letters of reference, not the originals. Bring only the letters that apply to the specific job interview.
- **Samples of your work.** Include any samples of your work that are relevant to the specific job. Be prepared to discuss these samples and to present them in the interview.
- **Blank notepaper and pen and pencil.** You should be prepared to take notes during an interview. Also try to write down the names and titles of everyone you meet, especially those of your interviewer(s).

CAREER SUCCESS TIP

If possible, videotape your practice interviews, particularly your dress rehearsal. You will be able to see for yourself any areas you need to improve.

Practice

Research, preparation, and practice are the keys to a successful job interview. After you have arranged an interview for a specific job, review the list of questions you may be asked and the list of questions you want to ask. Add some questions that relate to the specific job. Prepare answers and questions that relate to your research about the specific company. Then you will be able to show the interviewer that your interests and skills match the specific job and the goals of the company. To be thoroughly prepared, you may also want to include some questions about wages or salary.

Then practice interviewing again. In this practice, determine how you will use your portfolio to provide specific examples of your accomplishments. Your final practice interview should be a dress rehearsal. Wear the clothes you plan to wear to the interview, and project the image you want the interviewer to see.

Recheck Details

When you arranged your interview, you should have written down and saved:

- The date and time of the interview, the address, and directions to the interview location.
- The name and title of the interviewer and the title of the job.
- Any information about forms you should bring.

The day before the interview, call the company to confirm the date and time of the interview and check your portfolio. If you are unfamiliar with where the company is located, study a map to find the best route to get there and estimate the time you will need. Making a dry run a day or two before the scheduled interview will assure that you are not late for your appointment.

In Activity 15-4, "Research Wages and Salaries," you will use the Internet to find the amount of pay for jobs in your career field.

DIFFERENT LEARNING ABILITIES
Hearing Disabled/Visually Disabled
Hold a class discussion on what prospective employers can and cannot ask about disabilities during an interview. Tell students they will want to let the prospective employer know of their disability and how they can do the job for which they are applying in spite of the disability. Also let students know that during an interview, they may learn something about the job that would keep them from being able to do it well. Encourage students to be honest about their disability.

The Interview

You will probably be nervous before a job interview, especially if the interview is your first one. Nervousness and anxiety are normal in this situation. Your next interview will be easier because you have a better idea of what to expect. Keep in mind that your research and practice interviews have prepared you for the experience. Also, you know you have the basic qualifications for the job because you have been asked to come in for an interview. Arrive ahead of time, project a positive image, listen attentively, and try to relax.

Arrive Ahead of Time

Plan to arrive about 15 minutes before your scheduled interview. Arriving early will allow you some time to get comfortable in your surroundings before the interview actually starts. Use the time to relax and collect your thoughts.

Project a Positive Image

When you enter the building where your interview will be held, make sure your attitude, appearance, and posture convey a positive image of courtesy, enthusiasm, and self-confidence. Your positive image should be reinforced by what you say and how you say it.

> 66 **Never ask more or less of yourself than your best.** 99
>
> —*Proverb*

REAL PEOPLE
REAL CAREERS

Karate Teacher

Since age eight, karate has been a part of Lynn Mullen's life. Because karate is her passion, Lynn believes her career goal is to own a karate school. Before choosing karate, Lynn considered healthcare and job shadowed at a hospital. But being around sick people made Lynn sad. However, she enjoys babysitting and volunteering at the Boys and Girls Club. She likes working with children and helping people. She also likes physical activity, including karate. A strong family life is more important to her than money.

With a career in teaching karate and the independence that comes from owning her own business, Lynn can keep regular hours, work with young people, and do something she enjoys. In school, she is taking computer classes to learn how to set up an office and to learn web page design. She intends to pursue a college degree in business while teaching part-time at a karate studio. At age eighteen, Lynn has her black belt in karate. She can take her karate instructor's certification test after graduation.

For more information, investigate:
* *www.californiakarateclub.com*.
* a search engine such as *www.google.com*, using the keywords *teach karate*.

Source: "Kicking Off Your Career." *American Careers*, February 2002.

293

What do you think?

Use **TM15-09**.
Students' answers will vary.

▬▬ TEACH ▬▬

Discuss with students the impression employers receive from the following types of applicant behaviors.

Applicant's Behavior
1. Knows it all
2. Criticizes others
3. Talks too much
4. Says only *yes* or *no*
5. Plays down abilities and successes
6. Brings friends or parents to the interview

Employer's Impression
1. Applicant won't follow instructions.
2. Applicant is an immature complainer.
3. Applicant won't listen to customers/supervisors.
4. Applicant will do minimum amount to get by.
5. Applicant won't promote company's products and services.
6. Applicant is not confident is his or her ability to do the job.

Ask students what behavioral changes the applicant could make to improve the employer's impression.

What do you think?

What image do you communicate through your attitude, physical appearance, and body language? Is it the image you want to project?

Attitude

A positive attitude conveys self-confidence and will set you apart from other qualified applicants. To project a positive attitude:

- Demonstrate good posture in how you walk, sit, and stand.
- Smile when you meet someone and shake hands firmly.
- Show enthusiasm and energy.
- Be honest and sincere.
- Emphasize your best qualities and skills and your interest in the company.
- Be courteous, respectful, and friendly toward everyone you meet.

Appearance

Your appearance and dress will enhance or diminish the positive image you want to project. Although a bank requires employees to dress more conservatively than a manufacturer does, all employers want their employees to present a positive image to customers. The following guidelines will help you make a positive impression:

CAREER SUCCESS TIP

Dress better than the employees who have positions similar to the one for which you are interviewing, but avoid overdressing.

- Be freshly bathed and use an effective deodorant. Make sure your teeth are clean and your fingernails are clean and trimmed.
- Keep your hair neat, clean, and trimmed. A subdued, professional-looking style is best.
- Wear conservative clothing that is clean, pressed, properly fitted, and appropriate to the company. For example, if you are interviewing for a food-server position, don't wear a business suit. However, a suit is appropriate if you are interviewing for a receptionist or retail sales position.
- Wear few or no accessories. Men should limit their jewelry to a conservative ring. Women should wear simple jewelry and only moderate makeup. Neither men nor women should wear cologne. Also, both should remove any unusual piercings and cover any tattoos.
- Never chew gum, eat mints, or smoke during an interview.

Body Language

Your body language, or nonverbal communication, often sends a more accurate message than your verbal communication. Be sure your body language reinforces your positive image. Positive body language includes maintaining good posture, making eye contact with the interviewer, having a pleasant expression, shaking hands firmly, and using a pleasant tone of voice. Slouching, looking around the room, frowning, clenching your jaw, and crossing your arms will send a negative message to an interviewer. Also, an interviewer will be distracted if you tap your foot, gesture inappropriately, or constantly move around in your chair.

👉 CAREER SUCCESS TIP

Dress for Success

From magazines and catalogues, have students cut out, label, and mount on a poster pictures of appropriate and inappropriate interview clothing for three different careers in their career field. Display the posters and hold a class discussion on what is appropriate dress in the workplace. Tell students that dressing for success doesn't require a large wardrobe. What is required is being neat and dressing conservatively, rather than following fashion trends.

Spoken Language

The positive image you have projected by your attitude, appearance, and body language can be undermined by the way you speak. An interviewer will listen for a pleasant tone of voice and self-confidence in what you say. Practice making firm, confident statements. Avoid uncertain phrases, such as "I was only . . ." or "I guess . . . ." Speaking too quickly or too slowly can also transmit a lack of confidence. Answer questions concisely by giving sufficient information but sticking to the topic.

> How might your use of slang or words such as *like* or *you know* affect an interviewer's impression of you?

What do you think?

The most effective verbal communication is simple and straightforward. Use correct grammar and word choice and appropriate vocabulary. Avoid slang and fillers, such as "um," "like," and "you know." Pause briefly while you search for the best way to express yourself. Also show courtesy and respect through your language.

A Successful Interview

An interview will usually consist of three parts: beginning the interview, the questioning process, and ending the interview. Your performance in each of these parts will determine the success of the interview.

Beginning the Interview

Positive body language and a friendly smile will start your interview on the right track. Be sure you know how to pronounce the interviewer's name correctly, and greet the person by name. Use his or her last name preceded by Mr., Mrs., Ms., or Dr. The interviewer will set the tone of the interview in the beginning; adjust your behavior based on the cues the interviewer provides. For example, shake hands—firmly—if the interviewer offers a hand and wait for the interviewer to ask you to sit down. After this introductory stage, allow the interviewer to guide the conversation and try to relax.

The Questioning Process

You have prepared for this part of the interview through your research and practice interviews. So try to relax and act naturally. In most situations, interviewers understand you may be nervous and will try to make you feel comfortable. However, their purpose is to hire the best candidate for the position. Therefore, they will be analyzing your answers and behavior throughout the interview.

Listen carefully to each question; then answer honestly, concisely, and directly. Make certain the interviewer is aware of all your strengths and accomplishments, and provide concrete examples at appropriate places in the interview. You can also use the samples of your work in your portfolio to reinforce the presentation of your skills and experience.

> **66** Nothing great was ever accomplished without enthusiasm. **99**
> —*Ralph Waldo Emerson, Philosopher and Writer*

295

What do you think?

Use **TM15-10**.
Students' answers will vary. Answers may discuss an employer thinking a person using slang doesn't know the difference between formal and informal situations. Answers may also mention the fact that jobs involving working with the public require the use of little or no slang.

TEACH

The first impression people have of others often is based in part on how people shake hands. Have students practice shaking hands with one another and with you. Stress that they should make eye contact, smile, use a firm but comfortable pressure, and end the handshake after two to three seconds.

DIFFERENT LEARNING STYLES

Visual Learners

Have students work in groups. Have each group create a poster that illustrates and promotes a positive job interview. Student groups may use computer graphics or art materials. Display the posters around the room.

Mention that sometimes students may not be able to write down the name of the interviewer(s) during the interview itself. In this case, advise students to ask the interviewer(s) for business cards at the end of the interview. As a last resort, students could call the receptionist or administrative assistant and ask for the names and titles of the interviewers.

APPLY

Have students complete **Activity 15-5, "Case Challenges,"** that appears on pages 302–303. Teaching suggestions and the solution for this activity appear on page 303. An activity worksheet can be found on the Career Portfolio and Resource CD— **Text Activity 15-5.doc.**

Mickey knows his broadcasting skills are excellent. He has been taking television and radio broadcasting classes during high school. He is now ready for an interview at WDLB-TV, a small local television station. Mickey has applied for a broadcasting internship to work in entry-level announcing and production. He has excellent grades and his teachers' letters of recommendation emphasize his outstanding work. However, performance is what counts in broadcasting. Mickey must show his skills to the station's program director.

Mickey arrives at the interview with taped samples of his work. Mr. Mark, the program director, asks Mickey about his courses. Next, Mr. Mark looks at Mickey's grades and promises to call his teachers. Then Mickey asks Mr. Mark to view a tape of his video experience. Mickey introduces each element of the tape. One segment shows Mickey's interviewing skills, and another emphasizes his ability to describe a live-action play-by-play of the state baseball tournament. Then the tape's content switches, showing Mickey's skills as a director. The variety of the segments offers Mr. Mark a perspective of Mickey's skills in video broadcasting and production. Those are the skills needed in a small television station where flexibility is the key to success.

Throughout the interview, use your knowledge of the company to demonstrate your interest and enthusiasm about the company and the position. Relate your education/training and skills to the requirements of the job, and always be positive in your responses. Never make a negative comment about a situation or a former job or supervisor.

Ending the Interview

An interviewer will usually signal the end of the interview by making a concluding statement. At this time, if you want the job, state that you are very interested in the position and that you believe you can do the job well. Ask what the next step is and when you will be notified about a hiring decision. Thank the interviewer and maintain a positive expression and positive body language until you leave the building.

In Activity 15-5, "Case Challenges," you will have an opportunity to analyze some interview situations.

INTEGRATED ACADEMICS
Communication
Ask several businesspeople from the community to work with students on job interviews. Invite people who work in employment bureaus, who work in the human resources department of the local government and large corporations, and who own small businesses. Ask speakers to explain how they interview prospective employees and then to conduct mock interviews with some of the students. Remind students to write a thank-you note to each speaker.

After the Interview

As soon as possible after your interview, evaluate your performance and the results of the interview. Regardless of whether you believe your performance was good or poor, you will learn from writing down an evaluation. In addition, business courtesy demands that you write a thank-you letter to the interviewer. If you want the position, you should also follow up with a phone call.

Evaluate Your Performance

A written evaluation of an interview will provide valuable feedback for future interviews, assist in identifying follow-up activities, and help you analyze the position and the company. Illustration 15-3 on page 298 lists the information that you should include in your written evaluation.

> What a relief, thought Lorenzo. The interview is over! Mr. Sarra was very fair, and he seemed to like me as a person. But will he decide that I can make a good employee? Let's see. Maybe I can figure out how I did. I was on time—really, ten minutes early. I wore my sports jacket, dress pants, and a conservative tie. I know those clothes are a little dressier than what a pharmacy technician wears every day to work, but I wanted to dress a level above what I would wear on the job. I shook Mr. Sarra's hand firmly—but then I sat down before he did. Oh no—I just remembered—I put my portfolio on his desk! I should have kept it in my lap.
>
> Then when Mr. Sarra starting asking me questions, I hesitated because I was nervous. But I think he thought that I was just formulating my answers. I spoke in a strong voice and answered the questions truthfully, even the one about attendance. Mr. Sarra can't possibly think that missing two days of school this semester was too much. I had the flu! I really think I wowed him, though, when I starting talking about the equipment and formulas we use in health occupations class. The equipment is similar to what is right there in the hospital pharmacy. I can calculate dosages—ready to be checked by the pharmacist—so I think I got the answers perfect on the math test Mr. Sarra gave me. Well, I know my references will give me excellent recommendations, especially my teacher, Mrs. McCarren. I wish Mr. Sarra would make his decision today—I know I'll end up pacing for the next three days. Thank goodness Mr. Sarra said he would call whether or not I got the job.

Write a Thank-You Letter

To leave a positive and lasting impression, write a letter thanking the interviewer for meeting with you. Briefly refer to something specific you discussed in the interview to show that it made an impression on you. Your thank-you letter will provide the interviewer with a positive reminder and will be part of the employer's file about you.

> 66 Our greatest glory lies not in never falling, but in rising every time we fall. 99
>
> —*Confucius, Chinese Philosopher*

Arrange for students to participate in a dress rehearsal practice interview to help them polish their interview skills and gain confidence in their abilities. Make this practice interview as realistic as possible. Ask teachers, parents who work in the business community, and businesspeople to volunteer to be interviewers. Instruct interviewers to ask one illegal question and to request a copy of a portfolio item during the interview. Print blank evaluation forms from **Activity 15-3**. Provide a copy of the evaluation form for the interviewer to complete after each interview.

Videotaping these final practice interviews will give students the powerful experience of seeing and evaluating their own skills. In addition, if the first practice interviews from **Activity 15-3** were videotaped, students would be able to see how their performance has improved since the first interview. Being able to measure the improvement will help students see the benefits of practice and will add to their confidence in their abilities.

TEACH

You may wish to use **TM15-11** to show students how they can record their interview evaluation summary on a 4" by 6" index card. Suggest that students staple the completed evaluation card to the original tracking card for the company. With this method, all the tracking information for the application process is grouped by company and is easy to use.

DIFFERENT LEARNING ABILITIES

At-Risk and Reluctant-Reader Students

Have at-risk and reluctant-reader students work with a student mentor to role-play job interviews. Tell the mentors to make the job interview realistic. One question the mentor should ask is why the at-risk and reluctant-reader student plans to finish or not finish high school. Then have student pairs write a public service announcement (PSA) for radio that encourages students to stay in school. The PSA should be written from the perspective of the employer and should emphasize that the same skills needed in school are also needed for employment.

Illustration 15-3 Interview Evaluation Summary

Interview Evaluation Summary

1. Company name and address
2. Interviewer's name, title, and telephone number
3. Date, length, and style of interview
4. Names and titles of other employees you met
5. Your impressions of the company, including the work environment and the attitude and dress of employees
6. Questions the interviewer asked you (If you believe you answered any questions inadequately, write down the answer you should have given.)
7. Questions you asked the interviewer (If there are any questions you wish you had asked, write them down.)
8. How to present yourself more effectively in the areas of attitude, appearance, body language, and spoken language
9. Areas in which you think you performed well
10. Areas in which you think your performance could be improved (Write down how you can improve.)
11. Information you forgot to give the interviewer that could affect the hiring decision
12. Your overall evaluation of the interview
13. Your decision whether to accept the job if it is offered
14. When the hiring decision would be made
15. When you sent a thank-you letter and when you made a follow-up phone call

CAREER FACT

According to *National Business Employment Weekly,* only 36 percent of job applicants send a thank-you letter following an interview—despite the fact that many employers expect one.

For a group interview, write a different thank-you letter to each interviewer in the group. You can make each letter different by referring to a specific question or point made by the interviewer.

After evaluating your interview performance, you may find you need to clarify some information or correct a weak performance area. In this case, you can send a longer thank-you letter. In this letter, refer to the interview and the position, clarify the necessary information, express your enthusiasm about the company and the position, thank the interviewer, and mention that you expect to hear soon about the hiring decision. Illustration 15-4 is an example of this type of thank-you letter.

Even if you decide you do not want a position, you should write a letter thanking the interviewer for the time he or she spent with you. State that you do not wish to be considered for the specific job, and if appropriate, express your interest in future job openings that are a better match for your background and career goals.

CAREER TREND
Business Etiquette

At one time, formal business etiquette was expected in the United States. As the pace of doing business has increased, the small niceties, such as writing formal letters of introduction and thank-you notes, are being practiced less frequently. Yet in most European, Pacific Rim, and Latin countries, formal business etiquette is still important. Tell students that in the global economy, being too informal could cost them a job.

Illustration 15-4 Example of a Thank-You Letter

Mickey Diver

5967 Pathway Drive
Cincinnati, OH 45246-3484

(513) 555-0130
E-mail: Mickey_Diver@freemail.com

May 15, 20--

Mr. Joshua Mark
Program Director
WDLB-TV
P.O. Box 23
Cincinnati, OH 45201-0023

Dear Mr. Mark:

Meeting with you today and learning what it is like working at WDLB-TV has made me more eager than ever to join your station as a broadcasting intern. The way you and your staff manage to produce quality programs on a limited budget really impressed me. Thank you for a fascinating and informative tour of the station. Ms. Kaminski, Mr. Thomas, and Miss Santini made me feel most welcome.

During our interview, we discussed my educational background and the planning and production of each segment on my demonstration tape. However, we did not have a chance to review my experience researching background for specific programs. Last summer a local radio station produced an hour-long program called "So, You Wanna Be in Pictures." The program explored different ways well-known screen stars were cast in their first movies. I provided the research for the Charlie Chaplin and Katharine Hepburn segments. For your convenience, I have enclosed a copy of my report on Ms. Hepburn.

As we agreed, I will call you next Thursday, but you can reach me before then at (513) 555-0130. Thanks again for inviting me to interview. I look forward to talking to you next week.

Sincerely,

Mickey Diver

Mickey Diver

enclosure

TEACH

Recap for the students the essential points in a thank-you letter:
1. Thank the interviewer for the interview.
2. Refer to something specific discussed in the interview.
3. Make a positive reference to how your skills would benefit the employer.
4. Refer to your follow-up plan.

CLOSE

Have students complete **Project 5, "Identify Skills"** found in the *Investigating Your Career Activities & Projects* book.

In Part 1 of this activity, students reinforce their ability to identify personal characteristics and transferable skills requirements present in job ads. In Part 2, students prepare for interviews by identifying the personal attributes and transferable skills the students have that employers value. Students then write down examples they could use during interviews or in thank-you notes to tell how they have demonstrated each skill in the past. Project 5 may be done by individual students or by teams.
Solution: The solution for this activity appears in the *Teacher's Edition* of *Investigating Your Career Activities & Projects*.

DIFFERENT LEARNING STYLES

Auditory Learners/Print Learners

Provide students with several different samples of thank-you letters. Put letters on transparencies; then using an overhead projector, go over them with students. Give students different interview scenarios, and have them write thank-you letters. Tell students to trade their letters with another student and edit each other's work. Suggest that reading the letters aloud will help students find mistakes. Have students return the edited letters to the original writer.

TEACH

Advise students to ask at the interview whether they may call in a week to check on the status of the hiring decision. Students should then follow the interviewer's instructions.

Prepare students for the possibility that employers may wish to avoid the consequences of misunderstandings. As a result, employers may not be willing to tell applicants how to improve their qualifications or their interview skills. No matter how the employer responds, applicants should thank the employer and remain polite.

APPLY

Have students complete **Activity 15-6, "Learning from Others,"** that appears on page 303. Teaching suggestions and the solution for this activity appear on page 303. An activity worksheet can be found on the Career Portfolio and Resource CD— **Text Activity 15-6.doc**.

IN A NUTSHELL

Remind students about the objectives set forth at the beginning of the chapter, and use this summary to reinforce the concepts presented in this chapter.

Career Journal

Ask students to spend 10 minutes writing Career Journal entries that answer the following questions:
1. How well did what you thought you knew match what the chapter presented?
2. What questions do you now have about the chapter topics, and where do you think you can find the answers to those questions?
3. How will the content of the chapter help you investigate *your* career?

ASSESS

Administer the printed objective test for Chapter 15, available with this package. Test solutions are found in the *Teacher's Edition* of *Investigating Your Career Chapter Tests*. Use the **Exam***View*® CD to create your own objective test for this chapter.

300

Follow-up Phone Call

If you did not find out at the end of your interview when a hiring decision would be made, make a follow-up phone call to the interviewer in a week. Ask politely about the status of your application, remind the interviewer of your most important qualifications, and express your enthusiasm about the position. If you learn that the position has been filled, ask how you could have been more competitive. This information can help you be successful in future interviews.

In Activity 15-6, "Learning from Others," you will find out more about how you will be evaluated by an interviewer.

> ❝To avoid criticism, do nothing, say nothing, be nothing.❞
> —Elbert Hubbard, Publisher

IN A NUTSHELL

- **I can describe the purposes and styles of interviews.**

  An employer's purpose is to find out whether I am qualified for the job. My purposes are to find out whether I want the job and, if so, to convince the interviewer that I am the best applicant. Interviews may be unstructured or structured. Structured interviews may be behavioral, performance, stress, group, or screening interviews.

- **I can explain how to prepare for interviews.**

  Before an interview, I should review my resume, plan answers to common questions and illegal questions, plan questions to ask, and practice answering and asking questions.

- **I can describe my preparations before an interview.**

  After I arrange for a specific job interview, I should research the company, prepare to discuss wages or salary, organize my portfolio, practice for the specific interview, and recheck the interview details.

- **I can describe how to have a successful interview.**

  I should project a positive image throughout the interview. I need to be sure my attitude, appearance, body language, and spoken language convey a positive image of courtesy, enthusiasm, and self-confidence. I should listen carefully to questions, answer honestly and positively, and demonstrate my interest and enthusiasm about the company and the job.

- **I understand how to follow up after an interview.**

  After an interview, I should evaluate my performance and write a thank-you letter to the interviewer(s). If necessary, I will make a follow-up phone call to find out the hiring decision.

Suggestions for Parents and Family Members

Help with Job Interviews

Parents and family members need to support the career discovery process of teens. Ways they can assist teenagers in preparing for job interviews include:

1. Listening to your child deliver his or her one-minute summary.
2. Offering to play the role of an interviewer so your teen can practice answering interview questions.
3. Discussing how the benefits package you have through your employer affects the family.

ACTIVITY 15-1   Coming to Terms

The following terms are the seven styles of interviews defined in this chapter. Brainstorm with another person to describe a job search situation that is suitable for each type of interview. Discuss your results with the class.

1. Unstructured interview
2. Structured interview
3. Behavioral interview
4. Performance interview

5. Stress interview
6. Group interview
7. Screening interview

ACTIVITY 15-2   Your Answers to Common Questions

On a separate sheet of paper, write down your answers to the common interview questions listed below. Assume that the interview is with an employer in your chosen career. Be sure your answers are truthful and positive. Exchange your answers with another student, and discuss ways you could each improve your responses.

1. Tell me about yourself. How would you describe yourself?

2. What are your hobbies and interests?

3. What are your strengths?

4. What are your weaknesses?

5. Why are you interested in this job, company, or career?

6. What did you learn from one of the experiences listed on your resume?

7. What rewards are you looking for in a job, workplace, or career?

8. Give an example of a conflict you've had with a coworker, and explain how you handled it.

9. What courses did you like best (or least) and why?

10. What extracurricular activities did you like best (or least) and why?

11. What type of supervisor or management style do you prefer?

12. Why should I hire you?

13. Have you ever been fired from a job? If so, please explain.

14. What do you see yourself doing ten years from now?

15. What are your long-term career goals, and how do you plan to achieve them?

Activity 15-1: Coming to Terms
This activity helps students clarify the differences between the various types of interviews and the reasons why employers select specific types of interviews.

To increase the usefulness of the activity, pair students who have chosen the same career cluster. Encourage students to describe a job situation in their career field for each type of interview.

Solution: Answers will vary. Discuss in class how the type of job situation and the career field can affect the type of interview. Compare the job situations of students who have different career clusters but have chosen the same interview style.

Activity 15-2: Your Answers to Common Questions
This activity helps students develop effective answers for common interview questions before an actual interview.

Remind students of the importance of incorporating the employer's viewpoint into their answers. You may wish to hand out copies of **TM15-04** and discuss the teaching master in class. **TM15-04** lists effective answers to common interview questions and is based on the scenario and resume of Soo Lin Lee in Chapter 14 on text pages 268–269. Point out how Soo Lin tailors her responses to showcase her value as an employee. After students have exchanged their answers and discussed with their partners how to improve their responses, allow students to edit their answers to make them more effective.

Solution: Answers will vary. Discuss students' answers in class, emphasizing that the goal of this activity is for everyone to have effective answers to these important interview questions, not to criticize any specific answers. Ask students to share any answers that would get their attention if they were employers.

Activity 15-3: Interview Practice

This activity gives students their first opportunity to practice and evaluate interview skills and provides students with a "before" snapshot against which they can measure their improvement in subsequent interviews.

If possible, videotape these and subsequent practice interviews. Observing themselves helps students understand the evaluations of their peers. If videotaping is not possible, have students work in teams as described in the activity.

Discuss the evaluation form with students before they begin their interviews. Be sure students understand all the criteria and terms on the form. In particular, explain that fillers are words or sounds, such as *um, like,* and *you know,* that people may use to fill silences in conversations. Also remind students that employers value confidentiality and tact, and explain that this activity gives them an opportunity to practice both. To help them improve their interpersonal skills, you may require students to state their evaluation comments in a positive way. For example, instead of saying, "Applicant slouched and squirmed," an evaluator could say, "Straighter posture and fewer hand movements would improve the applicant's image."

Instruct interviewers to ask at least one illegal question so students can practice fielding such questions. **Solution:** Answers will vary. Explain to students that the purpose of this practice interview is to help them identify areas they need to improve. Focus your class discussion on any areas that gave students particular difficulties. If, as recommended, you plan to include the two additional practice interview opportunities (listed on page 288), explain that students will learn more interview techniques in the next sections and will be able to practice their interviewing skills further.

Activity 15-4: Research Wages and Salaries

This activity helps students obtain a realistic idea of how much money they can earn in various jobs in their career field and what level of lifestyle those earnings will support.

To obtain a fairly complete picture of the options available for their wage or salary range, encourage students to explore a number of locations where they might like to live and some places they may not have considered.

If you wish to find other web sites to use in this activity, try searching with the keywords *salary calculator, salary wizard,* or *relocation cost of living.*

ACTIVITY 15-3 **Interview Practice**

Form a small group to practice interviewing. Take turns playing the role of the interviewer and the role of the person being interviewed. Each person should play each role. The remaining members of the group are observers who will evaluate the performance of the person being interviewed. Print copies of the Interview Evaluation Form from your CD for the observers to use in their evaluations. If a computer is not available, use the handouts from your teacher. Your teacher may video your interview and show it to you so you can evaluate your own performance.

ACTIVITY 15-4 **Research Wages and Salaries**

Wages and salaries may vary depending on where you live, how much experience you have, the type of job, the company where you work, and many other factors.

1. Use the following web sites to find the possible wages or salaries for your chosen career. Write a summary of the information you find.
   - *http://careers.kansascity.com/salary_wizard.html*
   - *www.acinet.org*

2. Visit the web site *www.bankrate.com/oxm/movecalc.asp*. This site will show you how the cost of living changes in different parts of the country. Compare the costs of where you live now with the costs of several places where you think you would like to live. Will the expected wage or salary that you found in Question 1 allow you to live where you want?

ACTIVITY 15-5 **Case Challenges**

Each of the interview situations below seems headed for disaster. In small groups, discuss the following questions for each situation:

- What is the problem with the interview?
- How can the interviewee resolve the problem and make the interview a successful one?

Then share your group's decisions with the rest of the class.

1. Nina thought working in a bank would be ideal, and she was excited when she received a call to interview at Centerfield National Bank. Nina knew she had to dress up for an interview, so she wore her best Saturday night date clothes. What an outstanding candidate she would be, dressed in her black leather miniskirt and red crop top. Though she had a little trouble walking in the spiked heels, Nina knew they added to the outfit. Upon meeting Nina, Mrs. Hyden, the interviewer, appeared startled. Then she shook Nina's hand and began the interview.

Solution: Answers will vary. Focus a class discussion on how wages or salaries may vary in different locations. Point out that although earnings may be higher in some places, the cost of living also is likely to be higher in those locations.

2. As the interview progressed, Laeticia believed she was answering Mr. Steinum's questions honestly. She verified her experience by demonstrating several different hair weaves on the mannequin he provided. Laeticia knew she would be an asset to Mr. Steinum's shop. Then Mr. Steinum asked Laeticia if she had a boyfriend. When she didn't answer, he asked her if she ever stayed out late on Friday nights. "After all," he said, "I wouldn't want you to miss work on Saturdays. I would hate to lose you because of your social life." Laeticia really wanted to work in Mr. Steinum's shop, but she was at a loss for words.

3. Kisho was enjoying his interview with Mr. Olsen. They hadn't talked much about the job or Kisho's skills, but they had thoroughly discussed fly-fishing—both Kisho and Mr. Olsen loved the sport and were familiar with the creeks, rivers, and lakes in their part of the state. They had spent the better part of an hour discussing fishing trips, rods, and fly selection. Mr. Olsen said, "Well, Kisho, I've got another interview in 30 minutes, but I did want to ask if you've tried tying your own flies." Knowing Mr. Olsen had another applicant coming soon, Kisho began to wonder how to turn the conversation back to the job and his qualifications without upsetting Mr. Olsen.

ACTIVITY 15-6   **Learning from Others**

Listen carefully to the guest speaker, someone who regularly conducts interviews for a company. From the information shared during the presentation or the question-and-answer period, write the answers to the following questions:

• How many people do you usually interview in a month?
• For what types of jobs do you conduct interviews?
• What style(s) of interview do you use most often? least often?
• Do you usually conduct a screening interview before you set up an in-person interview? If not, how do you decide which applicants to interview in person?
• In your opinion, how important are honesty, dependability, and the ability to work with others? How do you interview for these qualities?
• What do you consider the most important question that you ask in an interview?
• What is the most important quality you look for in an applicant?
• How important is the attitude of an applicant? How important is appearance?
• What qualities or behaviors of an applicant would cause you *not* to consider the person for a job?
• Do you want applicants to ask questions during an interview? If so, what types of questions would impress you positively? If not, why not?
• Do you find it helpful in evaluating applicants if they provide samples of their work? If not, why not? If so, what do you look for in the samples?
• When do you discuss wages or salary with an applicant?
• Please describe some of your most positive interview experiences.
• Please describe some of your most negative interview experiences.
• Do you want applicants to call after an interview, or do you prefer to call them? Why?
• Do you expect to receive a thank-you letter from an applicant after an interview? How often do you receive one?

Write a summary of the results of your interview. Then share the information with your class.

Activity 15-5: Case Challenges

This activity helps students realize that interview problems can be overcome and job interviews are not judgments of a person's worth.

Solution: Answers will vary. Students should identify the following problems in the interviews:

1. Nina chose inappropriate clothing for the interview.
2. Laeticia needs to answer an illegal question in a way that preserves her privacy but does not alienate the employer.
3. Kisho needs to discuss his job qualifications without destroying the goodwill he has developed with the employer.

Class discussion should focus on how the person in each case study can overcome the problem identified above. For example, Nina could overcome her inappropriate clothing by impressing Mrs. Hyden with the enthusiasm, skills, abilities, and willingness to learn she can bring to the job. Mrs. Hyden should realize that Nina can learn to dress more appropriately after she is hired. Mrs. Hyden may bring up the issue of on-the-job attire later in the interview.

Activity 15-6: Learning from Others

This activity reinforces students' understanding of the interview process and assists them in preparing for all aspects of interviews.

Suggest that students try to interview someone who hires employees in the career cluster students have chosen.

Solution: Answers will vary. In a class discussion, compare the similarities and differences in the results of students' interviews. Encourage students to discover possible reasons for the differences, such as the types of jobs for which the various interviewers usually hire people or the personal preferences of the interviewers. Also emphasize that any similarities are likely common to many interviews.

Index